Distributed Operating Systems

Theory and Practice

NATO ASI Series

Advanced Science Institutes Series

A series presenting the results of activities sponsored by the NATO Science Committee, which aims at the dissemination of advanced scientific and technological knowledge, with a view to strengthening links between scientific communities.

The Series is published by an international board of publishers in conjunction with the NATO Scientific Affairs Division

A Life Sciences **B Physics**	Plenum Publishing Corporation London and New York
C Mathematical and Physical Sciences	D. Reidel Publishing Company Dordrecht, Boston, Lancaster and Tokyo
D Behavioural and Social Sciences **E Applied Sciences**	Martinus Nijhoff Publishers Boston, The Hague, Dordrecht and Lancaster
F Computer and Systems Sciences **G Ecological Sciences** **H Cell Biology**	Springer-Verlag Berlin Heidelberg New York London Paris Tokyo

Series F: Computer and Systems Sciences Vol. 28

Distributed Operating Systems:

Theory and Practice

Edited by

Yakup Paker

Polytechnic of Central London
115 New Cavendish Street
London W1M 8JS, United Kingdom

Jean-Pierre Banatre

IRISA, Campus Universitaire de Beaulieu
Avenue du General Leclerc
F-35042 Rennes Cedex, France

Müslim Bozyiğit

Middle East Technical University
Ankara, Turkey

Springer-Verlag
Berlin Heidelberg New York London Paris Tokyo
Published in cooperation with NATO Scientific Affairs Divison

Proceedings of the NATO Advanced Study Institute on Distributed Operating Systems: Theory and Practice held at Altinyunus, Çeşme, Turkey, August 18–29, 1986.

ISBN-13:978-3-642-46606-9 e-ISBN-13:978-3-642-46604-5
DOI: 10.1007/978-3-642-46604-5

Library of Congress Cataloging-in-Publication Data. NATO Advanced Study Institute on Distributed Operating Systems, Theory and Practice (1986 : Çeşme, Turkey) Distributed operating systems. (NATO ASI series. Series F, Computer and systems sciences ; v. 28) "Proceedings of the NATO Advanced Study Institute on Distributed Operating Systems, Theory and Practice, held at Altinyunus, Cesme, Turkey, August 18–29, 1986."—T.p. verso. 1. Electronic data processing—Distributed processing—Congresses. 2. Operating systems (Computers)—Congresses. I. Paker, Yakup. II. Banâtre, Jean-Pierre. III. Bozyiğit, Muslim, 1945- . IV. Title. V. Series: NATO ASI series. Series F, Computer and systems sciences ; vol. 28.
QA76.9.D5N377 1986 004'.36 87-9682

Softcover reprint of the hardcover 1st edition 1987

2145/3140-543210

NATO Advanced Study Institute "Distributed Operating Systems :
Theory and Practice", Altınyunus, Çeşme, Turkey, August 18-29, 1986

PREFACE

This text comprises the edited collection of papers presented at the NATO Advanced Study Institute which took place at Altınyunus, Çeşme (near İzmir), Turkey, 18-29 August 1986. The Institute was attended by nearly 80 participants from 18 countries. It is hoped that this book, which includes all the contributions to the Institute except one, will serve as a comprehensive record of the topics which were covered for those who could not attend, and, more importantly, for the wider audience of practitioners, researchers and students working, or considering working, in this complex field.

Recent technological trends and market demands have favoured the widespread design and building of distributed computing systems. Such systems consist of a set of nodes interconnected by communication lines. Each node is assumed to contain a computing resource which itself could be a distributed computer. Several reasons make us conclude that more and more such systems will form the mainstream of computer applications: (i) advances in VLSI and related technologies which make possible the large scale production of computer and communications equipment, (ii) the inherently distributed nature of many applications, and (iii) the need for concurrent processing.

Initially, the design approach adopted mostly concentrated on providing a communications infrastructure between autonomous computers. This led to the proliferation of Local Area Networks (LANs) and Wide Area Networks (WANs) and related services. Such a system essentially treats each computer as an individual resource managed by its own resident operating system. This restricted view has been clearly shown to be inadequate, since a distributed application requires the underlying structure of interconnected nodes to be transparent and appear as a unified, single computational resource. Therefore for the management and running of such applications on a network of computers a new approach is needed: the view of the operating system as a single facility spread over all the available (often diverse) nodes. This is not a straightforward transition; it poses a new set of problems such as synchronisation, control, security, and so on. Since as yet there is not a single universally accepted practice and most work is in the research phase, the field of distributed operating systems seems rather confusing for the novice and the related literature rather patchy or non-existent. Well-documented successful applications are difficult to find.

The objective of this Institute was to present the underlying state-of-the-art methodologies both in the research phase and already in practice in building distributed operating systems. This was done looking at this complex field from four viewpoints: (i) formal aspects, (ii) system structuring, (iii) hardware issues, and (iv) particular implementation experiences. We tried especially to emphasise the sharing of experiences gained in practice by including implementation projects. The reader will observe that this text has been organised in four parts to reflect the above structure.

Part 1, formal aspects of concurrent systems, starts with a paper by Lamport which addresses itself to the issues of describing complex systems in terms of behaviour and develops a description formalism. Roucairol considers the construction of correct programs in a distributed environment. Various approaches for constructing distributed algorithms for process synchronisation are described by Verjus, in particular with respect to mutual exclusion.

In Part 2, papers addressing themselves to the fundamental design issues are grouped. Baiardi and Vanneschi propose a concurrent language, ECSP, and programming environment to support parallelism in resource management and fault recovery. Communication aspects, in particular the "remote pipe and procedure" model are explained by Gifford. In order to describe parallel computations a concept called "multi-function" which generalises the function concept is proposed by Banatre (J-P).

Distributed Operating Systems run on hardware nodes interconnected by various network technologies explained by Bozyigit in Part 3 which also includes Manner's paper describing the hardware support incorporated to implement the Heidelberg Polyp processor.

A number of case studies constitute Part 4. Levine describes the Apollo DOMAIN system which is commercially available. Rozier and Legatheaux Martins' paper is on the CHORUS operating system which has been developed by INRIA, France, over a number of years and recently made available to run under Unix. CONIC represents a different approach, developed at Imperial College, London, to construct and operate software for embedded systems as described in Magee, Kramer and Sloman's paper. Banatre (M.) gives an example of a transaction system implemented for a distributed auction bidding system built at IRISA/INRIA, Rennes. Camelot is a general purpose system developed at Carnegie-Mellon University, described by Spector, as a distributed transaction facility. The Worm Programs paper by Kindberg, Sahiner and Paker describes an Operating System called WORMOS developed at the Polytechnic of Central London to run distributed applications.

We wish to acknowledge the support received from the NATO Science Programme and the other sponsors, namely the Polytechnic of Central London, IRISA/INRIA, Rennes, the US Army European Office, the Middle East Technical University, Ankara and the Turkish Scientific and Technical Research Council.

The editors
January 1987

Table of Contents

Part 4 Case Studies

Part 1

Formal Aspects of Concurrent Systems

A Formal Basis for the Specification of Concurrent Systems

Notes for the NATO Advanced Study Institute, Izmir, Turkey

Leslie Lamport

July 11, 1986

NATO ASI Series, Vol. F28
Distributed Operating Systems. Theory and Practice
Edited by Y. Paker et al.

Contents

1 Describing Complete Systems

1.1 Systems as Sets of Behaviors

We are ultimately interested in specifying systems—usually systems that are to be implemented as concurrent programs. We cannot claim to have written a formal specification of such a system unless we can formally state what it means for a program to satisfy the specification. Such a statement requires a formal *semantics* for programs—that is, the assignment to every program of some mathematical object that denotes the "meaning" of the program. We therefore begin with an informal sketch of a formal semantics for concurrent programs.

We will ignore many interesting aspects of program semantics, including the specification of most language constructs and the issue of compositionality. These questions are addressed in [6].

1.1.1 Behaviors

While sequential programs can often be described in terms of their input and output, concurrent programs must be described in terms of their behavior. A *behavior*, also called an *execution sequence*, is a sequence (finite or infinite)

$$s_0 \xrightarrow{\alpha_1} s_1 \xrightarrow{\alpha_2} s_2 \xrightarrow{\alpha_3} s_3 \ldots$$

where the s_i are states and the α_i are atomic operations. We claim, but will not attempt to justify this claim here, that the behavior of every discrete system, be it hardware or software, can be formally represented as such a sequence.

A triple $s \xrightarrow{\alpha} t$ is called an α *transition*; s is called the initial state and t is called the final state of the transition. The above behavior can be viewed as a sequence of transitions $s_{i-1} \xrightarrow{\alpha_i} s_i$ such that the final state of each transition is the initial state of the next transition.

As an example, we consider the simple program of Figure 1, where x and y are assumed to be integer-valued variables. The angle brackets indicate that each assignment statement is a single atomic operation. The statements are labeled α and β, and the control point following statement β is labeled γ. The state of the program consists of an assignment of values to the variables x and y and an assignment of one of the three values α, β, or γ to the "program counter" pc that defines the current locus of control. Let $(x = 4, y = -15, pc = \beta)$ denote the state in which the value of x is 4, the

$$\begin{aligned}&\alpha\colon \langle y := 7\ \rangle;\\ &\beta\colon \langle x := x^2 + y\rangle\\ &\gamma\colon\end{aligned}$$

Figure 1: A simple program.

value of y is -15, and control is right at the beginning of statement β. One possible behavior of this program is

$$(x = -2, y = 128, pc = \alpha) \xrightarrow{\alpha} \\ (x = -2, y = 7, pc = \beta) \xrightarrow{\beta} (x = 11, y = 7, pc = \gamma)$$

In fact, the set of all sequences of the form

$$(x = x_0, y = y_0, pc = \alpha) \xrightarrow{\alpha} \\ (x = x_0, y = 7, pc = \beta) \xrightarrow{\beta} (x = x_0^2 + 7, y = 7, pc = \gamma)$$

for arbitrary integers x_0 and y_0, are possible execution sequences of the program. (The value of an integer variable is assumed to be a mathematical integer, which can be arbitrarily large.) One might expect these to be the only possible behaviors of this program, but it is convenient to allow certain others that are described below.

In this example, the atomic-operation labels on the arrows in the execution sequence are redundant—just looking at the sequence of states allows us to fill in the arrow labels. In fact, this is true for any reasonable sequential or concurrent program. Labeling the transition with the action makes it easy to formalize the notion of who is performing an action. For now, these labels can be regarded as a harmless bit of redundancy.

No significance should be attached to the use of the same letters (α and β) to denote both atomic operations (arrow labels) and control point values (values of pc). We simply find it more convenient to overload these symbols than to introduce an extra set of program labels.

1.1.2 Behavioral Semantics

We define a semantics in which the meaning of a program is a set of behaviors—the set of all possible behaviors that the program is allowed to exhibit. There are usually considered to be two general approaches to describing a set of behaviors: constructive (or operational) and axiomatic. In the constructive approach, one gives rules for generating sequences. One can view the program of Figure 1 as a constructive specification by considering it to be a method for generating a behavior given initial values for x and y. The semantics of the program is the set of all sequences generated by this method starting from arbitrary integer value for x and y. In the axiomatic approach, one describes the set of behaviors by a collection of axioms. The meaning of the program is the set of all sequences that satisfy the axioms.

Formal mathematics is ultimately reducible to axiomatic reasoning, and a constructive method rests upon axioms. The distinction between constructive and axiomatic specifications is therefore illusory. When one formally describes a constructive method, it becomes axiomatic. However, there are axiomatic methods that are nonconstructive—that is, for which there is no clearly operational way to describe the set of behaviors that they define. Thus, constructive methods are really a special class of axiomatic ones.

Classifying constructive methods as a special case of axiomatic ones may seem like a dubious bit of reductionism, obscuring an essential distinction. We hope that the semantics described below will serve to counter that objection. It is certainly axiomatic, since every specification can be written as a formula in a formal logical system. However, most of the axioms will be written in a distinctly operational way.

1.1.3 Specifying Behaviors with Axioms—A Simple Approach

To provide an axiomatic specification of the above set of behaviors for the program of Figure 1, we first observe that this set of behaviors is determined by the following four separate rules:

- The initial state has $pc = \alpha$.
- When $pc = \alpha$, the next transition is an α transition that sets y to 7 and sets pc to β.
- When $pc = \beta$, the next transition is a β transition that sets x to $x^2 + y$ and sets pc to γ.
- When $pc = \gamma$, no more transitions can occur.

The four rules are informal axioms that specify the set of behaviors for the program. To turn them into a true axiomatic specification, they must be expressed in some formal system. Temporal logic is an excellent formal system for this purpose. We will not give a formal description of temporal logic here, and will write axioms using somewhat stilted English. All the properties in our specifications that are expressed informally in English can be translated into a temporal logic formula by anyone well versed in the temporal logic described in the appendix of [7].

The above four rules can be rewritten more precisely as the following temporal assertions.

> *Initial Axiom*: In the starting state, $pc = \alpha$ and x and y have integer values.
>
> α *Transition Axiom*: It is always the case that if $pc = \alpha$ and $x = x_0$, then the next action is labeled α and, in the next state, $pc = \beta$, $x = x_0$, and $y = 7$.
>
> β *Transition Axiom*: It is always the case that if $pc = \beta$, $x = x_0$, and $y = y_0$, then the next action is labeled β and, in the next state, $pc = \gamma$, $x = x_0^2 + y_0$, and $y = y_0$.
>
> *Termination Axiom*: It is always the case that if $pc = \gamma$, then there is no next state.

If we add the assumption that the state is specified by the values of x, y, and pc, then the set of execution sequences that satisfy these four axioms is precisely the set of sequences described above.

This is the obvious method of writing a temporal logic specification of the set of execution sequences described above. However, it turns out that this is the wrong way to do it. The use of the "in the next state" temporal operator raises serious difficulties in defining what it means to implement the program of Figure 1 by a lower-level program. Instead, we now describe a less obvious method that does not use this temporal operator.

Note that the "next action" operator causes no problem and will be used. The temporal logic of [7] can express the concept of the next action but not the concept of the next state.

1.1.4 Specifying Behaviors with Axioms—the Right Way

In the axiomatic approach, one usually specifies a set of behaviors by writing a list of properties, which specifies the set of all behaviors that satisfy all the properties. It is convenient to distinguish two types of properties: safety and liveness. Intuitively, a safety property asserts that something (presumably bad) will not happen, while a liveness property asserts that something (presumably good) will eventually happen. (A formal characterization of these properties can be found in [1].)

In specifying the set of behaviors for the program of Figure 1, safety properties assert that the program does not perform an incorrect action—for example, a safety axiom would rule out execution sequences whose first atomic action sets the value of y to 13, or changes the value of x. Liveness properties assert that the program does eventually make progress, unless it has reached its halting state. For example, a liveness axiom would assert that if control is at α, then eventually control will be at β.

In place of the "in the next state" temporal operator, we use the "until" operator, where "A until B" means that A remains true at least until the next time that B becomes true.

In our next attempt at specifying the program of Figure 1, we use the same initial and termination axiom as before, but, for each atomic operation, we have a pair of axioms, one for safety and one for liveness.

> α *Transition Axiom*: (Safety) It is always the case that if $pc = \alpha$, $x = x_0$, and $y = y_0$, then the next action is labeled α and $pc = \alpha$, $x = x_0$, and $y = y_0$ remain true until $pc = \beta$, $x = x_0$, and $y = 7$.
>
> (Liveness) It is always the case that if $pc = \alpha$ then eventually $pc \neq \alpha$.
>
> β *Transition Axiom*: (Safety) It is always the case that if $pc = \beta$, $x = x_0$, and $y = y_0$, then the next action is labeled β and $pc = \beta$, $x = x_0$, and $y = y_0$ remain true until $pc = \gamma$, $x = x_0^2 + y_0$, and $y = y_0$.
>
> (Liveness) It is always the case that if $pc = \beta$ then eventually $pc \neq \beta$.

Note the general pattern: instead of saying that if A holds then B holds in the next state, we say that A holds until B does (a safety property) and that if A holds then eventually A will cease to hold (a liveness property).

All the execution sequences described above for the program of Figure 1 satisfy these axioms. However, there are additional sequences that also satisfy the axioms. For example, the axiom for statement α states that, starting in a state $(x = x_0, y = y_0, pc = \alpha)$, the next arrow must be labeled α, and the only way that the state can change is for the next state to become $(x = x_0, y = 7, pc = \beta)$. However, it does not rule out "stuttering" actions labeled α that leave the state unchanged.

Assuming that the state is completely determined by the values of x, y, and pc, the above axioms specify the set of all execution sequences starting in state $(x = x_0, y = y_0, pc = \alpha)$, for arbitrary integers x_0 and y_0, followed by a finite number (possibly zero) of actions $\xrightarrow{\alpha} (x = x_0, y = y_0, pc = \alpha)$, followed by an action $\xrightarrow{\beta}$ $(x = x_0, y = 7, pc = \beta)$, followed by a finite number of actions $\xrightarrow{\beta}$ $(x = x_0, y = 7, pc = \beta)$, followed by an action $\xrightarrow{\beta}$ $(x = x_0^2 + 7, y = 7, pc = \gamma)$.

The extra stuttering actions allowed by this specification may seem burdensome. We shall see later that, on the contrary, they are the key to the proper definition of what it means to implement a program with a lower-level program. In fact, the "in the next state" temporal operator is bad precisely because it allows one to specify that there is no stuttering.

Although they may seem strange, there is no reason not to allow stuttering actions. The state includes all visible information about what the program is doing. An atomic action that does not change the state has no visible effect, and an action with no visible effect must be harmless.

Since stuttering actions are harmless, there is no reason not to allow behaviors of the program of Figure 1 to have extra stuttering actions labeled γ at the end. In fact, it turns out to be useful to assume that, instead of the execution sequences being finite, they all end with an infinite sequence of γ actions that do not change the state. Again, this creates no problems because there is no way to distinguish a program that has halted from one that is continually doing nothing. (Indeed, a *halt* instruction does not turn off a computer; it causes the computer to cycle endlessly, doing nothing.)

We now rewrite the above specification to require that execution sequences end with an infinite sequence of stuttering γ actions. This requires adding an axiom for the γ action. We also rewrite the axioms for the α and β actions in an even more baroque form that leads to the proper generalization for concurrent programs. To make the axioms easier to understand, we express them in a form that mentions the next state, although explicitly allowing stuttering actions. These axioms can be expressed in terms of the "until" operator without the "next state" operator, but doing so results in rather convoluted assertions. (In fact, the major problem with the "until" operator is that it leads to formulas that are hard to understand.) The same initialization axiom is used, but the Termination Axiom is replaced by the Completion Axiom.

> α *Transition Axiom*: (Safety) It is always the case that, if the next action is labeled α, then $pc = \alpha$ (in the current state) and the next state is either unchanged or else has pc set equal to β, y set equal to 7, and all other variables unchanged.
>
> (Liveness) It is always the case that, if there are infinitely many α actions, then eventually $pc \neq \alpha$.

β Transition Axiom: (Safety) It is always the case that, if $x = x_0$, $y = y_0$ (in the current state) and the next action is labeled β, then $pc = \beta$ and the next state is either unchanged or else has pc changed to γ, x set to $x_0^2 + y_0$, and all other variables unchanged.

(Liveness) It is always the case that, if there are infinitely many β actions, then eventually $pc \neq \beta$.

γ Transition Axiom: (Safety) It is always the case that, if the next action is labeled γ, then $pc = \gamma$ in the current state and the next state is unchanged.

Completion Axiom: It is always the case that the next action is labeled either α, β, or γ.

Note that there is no liveness axiom for the γ action, and the Completion Axiom expresses a safety property.

Most readers will not find it immediately obvious that this set of axioms specifies the same set of execution sequences described above; we now show that it does. The initial axiom implies that the first state has $pc = \alpha$. The Completion Axiom implies that the first action must be labeled α, β, or γ. However, the other axioms imply that only an α action can occur when $pc = \alpha$. Hence, the first action must be an α action, which can either leave the state unchanged or else set y to 7. The liveness axiom for α implies that there cannot be an infinite sequence of α actions that leave the state unchanged, because that would mean that there would be an infinite number of α actions and pc would remain forever equal to α, contrary to the axiom. Hence, there can be some finite number of α actions that do not change the state, but they must be followed by an α action that sets y to 7 and sets pc to β. Similar reasoning shows that there must then be a finite number (possibly zero) of β actions that leave the state unchanged followed by one that sets x to $x_0^2 + 7$ and sets pc to γ. Finally, the Completion Axiom implies that there must be an infinite number of actions (since there is always a next one), and the only action possible when $pc = \gamma$ is a γ action, so the sequence must end with an infinite sequence of γ actions that leave the state unchanged.

1.1.5 Concurrent Programs

Thus far, we have considered only a sequential program. Let us now turn to the simple concurrent program of Figure 2. In it, the program of Figure 1 is one process in a two-process program. A state of this program is an

```
cobegin
    α: ⟨y := 7 ⟩;
    β: ⟨x := x² + y⟩
    γ:
  □
        while δ: ⟨x ≠ 7 ⟩
            do ε: ⟨x := x + z ⟩od
    η:
coend
θ:
```

Figure 2: A simple concurrent program.

assignment of values to the integer variables x, y, and z, and to the "program counter" pc, which denotes the control state of the two processes, or else equals θ when both processes have halted. Let $(x = 7, y = -2, pc = (\beta, \delta))$ denote the state that assigns the value 7 to x, -2 to y, 4 to z, and in which control in the first process is at β and control in the second process is at δ. Let pc_1 and pc_2 denote the two components of pc, so, in this state, $pc_1 = \beta$ and $pc_2 = \delta$. For notational convenience, let $(\gamma, \eta) = \theta$, so if $pc = \theta$ then $pc_1 = \gamma$ and $pc_2 = \eta$.

An execution sequence of this program consists of an interleaving of atomic operations from the two processes. One such execution begins

$$
\begin{aligned}
&(x = 0, y = 1, z = 5, pc = (\alpha, \delta)) \xrightarrow{\alpha} (x = 0, y = 1, z = 5, pc = (\alpha, \delta)) \xrightarrow{\delta} \\
&\quad (x = 0, y = 1, z = 5, pc = (\alpha, \epsilon)) \xrightarrow{\alpha} (x = 0, y = 7, z = 5, pc = (\beta, \epsilon)) \xrightarrow{\beta} \\
&\quad (x = 7, y = 7, z = 5, pc = (\gamma, \epsilon)) \xrightarrow{\epsilon} (x = 12, y = 7, z = 5, pc = (\gamma, \delta)) \xrightarrow{\delta} \\
&\quad (x = 12, y = 7, z = 5, pc = (\gamma, \delta)) \xrightarrow{\delta} (x = 12, y = 7, z = 5, pc = (\gamma, \epsilon)) \xrightarrow{\epsilon} \\
&\quad (x = 17, y = 7, z = 5, pc = (\gamma, \delta)) \xrightarrow{\delta} \cdots
\end{aligned}
$$

and continues with the second process cycling forever through δ and ϵ actions (some of which may be stuttering actions).

This program also permits halting executions, which occur if statement δ happens to be executed when x has the value 7. Such execution sequences end with an infinite string of stuttering θ actions.

We specify the set of behaviors of this program with the following axioms. For convenience, pc_1 and pc_2 are considered to be variables when asserting that "no other variables" are changed. Note that the axioms for α and β

are almost the same as before, the only change being the substitution of pc_1 for pc.

Initial Axiom: In the starting state, $pc = (\alpha, \delta)$ and x, y, and z have integer values.

α *Transition Axiom*: (Safety) It is always the case that, if the next action is labeled α, then $pc_1 = \alpha$ (in the current state) and the next state is either unchanged or else has pc_1 set equal to β, y set equal to 7, and all other variables are unchanged.

(Liveness) It is always the case that, if there are infinitely many α actions, then eventually $pc_1 \neq \alpha$.

β *Transition Axiom*: (Safety) It is always the case that, if $x = x_0$, $y = y_0$ (in the current state) and the next action is labeled β, then $pc_1 = \beta$ and the next state is either unchanged or else has pc_1 set to γ, x set to $x_0^2 + y_0$, and all other variables are unchanged.

(Liveness) It is always the case that, if there are infinitely many β actions, then eventually $pc_1 \neq \beta$.

δ *Transition Axiom*: (Safety) It is always the case that, if the next action is labeled δ, then $pc_1 = \delta$ (in the current state) and the the next state is either unchanged or else only the value of pc_2 is changed and its value in the next state equals ϵ if $x \neq 7$ in the current state and equals η if $x = 7$ in the current state.

(Liveness) It is always the case that, if there are infinitely many δ actions, then eventually $pc_2 \neq \delta$.

ϵ *Transition Axiom*: (Safety) It is always the case that, if $x = x_0$ and $z = z_0$ (in the current state) and the next action is labeled ϵ, then $pc_2 = \epsilon$ and the next state is either unchanged or else has x set to $x_0 + z_0$, pc_2 changed to ϵ, and all other variables unchanged.

(Liveness) It is always the case that, if there are infinitely many ϵ actions, then eventually $pc_2 \neq \epsilon$.

θ *Transition Axiom*: (Safety) It is always the case that, if the next action is labeled θ, then $pc = \theta$ in the current state and the next state is unchanged.

Completion Axiom: It is always the case that the next action is labeled either α, β, δ, ϵ, or θ.

Note that there are no γ or η actions; when one process has terminated, all the actions are generated by the other process until it halts, at which time only stuttering θ actions occur.

The reader can check that these axioms permit all the execution sequences we expect. They also guarantee that nonstuttering actions keep happening unless the program halts—that is, until pc equals θ. However, they do not rule out the possibility that the second process loops forever and the first process never terminates. A **cobegin** statement whose semantics allows one process to be "starved" in this way is called an *unfair* **cobegin**. An alternative semantics for **cobegin** rules out that possibility, defining a *fair* **cobegin**. To specify the set of behaviors allowed by a fair **cobegin**, we must add another axiom. Let us say that control is in the first process if pc_1 equals α or β, and that control is in the second process if pc_2 equals δ or ϵ. Let us also say that α and β are the atomic operations of the first process, and that δ and ϵ are the atomic operations of the second process. Fairness is expressed by the following axiom:

> *Fairness Axiom*: For each process of the **cobegin**, if it is always the case that control is in the process then eventually there will be an action labeled with some atomic operation of the process.

The Fairness Axiom insures that the first process must terminate in any execution sequence of the program of Figure 2. To see this, observe that initially $pc_1 = \alpha$, and the Completion Axiom together with the safety axioms for all the actions imply that pc_1 must then remain equal to α unless an α action changes it. We show by contradiction that pc_1 cannot remain forever equal to α. Assume the contrary. Then the Fairness Axiom implies that it is always the case that there will eventually be an action of the first process, which means that there must be infinitely many actions of the first process. Since pc_1 always equals α, the transition axioms imply that the only actions of the first process that can occur are α actions, so there must be infinitely many α actions. The liveness axiom for α then implies that pc_1 must eventually become unequal to α, which is the required contradiction. Thus, we have proved that there must eventually be an α action that changes the value of pc_1. By the safety part of the Action α Axiom, pc_1 can be changed only to β. Hence, we must eventually have $pc_1 = \beta$. A similar argument then shows that pc_1 must eventually equal γ.

This reasoning may seem rather convoluted, but one expects proving properties of a program directly from an axiomatic semantics to be a long-winded affair. We could have written the axioms in a somewhat more straightforward way that would have simplified this proof. However, writing the axioms the way we did should make it clear how one writes similar axioms for any program built from simple sequential constructs and unfair **cobegins**. There is an axiom describing the initial state, a safety and liveness axiom for each atomic operation, a safety axiom for the stuttering action that represents termination (not necessary if termination is impossible), and a completeness axiom saying that the next action is always one of the program's atomic actions.

When a program contains fair **cobegins**, an additional fairness axiom is needed for each fair **cobegin**. If all **cobegins** are assumed to be fair, then the fairness axiom given above can be used. If a fair **cobegin** can be nested inside an unfair one, then the following axiom defines the most natural semantics.

> *Fairness Axiom*: If infinitely many actions are labeled with the atomic operations of the **cobegin**, then, for each process of the **cobegin**, it is always the case that if control is in the process then eventually there will be an action labeled with some atomic operation of the process.

This axiom asserts that no process in the **cobegin** is starved unless the entire **cobegin** is starved.

1.1.6 Programs as Axioms

One normally thinks of the program of Figure 2 as a machine for generating execution sequences—in other words, we base our understanding of the program upon an intuitive constructive semantics. The above discussion showed that we can represent our intuitive understanding (modified to allow stuttering actions) by a set of axioms. Thus, the program can equally well be thought of as an axiomatic description of a set of behaviors.

We ask the reader to change his way of thinking, and to regard the program in just this way: as an axiomatic specification of a set of execution sequences, not as a machine for generating behaviors. Pretend that someone has built a machine for generating execution sequences. We will use the program of Figure 2 to determine if this machine is correct, where correctness means that every execution sequence that it generates is in the set specified by this program. Instead of thinking of the program as a mechanism for generating behaviors, think of it as a filter for outlawing incorrect behaviors.

Of course, this way of thinking has no formal significance; formally, all that we have is a correspondence between the program text and the set of

$$
\begin{aligned}
a\colon & \langle\text{load } 7\rangle \\
& \langle\text{store } Y\rangle \\
b\colon & \langle\text{load } X\rangle \\
& \langle\text{multiply by } X\rangle \\
& \langle\text{store } X\rangle \\
& \langle\text{load } Y\rangle \\
& \langle\text{add } X\rangle \\
& \langle\text{store } X\rangle \\
g\colon &
\end{aligned}
$$

Figure 3: Implementation of the program of Figure 1.

behaviors. However, thinking of a program as an axiomatic specification of its set of possible behaviors is a crucial step in understanding hierarchical specification.

1.2 Correctness of an Implementation

Let us now consider what it means for one program to correctly implement another. For our example, we return to the simple sequential program of Figure 1 and consider its implementation with an assembly language program. For simplicity, assume that the assembly language implements infinitely large integers.

The program of Figure 3 is an implementation that might be produced by a very stupid compiler for a computer with a single accumulator. (There are two unnecessary instructions.) The assembly language variables X and Y implement the variables x and y of the higher-level program of Figure 1, statement α is implemented by the instructions at locations a and $a+1$, and statement β is implemented by the instructions at locations b through $b+5$. (We assume that each instruction occupies a single memory location.)

Formally, the programs of Figures 1 and 3 specify sets of execution sequences. We will not bother writing the axioms that define the set of behaviors of the assembly language program. Suffice it to say that the state consists of the values of the variables X and Y, the value of the accumulator, and the value of the program counter PC.

We must define what it means for one set of execution sequences to implement another. The basic idea is that every possible execution sequence of the assembly language program should, when viewed at the higher level, be a possible execution of the higher-level program. What does "viewing at the higher level" mean? We start with what is perhaps the most obvious approach, and show that it does not work.

First we must interpret the state of the lower-level program in terms of the state components of the higher-level one. The values of the assembly-language variables X and Y represent the values of the higher-level variables x and y. If control in the lower-level program is at a, b, or g, then control in the higher-level one is at α, β, or γ, respectively. But what happens when control is at some other point in the assembly language program—for example, at location $b+3$? At that point, X contains an intermediate value of the computation, and its value does not correspond to a valid value of x.

An execution of the higher-level program contains three distinct states, while an execution of the lower-level program contains nine. Three of those nine states, the ones with control at statements a, b, and g, correspond to the three correct states of the higher-level program. The other six states of the lower-level program are "intermediate" states that do not correspond to any states of the higher-level program. We define an implementation to be correct if we can partition the states of the lower-level program into "valid" and "intermediate" states, and define a mapping from valid states to states of the higher-level program such that throwing away the intermediate states and applying the mapping to the remaining sequence of valid states produces a sequence of higher-level states that is a possible behavior of the higher-level program.

This approach is quite natural, and captures the way most people think about implementations. Unfortunately, while it is adequate for sequential programs, it does not work for concurrent ones. In a concurrent program, it is possible for the entire program never to be in a valid state except at the beginning—there could always be some process in an intermediate state. Thus, throwing away the intermediate states leaves us with nothing. Therefore, we must eschew the obvious approach.

The proper approach is more subtle. We cannot throw away any "intermediate" states because, in a concurrent program, almost all the states could be intermediate ones. If we don't throw away any states, how can an execution of the lower-level program with eight different nonstuttering actions correspond to an execution of the higher-level program that has only three different nonstuttering actions? The answer is clear: five of the nonstuttering lower-level actions must correspond to higher-level stuttering actions. How is this possible when the value of X assumes an intermediate value that is never assumed by the higher-level variable x? The answer to this question is more subtle: the value of x is not defined to simply equal

X, but is a more complex function of the lower-level program state.

We will define the variables x and y and the control state pc of the higher-level program as functions of the lower-level program state such that: the execution of statement a corresponds to a nonstuttering high-level action α, the execution of statement $a+1$ corresponds to a stuttering action β, the execution of statement b corresponds to a high-level nonstuttering action β, and execution of the remaining statements in the implementation correspond to stuttering actions γ. This is done as follows:

- pc is defined to equal: (i) α if $PC = a$; (ii) β if $PC = a+1$ or $PC = b$; or (iii) γ if $PC > b$.
- x is defined to equal: (i) X if PC equals a, $a+1$, b, or c; (ii) $X^2 + Y$ if PC equals $b+1$ or $b+2$; or (iii) $X+Y$ if PC equals $b+3$, $b+4$, or $b+5$.
- y is defined to equal Y unless $PC = a+1$, in which case it equals 7.

The reader should check that, with these definitions, execution of the lower-level program statements has the higher-level interpretation indicated above—for example, that executing the store instruction at $b+2$ does not change the value of x, y, or pc, so it is a stuttering action.

Although this procedure for proving that an assembly language program implements a higher-level program works in this example, it is not obvious that it works in general. In fact, the method works only if every variable of the higher-level program can be represented as a function of the lower-level variables (including the "variable" PC). This is not always the case. For example, an optimizing compiler could discover that a variable is never used and decide not to implement it, making it impossible to represent that variable's value as a function of the assembly language program's state. In such a case, one must add "dummy variables" to the assembly-language program—variables and extra statements that are not actually implemented (and take up no memory), but which provide the additional state information needed to represent the higher-level variables. This is seldom necessary in practice and will not be explained in any more detail.

Let us examine more formally what we have done. We expressed each of the state components x, y, and pc of the higher-level program as a function of the state components X, Y, and PC of the assembly language program, and we expressed each of the actions α, β, and γ of the higher-level program as a set of actions of the lower-level one. This defines several mappings. First, there is a mapping F_{st} from states of the lower-level program to states of the higher-level one and a mapping F_{ac} from actions of the lower-level program to actions of the higher-level one. For example, if s is the state $(X = 2, Y = 5, PC = b+1)$ of the assembly language program, then $F_{st}(s)$ is the state $(x = 9, y = 5, pc = \gamma)$ of the higher-level program, and $F_{ac}(a+1) = \beta$—that is, F_{ac} maps the action $a+1$ of the assembly language program (the action corresponding to the *store* Y atomic operation) to the action β of the higher-level program. The mappings F_{st} and F_{ac} define a mapping F on execution sequences, where F maps an execution sequence

$$s_0 \xrightarrow{\xi_1} s_1 \xrightarrow{\xi_2} s_2 \xrightarrow{\xi_3} s_3 \ldots$$

of the assembly language program to the execution sequence

$$F_{st}(s_0) \xrightarrow{F_{ac}(\xi_1)} F_{st}(s_1) \xrightarrow{F_{ac}(\xi_2)} F_{st}(s_2) \xrightarrow{F_{ac}(\xi_3)} F_{st}(s_3) \ldots$$

of the higher-level program. The implementation is correct if, for every execution sequence σ that satisfies the axioms for the assembly language program, the execution $F(\sigma)$ satisfies the axioms for the higher-level program.

Expressing the state components and actions of the higher-level program as functions of the lower-level program state and actions defines a mapping F^* that maps assertions about the higher-level program into assertions about the lower-level program. For example, if A is the assertion (about the state of the higher-level program) that $y = y_0$, then $F^*(A)$ is the assertion (about the state of the assembly language program) obtained by substituting for y its expression as a function of PC and Y—namely, the assertion that if $PC = a+1$ then $7 = y_0$, else $Y = y_0$. If B is the assertion that the next action (in an execution of the higher-level program) is labeled β, then $F^*(B)$ is the assertion that the next action (in an execution of the lower-level program) is labeled either $a+1$ or b.

The mappings F and F^* are related as follows. If A is an assertion about execution sequences of the higher-level program, and σ is an execution sequence of the assembly language program, then the assertion A is true of the execution sequence $F(\sigma)$ if and only if the assertion $F^*(A)$ is true of σ.

1.3 The Formal Description of Systems

Let us now abstract the basic method underlying the above example programs. A *system* is a triple $(\mathcal{B}, \mathbf{S}, \mathbf{A})$, where $\mathbf{S}$ is a set of *states*, $\mathbf{A}$ is a set of *actions*, and $\mathcal{B}$ is a set of *behaviors* of the form

$$s_0 \xrightarrow{\alpha_1} s_1 \xrightarrow{\alpha_2} s_2 \xrightarrow{\alpha_3} s_3 \ldots \tag{1}$$

with each s_i an element of S and each α_i an element of **A**. The set $\mathcal{B}$ must also be ***invariant under stuttering***, which means that given any behavior (1) in $\mathcal{B}$, the behavior obtained by replacing $s_{i-1} \xrightarrow{\alpha_i} s_i$ with $s_{i-1} \xrightarrow{\alpha_i} s_{i-1} \xrightarrow{\alpha_i} s_i$ is also in $\mathcal{B}$.

We now explain how a system is formally described. This involves the formal specification of the sets S and **A** and of the set of behaviors $\mathcal{B}$.

1.3.1 Specifying States and Actions

Specification of the set **A** of actions involves simply naming all the actions. In other words, the set **A** is specified simply by enumerating its elements. This is easy for a finite set. Infinite sets of actions are also possible, and are usually enumerated in parametrized form—e.g., by including a set of actions α^i for every positive integer i.

The set S of states is described in terms of ***state functions***, where a state function is a mapping from S to some set of values called its ***range***. In our specification of the program of Figure 1, we used the three state functions x, y, and pc; the range of x and of y was the set of integers, the range of pc was the set $\{\alpha, \beta, \gamma\}$. In general, the set S is defined by giving a complete collection of state functions $f_1, \ldots, f_n$. An element s of S is uniquely determined by the n-tuple of values $(v_1, \ldots, v_n)$ such that $f_1(s) = v_1, \ldots, f_n(s) = v_n$.

One can further restrict the set S by defining a ***constraint*** that limits the possible sets of n-tuples $(f_1(s), \ldots, f_n(s))$. For example, consider a sequential program with an integer variable u whose scope does not include the entire program. We could define the range of u to consist of the integers together with the special element $\perp$ denoting an undefined value, and then require that the value of u be an integer for certain values of pc and that it equal $\perp$ for the remaining value of pc.

To express this formally, let R_i be the range of f_i. A constraint is a subset C of $R_1 \times \cdots \times R_n$. Given the functions f_i and the set C, S is effectively defined by the requirements: (i) for every element s of S, there is a unique element $(v_1, \ldots, v_n)$ in C such that $f_i(s) = v_i$; and (ii) for distinct elements s and t of S, the n-tuples $(f_1(s), \ldots, f_n(s))$ and $(f_1(t), \ldots, f_n(t))$ are unequal.

A subset C of $R_1 \times \cdots \times R_n$ is the same as a boolean-valued function on that set, where the function C is defined by letting $C(v_1, \ldots, v_n)$ equals *true* if and only if $(v_1, \ldots, v_n)$ is in the set C. A constraint C is usually expressed as the relation $C(f_1, \ldots, f_n)$ among the state functions f_i. For example, suppose there are three state functions f_1, f_2, and f_3, where the ranges R_1 and R_2 are the set of integers and R_3 is the set $\{\alpha, \beta, \gamma\}$. We write $[f_1 < f_2] \wedge [(f_3 = \gamma) \supset (f_1 = 0)]$ to mean the subset

$$\{(v_1, v_2, v_3) : v_1 < v_2 \wedge (v_3 = \gamma \supset v_1 = 0)\}$$

of $R_1 \times R_2 \times R_3$.

In the three programs considered above, the state functions consisted of the program variables and the program counter. With more complicated language constructs, other state functions may be needed to describe the program state. A program with subroutines requires a state function to record the current value of the "stack". A concurrent program that uses message-sending primitives may need state functions that record the contents of message buffers. In general, the state functions must completely describe the current state of the system, specifying everything that is necessary to continue its execution. For a deterministic system, such as the program of Figure 1, the current state completely determines its future behavior. For a nondeterministic system, such as the concurrent program of Figure 2, the current state determines all possible future behavior.

Observe that in giving the state functions and constraint, we are describing the essential properties of the set S, but we are not specifying any particular representation of S. In mathematical terms, we are defining S only up to isomorphism. This little mathematical detail is the formal reason why our specification of the program of Figure 1 does not state whether the variable x is stored in a binary or decimal representation. It doesn't matter whether the elements of S are strings of bits or decimal digits, or even sequences of voltages on flip-flop wires. All that the specification mentions is the value of the state function x, not the structure of the states.

New state functions can be created as combinations of the state functions f_i. For example, if f_1 and f_2 are integer-valued state functions, then we can define a new boolean-valued state function f by letting $f(s) = (f_1(s) < f_2(s) + 3)$, for any s in S. There are two ways to view the state function f. We can think of the f_i as *elementary* state functions and f as a *derived* state function, or we can consider f to have the same status as the f_i by adding the condition $f = (f_1 < f_2 + 3)$ to the constraint. Formally, the two views are equivalent. In practice, the first view seems more convenient and will be adopted.

1.3.2 Specifying Behaviors

Having specified the sets $\mathbf{S}$ and $\mathbf{A}$, we must now specify the set $\mathcal{B}$ of behaviors. The set of behaviors is described formally by a collection of axioms. Four kinds of axioms are used: initial axioms, transition axioms, liveness axioms, halting axioms, and completion axioms.

Initial Axioms A *state predicate* is a boolean-valued state function (either derived or elementary). We say that a predicate P is true for a state s if $P(s)$ equals *true*.

An initial axiom is a state predicate. It is true for the behavior (1) if and only if it is true for the initial state s_0. Initial axioms are used to specify the starting state of the system.

Transition Axioms A *relation* R on the set $\mathbf{S}$ consists of a set of ordered pairs of elements of $\mathbf{S}$. We write sRt to denote that (s, t) is in the relation $\mathbf{S}$. We say that the relation R is *enabled* in a state s if there exists a state t such that sRt. The relation R is said to be *self-disabling* if, for any states s and t such that sRt: R is not enabled in t.

A *transition axiom* is a pair (α, R) where α is an action in $\mathbf{A}$ and R is a self-disabling relation on $\mathbf{S}$. We write this pair as $\alpha : R$ instead of (α, R). The transition axiom $\alpha : R$ asserts the following for a behavior of the form (1):

> (Safety) For each i: if $\alpha_i = \alpha$, then R is enabled in state s_{i-1}, and either $s_{i-1}Rs_i$ or else $s_{i-1} = s_i$.
>
> (Liveness) If there exist infinitely many values of i such that $\alpha_i = \alpha$, then, for any i, there exists a $j > i$ such that R is not enabled in s_j.

This is the formal description of the kind of transition axioms we wrote for the programs of Figures 1 and 2. Each atomic operation of the programs was described by a separate transition axiom.

The behavior (1) can be thought of as an infinite sequence of transitions $s_{i-1} \xrightarrow{\alpha_i} s_i$ such that the final state of each transition equals the initial state of the next transition. A transition axiom describes the transitions that can appear in a behavior. The safety part of a transition axiom $\alpha : R$ asserts how an α transition can change the state. The conjunction of these assertions for all actions α describes all possible ways that the state can change. However, it does not assert that any change must occur. Asserting that something must change is a liveness property. Interesting liveness properties are asserted by special liveness axioms, described below. Being a liveness axiom, the liveness part of a transition axiom is more logically included with the other liveness axioms. However, it expresses a very weak liveness property—namely, that an infinite number of stuttering α transitions cannot occur with R continuously enabled. (Remember that R is self-disabling, so a nonstuttering α action must disable the transition.) We know of no cases in which one does not want at least this liveness property to hold, so it is easiest to include it as part of the transition axiom.

The requirement that R be self-disabling avoids certain formal difficulties, such as the ones pointed out in [3]. In specifying systems, it seems to be a bad idea to allow actions that could repeat themselves infinitely often with no intervening actions—except for a trivial halting action that denotes termination. Thus, this requirement is not a significant restriction.

A relation R on $\mathbf{S}$ is described as a relation on state functions subscripted *new* or *old*. For example, if f and g are state functions, then $f_{new} < g_{old}$ describes the relation R such that sRt is true if and only if $f(t) < g(s)$. In a practical specification language, one needs a convenient notation for expressing relations on state functions. One method is to write the relations using the *new* and *old* subscripts. Another method is to use ordinary programming language constructs. The assignment statement $x := x + y$ describes a relation such that $x_{new} = x_{old} + y_{old}$ and the new and old values of all other variables are the same. The use of *new* and *old* subscripts is more general, since a relation such as $x^2_{new} + y^2_{old} = x_{old}$ cannot be written conveniently as an assignment statement. On the other hand, sometimes the programming notation is more convenient. A specification language should probably allow both notations.

Liveness Axioms Liveness axioms are expressed with temporal logic. The time has come to describe this logic more formally. Fortunately, we need only a very restricted form of temporal logic—a form that is known in the trade as linear-time temporal logic with unary operators. In particular, we do not need the binary "until" operator, which can make formulas hard to understand. Of course, we do not include an "in the next state" operator.

A temporal logic formula represents a boolean function of behaviors. We write $\sigma \models U$ to denote that the formula U is true on the behavior σ. Recall that a state predicate is a boolean-valued function on the set $\mathbf{S}$ of states. An *action predicate* is a boolean-valued function on the set $\mathbf{A}$ of actions. We identify an action α of $\mathbf{A}$ with the action predicate that is true on an action β of $\mathbf{A}$ if and only if $\beta = \alpha$. The generalization of state predicates and action predicates is a *general predicate*, which is a boolean-valued function on the set $(\mathbf{S} \times \mathbf{A})$ of state, action pairs.

A formula of temporal logic is made up of the following building blocks: general predicates; the ordinary logical operators $\wedge$ (conjunction), $\vee$ (disjunction), $\supset$ (implication), and $\neg$ (negation); and the unary temporal operator $\Box$. To define the meaning of any formula, we define inductively what it means for such a formula to be true for a behavior σ of the form (1).

A general predicate G is interpreted as a temporal logic formula by defining $\sigma \models G$ to be true if and only if $G(s_0, \alpha_1)$ is true. Thus, a state predicate is true of a behavior if and only if it is true for the first state, and an action predicate is true of a behavior if and only if it is true for the first action.

The meaning of the ordinary boolean operators is defined in the obvious way—for example, $\sigma \models U \wedge V$ is true if and only if both $(\sigma \models U)$ and $(\sigma \models V)$ are true, and $\sigma \models \neg U$ is true if and only if $\sigma \models U$ is false.

The operator $\Box$, read "always" or "henceforth", is defined as follows. If σ is the behavior (1), then let σ^{+n} be the behavior

$$s_n \overset{\alpha_{n+1}}{\longrightarrow} s_{n+1} \overset{\alpha_{n+2}}{\longrightarrow} \cdots$$

for $n \geq 0$. For any formula U, $\sigma \models \Box U$ is defined to be true if and only if $\sigma^{+n} \models \Box U$ is true for all $n \geq 0$. For example, if P is a state predicate, then $\Box P$ is true for σ if and only if P is true for every state s_n in σ.

The derived operator $\Diamond$, read "eventually", is defined by letting $\Diamond U$ equal $\neg\Box\neg U$ for any formula U. Thus, $\sigma \models \Diamond U$ is true if and only if $\sigma^{+n} \models \Diamond U$ is true for some $n \geq 0$. In particular, if P is a state predicate, then $\Diamond P$ is true for σ if and only if P is true on some state s_n in σ.

The derived operator $\leadsto$, read "leads to", is defined by letting $U \leadsto V$ equal $\Box(U \supset \Diamond V)$. Intuitively, $U \leadsto V$ means that whenever U is true, V must be true then or at some later time. Thus, if P and Q are state predicates and σ is the behavior (1), then $P \leadsto Q$ is true for σ if and only if, for every n: if P is true on state s_n then Q is true on s_m for some $m \geq n$.

You should convince yourself that, for a state predicate P, the formula $\Box\Diamond P$ (read "infinitely often P") is true for the behavior (1) if and only if P is true on infinitely many states s_n, and $\Diamond\Box P$ is true if and only if there is some n such that P is true on all states s_m for $m \geq n$. With a little practice, it is easy to understand the type of temporal logic formulas one writes to specify liveness properties.

Most liveness properties are expressed with the $\leadsto$ operator. A typical property asserts that if a transition becomes enabled then it will eventually "fire". This property is expressed by a formula of the form $P \leadsto \neg P$, where P is the state predicate asserting that the transition is enabled. The liveness part of a transition axiom $\alpha : R$ is $\Box\Diamond A \leadsto \neg P$, where A is the action predicate that is true for action α and false for all other actions, and P is the predicate that is true for a state s if and only if R is enabled on s.

Halting and Completion Axioms A *halting axiom* consists of a pair $\alpha : P$ where α is an action in $\mathbf{A}$ and P is a state predicate. The halting axiom $\alpha : P$ is true for the behavior of (1) if the following condition is satisfied:

For every i: if $\alpha_i = \alpha$, then P is true in state s_{i-1} and $s_i = s_{i-1}$.

The γ Transition Axiom for the program of Figure 1 and the θ Transition Axiom for the program of Figure 2 are examples of halting axioms.

A halting axiom is needed to allow the possibility of halting—the absence of any more nonstuttering transitions. It turns out that, when writing descriptions of individual modules rather than of complete programs, one usually does not need a halting axiom.

The completion axiom defines the set $\mathbf{A}$ of actions, asserting what the possible actions α_i are in a behavior of the form (1). In writing specifications, a slightly different form of completion axiom will be used that asserts which actions are performed by which modules.

1.3.3 Completeness of the Method

Implicit in the work of Alpern and Schneider [2] is a proof that any system that can be described using a very powerful formal system for writing temporal axioms (much more powerful than the simple temporal logic defined above) can also be described by initial axioms, transition axioms, simple liveness axioms of the form $P \leadsto Q$ with P and Q state predicates, a halting axiom, and a completion axiom. Our method for describing systems can therefore be used to provide a formal description of any system that we would expect it to.

Of course, theoretically possible does not necessarily mean practical and convenient. The utility of our formal method as the basis for a practical method for specifying and reasoning about concurrent systems must be demonstrated with examples.

1.3.4 Programs as Axioms

It is customary to adopt the point of view that the transition axiom describes the semantics of the atomic operation. From now on, it will be useful to reverse this way of thinking and instead to think of the atomic operation as a convenient way to write the transition axiom. A program then becomes an easy way to write a collection of axioms.

When writing specifications, programs seem to be convenient for expressing the transition axioms but not so convenient for expressing other liveness properties.

1.4 Implementing One System with Another

1.4.1 The Formal Definition

Let $(\mathcal{B}, \mathbf{S}, \mathbf{A})$ and $(\mathcal{B}', \mathbf{S}', \mathbf{A}')$ be two systems. We now formally define what it means for the first to implement the second. We call $(\mathcal{B}, \mathbf{S}, \mathbf{A})$ the ***lower-level*** system and its state functions, behaviors, etc. are called lower-level objects; $(\mathcal{B}', \mathbf{S}', \mathbf{A}')$ is said to be the ***higher-level*** system and its state functions, etc. are called higher-level objects.

Recall the approach used in Section 1.2, where the lower-level system was an assembly language program and the higher-level one was a program written in a higher-level language. We defined a mapping F from lower-level behaviors to higher-level behaviors. More precisely, if σ is a behavior with lower-level states and actions, then $F(\sigma)$ is a behavior with higher-level states and actions. Correctness of the implementation meant that for any behavior σ of the lower-level system, $F(\sigma)$ is a behavior of the higher-level one. The mapping F was derived from mappings F_{st} from lower-level states to higher-level states and F_{ac} from lower-level actions to higher-level actions.

We generalize this definition slightly by allowing F_{ac} to be a function of both the action and the state of the lower-level system rather than just of the action. This generalization permits the same lower-level action to implement several different higher-level actions. For example, suppose the compiler translates (higher-level) exponential operations into calls of a single (assembly language) exponentiation subroutine. An atomic operation performed by the exponentiation subroutine can correspond to an execution of one of many different atomic operations of the higher-level program, which one depending upon the value of the register that contains the return address of the subroutine call.

The formal definition states that $(\mathcal{B}, \mathbf{S}, \mathbf{A})$ implements $(\mathcal{B}', \mathbf{S}', \mathbf{A}')$ if there exist mappings $F_{st} : \mathbf{S} \rightarrow \mathbf{S}'$ and $F_{ac} : \mathbf{A} \times \mathbf{S} \rightarrow \mathbf{A}'$ such that $F(\mathcal{B}) \subset \mathcal{B}'$, where the mapping F is defined by letting $F(\sigma)$, for the behavior σ given by (1), equal

$$F_{st}(s_0) \stackrel{F_{ac}(\alpha_1,s_0)}{\longrightarrow} F_{st}(s_1) \stackrel{F_{ac}(\alpha_2,s_1)}{\longrightarrow} F_{st}(s_2) \stackrel{F_{ac}(\alpha_3,s_2)}{\longrightarrow} \cdots \tag{2}$$

1.4.2 The Definition in Terms of Axioms

The Mappings The set of states is specified by elementary state functions and a constraint. Let $f_1, \ldots, f_n$ be the elementary state functions and C the constraint that define the set $\mathbf{S}$ of lower-level states, and let $f'_1, \ldots, f'_m$, C' be the elementary state functions and constraint defining the set $\mathbf{S}'$ of higher-level states. To define the mapping F_{st}, we must express each higher-level state function f'_j in terms of the lower-level ones f_i. That is, we must choose mappings $F_j : R_1 \times \cdots \times R_n \rightarrow R'_j$, where R_i is the range of f_i and R'_j is the range of f'_j, and define f'_j to equal $F_j(f_1, \ldots, f_n)$. The F_j must be constraint-preserving—that is, for any v in $R_1 \times \cdots \times R_n$, if $C(v) = \mathit{true}$ then $C'(F_1(v), \ldots, F_m(v)) = \mathit{true}$.

The mappings F_j define the mapping $F_{st} : \mathbf{S} \rightarrow \mathbf{S}'$ as follows. If s is the (unique) element of $\mathbf{S}$ such that $f_i(s) = v_i$, for $i = 1, \ldots, n$, then $F_{st}(s)$ is the element of $\mathbf{S}'$ such that $f'_j(F_{st}(s)) = F_j(v_1, \ldots, v_n)$, for $j = 1, \ldots, m$.

For any higher-level state function f, let $F^*_{st}(f)$ be the lower-level state function such that $F^*_{st}(f)(s)$ is defined to equal $f(F(s))$. It is a simple exercise in unraveling the notation to verify that, for the elementary higher-level state function f'_j, the lower-level state function $F^*_{st}(f'_j)$ is the function $F_j(f_1, \ldots, f_n)$. Thus, for the elementary higher-level state function f'_j, the lower-level state function $F^*_{st}(f'_j)$ is just the definition of f'_j as a function of the lower-level state functions. For a derived higher-level state function f, one can compute $F^*_{st}(f)$ in terms of the functions $F^*_{st}(f'_j)$. For example, $F^*_{st}(3f'_1 + f'_2)$ equals $F^*_{st}(3f'_1) + F^*_{st}(f'_2)$.

These definitions are basically quite simple. Unfortunately, simple ideas can appear complicated when they are expressed in the abstract formalism of n-tuples and mappings. The mapping F_{st} from lower-level states to higher-level ones and the mapping F^*_{st} from higher-level state functions to lower-level ones are the basis for our method of verifying the correctness of an implementation. To fully understand this method, the reader should develop an intuitive understanding of these mappings, and the relation between them. This is best done by expressing the mappings from the example in Section 1.2 in terms of this formalism.

Our specifications talk about state functions rather than states. Hence, it is the mapping F_{st}^* from higher-level state functions to lower-level ones that we must use rather than the mapping F_{st} from lower-level states to higher-level ones.

For any action α, let $A(\alpha)$ be the action predicate such that $A(\alpha)(\xi)$ is true if and only if $\xi = \alpha$. Action predicates of the form $A(\alpha)$ are called *elementary* action predicates; they play the same role for the set of actions that the elementary state functions play for the set of states. Any action predicate can be expressed as a function of elementary action predicates.

Just as the mapping F_{st} is defined by expressing the higher-level elementary state functions in terms of the lower-level ones, the mapping F_{ac} from $\mathbf{A} \times \mathbf{S}$ to $\mathbf{A}'$ is defined by expressing each higher-level elementary action predicate as a function of the lower-level elementary action predicates and state functions. This defines a mapping F_{ac}^* from higher-level action predicates to lower-level general predicates such that $F_{ac}^*(A')(\sigma, s) = A'(F_{ac}(\alpha, s))$ for any higher-level action predicate A. (Recall that a lower-level general predicate is a boolean function on $\mathbf{S} \times \mathbf{A}$.) The formal definitions are analogous to the ones for F_{st} and F_{st}^*, and we won't bother with the details.

The mappings F_{st}^* and F_{ac}^* induce a mapping F^* from higher-level general predicates to lower-level ones, where, for any higher-level general predicate G, $F^*(G)$ is the predicate whose value on (s, α) equals $G(F_{st}(s), F_{ac}(s, \alpha))$. For a high-level state predicate P, $F^*(P)$ is the same as $F_{st}^*(P)$, and, for a high-level action predicate A, $F^*(A)$ is the same as $F_{st}^*(A)$.[1] Any general predicate is represented as a function of elementary state and action predicates, so F^* can be computed from the $F_{st}^*(f_j')$ and the $F_{ac}^*(A(\alpha))$ for the higher-level elementary state functions f_j' and action predicates $A(\alpha)$. For example, $F^*(A(\alpha) \supset f_1 < f_2)$ is the lower-level general predicate $F_{ac}^*(A(\alpha)) \supset F_{st}^*(f_1) < F_{st}^*(f_2)$.

The mapping F^* is extended to arbitrary temporal formulas in the natural way—for example, for general predicates G and H,

$$F^*(\Diamond(\Box G \vee \Diamond H)) = \Diamond(\Box F^*(G) \vee \Diamond F^*(H))$$

Thus, F^* maps higher-level temporal logic formulas into lower-level ones. It is a simple exercise in untangling the notation to verify that, for any lower-level level behavior σ and any higher-level temporal logic formula U: $F(\sigma) \models U$ is true if and only if $\sigma \models F^*(U)$ is.

[1] Formally, this requires identifying the state predicate P with the general predicate $\overline{P}$ such that $\overline{P}(s, \alpha) = P(s)$, and similarly for the action predicate A.

For later use, we note that F_{st} also induces a mapping F^* from higher-level relations on $\mathbf{S}'$ to lower-level relations on $\mathbf{S}$, where $s\,F^*(R)\,t$ is defined to equal $F_{st}(s)\,R\,F_{st}(t)$. The mapping F^* on relations is easily computed from the mapping F^*_{st} on state functions. For example, if R is the higher-level relation defined by $f_{new} < g_{old}$ for higher-level state functions f and g, then $F^*(R)$ is the lower-level relation defined by $F^*_{st}(f)_{new} < F^*_{st}(g)_{old}$.

Mapping the Axioms Suppose that the sets of behaviors $\mathcal{B}$ and $\mathcal{B}'$ are specified by sets of axioms $\mathcal{U}$ and $\mathcal{U}'$, respectively. Thus, a behavior σ is in $\mathcal{B}$ if and only if $\sigma \models U$ is true for every axiom U in $\mathcal{U}$, and similarly for the behaviors in $\mathcal{B}'$. Recall that the lower-level system implements the higher-level one if and only if, for every behavior σ in $\mathcal{B}$, $F(\sigma)$ is in $\mathcal{B}'$. The behavior $F(\sigma)$ is in $\mathcal{B}'$ if and only if $F(\sigma) \models U$ is true for every axiom U in $\mathcal{U}'$, which is true if and only if $\sigma \models F^*(U)$ is true. Hence, to show that $\sigma \in \mathcal{B}$ implies $F(\sigma) \in \mathcal{B}'$, it is necessary and sufficient to show, for all U in $\mathcal{U}'$, that $\forall V \in \mathcal{U} : \sigma \models V$ implies $\sigma \models F^*(U)$, which is the same as showing $\sigma \models (\forall V \in \mathcal{U}) \supset F^*(U)$. Proving that $\sigma \models (\forall V \in \mathcal{U}) \supset F^*(U)$ for all σ means showing that the axioms of $\mathcal{U}$ imply $F^*(U)$.

Thus, to show that the lower-level system implements the higher-level one, we must show that for every higher-level axiom U, the lower-level temporal logic formula $F^*(U)$ is provable from the lower-level axioms. We now consider what this means for the different kinds of axioms that constitute the formal description of a system.

An initial axiom is simply a state predicate. For each higher-level initial axiom P, we must prove that the state predicate $F^*_{st}(P)$ follows from the lower-level initial axioms.

A higher-level liveness axiom is a temporal logic formula, and for each such axiom U we must prove that $F^*(U)$ is a logical consequence of the lower-level liveness axioms. The liveness part of a transition axiom is also considered to be a liveness axiom, and is handled in this way.

If U is the higher-level completion axiom, then $F^*(U)$ follows immediately from the lower-level completion axiom and the fact that the range of values assumed by F_{ac} is contained in the set $\mathbf{A}'$.

Finally, we consider the conjunction of the halting axioms and the safety part of the transition axioms as a single higher-level axiom U. The axiom U asserts that for any higher-level transition $s' \xrightarrow{\alpha'} t'$:

- If there is a transition axiom $\alpha' : R'$ then R' is enabled in state s' and either $s' R' t'$ or $s' = t'$.

- If there is a halting axiom $\alpha' : P'$ then P' is true for state s' and $s' = t'$.

The formula $F^*(U)$ asserts that for any lower-level transition $s \xrightarrow{\alpha} t$:

- If there is a transition axiom $F_{ac}(\alpha, s) : R'$ then R' is enabled in state $F_{st}(s)$ and either $F_{st}(s)\, R'\, F_{st}(t)$ or $F_{st}(s) = F_{st}(t)$.
- If there is a halting axiom $F_{ac}(\alpha, s) : P'$ then P' is true for state $F_{st}(s)$ and $F_{st}(s) = F_{st}(t)$.

The lower-level transition axioms determine the possible lower-level transitions $s \xrightarrow{\alpha} t$. Assume that for each action there is exactly one transition or halting axiom.[2] Then a lower-level transition $s \xrightarrow{\alpha} t$ must satisfy either a transition axiom $\alpha : R$ or a halting axiom $\alpha : P$. It follows from the above characterization of the formula $F^*(U)$ that the lower-level transition and halting axioms imply $F^*(U)$ if and only if the following conditions hold:

- For every lower-level transition axiom $\alpha : R$, if sRt then:
  - If there is a transition axiom $F_{ac}(\alpha, s) : R'$ then R' is enabled in state $F_{st}(s)$ and either $F_{st}(s)\, R'\, F_{st}(t)$ or $F_{st}(s) = F_{st}(t)$.
  - If there is a halting axiom $F_{ac}(\alpha, s) : P'$ then P' is true for state $F_{st}(s)$ and $F_{st}(s) = F_{st}(t)$.
- For every lower-level halting axiom $\alpha : P$, if P is true on a state s then there is a halting axiom $F_{ac}(\alpha, s) : P'$ and P' is true on state $F_{st}(s)$.

These conditions imply that for every transition $s \xrightarrow{\alpha} t$ satisfying the lower-level transition or halting axiom for α, the transition $F_{st}(s) \xrightarrow{F_{ac}(\alpha,s)} F_{st}(t)$ satisfies the higher-level transition or halting axiom for $F_{ac}(\alpha, s)$.

The above conditions can be written more compactly in the common case when $F_{ac}(\alpha, s)$ depends only upon the action α. In that case, the conditions can be expressed as follows, where $=$ denotes the equality relation (the set of pairs (s, s)) and enabled(R) is the predicate that is true for state s if and only if R is enabled in s. (Recall that $F^*(R')$ is the relation such that $s\, F^*(R')\, t$ if and only if $F_{st}(s)\, R'\, F_{st}(t)$.)

- For every lower-level transition axiom $\alpha : R$:

[2] It makes no sense to have both a transition and a halting axiom for the same transition, and the conjunction of two transition axioms $\alpha : R$ and $\alpha : R'$ is equivalent to the single transition axiom $\alpha : R \cap R'$.

- If there is a transition axiom $F_{ac}(\alpha)$: R' then enabled$(R) \supset F^*(\text{enabled}(R'))$ and $R \subset F^*(R' \cup =)$.
- If there is a halting axiom $F_{ac}(\alpha) : P'$ then enabled$(R) \supset F^*(P')$ and $R \subset F^*(=)$.

- For every lower-level halting axiom $\alpha : P$, there is a halting axiom $F_{ac}(\alpha) : P'$ such that $P \supset F^*(P')$.

2 Specification

Thus far, we have been discussing the formal description of a complete system. A prerequisite for a *specification* is the splitting of a system into two parts: the part to be specified, which we call a *module*, and the rest of the system, which we will call the *environment*. A Modula-2 [11] module is an example of something that could qualify as a "module", but it is not the only example. A piece of hardware, such as RAM chip, could also be a module. The purpose of a specification is to describe how the module interacts with the environment, so that (i) the environment can use the module with no further knowledge about how it is implemented, and (ii) the module can be implemented with no further knowledge of how it will be used. (A Modula-2 definition module describes the "syntax" of this interaction; a complete specification must describe the semantics.)

One can regard a Modula-2 module as a module, with the rest of the program as the environment. A specification describes the effects of calling the module's procedures, where these effects can include the setting of exported variables and **var** arguments, calls to other procedures that are part of the environment, and the eventual setting of the "program counter" to the location immediately following the procedure call. The specification describes only the procedure's interaction with the environment, not how this interaction is implemented. For example, it should not rule out the possibility of an implementation that invokes machine-language subroutines, or even special-purpose hardware. Any other requirements—for example, that the procedure be implemented in ASCII standard Pascal, or that it be delivered on 1600 bpi magnetic tape, or that it be written on parchment in green ink—are not part of the specifications that we will write. This omission is not meant to imply that these other requirements are unimportant. Any formal method must restrict itself to some aspect of a system, and we choose to consider only the specification of the interface.

It is reasonably clear what is meant by specifying a Modula-2 module because the boundary between the module and the environment is evident. On the other hand, we have no idea what it would mean to specify the solar system because we do not know what is the module to be specified and what is its environment. One can give a formal description of some aspect of the solar system, such as the ones developed by Ptolemy, Copernicus, and Kepler. The distinction we make between a specification and a formal description appears not to be universally accepted, since a workshop on specifying concurrent systems [4] was devoted to ten "specification" problems, only three of which had moderately clear boundaries between the module to be specified and its environment.

2.1 The Axioms

As we have seen, the complete system is described formally by a triple $(\mathcal{B}, \mathbf{S}, \mathbf{A})$, where $\mathcal{B}$ is a set of behaviors. A behavior is a sequence of transitions $s \xrightarrow{\alpha} t$, where α is a transition in $\mathbf{A}$ and s and t are states in $\mathbf{S}$. When specifying a module, we don't know what the complete set of states $\mathbf{S}$ is, nor what the complete set of actions $\mathbf{A}$ is. All we can know about are the part of the state accessed by the module and the subset of actions that are relevant to the module's activities, including those actions performed by the module itself.

A complete system $(\mathcal{B}, \mathbf{S}, \mathbf{A})$ is specified by a collection of axioms. This collection of axioms should be partitioned into two subcollections: ones that specify the module and ones that specify the rest of the system. Our task is to write the axioms that specify the module without making any unnecessary restrictions on the behavior of the rest of the system.

A major purpose of labeling the arc in a transition $s \xrightarrow{\alpha} t$ is that it allows us to identify whether the transition is performed by the module or the environment. The operation of the module is specified by axioms about transitions performed by the module—usually describing how they change the state. The specification of the module must also include axioms about transitions performed by the environment, since no module can work properly in the face of completely arbitrary behavior by the environment. (Imagine trying to write a procedure that works correctly even though concurrently operating processes are randomly modifying the procedure's local variables.) Axioms about the environment's transitions usually specify what the environment cannot do—for example, that it cannot change parts of the state that are local to the module.

We will partition a module's specification into axioms that constrain the module's behavior and ones that constrain the environment. This will be done by talking about transitions—axioms that describe the module's transitions constrain the module's behavior, and ones that describe the environment's transitions constrain the environment's behavior. However, this is not as easy as it sounds. The implications of axioms are not always obvious, and axioms that appear to specify the module may actually constrain the behavior of the environment. For example, consider a specification of a Modula-2 procedure that returns the square root of its argument, the result and argument being of type **real**. Neglecting problems of round-off error, we might specify this procedure by requiring that, if it is called with an argument x, then it will eventually return a value y such that $y^2 = x$. Such a specification contains only axioms specifying the module, and no axioms specifying the environment. However, observe that the specification implies that if the procedure is called with an argument of -4, then it must return a real value y such that $y^2 = -4$. This is impossible. The axioms specifying the module therefore constrain the environment never to call the procedure with a negative argument.

In general, for an axiom that specifies a safety property, it is possible to determine if an axiom constrains the module, the environment, or both. However, it appears to be impossible to do this for a liveness axiom.

In practice, one specifies safety properties by transition axioms, and it is easy to see if a transition axiom constrains the module or the environment; a transition axiom for a module action constrains the module and one for an environment action constrains the environment. Liveness properties are more subtle. A liveness property is specified by an axiom asserting that, under certain conditions, a particular transition must eventually occur. For example, when the subroutine has been called, a "return" action must eventually occur. We view such an axiom as constraining the module in question if the transition is performed by the module, and as constraining the environment if it is performed by the environment. However, we must realize that a liveness axiom could have nonobvious implications. In the above example, a simple liveness property of the module (that it must return an answer) implies a safety property of the environment (that it may not call the module with a negative argument).

2.2 The Interface

The mechanism by which the module and the environment communicate is called the *interface*. The specification should describe everything that the environment needs to know in order to use the module, which implies that the interface must be specified at the implementation level. A procedure to compute a square root will not function properly if it expects its argument to be represented as a double-word binary floating point number and it is called with an argument represented as a string of ASCII characters.

The need to specify the interface at the implementation level is not restricted to the relatively minor problems of data representation. See [8] for an example indicating how the interface's implementation details can influence the specification of fundamental properties of concurrent systems.

In practice, specifying the interface at the implementation level is not a problem. When writing a specification, one generally knows if the implementation is going to be in Modula 2, Ada, or CMOS. One can then specify the interface as, for example, a collection of procedure calls with arguments of a certain type. For a Modula 2 module, the definition module will usually provide the interface specification. (Unfortunately, it is unlikely that the semantics of any existing concurrent programming language are specified precisely enough to insure that specifications are always independent of the particular compiler.)

We shall see that the specification can be decomposed into two parts: the *interface* specification and the *internal* specification. The interface specification is implementation dependent. In principle, the internal specification is independent of the implementation. However, details of the interface are likely to manifest themselves in the internal specification as well. For example, what a procedure does when called with incorrect input may depend upon whether or not the language provides an exception-handling mechanism.

The need to specify the interface at the implementation level was recognized by Guttag and Horning in the design of Larch [5]. What they call the language-dependent part of the specification corresponds to the interface specification. The language-independent part of a Larch specification includes some aspects of our internal specification. However, to handle concurrency, we need to describe the behavior of the module during a procedure call, a concept not present in a Larch specification, which describes only input/output relations.

2.3 State Functions

2.3.1 The Module's State Functions

To describe the set S of states of the complete program, we give a collection of state functions $f_1, \ldots, f_n$, and a constraint C, and assert that S is determined by the values of these functions—for every n-tuple $(v_1, \ldots, v_n)$ of values that satisfies the constraint C, there is a *unique* element s of S such that, for all i, $f_i(s) = v_i$.

When specifying a module, we do not know the complete state because we know very little about the environment. We can only know about the part of S that is relevant to the module. Fortunately, this causes no difficulty. To specify a module, we specify n state functions f_i and constraint C that describe the relevant part of the state, and we drop the requirement that the n-tuple of values $f_i(s)$ uniquely determines the state s. There can be many states s that have the same values $f_i(s)$, but have different values of $g(s)$ for some state function g that is relevant only to the environment. For example, if our module is a Modula-2 module, g could represent the value of a variable local to some separate module.

2.3.2 Interface and Internal State Functions

The decomposition of the system into environment and module implies that there are two different types of state functions: *interface* state functions and *internal* state functions. Interface state functions are part of the interface. They are externally visible, and are specified at the implementation level. To explain why they are needed, we briefly discuss the nature of communication.

Synchronous processes can communicate through transient phenomena; if you are listening to me, waiting for me to say something, I can communicate by sound waves, which are a transient disturbance in the atmosphere. However, if we are not synchronized in this way, and I don't know whether or not you are listening to me, we cannot communicate in this way. In the asynchronous case, I have to make some nontransient state change—for example, writing a message on your blackboard or magnetizing the surface of the tape in your answering machine. You can receive my communication by examining the state of your blackboard or answering machine. Communication is effected with a nontransient change to a communication medium. In computer systems, we sometimes pretend that asynchronous processes communicate by transient events such as sending a message. However, a closer examination reveals that the transient event actually institutes a nontransient state change to a communication medium—for example, by putting a message in a buffer. Communication is achieved through the use of this medium. We specify the communication between the environment and the module in terms of the state of the communication medium.

The interface state functions represent the communication medium by which the environment and the module communicate. In the specification of a hardware component, the interface state functions might include the voltage levels on certain wires. In the specification of a procedure, the interface state functions might include parameter-passing mechanisms. For example, immediately after the environment executes a call to this procedure, there must be some state component that records the fact that the procedure has just been called and the argument with which it was called. The state functions that provide this information are part of the interface specification. For a Modula-2 module, the interface functions are implicitly specified by the definition module. Fortunately, there is usually no need explicitly to describe those interface state functions in detail.

Interface state functions can be directly observed or modified by the environment; the environment can read the voltage on the wires leading to the hardware device, or set the value of the state function that describes the argument with which a procedure is called. Internal state functions are not directly observable by the environment. Their values can only be inferred indirectly, by observing the external behavior of the module as indicated by the values of its interface state functions. For example, consider the specification of a Modula-2 module that implements a queue, having a procedure that adds an element to the end of the queue and one that removes an element from the head of the queue. Its specification will include, as an internal state function, the value of the queue—that is, the sequence of elements comprising the current contents of the queue. This state function is probably not directly observable; the queue is probably implemented by variables that are local to the module and not visible externally. One can only infer the contents of the queue by the module's response to a sequence of procedure calls.

2.3.3 Aliasing and Orthogonality

In a program, we usually assume that distinct variables represent disjoint data objects—that is, we assume the absence of *aliasing*. Given a complete program, without pointers and dereferencing operations, aliasing can be handled by explicitly determining which variable is aliased to what. However, with the introduction of pointers or, equivalently, of procedures with "var" parameters, aliasing is no longer such a simple matter. Two procedure parameters with different names may, in a particular call of that procedure, represent the identical data object.

In programming languages, aliasing manifests itself most clearly in an assignment statement—x and y are aliased if assigning a value to x can change the value of y. The usual case is the absence of aliasing, which we call *orthogonality*. In an ordinary programming language, two variables x and y are said to be orthogonal to one another if assigning to one of them does not change the value of the other. The concepts of aliasing and orthogonality must be precisely defined in any specification language. Any method for specifying a transition must describe both what state functions change and what state functions do not change. Specifying what state functions change, and how they change, is conceptually simple. For example, we can write the assignment statement $x := x + y$ to specify that the value of x changes such that $x_{new} = x_{old} + y_{old}$. However, describing what state functions don't change is more difficult. Implicit in the assignment statement $x := x + y$ is the assumption that state functions orthogonal to x are not changed. However, a precise definition of orthogonality is difficult—especially when the state includes pointers and transient objects. A complete discussion of the problem of aliasing is beyond the scope of this paper. See [9] for an introduction to aliasing and orthogonality in sequential programs.

Just as with program variables, different state functions are usually orthogonal. The constraint determines any "aliasing" relations that may exist between state functions in the same module. A constraint such as $f > g$ may be regarded as a general form of aliasing, since changing the value of f might necessitate a change to g to maintain this constraint. Aliasing relations between state functions from different modules are what makes intermodule communication possible. If two modules communicate through the value of a voltage on a wire, then that value is an interface state function in each of the modules, those two state functions being aliases of one another. As another example, suppose a procedure in a module A calls a procedure in another module B. The interface state function of module A that represents the argument with which A calls B's procedure is aliased to the state function of module B that represents the value of the argument parameter.

Internal state functions of one module are assumed to be orthogonal to internal state functions of any other module and to any interface state functions, including the ones of the same module. By their nature, internal state functions are not directly accessible from the environment, so they cannot be aliased to state functions belonging to or accessible from the environment.

2.4 Axioms

2.4.1 Concepts

Recall that, to specify a complete system, we had the following classes of axioms: initial axioms, transition axioms, liveness axioms, halting axioms and completion axioms. In order to specify a module, which is only part of the complete system, some modifications to this approach are needed.

No change is needed to the way we write initial axioms and liveness axioms. Of course, when specifying liveness properties, we must remember that the module is not executing in isolation. The discussion of the fairness axioms in Section 1.1.5 indicates the type of considerations that this involves.

A halting axiom does not seem to be necessary. The module halts by performing no further transitions; halting transitions can be provided by the environment.

Recall that, for a complete system, the completion axiom specified the set of all actions. In specifying a module, we obviously do not know what the set of *all* actions is; we can specify only what the module's actions are. Thus, the completion axiom asserts that every action of the module is an element of some set $\mathbf{A}_m$ of actions.

Fundamental to splitting the system into module and environment is the ability to distinguish the module's actions from the environment's actions. For example, when presented with a machine-language implementation of a program containing a Modula-2 module, we must be able to determine which machine-language statement executions belong to the module, and which to its environment (the rest of the program). To understand why this is important, consider a specification of a queue, where the interface contains two procedures: *put* to insert an element at the end of the queue and *get* to fetch the element at the front of the queue. An important part of the specification that is often overlooked is the requirement that the *put* and *get* procedures be called by the environment, not by the module. Without this requirement, a "correct" implementation could arbitrarily insert and delete elements from the queue by calling the *put* and *get* procedures itself.

The specification must specify actions performed by the environment as well as those performed by the module. The environment actions that must be specified are the ones by which the environment changes interface functions—for example, the action of calling a procedure in a Modula-2 module. An external action in the specification of a module will be a module action in the specification of some other module.

Environment actions should not change internal state functions. Indeed, allowing the environment to change an internal state function would effectively make that state function part of the interface.

2.4.2 Notation

A specification language requires some convenient notation for writing axioms. As we have seen, the subtle issue is the specification of the relation R of a transition axiom (α, R). For a complete system, we could write R as a simple relation on n-tuples of state function values. This doesn't work specifying a module in a larger system because we don't know what all the state functions are. Therefore, we must write the relation R in two parts: one specifying what state functions it can change, and the other specifying how it can change those state functions. The first part is specified by simply listing the state functions; the second is specified by writing a relation between the old and new values of state functions. One could write a transition axiom in the following fashion:

module transition α **changes only** f, g:

$$(f_{old} = 1) \wedge (f_{new} = g_{old}) \wedge (g_{new} = h + g_{old})$$

This axiom specifies that an α transition, which is a transition performed by the module rather than the environment, is enabled for a state s if and only if $f(s) = 1$, and a nonstuttering α transitions sets the new value of f to the old value of g, sets the new value of g to its old value plus the value of h, and changes no other state functions. Since α does not change h, the new and old values of h are the same, so no subscript is needed. As before, this axiom also includes a liveness part that asserts that there cannot be an infinite number of α transitions without the transition becoming disabled (f assuming a value different from 1).

We could also adopt a more programming language style of notation and write this transition axiom as follows:

$$\begin{array}{l}\alpha\text{: } \langle\, f = 1 \rightarrow f := g; \\ \quad g := h + g \\ \quad \rangle\end{array}$$

This assumes a convention that only state functions appearing on the left-hand side of an assignment statement may be changed.

To be more precise, the above transition axioms do not say that an α transition changes only f and g; it could also change the value of state functions aliased to f or g. What it actually asserts is that any state function orthogonal to both f and g is left unchanged by an α transition.

It is often convenient to use parametrized transition axioms, such as:

module transition $\alpha(x : \textbf{integer})$ **changes only** f, g:
$$(f_{old} = x) \wedge (f_{new} = g_{old}) \wedge (g_{new} = h + g_{old})$$

Formally, this specifies a set of transition axioms—one for each (integer) value of x. It is simply a way of saving us from having to write an infinite number of separate axioms. Thus, $\alpha(-5)$ and $\alpha(7)$ are two completely different actions; they are not "invocations" of any single entity α.

For any state function f, the transition axioms for the complete system describe what transitions can change f. If f is an internal state function, then we know that only the module's transitions can change its value. However, an interface state function can be changed by actions of the environment. We need some way to constrain how the environment can change an interface state function. We could use transition axioms to specify all possible ways that the environment can modify an interface state function. However, it is more convenient to write the following kind of axiom:

f **changed only by** $\alpha_1, \ldots, \alpha_m$ **while** P

where f is a state function, the α_i are transitions, and P is a state predicate. This asserts that if a behavior includes a transition $s \xrightarrow{\alpha} t$ for which $f(s) \neq f(t)$, then either $P(s)$ is false or else α is one of the α_i. Of course, one can find syntactic "sugarings" of this type of axiom, such as omitting the **while** clause when P is identically true, thereby asserting that f can be changed only by the indicated transitions and by no others.

A **changed only by** axiom is needed for every interface state function; without one, the environment would be allowed to change the function at any time in any way. Since internal state functions can be changed only by the module's transitions, they do not need a **changed only by** axiom—the module's transition axioms explicitly state what state functions they can change. However, it would probably be a good idea to include one for redundancy.

2.4.3 Formal Interpretation

In Section 1.3, we defined a system to be a triple $(\mathcal{B}, \mathbf{S}, \mathbf{A})$, where $\mathbf{S}$ is a set of states, $\mathbf{A}$ is a set of actions, and $\mathcal{B}$ is a set of behaviors. The set of states was specified by giving the ranges of the state functions $f_1, \ldots, f_n$ and a constraint C that they satisfy. For simplicity, we will drop the constraint C from here on, assuming that it is the trivial constraint that is satisfied by all n-tuples. (It is a simple matter to add the constraint to the formalism.) By requiring that the n values $f_1(s), \ldots, f_n(s)$ uniquely determine s among all the elements of $\mathbf{S}$, we determined $\mathbf{S}$ up to isomorphism. Here, we drop that requirement, so specifying the ranges of the state functions f_i still leaves a great deal of freedom in the choice of the set $\mathbf{S}$.

Instead of a single collection of state functions, we now have two kinds of state functions: the internal state functions, which we denote $f_1, \ldots, f_n$, and interface state functions, which we denote $h_1, \ldots, h_p$. Similarly, there are two types of actions: internal actions $\alpha_1, \ldots, \alpha_s$ and interface actions $\gamma_1, \ldots, \gamma_t$.[3] The specification consists of initial axioms, transition axioms, etc., which can all be expressed as temporal logic formulas. Let $\mathcal{U}$ denote the temporal logic formula that is the conjunction of all these axioms. Then the free variables of this formula are the f_i, h_i, α_i, and γ_i. Formally, the specification is the formula[4]

$$\exists f_1 \ldots f_n \alpha_1 \ldots \alpha_s : \mathcal{U}$$

Thus, the interface state functions h_i and actions γ_i are the free variables of the specification, while the internal state functions and actions are quantified existentially. As we shall see, this is the mathematical expression of the fact that one is free to implement the internal state functions and actions as one chooses, but the interface state functions and actions are given.

What does it mean for a system $(\mathcal{B}, \mathbf{S}, \mathbf{A})$ to satisfy this formula? Since $\mathcal{U}$ has the h_i and γ_i as free variables, these state functions and action predicates must be defined on $\mathbf{S}$ and $\mathbf{A}$, respectively. If that is the case, then it makes sense to ask if the temporal logic formula $\mathcal{U}$ is true for a behavior in $\mathcal{B}$. We therefore say that $(\mathcal{B}, \mathbf{S}, \mathbf{A})$ satisfies this formula if and only if the state functions h_i are defined on $\mathbf{S}$, the γ_i are elements of $\mathbf{A}$, and the formula is true for every behavior in $\mathcal{B}$.

There is one problem with this definition: we have not yet defined the semantics of the temporal logic formula $\exists x : U$ when x is a state function or action predicate. We give the definition for x a state function; the definition for action predicates is similar. Let σ be the behavior $s_0 \xrightarrow{\alpha_1} s_1 \xrightarrow{\alpha_2} \ldots$ and let σ' be the behavior $s'_0 \xrightarrow{\alpha_1} s'_1 \xrightarrow{\alpha_2}$. We say that σ and σ' are equivalent

[3]For notational convenience, we are assuming that there are a finite number of state functions and actions; however, there could be infinitely many of them.

[4]The formula $\exists x_1 \ldots x_q : X$ is an abbreviation for $\exists x_1 : \exists x_2 : \ldots \exists x_n : X$.

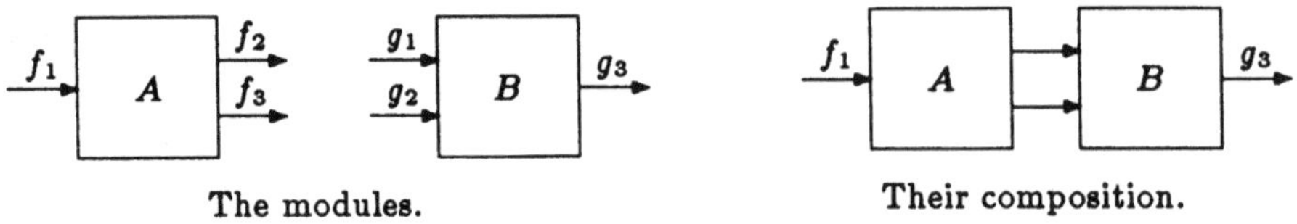

Figure 4: Two hardware modules and their composition.

except for x if, for every i and every state function f that is orthogonal to x, $f(s_i) = f(s'_i)$. We define a *stuttering* behavior of σ to be a behavior obtained from σ by replacing each transition $s_{i-1} \xrightarrow{\alpha_i} s_i$ by a nonempty finite sequence of transitions of the form $s_{i-1} \xrightarrow{\alpha_i} s_{i-1} \xrightarrow{\alpha_i} \ldots \xrightarrow{\alpha_i} s_{i-1} \xrightarrow{\alpha_i} s_i$. We then define $\sigma \models \exists x : U$ to be true if and only if there exists a behavior σ' that is equivalent except for x to some stuttering behavior of σ such that $\sigma' \models x : U$ is true. In other words, $\exists x : U$ is true on a behavior if and only if we can make U true by adding stuttering actions and arbitrarily changing the value of x on each state.[5]

2.5 The Composition of Modules

One builds a system by combining (composing) modules. As an example, consider two hardware modules, A and B, and their composition, illustrated in Figure 4. The specification of module A has three interface state functions, f_1, f_2, and f_3, whose values represent the voltage levels on the indicated wires. Similarly, module B's specification has the interface state functions g_1, g_2, and g_3.

Connecting the two modules as shown in the figure means identifying the state functions f_2 and f_3 of A's specification with the state functions g_1 and g_2 of B's specification—that is, declaring $f_2 \equiv g_1$ and $f_3 \equiv g_2$. Suppose the specification of A includes a single transition α of A that can change f_2 and f_3. The specification of B might include a transition axiom for a transition β of B's environment describing how g_1 and g_2 are allowed to change. (The fact that A changes f_2 and f_3 while the environment changes g_1 and g_2 means that f_2 and f_3 are outputs of A while g_1 and g_2 are inputs to B.)

The formal specification of the composition of the two modules is the conjunction of their specifications—that is, the conjunction of the axioms

[5] I wish to thank Amir Pnueli for pointing out this definition to me.

that make up their specifications—conjoined with the aliasing relations $f_2 \equiv g_1$ and $f_3 \equiv g_2$.

2.6 The Correctness of an Implementation

In Section 1.4 we defined what it meant for one complete system $(\mathcal{B}, \mathbf{S}, \mathbf{A})$ to implement another complete system $(\mathcal{B}', \mathbf{S}', \mathbf{A}')$. The definition was based upon mappings $F_{st} : \mathbf{S} \to \mathbf{S}'$ and $F_{ac} : \mathbf{A} \times \mathbf{S} \to \mathbf{A}'$. From these mappings, we defined mappings F_{st}^* from state functions on $\mathbf{S}'$ to state functions on $\mathbf{S}$ and F_{ac}^* from action predicates on $\mathbf{A}'$ to functions on $\mathbf{A} \times \mathbf{S}$.

If we examine how all these mappings are actually defined for a real example, we discover that it is the mappings F_{st}^* and F_{ac}^* that are really being defined. This is because we don't know what the actual states are, just the state functions. Let $f_1, \ldots, f_n$ be the state functions of the first system and $f_1', \ldots, f_m'$ be the state functions of the second system. To define the mapping F_{ac}, we must express the values of each f_i' in terms of the f_j, which means defining the state function $F_{st}^*(f_j')$.

The mappings F_{st}^* and F_{ac}^* in turn define a mapping F^* from temporal logic formulas about behaviors in $\mathcal{B}'$ to temporal logic formulas about behaviors in $\mathcal{B}$. If the sets of behaviors $\mathcal{B}$ and $\mathcal{B}'$ are defined by the axioms $\mathcal{U}$ and $\mathcal{U}'$, respectively, then $(\mathcal{B}, \mathbf{S}, \mathbf{A})$ correctly implements $(\mathcal{B}', \mathbf{S}', \mathbf{A}')$ if and only if $\mathcal{U}$ implies $F^*(\mathcal{U}')$.

Now let us turn to the question of what it means for a specification of one or more modules to implement a specification of another module. As we have seen, the formal specification of a module or collection of modules is a formula of the form

$$\exists f_1 \ldots f_n \alpha_1 \ldots \alpha_s : \mathcal{U} \tag{3}$$

where the f_i and α_i are the internal state functions and actions, and $\mathcal{U}$ is a temporal logic formula that depends upon the f_i and α_i as well as on interface state functions h_i and actions γ_i.

Let $\mathcal{M}$ be the formula (3) and let $\mathcal{M}'$ be the similar formula

$$\exists f_1' \ldots f_m' \alpha_1' \ldots \alpha_r' : \mathcal{U}' \tag{4}$$

so $\mathcal{M}'$ specifies a module with internal state functions f_j' and internal actions α_j'. There are two characterizations of what it means for the module specified by $\mathcal{M}$ to implement the module specified by $\mathcal{M}'$:

1. Every system $(\mathcal{B}, \mathbf{S}, \mathbf{A})$ that satisfies the formula $\mathcal{M}$ also satisfies the formula $\mathcal{M}'$.

2. $\mathcal{M}$ implies $\mathcal{M}'$.

Since one temporal logic formula implies another if and only if every behavior that satisfies the first also satisfies the second, it is easy to see that these two characterizations are equivalent.

To prove that the module specified by $\mathcal{M}$ implements the module specified by $\mathcal{M}'$, we must prove that $\mathcal{M}$ implies $\mathcal{M}'$. Recall that these two formulas are given by (3) and (4). To prove that $\mathcal{M}$ implies $\mathcal{M}'$, it suffices to construct mappings F^*_{st} and F^*_{ac}, which define the mapping F^*, as above so that $\mathcal{U}$ implies $F^*(\mathcal{U}')$. This is exactly the same procedure used in Section 1.4 to prove that one system implement another. The only difference is that, in addition to the internal state functions and actions f_i, α_i, f'_i, α'_i, the axioms also involve the interface state functions and actions. (Another way of viewing this is to say that F^*_{st} and F^*_{ac} are defined so they map each interface state function h_i and interface action γ_i into itself.) Thus, the method of actually verifying that one module implements another is the same one used to show that one concurrent program implements another.

As we observed earlier, it is not always possible to define the f'_j as functions of the f_i. In this case, it is necessary to add "dummy" internal state functions $g_1, \ldots, g_d$ to the system specified by $\mathcal{M}$, and to define the f'_j as functions of the f_i and the g_i. For notational convenience, suppose that one introduces a single dummy state function g. Let $\mathcal{M}_d$ be the temporal logic formula that represents the new specification. We want to prove that the new specification $\mathcal{M}_d$ correctly implements $\mathcal{M}'$ and infer from that $\mathcal{M}$ correctly implements $\mathcal{M}'$. This means that we must prove that $\mathcal{M}$ implies $\mathcal{M}_d$. If $\mathcal{M}$ is the formula (3), then $\mathcal{M}_d$ is the formula

$$\exists g : \exists f_1 \ldots f_n \alpha_1 \ldots \alpha_s : \mathcal{U}_d$$

Assume that the dummy state function g is orthogonal to all other state functions, both internal and external. (The specification language will have some notation, analogous to variable declarations in programming languages, for introducing a new state functions that is orthogonal to all other state functions.) To prove that $\mathcal{M}$ implies $\mathcal{M}_d$, we must show that $\mathcal{U}_d$ must has the following property: if σ is any behavior that satisfies $\mathcal{U}$, then there is a behavior σ' that is equivalent except for g to some stuttering behavior of σ such that σ' satisfies $\mathcal{U}_d$.

The condition for the specification with the dummy state function to be equivalent to the original specification is stated in terms of the semantics of the temporal logic—whether or not a behavior satisfies an axiom—rather than within the logic itself. One wants syntactic rules for adding dummy state functions that ensure that this condition is satisfied. the specification. These rules will depend upon the particular specification language; they will correspond to the rules given by Owicki [10] for a simple programming language.

References

[1] Bowen Alpern and Fred B. Schneider. Defining liveness. *Information Processing Letters*, 21:181–185, October 1985.

[2] Bowen Alpern and Fred B. Schneider. *Verifying Temporal Properties without using Temporal Logic.* Technical Report TR85-723, Department of Computer Science, Cornell University, December 1985.

[3] Howard Barringer, Ruurd Kuiper, and Amir Pnueli. A really abstract concurrent model and its temporal logic. In *Thirteenth Annual ACM Symposium on Principles of Programming Languages*, pages 173–183, ACM, January 1986.

[4] B. T. Denvir, W. T. Harwood, M. I. Jackson, and M. J. Wray, editors. *The Analysis of Concurrent Systems.* Volume 207 of *Lecture Notes in Computer Science*, Springer-Verlag, Berlin, 1985.

[5] J. V. Guttag, J. J. Horning, and J. M. Wing. *Larch in Five Easy Pieces.* Technical Report 5, Digital Equipment Corporation Systems Research Center, July 1985.

[6] Leslie Lamport. *An Axiomatic Semantics of Concurrent Programming Languages*, pages 77–122. Springer-Verlag, Berlin, 1985.

[7] Leslie Lamport. Specifying concurrent program modules. *ACM Transactions on Programming Languages and Systems*, 5(2):190–222, April 1983.

[8] Leslie Lamport. What it means for a concurrent program to satisfy a specification: why no one has specified priority. In *Proceedings of the Twelfth ACM Symposium on Principles of Programming Languages*, pages 78–83, ACM SIGACT-SIGPLAN, New Orleans, January 1985.

[9] Leslie Lamport and Fred B. Schneider. Constraints: a uniform approach to aliasing and typing. In *Proceedings of the Twelfth ACM*

Symposium on Principles of Programming Languages, ACM SIGACT-SIGPLAN, New Orleans, January 1985.

[10] S. Owicki. *Axiomatic Proof Techniques for Parallel Programs*. PhD thesis, Cornell University, August 1975.

[11] Niklaus Wirth. *Programming in Modula-2*. Springer-Verlag, third edition, 1985.

ON THE CONSTRUCTION OF DISTRIBUTED PROGRAMS

G. Roucairol
BULL S.A.
68, route de Versailles
78430 Louveciennes, France

1. INTRODUCTION

The construction of correct sequential programs requires generally that two main objectives have to be achieved.
The program must be partially correct : if the program terminates then the contents of its variables must satisfy some property for which the program has been built.
The program must be totally correct i.e. it must be partially correct and it terminates.
When considering programs expressed as sets of concurrent processes, each one being able to loop for ever (as behave some service process in an operating system) some other partial correctness criteria can be useful as, for instance : some property is always verified whatever the evolutions of the processes (a mutual exclusion property is an example of such criteria).

Existence or absence of deadlocks as well as correct termination may also become total correctness criteria. An extensive literature has been written concerning the different ways correctness can be achieved or proved for sequential programs and even for systems of concurrent processes sharing a common memory.
For distributed programs, the correctness problem becomes far more complicated.

NATO ASI Series, Vol. F28
Distributed Operating Systems. Theory and Practice
Edited by Y. Paker et al.

We mean by a distributed program a program considered as a set of sequential processes, each of these processes being executed by a node of a computer (or processor) network.

As a matter of fact, computer networks have two main characteristics from the point of view of program construction :

. there is no shared memory between the nodes

. there are no physical means for a node to force or to hinder any other action by any other node (no common physical clock is accessible).

These two characteristics prevent any process to obtain instantaneously a global view of the state of the network. Information can only come through the network communication lines by means of message exchanges between the nodes. Hence this information when arriving at a node can be only partial and even perempted.

In this paper, two problems are considered :

The first problem is related to partial correctness : we describe a systematic procedure which allows to build distributed programs which maintain invariant over the evolutions of the network, some global property of its states. This method is applied to the counter (clock)-synchronization problem as well as the distributed mutual exclusion problem.

The second aspect is related to total correctness : we define an algorithm which allows one node in a network to detect whether a global termination condition has been achieved by the network. This algorithm gives a general framework which can be also applied to deadlock detection for instance, but also to insure atomicity of a set of distributed operations.

2. DISTRIBUTION OF AN ASSERTION

Let us consider a (fully connected) n node network.

Being given the sets of states of the nodes : $E_1, \dots, E_n$ and a global predicate G over these sets of states : $G : \underset{i=1,n}{X} E_i \dashrightarrow \{true, false\}$;

the problem is to find a method which insures G can be kept invariant over the current evolutions of the nodes. But a node cannot obtain an instantaneous state of the whole network. The only operation a node can do is either local computation or sending or receiving a message to or from only one other node at a time.

These considerations lead to the need to transform G into a conjunction of new assertions. Each of these new assertions must involve at most the states of two nodes only.
So we describe a systematic procedure to realize this transformation and we point out a communication protocol which guaranties the invariance of an assertion involving two nodes.
By the mean of examples we start this description for a 2-node network only and then we generalize the procedure to an n-node network.
Results presented herein have been obtained by Carvalho, Roucairol [3], [4] and Carvalho [5].

2.1. Synchronization of two counters

Let us consider a 2-node network where each node performs the following operations expressed in a CSP-like language :
node 1 : $P_1 :: h_1 := o \; ; \; ^{*}[h_1 := h_1 + 1]$
node 2 : $P_2 :: h_2 := o \; ; \; ^{*}[h_2 := h_2 + 1]$
we would like to insure that at any time the following assertion remains true :

(A) $\quad |h_1 - h_2| \leqslant K$ where K is a positive constant

One can find many applications of this problem in the framework of communication protocols, distributed real-time control, clock synchronization,...

The absence of shared memory implies that assertion A cannot be used directly in order to control the evolution of the two counters. We are going to transform assertion A in a way more adapted to the context of distributed computing.

2.1.1. Assertion transformation

First we describe the principle of this transformation
Let E_1, E_2 be the sets of possible states of P_1 and P_2. In our example we have $E_1 = E_2 = \mathbb{N}$ the set of positive integers.
Assertion A is an instance of the general predicate :
$G : E_1 \times E_2 \dashrightarrow \{\text{true, false}\}$

Let us define the transform of this predicate with respect to one node :

for i $\in$ [1,2] we define the mappings

$g_i : 2^{E_i} \dashrightarrow 2^{E_j}$, $j \in [1,2]$ $i \neq j$ such that

$$\forall\ S_i \subseteq E_i \quad g_i(S_i) = \left\{ e_j \in E_j \ / \ \forall\ e_i \in S_i\ G(e_i, e_j) = \text{true} \right\}$$

$$g_i(E_i) = \emptyset \text{ and } g_i(\emptyset) = E_i$$

(The g_i's define a so-called Gallois connection between the lattices of subsets of E_i and E_j).

Coming back to our example the transform of a singleton $\{k\} \subseteq \mathbb{N}$ is the interval [max (o,k-K), k+K].

Let S be a set of positive integers, we have also

$g_i(S)$ = [max(o, max(S)-K), min(S)+ K] if it is defined, the empty set otherwise.

This is due to the property.

$g_i(S \cup S') = g_i(S) \cap g_i(S')$

Other properties of the transforms are :

- $S \subseteq S' \Longrightarrow g_i(S) \supseteq g_i(S')$
- $S \subseteq g_j(g_i(S))$

Then we can deduce

$\forall\ S_1 \times S_2 \subseteq E_1 \times E_2$

$S_1 \subseteq g_2(S_2) \Longleftrightarrow S_2 \subseteq g_1(S_1) \Longleftrightarrow G((e_1,e_2))$ = true for any pair $(e_1, e_2) \in S_1 \times S_2$

Let us assume now that at each node is located one variable W_i ranging over the subsets of E_i, and let us call s_i the current state of node i. If at any time we have for i, j $\in \{1,2\}$ and $i \neq j$

$$W_i \subseteq g_j(W_j) \text{(B)}$$

$$s_i \in W_i,\ s_j \in W_j \text{ (C)}$$

then the initial assertion remains always true.

These three assertions imply that :

a) whenever the first assertion B is true, node i and j can evoluate in the subsets designated by the W_i's while maintaining the global assertion invariant .

b) Whenever a node needs to go out of its current authorized subset of states then an information exchange must take place in order to update the values of the W_i's in a way consistent with the first assertion.

However the type of assertion B is very interesting from the point of view of distribution : this is an inequation between two terms,each one involving only a variable local to one node.

A simple protocol can be found to maintain invariant such an inequation, it will be described later on.

Let us come back to statement a) above and remark that the larger is the value of W_j, the wider is the degree of freedom given to the evolution of node j. Particularly, with respect to i it is not necessary at all to restrict the value of W_j to a smaller one (for the inclusion) which has the same transformed value.

Moreover, it can be easily observed that for any subset $\mathcal{S}$ of E_j $g_i(g_j(S))$ has the same transformed value as $\mathcal{S}$, and that $\mathcal{S} \subseteq g_i(g_j(\mathcal{S}))$.
Let us call <u>closed</u> a subset $\mathcal{S}$ of E_j such that $\mathcal{S} = g_i(g_j(\mathcal{S}))$.

According to the equivalence between inequations, we have stated in the previous page the same reasonning holds for node i, therefore we shall assume that the W_i's will range over closed subsets.

Hence, restricting the evolution of a node to be at any time inside a subset of states smaller than a closed subset is totally unecessary with respect to the invariance of the inequation.

(It is interesting to remark that the set of closed subsets is a lattice, and that the g_i's induce a dual isomorphism between these lattices).

Let us apply to assertion A the transformation we have described.

It can be easily shown that closed subsets are intervals of positive integers of the form [l,u] such that $u \geqslant K$, $l > 0$, $u-l \leqslant 2K$ (1)

Then the assertions B become :

$[l_1, u_1] \subseteq g_2([l_2, u_2,])$ (2)

and the assertions C are :

$h_1 \in [l_1, u_1]$, $h_2 \in [l_2, u_2,]$ (3)

(2) can be rewritten as

$[l_1, u_1] \subseteq [u_2 - K, l_2 + K]$

which is equivalent to

$u_2 - K \leqslant l_1$ and $u_1 \leqslant l_2 + K$

in other words :

$u_i \leqslant l_j + K$ for $i,j \in [1,2]$ $i \neq j$ (4)

which implies with the help of $l_i \leqslant u_i$, $u_i - l_i \leqslant 2K$

(3) and (1) then become :

$u_i \geqslant K$, $l_i \geqslant 0$ and $l_i \leqslant h_i \leqslant u_i$ for $i \in [1,2]$ (5)

2.1.2 Protocol for maintaining an inequation invariant

Recall that the type of inequation we consider is

node i : $x \leqslant y$: node j

where x and y are ranging over the same partially ordered set, (inequation (4) is also of this type with $y = l + K$)

We remark that :

a) whenever node i needs to change x into x' with $x' \nleqslant x$, then node j must have changed y into y' before, with $y' \geqslant$ lub (x, x') (lub : least upper bound).

b) whenever node j needs to change y into y' with $y \nleqslant y'$, then node i must have changed x into x' before, with $x' \leqslant$ glb (y, y') (glb : greatest lower bound).

These observations lead to the following general protocol :

- whenever a change has to be made (cases a) and b)) at a node, this node must send to the other node a request message indicating the next desired value of it local variable ;
- upon reception of this message the other node tries to modify its own local variable according to cases a) or b) ; when it is done an acknowledge message is sent back ;
- upon reception of this last message, the first node can actually perform the change of its local variable.

However this general protocol can be simplified in the following case. Suppose that the consecutive values which have to be taken by y and by x form an ascending chain.
Then it is enough to node j to send to i the new value of y each time it updates it. Upon reception of this value x can be updated to its next value immediately inferior or equal to the one which has been just received .

This latter protocol can be made also resistant to disordering or losses of messages by the communication medium. As a matter of fact if node i receives a value of y smaller than a previously received one, then this new value corresponds to an old message sent by j which does not reflect the actual set of states where j can be. This message must not be taken into account.

In the first protocol such a mechanism can be superimposed to the exchange of messages in order to be sure that the correct order of these messages can be recognized.
As a matter of fact the necessity to treat messages in a way consistent with the order they have been sent can also be expressed in terms of an inequation.

Let seq_i be the sequence of messages sent by j to i since the initialization of the system and let rec_j be the sequences of messages received from j and treated by i. (to treat a message means a local change of the state). The consecutive values of these variables are ascending chains (for the prefix order). Then the assertion to maintain is : rec_j is a sub-sequence of seq_i. However it is not necessary to keep track of all messages exchanges, stamping messages with integers is enough : this corresponds to the notion of time-stamp of Lamport [8] or the notion of acceptance threshold of Carvalho, Roucairol [4].

Coming back to our example and looking at assertion 4, one can deduce that only the simplified version of the protocol is necessary. The general version will be used in section 2.2.

2.1.3 The algorithm

Now we can express the algorithm corresponding to the solution of the synchronization of the two counters. It will be done using a CSP-like language but with asynchronous communication primitives. In order to distinguish these primitives from those of CSP we shall note them :

P!!x : send x to P and continue ; when arriving at P this message is put in some buffer local to P

P??y : extract one item in the buffer of messages coming from P and assign this item to y or wait for a message coming from P if the buffer is empty.

The algorithm for node i is then :
In this algorithm, the variable W_i is replaced by two variables l_i and u_i whose values represent respectively the lower bound and the upper bound of an interval.

```
Pi  ::   li:= hi:= o ; ui:= K

         *[hi  < ui ---> li:= hi:= hi + 1
           ▯
           Pj!!li
           ▯
           Pj??lj ---> [ ui < lj + K ---> ui:= lj + K
                         ▯
                         ui ≥ lj + K ---> skip

                       ]

           ]
```

(In this program l_j is a variable local to P_i).

Let us remark that if messages are not disordered, then it is possible to bound the amount of information which can be exchanged (Carvalho [5]).

2.2 A distributed mutual-exclusion problem

Let us consider three processes performing the following operations.

P_i :: s_i:= o ; * [s_i:= 1 ; critical section_i; s_i:= o]

for i ∈ [1,2,3,].

We would like to insure that at any time

(A) $s_1 + s_2 + s_3 \leqslant 1$

Like in the previous section we are going to transform this assertion.

2.2.1 Assertion transformation

The transformation of the initial assertion is more complicated with an n-node network.

Firstly we extend our notations and definitions.

The general assertion to be transformed is :

$$G : \underset{i=1,n}{X} E_i \text{ ---> } \{\text{true, false}\}$$

Let I be a subset of the set $\{1,\dots,n\}$ of indices of nodes, we write :

. S_I for a subset of $\underset{i \in I}{X} E_i$;

. e_I for any item of S_I ; e_I is called a I - tuple

. $(e_I//e_J)$, $J \cap I = \emptyset$, for the (IUJ) - tuple obtained by a coherent merge of the I-tuple together with the J-tuple wich preserves the index order ;

. $\bar{I}$ for the complement subset of I ($\bar{I} = \{1,\dots,n\} - I$)

. ΓI for the projection of G over I :

$$\Gamma I = \{ e_I / \exists e_{\bar{I}}, G((e_I//e_{\bar{I}})) = \text{true} \}$$

Using this notation we can now express the transformation of G with respect to one part of the network.

$$g_I(S_I) = \{ e_{\bar{I}} / \forall e_I \in S_I \; G((e_I//e_{\bar{I}})) = \text{true} \}$$

$$g_I(\emptyset_I) = \underset{i \in \bar{I}}{X} E_i \text{ and } g_I(\underset{i \in I}{X} E_i) = \emptyset_{\bar{I}}$$

Coming back to our example we have :

$E_i = \{0,1\} \quad i \in \{1,2,3\}$

$g_1(\{0\}) = \{(0,0),\ (0,1),\ (1,0)\}$

$g_1(\{1\}) = \{(0,0)\}$

$g_1(\{0,1\}) = \{(0,0)\}$

Let us remark that it is easy to show that g_I and $g_{\bar{I}}$ together have the same properties as the transforms we have exhibited in the previous section.

For these transforms closed subsets are subsets of the form $g_I(g_{\bar{I}}(S_{\bar{I}}))$. For instance $\{1\}$ is not a closed subset of E_1 because we have $g_{23}(\{0,0\}) = \{0,1\}$. But $\{0\}$ and $\{0,1\}$ are closed subsets of E_1. However, the initial assertion cannot be directly transformed as we have done in the previous section. As a matter of fact, maintaining invariant an assertion which involves one node and a set of other nodes is the same problem as the one we are trying to solve.

Hence, we define for each node i, and every pair (i,j) two variables local to node i, W_{ij} and M_{ij} which have the following meaning :

- M_{ij} is an upper bound, seen by i, of the subset of states where currently node j can be.
- W_{ij} is a lower bound of the subset of states where node j expects that node i can be (or where node i is engaged to stay with respect to node j).

Then we can show [4], that the initial assertions remain invariant if the following is true at any time :

. $M_{ij} \supseteq W_{ji}$ for all $i, j \in \{1,\ldots,n\}$, $i \neq j$ (B)

. $s_i \in \bigcap_{j\in\{\bar{i}\}} W_{ij} \cap g_{\{\bar{i}\}}\left(\mathop{X}_{j\in\{\bar{i}\}} M_{ij} \cap \Gamma_{\{\bar{i}\}}\right)$ (C)

The assertion C is only a local assertion. The B assertions are assertions involving only two nodes at a time. These assertions are inequations as the ones we have already obtained in the previous section.

Let us apply these formulae to our example. We have already seen that each set of states has only two closed subsets $\{0\}$ and $\{0,1\}$. Let us code these subsets by false and true respectively, and consider the W and M variables as boolean variables.

Then the assertions B are :

$W_{ji} \Longrightarrow M_{ij}$ (1)

For the assertion C we have :

$\Gamma\{\bar{i}\} = \{(0,0),\ (0,1),\ (1,0)\}$

by inspecting all the different cases, C can be rewritten as :

$s_i = 1 \Longrightarrow (W_{ij} \wedge W_{ik}) \wedge \neg(M_{ij} \vee M_{ik})$ for $i,j,k \in \{1,2,3\}$,
$i \neq j,\ i \neq k$ and $j \neq k$ (2)

2.2.2 The algorithm

In order to maintain assertions (1) we are going to use the general protocol we have exhibited in section 2.1.2. For sake of simplicity, we shall assume that the messages will not be disordered by the communication medium. However, the time-stamping mechanism of Lamport [8] will be used in order to arbitrate between concurrent requests to enter a critical section. Hence messages will have one of the following type :

- ('req', ts), where ts is a value of a time-stamp ; sent by node i to a node j, it means i wants to enter its critical section ; according to assertion (2), this signifies that i wants to assign true to W_{ij} and false to M_{ij}.
- ('ack'), sent by node j to a node i, it means j authorizes i to set the value of W_{ij} to <u>true</u> and the value of M_{ij} to <u>false</u> ; but before sending this message j must have set M_{ji} to <u>true</u> in order to keep the inclusion assertion correct ; moreover before giving this authorization node j must have engaged itself not to be inside the critical section for a while so it must have set W_{ij} to <u>false</u>.

In the following program for the node i, we shall use auxiliary variables and function :

<u>waiting</u> is a boolean variable set to true whenever P_i waits to enter its critical section ;

<u>hts</u> contains the highest time-stamp for messages received by P_i ;

<u>lts</u> contains the value of the local time-stamp ;

<u>prio</u> (j) is a boolean function used to arbitrate between node i and node j waiting together to enter their critical section :

```
prio (j) : = if (lts < ts) or ((lts = ts) and (i < j )) then true else
false fi
```

where ts is the value of the time-stamp sent by node j to i.

```
P_i:: s_i:= 0 ; w_j:= w_k:= false ; m_j:= m_k:= true ; waiting := false ;
    lts := hts := 0 ;

* [¬ waiting ----> waiting:= true ; lts:= hts + 1 ;
   ▯                P_j!! ('req', lts) ; P_k !! ('req', lts)
   waiting ∧ (w_j ∧ w_k) ∧ (¬ (m_j ∨ m_k)) ---> waiting:= false ; s_i:= 1 ;
                                                critical section_i ; s_i:= 0 ;
                                                wj:= w_k:= false ;
                                                m_j:= m_k:= true;
                                                P_j!!('ack') ; P_k!!('ack')
   ▯  P_h?? ('req',ts)----> hts:= max (hts,ts) ;
   h=j,k
                            [waiting ∧ prio(h) ---> skip
                              ▯
                            ¬(waiting ∧ prio(h))---> w_h:= false ; m_h:= true ;
                                                     P_h!! ('ack')
                            ]
   ▯ P_h?? ('ack') --->     [waiting ---> w_h:= true ; m_h:= false
  h=j,k                      ▯
                            ¬waiting ---> skip

                            ]
]
```

This algorithm can be improved in several ways ; the number of exchanged messages can be reduced and upon reception of a request message it is possible to take care of this information about the state of the sending node.

In [2] the reader will find such improvements. As an exercise, the reader is also invited to consider the case where the global assertion is $s_1 + s_2 + s_3 \leqslant 2$ (the 2-out-3 problem).

3. TERMINATION OF DISTRIBUTED PROGRAMS

We consider a fully connected network of n nodes, each one carrying some local computation and exchanging messages with the others.
We shall say that the global computation supported by the network is terminated whenever every node has achieved some local termination condition and there are no messages in transit between the nodes.
The problem we study is the detection by each node of termination of the global computation and the eventual stop of the nodes.
Let us redefine this more precisely.
We assume that each node can be in one of the following states :

- active : it is carrying some local computations and it can exchange messages with the other nodes ; such messages are called "work" messages
- idle : the node has achieved some local termination condition ; it can become active upon reception of a "work" message
- complete : every node is idle or complete and there are no "work" messages in transit.

Hence, coding by 0, 1, 2 respectively the three successive states above, the state diagram of a node is the following :

If the current state of a node i is recorded in a variable h_i local to i, then at any time the following invariant must be true :

$\forall\, i,j \in [1,n]\ i \neq j$

. $|h_i - h_j| \leqslant 1$ (A)

. $h_i = 2 \Longrightarrow$ no "work" messages are in transit (B)

Therefore we are looking for a distributed algorithm which maintains the previous assertions invariant and which insures that each node will eventually go in a complete-state if a global termination condition is reached.

We have already seen in section 2 how to maintain assertion A. Of course the difficulty lies in assertion B.

In order to check whether there are no "work"-messages in transit a solution is the following. Each time a node receives a "work" message then it sends back to the sender an acknowledge message. At any node i, let d_i be a variable which counts the difference between the number of "work" messages sent and the number of received acknowledgements. Then assertion B becomes $h_i = 2 \Longrightarrow \sum_{i=1,n} d_i = 0$. Then the assertion distribution procedure we have described can be used to determine for which local condition a node can go into a complete state. However it may be the case that for one "work" message too much control messages have to be exchanged in order to maintain the inequalities invariant. (The application of the distribution procedure is left as an interesting exercise to the reader).

Therefore we are going to define in this case an ad'hoc strategy.

Each time a node i enters in state 1 we shall say it starts a new iteration ; this iteration is divided into two steps :

- step 1 : node i establishes the fact that all "work"-messages it has sent are no longer in transit ; moreover it collects from all other nodes their current number of iteration
- step 2 : node i asks to every other nodes whether they have terminated or not their first step ; an answer sent by a node j to i is considered as positive by i iff : node j has terminated its first step and the set of iteration numbers collected by j is the same as the one i has collected in step 1 of i ; step 2 terminates successfully whenever i has received positive answers from every node.

An iteration terminates unsuccessfully whenever i receives a work message or an answer considered as negative.

Proposition 1

Whenever step 2 terminates successfully for node i then there are no "work" messages in transit and every node is not in an active state.

Proof

Let us call consistent for a node j an interval of time of the same iteration starting at the time when j has sent its iteration number for the first time to i and ending at the time when j has sent to i an answer considered as positive.

If the iteration of node i terminates successfully, then every node has been previously in a consistent interval of time. But all these consistent intervals have together a non empty intersection which contains the time when step 2 of i has begun. Since that time, we are going to show that no "work" messages are in transit. Assume the contrary, then after its step 1 a node, say j, will send to i some iteration number of some node k different from the one i has collected in its first step. Therefore, step 2 of i does not terminate successfully. Q.E.D.

Of course, for the proof to be correct it is supposed that messages arrive at a node in the order they have been sent. We are going to use this property in the step 1 of a node i to establish the fact that every "work" messages sent by i are no longer in transit. As a matter of fact it is enough for i to send every node j a "push" message and wait for an answer from j about the arrival of this message.

Now we are able to write the program for a node i which detects the global termination condition.

Besides "work" type messages, a node can either send or receive four different types of messages :

- type "step 1" : the "push" message sent by a node in its first step
- type "ok 1" : sent by a node in response to the previous message
- type "step 2" : sent at the beginning of step 2
- type "ok 2" : the answer to the previous message

Together with their type :

- ok messages will carry an array of iteration numbers
- step messages will carry the iteration number of the sender ; when reflected in an "ok" message, this number will be used to detect if an ok message is an answer to a "step" message sent in the same iteration.

Moreover a node i uses the following local variables :

lt : it is true whenever a local termination has been detected ; initial value is false ;

step [1:n] : array of step numbers which are either 1 or 2 once the corresponding step has been reached and 0 otherwise ; the initial values are 0

it[1:n] : array of iteration numbers ; <u>initial values</u> are 0

h contains the current state of i.

Finally we shall use the following instructions :

. In a process i, A_j "statement" : means <u>for all</u> j ∈ [1, n] j ≠ i <u>do</u> "statement"

. if x and y are two arrays of the same size n : x = y means for all j ∈ [1,n] x(j) = y(j) ; x ≠ y means there exists a j, x(j) ≠ y(j).

```
*[¬lt ---> ... local computation...
 []
(a)lt∧(h=o)-->it(i):= it(i)+1 ; h:= 1 ; step(i):= 1 ; A step(j):= o ;
                                                        j
                     A Pj!!("step 1", it(i))
                     j

 [] lt,Pj?? ("ok1", y) -->[ y(i) ≠ it(i) --> skip
j≠i                         []
                            y(i) = it(i) --> it(j):= y(j) ; step(j):= 1
                                        [ ∧ step(j)= 1-->step(i):= 2 ;
                                          j    APj!!("step 2",it(i))
                                                 j
                                           []
                                          else skip
                                        ]
                            ]
```

```
[] lt,Pj?? ("ok2", y) -->[ y(i) ≠ it(i) -->  skip
j≠i                      []
                          y(i) = it(i) --> [ y≠it --> as in statement (a)
                                                      above (initiation of
                                              []      a new iteration)

                                              y=it  --> step(j):= 2
                                                        [ ∧ step(j)=2 -->
                                                         j   ...h:=2 stop(b)
                                                          []
                                                         else skip

                                                        ]
                                              ]
                          ]


[]  lt,Pj??("step 1",x) --> it(j):=x ; Pj!!("okl",it)
j≠i

[]  lt,Pj??("step 2",x) --> it(j):=x ; Pj!!("ok2",it)
j≠i

[]  lt,Pj??("work") --> h:=o ; lt:= false
j≠i
]
```

Looking at the program above and considering the fact that iteration numbers are strictly <u>increasing</u> allow us to conclude :

<u>Proposition 2</u>

Whenever a global termination condition is reached, some node will eventually terminates.

If a node can halt, then it is easy to find simple solutions to tell the others that they must halt also. These solutions have to be implemented especially in statement (b) of the program above. For sake of clarity we omitted them.

Let us remark that this algorithm is based upon a principle very similar to the one of the two-step commit protocol used in the framework of distributed data-base in order to insure atomicity of a transaction [1]. As a matter of fact this algorithm can be used as a framework in order to insure the global atomicity of a set of distributed transitions (in our case transitions between states 1 and 2). Several authors have considered the distributed termination problem [6], [7], [10]. Most of them suppose a particular structure is superimposed over the graph of the network : it is generally a spanning tree or a circuit covering the edges or the vertices of the graph. Exchanges of control messages use only this structure. The solution we have presented does not need such a structure. It is interesting also to notice that the previous algorithm can also be used as a framework for detecting properties of a network which remain true once they have been satisfied. Deadlock situations fall in that class of properties.

Finally, let us remark that the algorithm we described can be easily generalized to a (non fully) connected network.

BIBLIOGRAPHY

[1] Bernstein P.A., Goodman N. Concurrency Control in Distributed Database Systems, ACM, Computing Surveys, Vol. 13, 2 (June 1981), pp. 185-201.

[2] Carvalho O., Roucairol G. On the distribution of an assertion. In "Proc. ACM-SIGACT-SIGOPS Symposium on Principles of Distributed Computing". Ottawa, Canada. 1982.

[3] Carvalho O., Roucairol G. On mutual exclusion in Computer Network. Comm. ACM Vol. 26,2. 1983 pp. 146-147.

[4] Carvalho O., Roucairol G. Assertion Decomposition and Partial Correctness of Distributed Control Algorithms. Distributed Computed Systems. Paker and Verjus eds. Academic Press London. 1983. pp. 67 - pp. 92.

[5] Carvalho O. Une contribution à la programmation des systèmes distribués (Thèse d'Etat). Internal Report L.R.I. 224, Université Paris 11 Orsay. 1985.

[6] Dijkstra E.W., Feijen W.H.J., Van Gasteren A.J.M. Derivation of a Termination Detection Algorithm for Distributed Computation, Inf. Proc. Letters, Vol. 16, (June 1983), pp. 217-219.

[7] Francez N. Distributed Termination, ACM Toplas, Vol. 2,1, (January 1980), pp. 42-55.

[8] Lamport L. Time, clocks and the ordering of events in distributed systems. Comm. ACM 21,7. 1978.

[9] Lavallée I., Roucairol G. A fully distributed (minimal) spanning tree algorithm. Inf. Proc. Letters to appear in 1986.

[10] Misra J., Chandy K.M. Termination Detection of Diffusing Computation Using Markers, Proc. of the 2nd annual ACM Symposium on Principles of DC, Montreal, (August 1983), pp. 290-294.

[11] Raynal M. Algorithmes Distribués et Protocoles. Eyrolles Publ. Paris. 1985.

DERIVATION OF DISTRIBUTED ALGORITHMS

J.P. VERJUS

IRISA
Campus de Beaulieu
35042 Rennes-Cedex
France

Abstract

For ten years, we have studied and analysed some distributed algorithms for process synchronization. In various papers (see references), we have shown methods for transforming centralized algorithms into distributed ones, with simple techniques. In the first part of this paper, we are going to show how to generate a mutual exclusion algorithm from an expression written with monotonically increasing counters. We show then that other well known mutual exclusion and resources allocation algorithms can be derived from this one. In the second and third parts, we show how to generate distributed mutual exclusion algorithms using other basic tools : queues, distributed variables ... from some kernel algorithm.

The thread of this paper is mutual exclusion, and in each part, we present a class of algorithms. In preamble, we shall give an illustration to serve as the key to understanding the algorithms of each class.

NATO ASI Series, Vol. F28
Distributed Operating Systems. Theory and Practice
Edited by Y. Paker et al.

Introduction

For ten years, we have studied and analysed some distributed algorithm for process synchronization. In various papers ([1], [2], [3] and [4]), we have shown some methods for transforming centralized algorithms into distributed ones, with simple techniques.

This method consists in giving an abstract expression of the solution to the given problems. In a centralized system, this expression is translated very simply : we use variables to represent the abstract expression and we manipulate these ones in critical section, using, for exemple semaphores, monitors or some special control process. In a distributed system we express the abstract expression with very simple objects which have good distribution properties. Examples of these objects are :

- Eventcounts, i.e. monotonically increasing counters, or time stamps,
- waiting queues.

Examples of distribution techniques are :

- Distributing the variables among the processes,
- distributing n copies of them among the processes.

In this paper, we are going to show how to generate a distributed algorithm from an abstract expression, then we will show that other well known algorithms can be derived from this one.

In the first part, we show how to generate mutual exclusion algorithms using monotonically increasing counters and we deduce fair distributed resource allocation algorithms, one of these being Dijkstra's mutual exclusion Algorithm. [7]

In the second part, we will show how to reconstitute very easily the well known mutual exclusion algorithms of Lamport [13], Ricart and Aggrawala [14] and their derivatives ([15], [16]) using the distribution of one queue. We can mention in passing that such a method is used for designing an algorithm which maintains the consistency of multiple copies [6].

Lastly, in the third part, we will give the Kernel of algorithms which have given rise to numerous publications ([17] to [24]) and some indications on derivations and variations which can be made from this Kernel. We sum up, in this part, the work which will be presented by Thoraval in his thesis ([11], [17]).

The thread in this paper is mutual exclusion : in each part a class of algorithms is presented.

The first one (Part 1) has given rise to little work from the time of the original one by Dijkstra [7] that we have proved and made relatively fault tolerant [9] (in a recent article, Dijkstra [25] proves one of the three algorithms given in his 74 paper but it's not the one considered here) and which constitute the kernel of this class. Even though it's a very simple class of algorithms, we think that there is still a lot of work to be done. The essential part of this paper is devoted to that.

The second class (Part 2) is the simplest, the better known and which, in our mind, is "classed". We just mention it for completeness.

The third class (Part 3), as mentionned above, has given rise to lots of studies, which in the end and in our opinion ressemble each other even if it is not always syntactically visible. It is up to Thoraval to conclude on the properties of and the perspectives opened by these algorithms [11, 17].

By way of a preamble, we shall give an example to serve as the key to understanding the algorithms of each class.

Let's consider an arena (or a stadium) with n gates and a circular track. The persons who try to enter are similar to concurrent processes. The rule is that one and only one person can be in the center of the stadium (i.e.

in critical section). We suppose that the fact of one person being in the center of the stadium cannot be seen from a gate : for example, there is a wall on the inside of the circular track.

The first class of algorithms works in the following way. There is a watchman at each gate. A baton is circulated between the watchmen around the track. When somebody stands at the gate, the watchman makes him wait until the baton arrives : he gives it then to the person who penetrates into the stadium holding the baton. When he leaves, by the same gate, he gives the baton back to the same watchman who passes it along.

In the second class of algorithms, the watchman is in touch with each other watchman by a communication medium. A good example would be the express letter system called "Parisian Tube" : the messages arrive at variable speed but they cannot overtake each other on the same line. Each watchman has a clock, but these are not necessarily synchronous. When somebody comes to a gate, the watchman timestamps his arrival on a letter which is sent to all the other watchmen. When a message gets to another watchman, he, if necessary sets his watch after the timestamp on the letter. By this means, the watchmen can decide a coherent order of priority between those who want to get in.

In the third class of algorithms, we do away with the watchmen. Anybody who comes along goes onto the circular track, leaves a beacon and starts to go around (without overtaken by others). If he does not come across another beacon, he goes into the center of the stadium, his beacon stays where he left it until he leaves. If, on the contrary, he comes across another beacon, then there is a conflict which is solved depending on rules of priority.

By keeping these images in mind, we can technically start on the algorithms.

Part 1. Generating Distributed Algorithms with counters.

In this part, we show how to generate a mutual exclusion agorithm from an expression written with monotically increasing counters, which, from now on, we will call *counters*. First, we construct a mutual exclusion algorithm between n processes distributed around a virtual ring. Secondly, we show that other well known algorithms can be derived from this one.

The hypotheses on the distributed system which we use are the following (Fig. 1).

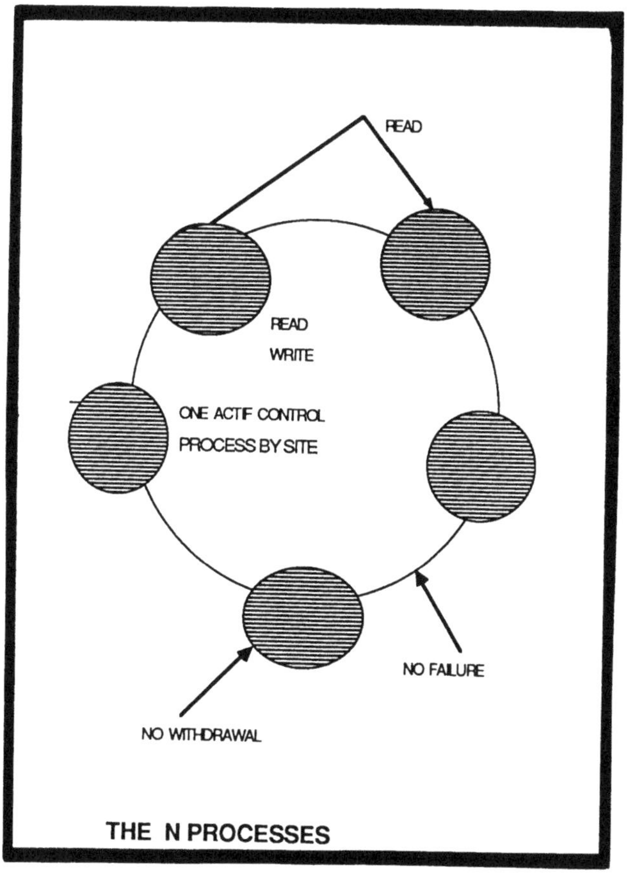

Figure 1

a) The sites of the distributed system are supposed to be arranged in an unidirectional communication ring. Each site can only communicate with its immediate neighbor.

b) Each site is supposed to have one permanently active control process. Each process can read and write its own local variables but can only read those of its neighbor.

c) There is neither failure of the message passing nor withdrawal from a site.

In the present chapter, we have especially two purposes : (1) to show that some algorithms can be reduced one to another and (2) to show that we can easily build an algorithm from an abstract expression. Of course, the chosen algorithms are relatively simple.

Herein, the abstract tool is the *counter* and the used method is their controlled distribution. So we are going to recall some of their properties.

The first advantage of the counters is that, on each site, we can know a lower bound of the value of a counter implemented on another site. The use of such a lower bound is often sufficient to check a synchonization condition.

For example, let's consider two increasing integers a and ℓ such that

$$0 \leqslant a - \ell \leqslant n$$

(For example, a is the number of entries into a parking lot, ℓ is the number of exits and n the number of spaces). Let's consider two distant sites S_a and S_ℓ, where we know the exact values of a and ℓ. A controller, located on S_a must, before allowing another car into the lot, check that

$$a - \ell < n \tag{1}$$

Unfortunately, here, he cannot know the exact value of ℓ, but only a lower bound. But, he can without fear check that

$$a - lowerbound\,(\ell) < n$$

which guarantees that (1) is true.

The second advantage of increasing counters is that, when their differential evolution is bounded (for example : $0 \leqslant a - \ell \leqslant 4$) and when they increase by step of one, we can implement them modulus K ($K=5$ here, and, in general, K equals the maximal difference between the two counters plus one) and we can deduce the new constraints.

In Fig. 2a, the two counters a and ℓ evolve inside the non shaded area, between the two parallel lines. In Fig. 2b, we can see that the evolution of counters A and L can happen inside the square except in the shaded area. The step function represents the evolution of a and ℓ. In the point b for example, we must forbid the increasing of ℓ.

The constraints become :

. Condition for increasing A : $A - L \neq 4$
(or $A - L \neq -1$)

. Condition for increasing L : $A - L \neq 0$

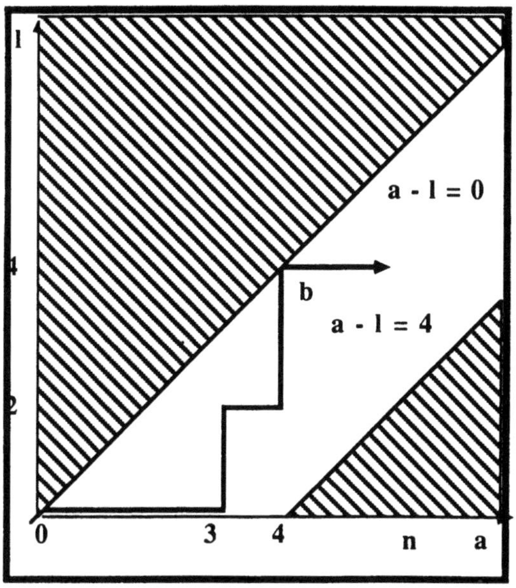

Figure 2a

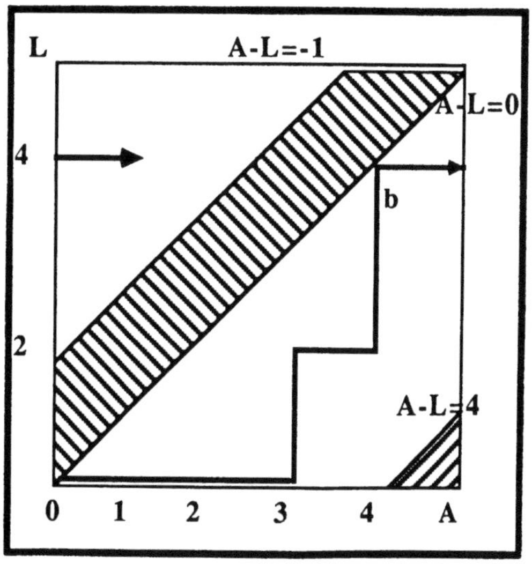

Figure 2b

So, we can see that the counters can be used in a distributed system without being bothered by communication delays, and can be implemented in any computer memory given that their evolution is bounded.

1.1. Arbitration between n processes around a ring

In this section, we are going to design a distributed algorithm of arbitration (or mutual exclusion) between n processes around a ring. We have shown on several occasions ([1], [2], [3]) that a set of distributed processes can be controlled by the use of a special message which we have called **privilege** or **right.** We have shown also that there is an advantage, in case of failure or removal of a process, to express the privilege by a particular combination of some state variables ([1], [2]). Lastly, we are only concerned with showing a derivation methodology and not with producing the most efficient algorithm.

1.1.1. Basic algorithm

We consider n processes $P_0, P_1 \dots P_{n-1}$, and the abstract expression given in Fig. 3.

Let's be n processus P_i, $0 <= i <= n-1$

```
Pi : repeat                          ∔ <=> + modulus n
   | wait PRIORITY = i
   |      SCi
   | PRIORITY := i ∔ 1
   | end
```

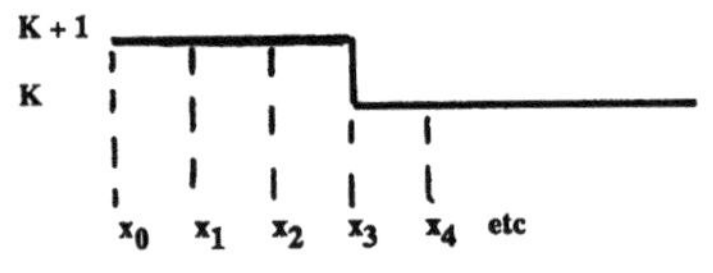

<u>initially</u> $x_i = 0$

$0 <= i <= n-1$

$1 <= j <= n-1$

PRIORITY = j <===> $x_{j-1} = x_j + 1$

PRIORITY = 0 <===> $x_0 = x_{n-1}$

PRIORITY := i ∔ 1 <===> $x_i := x_i + 1$

Figure 3

1) Each process P_i waits until its predecessor sets $PRIORITY := i$. Note that $PRIORITY$ is, in this abstract expression, a common variable : it will be distributed below.

2) SC_i represents a critical section, that is the fact that the process P_i is the only process to be privileged.

3) At the start, $PRIORITY = 0$: P_0 is the first to have the privilege.

4) The statement $PRIORITY := i + 1 \underline{mod}\ n$ allows the following process on the ring to go into critical section.

It is easy to express this protocol with increasing counters x_i which count the entries of each process in critical section. So, the evolution of the system can be represented by the wavefront (see Fig. 3), where P_3 has the privilege. In Fig. 3, the first four processes have had (K+1) times the privilege, the other ones K times only.

Inside the frame (Fig. 3), we have translated the abstract protocol under a form which we shall use from now on. We paraphrase this protocol :

1) The variables x_i are zero at the beginning.

2) In the first equality, we express the condition for having the privilege, which is valid for all the processes except P_0. For each one of these processes, this condition shows a difference of one between the variable of its left neighbor and its own. For P_0, this condition shows an equality.

3) For all the processes, yielding the privilege consists in adding one to its own variable.

The difference between two neighboring variables takes the values 0 or 1 : following on what we saw earlier, x_i can be implemented modulus 2. And so, we derive the algorithm given in Fig. 4, which is just the one given by Dijkstra [7]. In Fig. 4, we have substituted the condition on PRIORITY

LET

X_i : representation of x_i modulus 2(=0,1)

$+^2$: notation of + modulus 2

P0: $X_0 := 0$	P_i: $X_i := 0$
<u>repeat</u>	<u>repeat</u>
<u>wait</u> $X_0 = X_{n-1}$	<u>wait</u> $X_i = X_{i-1} +^2 1$
SC_0	SC_i
$X_0 := X_0 +^2 1$	$X_i := X_i +^2 1$
<u>end</u>	<u>end</u>

(DIJKSTRA 74 CACM 17, 11) ALG V

Figure 4

for the condition on the x_i's given in Fig. 3, and we substitute then X_i for x_i . The algorithm is distributed : each variable is accessible to its owner and can be read only by its right-hand neighbor.

The evolution of the system is shown in Fig. 5 :

- at the beginning, all the $x_i = 0$ and P_0 has the privilege (*)
- then, P_0 increases x_0 by 1 and P_1 can have the privilege
- then P_1 does the same
- ... and so on, until we find the situation like at the start.

From now on, we will use the representation of Fig. 5 : along the x-axis, we represent the different sites on the ring ; in ordinate, we represent the value of the variables.

N.B. Incidently, we can see (Fig. 5) that if a site, except P_0 , is withdrawn, the configuration remains the same. But, if P_0 is withdrawn, then P_1 must do what P_0 had to do. P_1 knows that P_0 is out because it is the only site such as its left neighbor's number is greater than itself. (See [1], [2]).

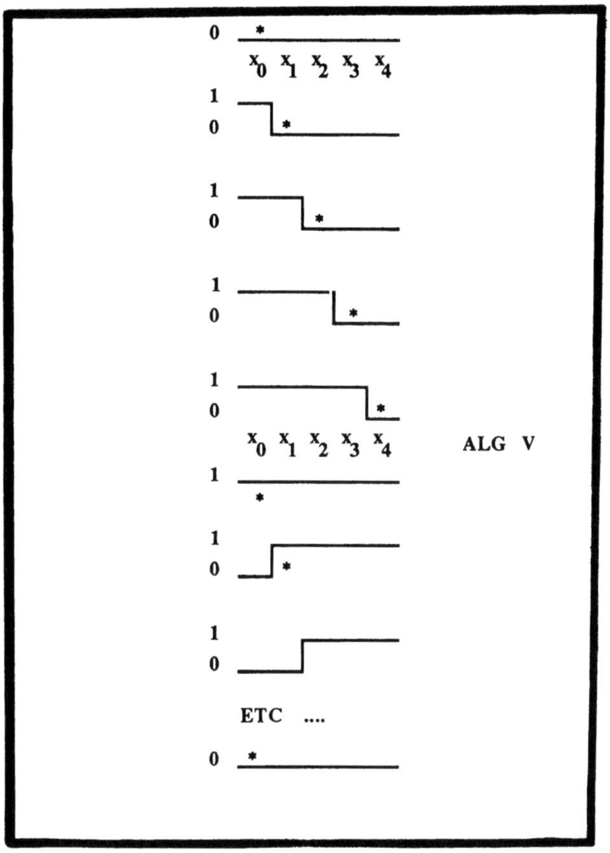

Figure 5

1.1.2. Variations

As in music, we can have possible variations on this theme. We are going to change the rules of the game.

For example, initially, all the processes are in a state such as :

- between two neighbors, there is the same difference K
- except for a pair where the difference is K'.

The right-hand neighbor, in this pair, is then privileged (note : in Fig. 4 : K=0, K'=1).

Let K = 1, K' = 0 (see Fig. 6)

X_i = i mod p (for example).

EXAMPLE : **K = 1 K' = 0**

∘ <=> - modulus n

VI

Initially X_i = i modulus p
0 <= i <= n-1, n > 2, p divides n-1 , p<> 1

PRIORITY = i <==> $X_{i∘1} = X_i$

PRIORITY := i + 1 <==> $X_i := X_i + 1$ mod p

Initialisation ==> $X_{n-1} = X_0$ ==> p divides n-1

If n is odd ==> p = 2 is adequate and we obtain battlements

WITH K = 1 and K' = 1 - n , we obtain

RAYNAL's ALGORITHM where $p = n^2$

Figure 6

So, all the processes are in a different state : for two neighboring processes to be in the same state (for example P_0 and P_{n-1}), we must establish that :

$$X_{n-1} = X_0$$

that is :

$$(n-1) \text{ mod } p = 0$$

which implies

p divides n-1 and $p \neq 1$

For example, in Fig. 7, we observe :

- on the first schema : $X_0 = X_{n-1} = 0$ and P_0 has the privilege
- on the second schema, n=5 and p can be equal to 4 or 2 but not 3
- on the third schema, n=7 and p can be indifferently equal to 6, 3 or 2.

If n is odd, then *p = 2* is sufficient and we obtain a battlement figure (Fig. 8) : at the beginning, P_0 has the privilege ; then P_0 increases its variable by one ; in its turn, P_1 has the privilege ... and so on until we get the same situation as at the beginning.

If we choose K = 1 and K' = 1-n, we obtain Raynal's algorithm. In his algorithm, Raynal took $p = n^2$. But it is not necessary. It is easy to demonstrate that the necessary and sufficient condition is that n is not divisible

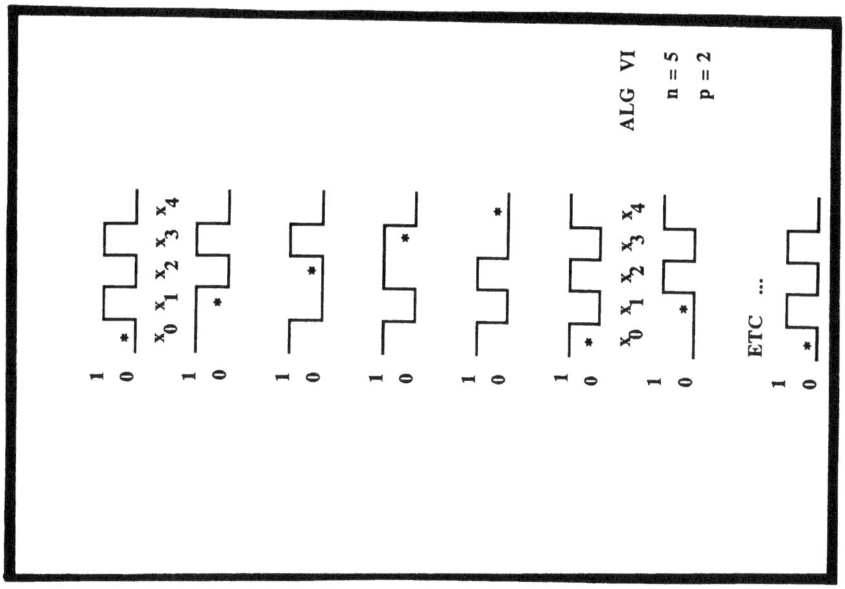

Figure 8

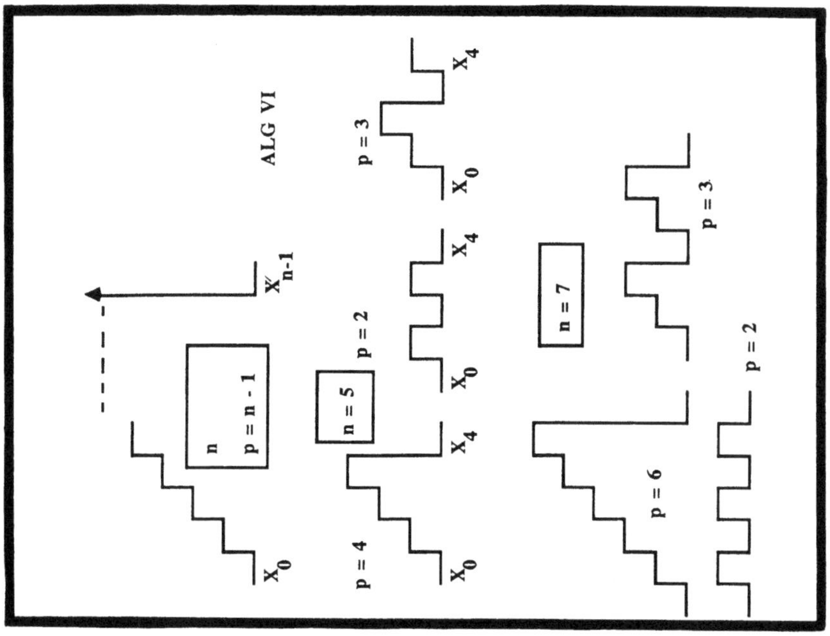

Figure 7

by p. The algorithm is then expressed in Fig. 9 and the behaviour of the system is given in Fig. 10 ($n = 6$, $p > 7$) and in Fig. 11 ($n = 5$, $p = 3$).

N.B. The condition "p does not divide n" is necessary because if p divides n then $K = K'$ mod p and all the pairs are in the same situation. It is sufficient by construction.

VII

Initially $X_i = i$ **mod** p
$0 <= i <= n-1$, $n > 1$, p does not divide n

PRIORITY = i <==> $X_{i-1} - X_i = n-1$ **mod** p

PRIORITY := i + 1 <==> $X_i := X_i + n$ **mod** p

Figure 9

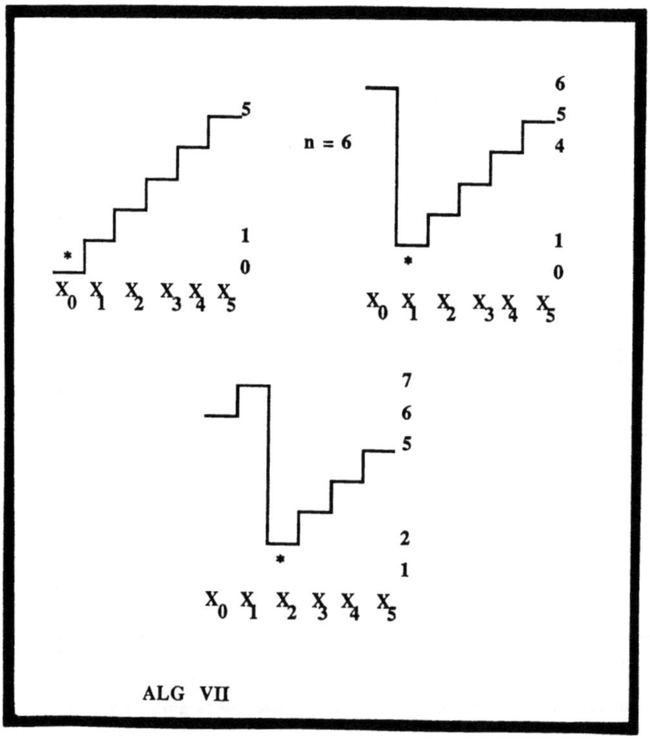

Figure 10

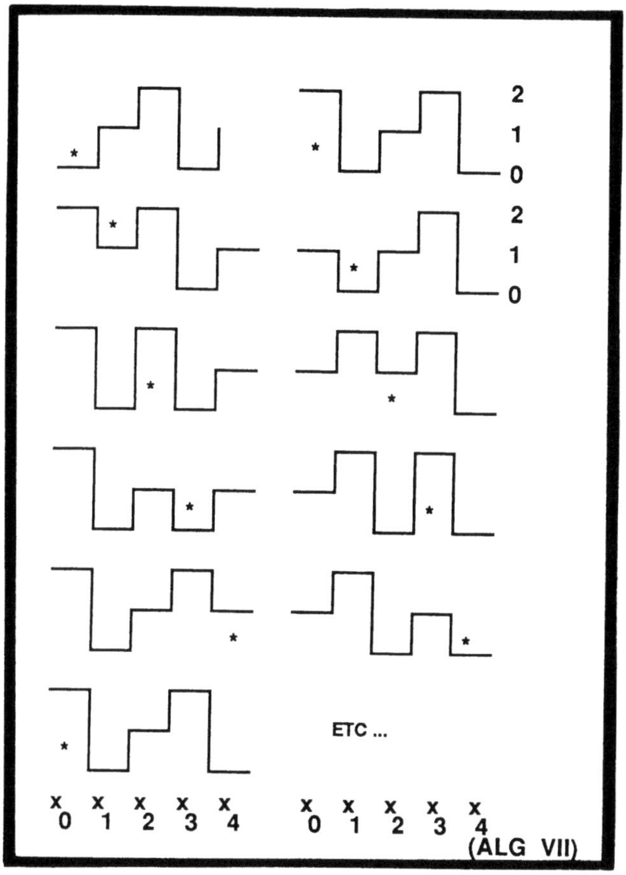

Figure 11

1.1.3. Generalization

In fact, all these algorithms have a common base. As we can see on Fig. 12, if we take :

$$Y_i = n * X_i + i$$

we can derive the last algorithm from the first shown in Fig. 4 and 5. Moreover, let's note that :

if p divides n-1 and n > 2

then p does not divide n

All these algorithms have a common base : with

$Y_i = n * X_i + i$

we derivate VII from V

	V	VII
Initially $0<=i<=n-1$	$X_i := 0$	$Y_i := i$
PRIORITY = 0	$X_{n-1} - X_0 = 0$	$Y_{n-1} - Y_0 = n-1$
PRIORITY = i $1<= i <= n-1$	$X_{i-1} - X_i = 1$	$Y_{i-1} - Y_i = n+(i-1)-i$ $= n - 1$
PRIORITY:=i+1 $0 <= i <= n-1$	$X_i := X_i + 1$	$Y_i := Y_i + n$

Figure 12

In such a case :

$$n-1 = 0 \ \underline{\text{mod}}\ p$$

and the algorithm VII (Fig. 9) becomes the algorithm VI (Fig. 6) - See Fig. 13 (n=5, p=4).

In other words, all these algorithms can be derived from an initial germ : the algorithm V.

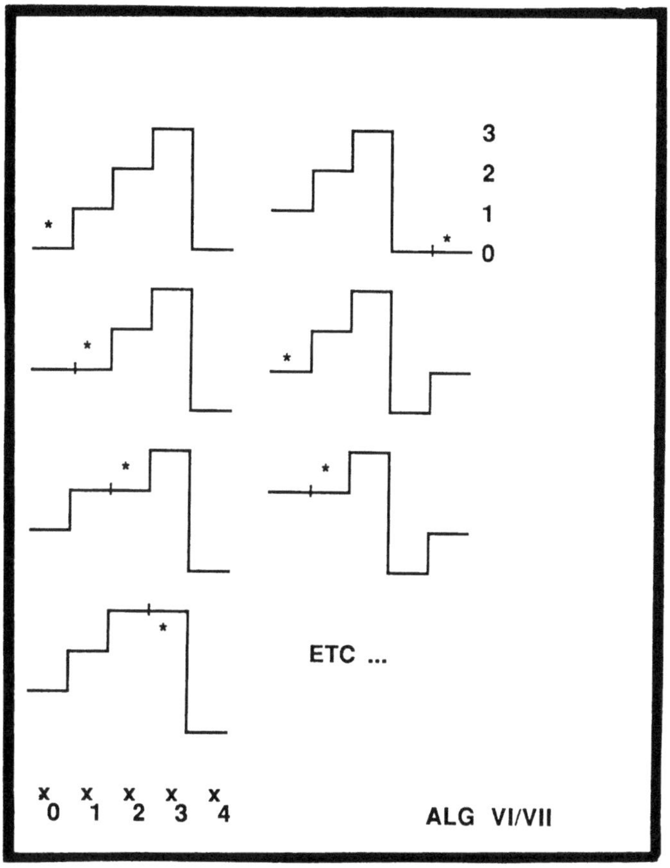

Figure 13

1.2. Distributed resources allocation

In this section, we are going to design distributed algorithms of resources allocation from the last ones (§ 1.1) or according to the same principles.

If we have 2 privileges (or n) circulating among the processes according to our model (ALG V), we resolve elegantly the fair allocation of 2 (respectively n) resources. Let's note that when a process has a privilege, then a resource can be allocated if and only if it is asked by a user. Therefore, each process P_i gives, recovers and circulates the right to use the resources. These rights are running fairly.

We note that only one resource can be allocated at the same time to one user, but more than one user can make a request onto a site.

1.2.1. Fair allocation of 2 resources

Let (X_i) and (Y_i) be two counters' sets evolving around the ring according to ALG. V (Fig. 14). We can solve the given problem by checking either X_i or Y_i on each site. But it is possible to take, on each site :

$$Z_i = X_i + Y_i$$

which allows us to check just the variable Z_i.

Given that :

$$0 \leqslant Z_i - Z_{i \boxminus 1} \leqslant 2$$

it may be seen that Z_i can be evolved modulus 3, according to the algorithm VIII (Fig. 14).

LET'S BE (X_i) and (Y_i) two counters' sets evolving according to V

Let's set $Z_i = X_i + Y_i$

We have $0 <= Z_i - Z_{i-1} <= 2$

and we deduce (Z_i) **can evolve according to :**

VIII

<u>initially</u> $Z_i = 0$
$0 <= i <= n-1, n > 1$

P_0 has 2 rights $<==> Z_{n-1} - Z_0 = 0$

P_0 has 1 right $<==> Z_{n-1} - Z_0 = 2$

P_i has 2 rights $<==> Z_{i-1} - Z_i = 2, 1 <= i <= n-1$

P_i has 1 right $<==> Z_{i-1} - Z_i = 1, 1 <= i <= n-1$

P_i leaves 1 right $<==> Z_i := Z_i +^3 1, 0 <= i <= n-1$

CONSULTATION of BOTH NEIGHBORS

Figure 14

On the assumption that P_0 has, at the beginning, both the rights, it may be seen that the evolution of the system is the following (Fig. 15) ; there is more than one path to come in a given configuration. In the left-hand path, P_0 keeps a right, the other right goes on until P_4, then P_1 obtains the right, then P_2. In the right-hand path, the two rights go on together until P_2, then a right goes onto P_3, next P_4.

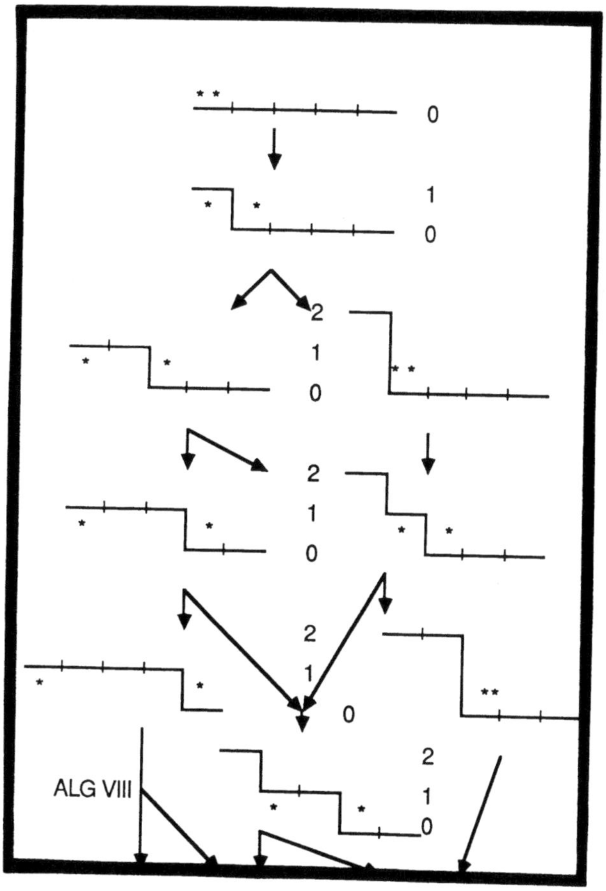

Figure 15

Note that each configuration Z_i is the sum of X_i and Y_i. There is never any ambiguity to find who has one or two rights (Fig. 16).

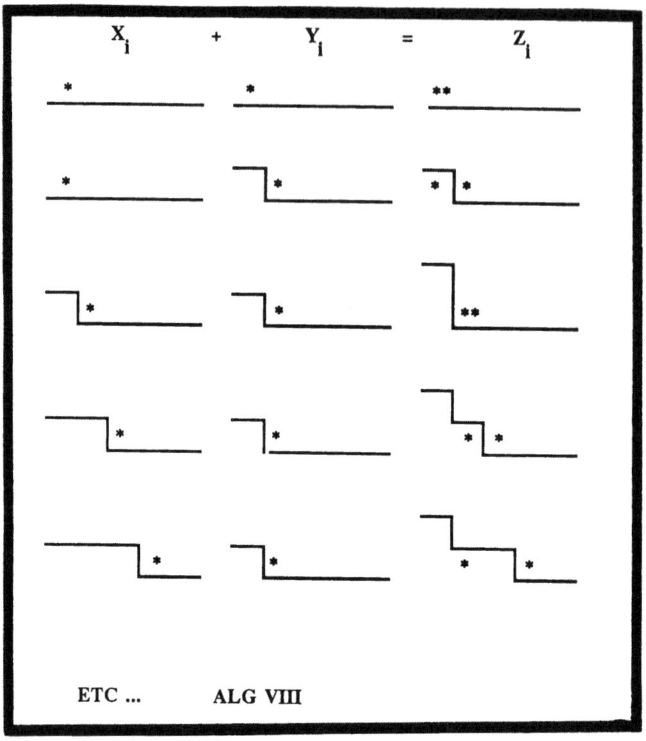

Figure 16

1.2.2. Consultation of both neighbors

As in the section 1.1.2., we can generate some variations. For example, assume only one right to be given each site. Then, we consider the evolution of the variable Z_i , seen in the preceding algorithm, according to the following conditions (Fig. 17).

IX

Initially $Z_0 = 1, Z_i = 0 \ , 1 <= i <= n-1$

P_i **has 1 right** $\quad <==> \quad Z_i <> Z_{i-1}$

P_i **leaves its right** $<==>$ **when** $Z_i = Z_{i+1}$

do $Z_i := Z_i +^2 1$

$0<=i<=n-1$

Figure 17

- Given that $Z_i - Z_{i-1}$ takes the values 0 and 1, it follows that the addition evolves modulus 2.

- When P_i wants to give its right, it must check that its right-hand neighbor has not already got a right.

We obtain then the algorithm IX (Fig. 17), described on the figure 18.

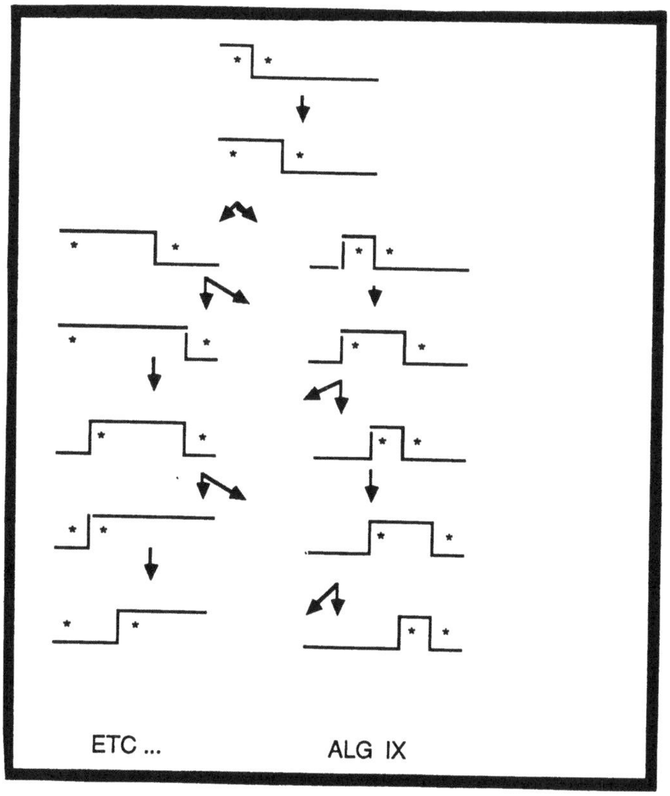

Figure 18

1.2.3. Five philosophers : derivation

From algorithm IX, we can easily derive a solution to the well-known Five Philosophers problem. A philosopher can have a right if and only if each of his neighbors has not a right. As shown earlier, we can see that we must forbid certain situations (Fig. 19, 20). At the beginning, assume that P_0 and

P_2 have each a right. So, P_i can use a right if and only if :

- $P_{i \ominus 1}$ has not got the right anymore
- $P_{i \oplus 1}$ has not got a right either

X (The 5 Philosophers)

<u>Initially</u> $Z_0 = Z_1 = 1$, $Z_i = 0$, $2 <= i <= 4$

P_i has 1 right $<==>$ $Z_i <> Z_{i-1}$ <u>and</u> $Z_i = Z_{i+1}$

P_i leaves its right $<==>$ $Z_i := Z_i +^2 1$

$0<=i<=4$

Figure 19

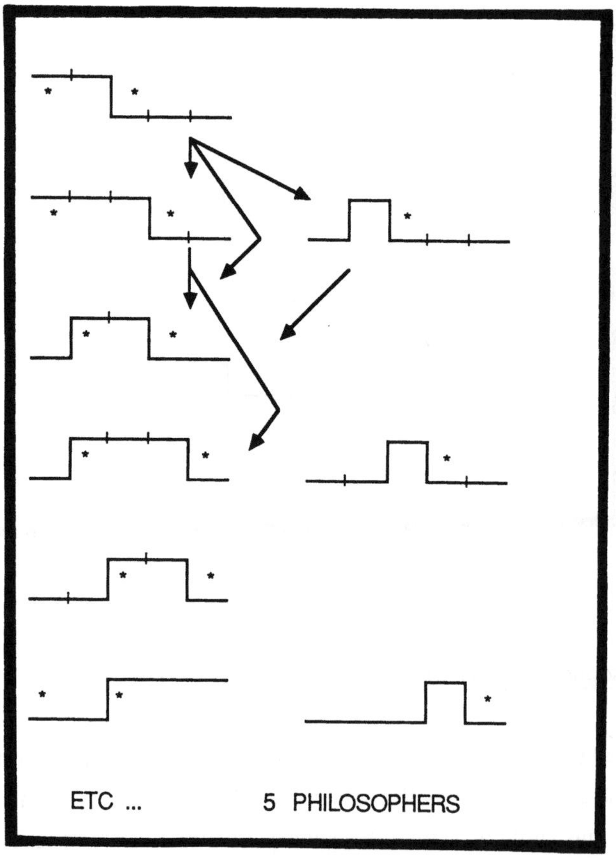

Figure 20

The first condition is translated in : $Z_i \neq Z_{i \ominus 1}$
The second in : $Z_i = Z_{i \oplus 1}$
P_i leaves its right by making : $Z_i := Z_i + 1 \underline{\text{mod}}\ 2$

N.B. Recall that "having a right" must be understood in this case like having the right to "eat". There are 5 philosophers and 5 forks : each philosopher has a left fork and a right one, and, to eat, he must use both of them.

In the figures 20 and 21, we see the evolution of the system. This solution can be generalized to any number of philosophers.

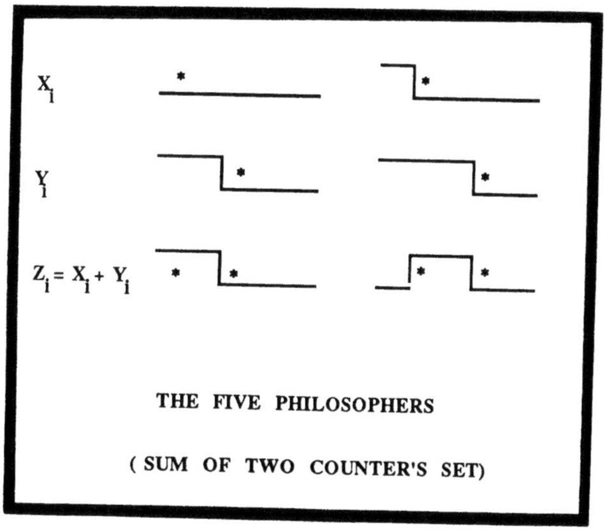

Figure 21

1.2.4. Five philosophers : direct design

We can directly obtain the Five Philosophers protocol. Each philosopher P_i is associated with a counter x_i ; x_i counts each entry of P_i in critical section (that is the right to use a resource). Initially all the x_i are zero and we assume that this configuration gives a right to P_0 and P_2. When a process gives its right, it increases by one x_i.

The game rule stays the same : each process is served fairly. We deduce the five rules (Fig. 22) and we find that x_i can be implemented modulus 2.

x_i counts each entry of P_i in critical section
(= the right to use a resource)

Initially $x_i = 0$ ==> P_0 & P_2 have a right

P_i gives its right ==> it increases by 1 x_i

WE DEDUCE

P_0	privileged iff	$x_0 = x_4 = x_1$
P_2	"	$x_2 = x_1 = x_3$
P_1	"	$x_1 = x_0 - 1 = x_2 - 1$
P_4	"	$x_4 = x_3 - 1 = x_0 - 1$
P_5	"	$x_3 = x_2 - 1 = x_4$

Figure 22

We obtain then an algorithm evolving according to the algorithm X with the change of variable

$$X_i + Z_i = C \qquad \text{(Fig. 23)}$$

i.e. $$X_i = Z_i + C$$

where C is a constant and Z_i the counters of Algorithm X.

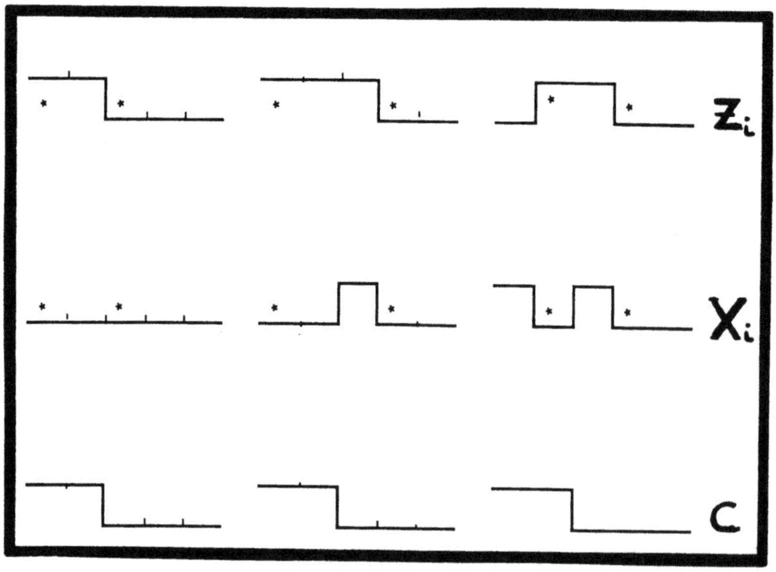

Figure 23

1.3. Conclusion

We have shown in this presentation that, from tools like counters, we can design distributed and fair resources allocation algorithms.

First, we found already known mutual exclusion algorithms based on the principle of privilege circulation, we derived new ones and we showed that they all belong to the same variety.

Secondly, we showed that thanks to additive operations on the counters, we can obtain elegant solutions to the production of fair allocation resources algorithms. Thus, from a set of counters (X_i), we can design two sorts of expressions :

(1) $(Y_i) = n * (X_i) + a_i$

(2) $(Z_i) = \sum_j (X_i^j)$

defining new sets of counters. These operations on the counters look like operations on an algebra.

To finish, let's draw our attention to some particular items.

About Counters

Counters are simple and powerful tools representing in a condensed form the history of a process. The fact that they evolve modulus K can be seen as the fact that, periodically, we can forget the history : we reset the counters. This is a good property for a process which repeats itself infinitely. To this property, we can add a practical interest : we can implement each counter with a variable.

About Fault-Tolerance

We have shown [1], [2], [9] that algorithms like those we have just studied present a good fault-tolerant capability to the withdrawal of a site. Such a capability justifies the practical interest of these algorithms rather than those which run by simple token passing.

About mutual exclusion algorithms

We have also studied [10], [11], how to derive mutual exclusion algorithms for two processes or when the processes are ordered on a binary tree structure : we retrieve then Kessel's algorithm [12].

In the next sections, we shall study mutual exclusion algorithms : in these, each process **must request** the entry into critical section before being considered for competition. Much has been written about this. We shall derive the generical algorithm for all of them.

Part 2. Generating Distributed Algorithms using replication of Queues

In a centralized system, it is often convenient to use queues to solve problems of fairness and priority. Some distributed algorithms use a set of queues, one for each site and service messages to maintain coherence : these can all be regarded as copies of a single abstract queue. We now use an example concerning **mutual exclusion** to demonstrate a method for replication of queues which can be adapted to other problems : For example, in [6], we use the same basic tools for maintaining the consistency of multiple copies of the same data. This chapter is only devoted to the mutual exclusion algorithms.

2.1. Abstract expression for the problem

We consider the sharing of a single resource among a set of processes, in which only one process at a time may occupy the resource and may do so for only a finite time (condition C1). The algorithm must also satisfy the fairness condition (C2). For this last condition, we set up a FIFO queue : requests are then dealt with in the order in which they are received. The abstract expression for the problem is straightforward (Fig. 24).

```
Q : queue FIFO
Pi :
|  REQi  : Put ( REQ,i) into Q
|
|           wait (REQ,i) at the head of Q
|           SC
|  RELi  : Remove (REQ,i) from Q
```

Figure 24

2.2. The distributed algorithm

We consider a distributed system with a single process P_i implemented at each site S_i . We assume :

(i) Every site can communicate with every other site.

(ii) Transmission is error-free, there is no loss of messages.

(iii) For transmission between any pair of sites i and j, the order in which i sends messages to j is the same as the order in which j receives the messages.

(iv) There is no breakdown (or physical isolation) of a site.

We assume that some system for time-stamping is provided [13] ; in the absence of a single physical clock, condition C2 must be interpreted in terms of a logical clock.

The abstract queue Q is replicated, so that at each site S_i, there is a queue q_i holding the markers (REQ, j).

As a first approach, we look for a method for processing Q which is as natural as possible :

1) At site i, when process P_i arrives at the point REQ_i (Fig. 24), the marker is put into the local queue q_i and a message (REQ, i, t) is broadcast to all the other sites, where t is the logical time at which the request is made.

2) At site j, when this message is received, marker (REQ, i, t) is put into queue q_j. The aim is that the q_i shall all be images, possibly delayed, of the abstract queue Q ; because of the variable delays experienced by the different messages, a FIFO organization of the q_j is inappropriate, so the decision is to deal with these in increasing order of the timestamps in the marker (REQ, i, t).

3) When the process at site i arrives at the point REL_i, a message (REL, i, t) is broadcast to all the other sites, which can then remove the corresponding marker from their queues q_j.

We now have to determine local conditions (which will assure that C1 and C2 are satisfied) ; the requirement is that the request for access to the resource by the local process will be granted if it has been outstanding for longer than any of the other requests still waiting. The local condition for entering in critical section is the following :

(CW1) : **wait** (REQ, i, t) is at the head of q_i
and
$site_i$ has received, from each other site, one (at least) message time-stamped later than t

The second part of this condition is intended to prevent the allocation of the resource in a situation such as that represented by Fig. 25. Since the messages cannot overtake one another on the point-to-point channels, if site 1 had received any message whatever from site 2, timestamped 7, it would be certain that all earlier messages from that site had already been received and, therefore, that a message such as (REQ, 2, 4) could not be in transit.

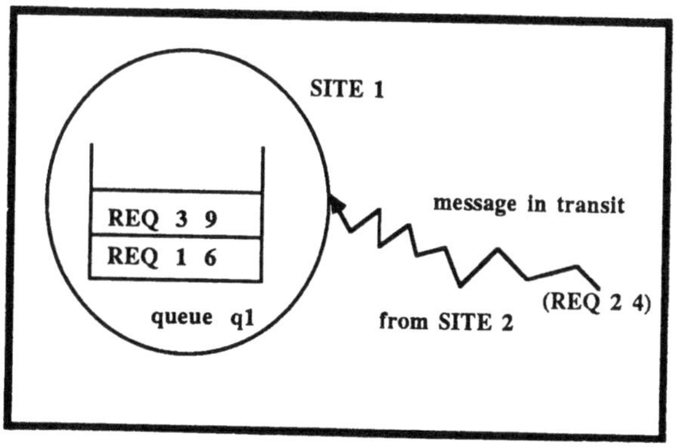

Figure 25

Condition (CW1) can be expressed more simply if the release markers are retained in the local queues. Assuming that initially every process sends a release message, the condition becomes

(CW2) : **wait** (REQ, i, t) is at the head of q_i

In the situation of Fig. 25, the queue q_1 is as shown in Fig. 26; the resource cannot be allocated to P_1, whether or not there is a message (REQ, 2, 4) in transit.

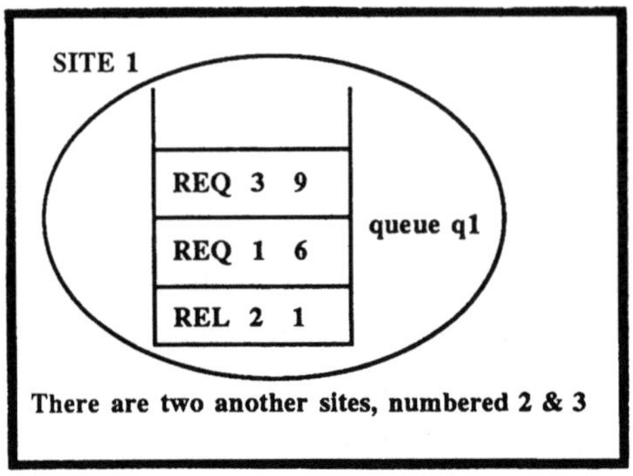

Figure 26

To avoid permanent denial of service to a process, as could happen in this case if P_2 had finished executing, or even excessively long waits, messages of the form (REL, i, t) can be issued in response to requests, and are dealt with as follows

2bis) When site j receives the message (REQ, i, t), there are two possibilities

a) There is an unsatisfied request (REQ, j, t') with t' < t : site j then delays its response until it has accessed and then released the resource ;

b) There is no earlier request from site j, so the message (REL, j, t") is sent to site i. The system for time-stamping ensures that t < t", consequently (REQ, i, t) can move up the queue in q_i.

2.3. Variations

This algorithm is just the one given by Lamport [13] [2]. Ricart and Aggrawala [14] move an amendment : a process which releases the resource sends the message REL only to those sites from which it has received requests. The cost corresponding to a request for the resource is therefore :

N-1 request messages sent out by the requesting site

plus N-1 messages advising release, which must be received before the resource can be accessed.

This is the minimum cost under the present assumptions. Carvalho and Roucairol [15] move another amendment which gives 2(N-1) as the upper limit for the cost, but which requires a special interpretation of condition C2 : some priorities are introduced dynamically, but do not lead to starvation. In turn, Ricart and Aggrawala [16] move a new amendment where they substitute the timestamps for simple increasing counters (without updating when messages are exchanged) (see Part 3).

2.4. Conclusion

This example has made use of general principles according to which the abstract queue Q can be replicated ; these are illustrated by condition (CW1) of section 2.2. :

a) The time-stamping system ensures that the order in which requests are put into the local queues is the same for all sites : this is the first part of CW1.

b) The abstract condition is strengthened in order to compensate for the uncertainties in specifying the actual state of the system, such as the possibility of messages in transit : this is the second part of CW1.

The application of such a technique is illustrated in [1], [6], for the maintenance of consistency among copies of the same information.

Part 3. Generating fair distributed mutual exclusion algorithms using distributed variables.

In this part, we shall give some indications on Thoraval's proposition [11, 17] for the uniform way of expressing third class algorithms (see introduction).

3.1. Abstract Expression

Let's consider n parallel processes, each based on model in Fig. 27. Each process can be invoked infinitely often. The expression given in Fig. 27 does not have to be explained.

```
Process P_i
STATE_i : local variable ∈ {waiting, ready, ending}
initially STATE_i = ending

    (n)   repeat
              STATE_i := waiting

              STATE_i := ready
          until {STATE_j ≠ ready ∀j ∈ E-{i}}

    SC_i

    STATE_i := ending
endprocess

    i ∈ E
    E = {0, 1, ... n-1}
```

Figure 27

Let's simply note that the evaluation of the variables $STATE_i$ in the loop exit condition is not necessarily atomic and can be carried out in any order.

3.1.1. Algorithm (Fig. 27) ensures mutual exclusion but not absence of deadlock

Let's suppose that there is not mutual exclusion between P_i and P_j Let's consider the moment t where P_i and P_j run respectively and simultaneously SC_i and SC_j. Let t_i (resp. t_j) be the moment where P_i (resp. P_j) has read for the last time $STATE_j$ (resp. $STATE_i$) before going into its critical section. Then by construction :

$$\begin{aligned} \text{at time } t_i : \ & STATE_j \neq \text{ready} \\ & STATE_i = \text{ready} \\ \text{at time } t_j : \ & STATE_i \neq \text{ready} \\ & STATE_j = \text{ready} \end{aligned}$$

Let t_j be the later time. Then, between t_j and t :

$$STATE_i \neq \text{ready} \ \underline{\text{and}} \ STATE_i = \text{ready}$$

which contradicts our hypothesis.

This algorithm (Fig. 27) has obviously a deadlock situation since, if two processes are evolving at the same speed, they do not have any means of differentiating themselves from each other (see [18]) and the loop exit condition (a) may happen to be false at each evaluation.

3.1.2. Algorithm (Fig. 28) ensures mutual exclusion deadlock but with a possibility of starvation

```
Process Pi

STATEi : local variable ∈ {waiting, ready, ending}

initially STATEi = ending

     (a)    repeat
                STATEi := waiting
     (b)        wait { STATEj = ending ∀ j ∈ PRIORi }
                STATEi := ready
            until {STATEj ≠ready ∀j ∈ E-{i}}

     SCi

     STATEi := ending

endprocess

     i ∈ E
     E = {0, 1, ... n-1}
     PRIORi = {0,1, .... i-1}
```

Figure 28

To remove the risk of deadlock, it is sufficient for the processes to choose a priority process. Instruction (b), added to algorithm (fig. 27), allows this choice (see Fig. 28) by giving priority to the process which has the smallest number of those in their cycle (a).

However, this algorithm presents rules of strict priority and is not fair : any process except P_0 can wait indefinitely.

3.1.3. Algorithm (Fig. 29) ensures fair mutual exclusion

```
Process Pi
  STATEi : local variable ∈ {waiting, ready, ending}
  initially STATEi = ending
  (c) repeat
        (a) repeat
                  STATEi := waiting
            (b)   wait { STATEj = ending ∀ j ∈ PRIORi }
                  STATEi := ready
            until {STATEj ≠ready ∀j ∈ E-{i}}
      until {STATEk = ending , Pk is the highest priority process }
      SCi
      TRANSLATE PRIORITYi
      STATEi := ending
endprocess

      i ∈ E
      E = {0, 1, ... n-1}
      PRIORi = see text
      TRANSLATE PRIORITYi = see texte
```

Figure 29

The kernel algorithm (Fig. 27) is the abstraction of a mechanism which can be seen in Burns [18], Dijkstra [20] and Pnueli [24]. Algorithm (Fig. 28) is an abstraction of Katseff's [22] and constitutes the germ of De Bruijn [19], Eisenberg [21] and Knuth [23], the aim of which is to offer fair extensions by dynamising the set $PRIOR_i$.

And, in fact, Thoraval's work consists in showing that we can generate, on demand, very numerous fair variations of algorithm (Fig. 28). As an example we give one of this (Fig. 29), which is original and efficient in comparison with others.

The implementation of fairness is based on two mechanisms.

The first translates the relation of priority around a virtual ring using the instruction TRANSLATE $PRIORITY_i$. The highest priority process is no longer systematically P_0 but any process P_k and the set $PRIOR_i$ becomes :

$$\begin{array}{ll} \{ k, k+1, \ldots i-1 \} & \text{if } k < i \\ E - \{ i, i+1, \ldots k-1 \} & \text{if } k > i \\ \emptyset & \text{if } k = i \end{array}$$

Any process P_k thus becomes priority, after finite time.

The second mechanism forbids an elected process (i.e. the one which exited from loop (a)) to enter in critical section if the highest priority process is waiting or ready, which enforces the validity of its election.

3.2. Distributed implementation

Algorithm (Fig. 29) can be easily distributed. In fact, the local state variables are naturally distributed and their reading, possibly delayed, is not a problem.

As far as the calculation of the set $PRIOR_i$ is concerned, the number of the highest priority process must be calculated. To do this, we adopt the now well-known mechanism of privilege circulation (see Part1).

Let N_i be the counter which calculate the ending of each TRANSLATE PRIORITY$_i$, i=0, 1, ... n-1. P_k is then priority when :

$$\sum_{j=0}^{n-1} N_j = K$$

if we choose, at the beginning, P_0 as initially the priority process, and N_j =0.

TRANSLATE PRIORITY$_i$ can be expressed by :

$N_i = N_i + 1$

Let's note that these additions can be made modulus n.

3.3. Variations

In algorithm (Fig. 29), Thoraval distinguishes three basic tools :

- the mode of translation of priority relations
- the representation of priority relations, thanks to counter, common variables, etc...
- the control mechanism, represented by instruction (c)

and he shows that we can derive (and evaluate) by composition, a very great variety of algorithms. All the algorithms mentionned can thus be found, with minor syntactical differencies.

Conclusion

In this paper, only the first part has an exhaustive development, and the reader can consult its conclusion.

With the two following parts, we wanted to make the foundations of a thesis in which any distributed mutual exclusion algorithm can be reduced to one of three classes. We think moreover that these three classes, apparently distincts, especially if you refer back to the introductory image, can be linked to each other.

Anyway we think that we have made some distributed (mutual exclusion) algorithms that we have seen (for example in [7], [8], [14], [19], [20], [21], [22], [23]) easier to understand. Of course, our ambition is that this better understanding can be applied to the way in which we design, prove and evaluate these algorithms.

Bibliography

1. Fair Distributed Algorithms with counters

[1] F. ANDRE, D. HERMAN, J.P. VERJUS
Synchronisation of parallel programs
North Oxford Academic, OXFORD, ENGLAND 1985
M.I.T. Press, CAMBRIDGE, USA 1985

[2] CORNAFION
Distributed Computing Systems : Communication, Cooperation, Consistency
Elsevier S.P., AMSTERDAM NEW YORK 1985

[3] J.P. VERJUS
Synchronisation in distributed systems : an informal introduction
in (4)

[4] Y. PAKER, J.P. VERJUS Eds
Distributed computing systems :
Synchronisation, Control and Communication
Academic Press LONDON 1983

[5] D. HERMAN
Towards a systematic approach to implement distributed control of synchronisation
in (4)

[6] D. HERMAN, J.P. VERJUS
An algorithm for maintening the consistency of multiple copies
IEEE Proc of the 1st Int. Conf. on Distributed Computing Systems, Huntsville 1979

[7] E.W. DIJKSTRA
Self stabilization in spite of distributed control
Comm. of the ACM, 17 (11), nov. 1974

[8] M. RAYNAL
Un algorithme d'exclusion mutuelle pour une structure logique en anneau
T.S.I., 4 (5), 1985, pp 471-474

[9] J.MOSSIERE, M.TCHUENTE, J.P. VERJUS
Sur l'exclusion mutuelle dans les réseaux informatiques
Pub IRISA n° 75 (1977)

[10] J.P. VERJUS, R.THORAVAL
Dérivation d'algorithmes distribués d'arbitrage
T.S.I., 5(1), jan.-fév. 1986, pp. 37-47

[11] R. THORAVAL
Dérivation de protocoles distribués et équitables d'exclusion mutuelle
A paraitre Rennes 1986

[12] J.L.W. KESSELS
Arbitration without common modifiable variables
Acta informatice 17, pp. 135-141, Springer-Verlag 1982

2. Fair Distributed Algorithms with Queues and Timestamping

[13] L.LAMPORT
Time, clocks and the ordering of events in a distributed system
Comm. of the ACM, 21 (7), july 1978, pp. 558-565

[14] G RICART and A AGRAWALA
An optimal algorithm for mutual exclusion
Computer Network CACM, 24 (1), jan. 1981

[15] O.S.F. CARVALHO and G .ROUCAIROL
Une amélioration de l'algorithme d'exclusion mutuelle de Ricart et Agrawala
Report 81.58, L.I.T.P., Paris, nov. 1981

[16] G. RICART, A.K. AGRAWALA
Author's responseto "On mutual exclusion in computer networks" by Carvalho and Roucairol
Comm. of the ACM, 26 (2), feb. 1983, pp. 147-148

3. Fair Distributed Mutual Exclusion Algorithms with Dynamical Priority

[17] R.THORAVAL
Derivation de protocoles d'exclusion mutuelle équitables à partir de protocoles d'exclusion mutuelle inéquitables
Rapport IRISA, 1986, à paraître

[18] J.E. BURNS
Symmetry in systems of asynchronous processes
Proc. of the 22nd Ann. Symp. on Found. of Comp. Sci., oct 81 pp. 169-174

[19] N.G. de BRUIJN
Additional comments on a problem in concurrent programming control
Comm. of the ACM, 11 (1), jan. 1968, pp. 55-56

[20] E.W. DIJKSTRA
Solution of a problem in concurrent programming control
Comm. of the ACM, 8 (9), sept. 1965, p 569

[21] M.A. EISENBERG, M.R. Mc GUIRE
Further comments on Dijkstra's concurrent programming control problem
Comm. of the ACM, 15 (11), nov. 1972, p. 999

[22] H.P. KATSEFF
A new solution to the critical section problem
Conf. Rec. of the 10th Ann. ACM Symp. on Th. of Comp.
San Diego, Calif., may 1-3, 1978, pp. 86-88

[23] D.E. KNUTH
Additional comments on a problem in concurrent programming control
Comm. of the ACM, 9 (5), may 1966, pp.321-322

[24] A. PNUELI, L. ZUCK
Verification of multiprocess probabilistic protocols
Proc. of the 3rd ACM SIGACT-SIGOPS Symp. on Princ. of Distr. Comp., Vancouver, Canada, aug. 27-29, 1984, pp. 12-17

4. General

[25] E.W. DIJKSTRA
A belated proof of self-stabilization
Distributed Computing (1986) 1 : 5-6

[26] M. RAYNAL
Algorithmique du parallélisme
-le problème de l'exclusion mutuelle-
Dunod informatique, Paris 1984

[27] M. RAYNAL
Algorithmes distribués et protocoles
Eyrolles, Paris 1985

Part 2

Design Issues for Distributed Operating Systems

DESIGN OF HIGHLY DECENTRALIZED OPERATING SYSTEMS

Fabrizio Baiardi and Marco Vanneschi
Dipartimento di Informatica
Universita' di Pisa, Italy

Keywords
distributed computer / decentralized operating system / concurrency / fault tolerance / integrated design / concurrent programming environment / forward - backward recovery / optimistic approach.

Abstract
In the decentralized operating system approach all the resources of a distributed system are considered as belonging to a single, very reliable, machine. To fully exploit the high potential for performance of such a machine, we need a methodology able to express high parallelism in resource management policies. Also recovery policies should be expressed without constraining real parallelism.
The proposed solution is based upon the definition of a concurrent language and of the corresponding programming environment. The language supports the integration of concurrency and fault tolerance through the optimistic approach to process synchronization.

1. INTRODUCTION

In the field of distributed systems architecture one of the most interesting solutions is that of distributed computers [2,19,20,21,32]. A *distributed computer* is characterized by the fact that all resources in the system are globally managed by a single operating system,

NATO ASI Series, Vol. F28
Distributed Operating Systems. Theory and Practice
Edited by Y. Paker et al.

called *global operating system*. By global management we mean that the scheduling policies take into account the influence of choiches on all the users of the system. This is in contrast with the point of view of "network" operating systems where each node has its own local policies not necessarily integrated with those of other nodes. Of course, some resources might be globally managed also in network systems, but this is not the general situation.

Furthermore, we are interested in *decentralized* global operating systems *(DGOS)*. A DGOS consists of several instances of the same set of processes: each instance is allocated to a distinct node, and every decision about the system behaviour is taken through the cooperation among several (or even all) instances, since none of them has authority over the others.

Taking into account the existence of several instances and the global management of resources, the behaviour of a DGOS may be sketched as follows: when some scheduling is required, at first each instance determines the scheduling according to its own view of both the actual system state and requests (*local decision*). Then the various schedulings and views are integrated trying to overcome discrepancies and incongruities, due to distribution and/or delays of the interconnection structure (*global decision*). Of course the two steps (local and global decision) might be interleaved in several ways.

It should be fairly obvious that this behaviour has a great potential for both high reliability and optimal resource usage, but it is also obvious that the counterpart is a large increase in the amount of interactions among components of the DGOS. This increase can strongly reduce the performance of the system, thus making more questionable the adoption of the distributed computer approach.

Our approach to the design of distributed computers proposes to improve the DGOS performance by two interrelated guidelines:

a) *increasing the actual concurrency* among software components, both within an instance of the DGOS and among distinct instances;

b) *employing more hardware units* to better exploit the real parallelism.

As an example, after having recognized that some functionalities are critical for any instance of the DGOS, we can implement them by a set of concurrent processes and build each node of the system as a set of processors dedicated to the execution of such processes.

Increasing the performance of a system through real parallelism is, in our opinion, one of the most structured as well as the most coherent approaches, due the evolution of technology [32]. Of course, the performances/cost trade off increases when the processes, supported by dedicated processors, are largely asynchronous (loosely coupled). As detailed in the next sections, the classical approach to the definition of concurrent programs, that guarantees a step-by-step consistency among the various processes, may not be able to express the required degree of concurrency. A solution might be found in the so called *optimistic* approach to synchronization: in this approach the requirement of a strict consistency is relaxed, and some synchronizations are thus removed, since any error that may arise is detected and recovered. Several cases exist where the cost of detection and recovery is lower than the overhead associated with synchonization because of the low probability of an inconsistency.

Another constraint on exploitable concurrency arises because of recovery policies. As a matter of fact, the recovery policies adopted in network systems strongly reduce the degree of concurrency among operations. A typical example is given by distributed atomic actions: all processes and/or resources involved in an action are forced to enter and leave an action simultaneously, independently of the time required by their own computation. Hence, only *recovery policies that do not bound existing parallelism* are to be adopted. In general, an *integrated solution to synchronization and recovery* should be defined: in fact, by taking into account recovery already in the definition of synchronization mechanisms, it is possible to reduce the emulation of those mechanisms required for the implementation of recovery policies.

In the definition of a solution to the various outlined problems, a *"language-first"* approach will be adopted. That is to say, we do not aim to define a set of decentralized or distributed algorithms to solve specific problems, instead we are interested in defining a concurrent language able to express a large set of alternative solutions. This implies that all the adopted mechanisms should correspond to language constructs and hence, first of all, their semantics can be defined in terms of a formal model. Furthermore, being in correspondence to language constructs, the mechanisms should satisfy the orthogonality requirement.

It is worth stressing here two main consequences of the language first approach:

a) the *hardware structure* should be designed mainly with the aim of efficiently supporting the programming language of the operating system. As a matter of fact, the performance of the operating system is critical since it influences other system components;
b) a *programming environment* may be defined starting from the formal semantics of the language [3,8,13,25]. Several static checks on program correctness may be implemented by the tools of the environment, thus reducing program development costs. Since both the amount of processes and the actual concurrency increase, most tests are significant only when they are formalized and delegated to a tool.

In the next two sections we will discuss the parallelism and reliability issues in isolation. A design methodology to obtain solutions to the two problems will be discussed in sect. 4; the solution will be also compared with previous proposals [18,21,22,23,27,31]. Sect. 5 introduces the ECSP programming language and its programming environment.

Sect. 6 includes some examples of the application of the methodology to ECSP programs.

2. PARALLELISM AND PROGRAMMING ENVIRONMENT

In the discussion of this section we will consider only languages that are based upon the *local environment model* of cooperation (i.e. message-oriented) [10]. As a matter of fact, the existence of a global environment introduces a bottleneck in the system which bounds the amount of effective concurrency.

When aiming to decompose a computation into a large number of concurrent processes, a very important issue is the feasibility of a *top-down approach* to the design: after decomposing a computation into a given set of processes, each of these processes may in turn be decomposed into further processes. A top-down approach requires a *hierarchical model of parallelism* , and in particular the adoption in the programming language of a construct to dynamically activate a set of processes and to wait for their termination. By this construct it is possible to fully exploit those situations where some operations can be concurrently executed depending on the actual state of some process. This requires also:

a) constructs to transmit some values to the activated processes. In fact, due to the local environment model of cooperation, the activated processes cannot have access to the state of the activating one;

b) the ability to *terminate* the (sub)computation as soon as some dependencies arise between distinct processes.

It is important to stress here the importance of point b): the availability of constructs that precisely define when, and under which conditions, a process P should terminate its execution, as well as the influence of this termination on the partners of P, is essential to coordinate the computation. We believe that the view of a computation as a set of processes that are executed forever is no longer applicable when designing systems aiming to exploit concurrency at best.

As an example of the feasibility of using process activation and termination to exploit concurrency, let us consider a process P that implements four operations, op_1, ...op_4, and suppose that they are scheduled according to relations among integer values of h_1,l_2 (constants) and x_1,x_2 (variables) as follows:

i) op_1 can be executed when $x_1 < h_1$. After the execution x_1 is incremented;

ii) op_2 and op_3 can be executed only when $x_1 > x_2$. After the execution of op_2 x_1 is decremented, while x_2 is incremented after that of op_3 ;

iii) op_4 can be executed only if $x_2>l_2$ and then x_2 is decremented.

In general the four operations are to be sequentialized because the condition $x_1>x_2$ cannot be evaluated concurrently in distinct processes:however, if at some time $x_1-x_2=k>>0$ then P can activate two processes, executing op_1 and op_2 or op_3 and op_4 respectively ; a process will be executed till the corresponding x_i is decreased, or increased, by a given constant d_i such that $d_1+d_2 \leq k$. As soon as both processes are terminated, the execution of P will be resumed, the operations executed sequentially, and so on.

Another noticeable advantage of a hierarchical parallel model is that it is easier to analyze the program provided that the parallel structure of a process P is hidden to the environment of P. This means that from the point of view of the environment any interaction has place with P, even when the actual partner is a process activated by P or by one of the descendants of P. Hence, only the interface defined by a process, and not its internal structure, is to be considered when analyzing a program. This reduces the number of processes that have to be taken simultaneously into account, thus decreasing the complexity of the analysis. As a consequence, the tools of the programming environment are easier to design and more efficient when their analysis can be defined in terms of the hierarchical structure of programsand their interfaces.

The notion of a computation as composed of a hierarchy of process, each of which knows only the interfaces defined by the others and not their internal structure, strongly resembles the one where a computation is seen as a collection of *instances of abstract data types*. As a matter of fact we believe that this similarity should be stressed and exploited, since during the design each process may be considered as an instance of an abstract data type [26,29] implementing a set of operations that can be invoked by the partners through proper interactions. With respect to the one of abstract data type, the notion of process includes that of *autonomous execution* (i.e. objects are active entities represented by processes): this makes it easier to determine when and under what conditions an operation should be executed.

Hence we can distinguish in any process, at any abstraction level, the functions that determine the scheduling of the invocations of the operations implemented by the process. Any process P can, at least in principle, be decomposed into two processes: one for the *scheduling* of the invocations and the other for the *execution* of the operation themselves.

Taking into account the similarity between processes and abstract data types, the decomposition of a program into a large set of processes has also noticeable advantages in terms of program modifiability since it is easier to select the processes that are to be modified to define a different version of the system.

The issue of a set of tools supporting the analysis of program behaviour cannot be completely satisfied only by requirements on the program structure: it is also essential to be able to *statically deduce the maximum amount of information on process interactions*. First of all this requires that the notion of data type is exploited in the definition of interactions: for example any exchange of values among processes should satisfy the same typing rules of an assignment among variables of a single process. Under this assumption, the tools are able to recognize which are the possible partners for a given interaction of a process and determine whether an interaction can be successfully completed.

Another important point is that the constructs should avoid *hidden or unbounded nondeterminism* and time dependent behaviour, as much as possible. Assume that the implementation of a construct requires a nondeterministic choice whose domain is not determined by the construct definition or it depends upon the definition or the behaviour of other processes. In this case a static analysis of the construct either is possible only by extending the analysis to several other processes, and this hinders design modularity, or is not able to convey any useful information since the program behaviour is completely dependent upon run time choices. Consider as an example the problem of choosing one message to be received among those of a given set. In languages such as CSP or Ada this is expressed in the receiver as a guarded nondeterministic construct, where each guard corresponds to a distinct message; instead in languages using the concept of a single port for each process, where all messages to be received are queued, only the name of the port appears, and the rest of the program has to be considered in order to discover a nondeterministic behaviour.

Of course some trade offs should be adopted since some kinds of unbouded nondeterminism may improve program modularity. We believe that these situations should be derivable as a particular case by relaxing some constraints: in this way it is easier to avoid unwanted nondeterminism than when introducing further constraints on constructs not suitable for static analysis.

A distinct problem related to concurrency is the *allocation of processes to nodes* of the system or to processors within a node. This problem arises since in general a system is not fully connected and then some kind of routing is required when communicating processes are not allocated to directly connected nodes. To reduce communication costs, processor allocation should be driven by both the system topology and the communications of the program, and because of the complexity of the problem the solution should be delegated to a tool of the environment.

Also in the definition of such a tool we may take into account the program structure. First of all we may extend the notion of *locality* and of *working set* to partners of the communications of a process, and try to allocate the processes in the working set of P to nodes directly connected to the one where P has been allocated. Notice that the structure of a concurrent program may be described by a tree representing process decomposition.Then we could assume that most of the computation is carried out by processes corresponding to *leaves of the tree* and allocate also these processes to connected nodes. Of course this is not sufficient to solve the problem, but it enables us to strongly reduce the solutions to be considered in the search for an optimal one, with respect to the case of a large flat set of processes.

Furthermore, the tree representation of a program allows us to partition processes into *classes* so that two processes belong to the same class only if they cannot be concurrently executed (consider as an example the case where a process activates either the processes in a set S_1 or those in a set S_2 but never processes in both S_1 and S_2). Afterwards, we can allocate processes belonging to distinct classes to the same node without loosing any concurrency because of multiprogramming.

3. FAULT TOLERANCE POLICIES

As already mentioned, fault tolerance policies should not introduce further constraints on existing concurrency.

As a first consequence, using backward recovery [30], the semantics of the involved actions should be exploited in order to avoid those mechanisms (such as the two phase lock protocol) that guarantee the feasibility of a recovery independently of the semantics but at the expence of parallelism.

As an example, consider a set of cooperating processes $P_1,...,P_n$. Backward recovery policies require that, before taking part in the cooperation, a P_i has to save its state in a stable memory and all the processes have to decide whether to successfully complete the action or to restore the state saved in the stable memory. This is not necessary when the semantics of the actions of a P_i guarantees idempotency (such as when P_i is functional) at least as far as is concerned the considered computation.

Furthermore, also the implementation of a distributed stable memory in a system including a large number of nodes may introduce some centralization points because of the uncertainty principle or due to the fact that only a few nodes are connected to i/o devices: this gives rise to more serious drawback than in the case of network systems.

To be able *to exploit the semantics of actions* [21] in order to decrease the recovery cost, the notion of atomic actions or transactions should not be primitive in the programming language since this prevents any optimization of the implementation. Instead, the language constructs should support several alternative implementations of these notions so that the designer might choose the most suitable one with respect to the considered problem.

Forward recovery should be adopted as the main mechanism to restore a global consistent state. Two main principles should be taken into account:

a) the adoption of *copy processes*, i.e. processes managing a copy of the internal state of critical processes. If C(P) is the process managing the copy of the state of P, a fault affecting P is recovered by switching from P to C(P). The amount of interactions required to update C(P) can be reduced if we do not assume that the copy of C(P) is always consistent and hence some computation is required after the switch in order that C(P) can actually replace P. In contrast with backward recovery, the designer is able to establish a trade off between the cost of interactions to update C(P) and the interval of time required to replace P by C(P);

b) *stressing the autonomy* of each process. One of the main problem of any recovery policy in any concurrent system is the propagation of recovery actions: if a fault in a process P is not detected by processes $P_1,\ldots,P_n$ interacting with P, a recovery action in P may produce corresponding actions in $P_1, \ldots, P_n$.

Even by not taking into account the domino effect, that can usually be avoided by forward recovery, it is obvious that the cost of recovery is determined essentially by the amount of involved processess. To decrease this cost each process should test, in the most complete way , all data received from other processes to detect faults in the sender. As an example, the adoption of typed messages might be seen as a first simple check on values since a value will be assigned to a variable of the receiver only when its type corresponds to that of the variable. In the more general case, recalling the similarity between processes and abstract data types, for each process we can introduce a set of functions to protect the operations implemented by the process itself. These functions may be implemented, as in the case of scheduling, by one of the processes into which the considered one can be decomposed.

As far as point b) is cocerned notice that, since any interaction includes a consistency check on the state of involved processes, the degree of error detection and confinement increases when the domain of each process is small and so the frequency of interactions is high. The reduction of the domains of the processes is required also to improve the concurrency of the program.

Points a) and b) are strongly related: as a matter of fact if we assume that the copy C(P) may be out-of-date with respect to P, then all the partners of P should maintain some data , about its past operations, to update C(P) consistently.

Consider, as an example, the case where P implements a data structure S on which processes $P_1, ..., P_n$ may operate through interactions with P. Assume also that P updates C(P) only when a given fixed number of operations has been executed. We can structure the recovery of a crash of P by assuming that P informs any P_i when C(P) has been updated, and that a P_i records its own requests satisfied by P till C(P) has been updated. In this way, when C(P) has to replace P, it can be required that $P_1, ..., P_n$ repeat their operations. In this solution the data required to restore a consistent state are distributed among a set of processes instead of being centralized in a single process or in a stable storage [24].

Through this structuring, recovery policies can exploit the parallelism supported by the system without introducing singularity points.

When designing fault tolerance policies according to a language first approach, any fault in the system is *modeled* by the failure of one or more language constructs. Thus the basic mechanism for the definition of such policies is a construct to express the handling of a failure by the execution of a proper command list. Of course, ad hoc error detection constructs such as acceptance tests, may also be introduced in the language, but error coverage increases when any construct can be exploited for error detection.

The checks to be executed to determine the failure of a construct may either be derived from the dynamic semantics of the language or be a repetition of those implemented by the tools of the environment. A typical example is the pattern matching between the type of a message and the one of a variable assigned to the value of the message: by executing again this checking at run time, and including also checks on the actual value of the message, it is possible to detect errors in the sender or in the receiver or in the interconnection structure.

A case of particular importance arises when the failure of a command leads to the *termination with failure* of a process P executing the command. The partners of P should be able to detect the anomalous termination of P, as well as to state an alternative continuation when an interaction with P cannot have place.

It should be stressed that a language first approach is able to fulfil the principles stated in [11] for the definition for a robust cooperation environment, namely:

a) process isolation;

b) resource control in absence of side effects;

c) decision verification in a failure independent way.

Process isolation and control in absence of side effects may be naturally achieved by adopting the local model of cooperation, provided that the language does not introduce mechanisms that allow a process *to force* the behaviour of the other ones. Examples of this mechanisms are the *abort* construct of Ada [12] or the existence of a single input queue for each process where the ordering of messages cannot be controlled by the receiver.

Decision verification is based essentially, from the point of view of the language, upon the fact that the constructs for interactions require some kind of *consensus* among all the involved processes for the interactions to be successfully completed. As an example, the adoption of *explicit naming* in interactions allows any process to determine which processes may be its partners in an interaction.

Other conditions, such as the "minimum privilege" and the absence of default privileges, are satisfied when the name of the partner in an interaction construct may be given by the value of a *variable*. By updating this variable, the process is able to change the partner of the interaction and this may be exploited both to grant a process the right to interact or to reconfigure the system after a fault, i.e. to switch from P to C(P).

4. INCREASING THE DEGREE OF CONCURRENCY

It is possible that some system or applicative programs are not able to fully exploit the parallelism of a distributed computer architecture and/or of each node, since they do not have an inner degree of concurrency sufficient to guarantee an appropriate performance. To enlarge the set of applications that can be supported , we need a formal methodology able to increase such a degree.

The methodology should produce the definition of a tool of the programming environment to implement the transformation of a concurrent program into one with the required degree of concurrency. The role of such a tool might be compared to that of the *optimizer* in an environment for a sequential language. This tool may execute some *pattern driven optimizations*,that is to say it may search for some patterns each of which can be replaced by a more efficient one.

A typical example is the replacement of a synchronous communication by an asynchronous one or the permutation of instructions. Consider as an example the following CSP program fragment

P:: ... x:=f_1(...); y:=f_2(x); Q!x; Q?z; ...

The computation of f_2 and the output command may be exchanged, leading to

P:: ... x:= f_1(...); Q!x; y:=f_2(x); Q?z; ...

Furthermore, the transmission of the value of x to Q might be asynchronous since P will wait anyway for the value of z .

In general, such a tool should analyze several processes simultaneously in order to guarantee that the semantics of the program is preserved. To be able to express a large set of optimizations, the programming language should offer several interactions constructs with *different degrees of synchronization* among the involved processes. Few optimizations are possible if the language offers a single mechanism, e.g. requiring a tight synchronization.

This pattern driven optimization could not be sufficient since, at best, it can reduce the synchronization among already defined processes. The starting point for the definition of the required methodology is *to fully exploit the feasibility of activating and terminating processes*, in order to express all the concurrency still implicit in the program.

Consider as an example the process P in fig. 1, which is a CSP implementation of the one already discussed in sect. 2. In process P, the values of the two variables x_1 and x_2 determine the total ordering of the execution of the four alternatives.

```
P:: var  x1=l1..h1:=h1;                                        / l1<=h2  /
         x2=l2..h2:=h2;

  *[  (x1<h1), U1?c1(...)                    → ...; x1:=x1+1
   □  (x1>x2) and (x1>l1),  U1? c2(...)      → ...; x1:=x1-1
   □  (x1>x2) and (x2<h2), U2? c3(...)       → ...; x2:=x2+1
   □  (x2>l2), U2?c4(...)                    →..., x2:=x2-1
   ]
```

Fig. 1. Sequential version of a resource manager.

The decomposition of P into two fully asynchronous processes, P_1 and P_2, executing respectively the first and the second, or the third and the fourth alternative, is not possible since they both need the values of x_1 and x_2. Some communications should be introduced so that both P_1 and P_2 are able to evaluate the condition $x_1>x_2$; these communications could introduce an overhead larger than the increase in performance due to concurrency.

A first solution to avoid interactions between P_1 and P_2 consists in partitioning the space of the range of x_1 and x_2 into two subsets, namely $S_{11}=(h_2+1, h_1)$ and $S_{12}=(l_1, h_2)$ for x_1 and $S_{21}=(l_1, h_2)=S_{12}$, $S_{22}=(l_2,l_1-1)$ for x_2. As long as

$$\text{cond} = (x_1 \in S_{11}) \textit{ and } (x_2 \in S_{22})$$

holds, then P_1 and P_2 may be fully asynchronous since $x_1>x_2$ surely holds too, and each P_i can evaluate autonomously the condition $x_i \in S_{ii}$.

This can be exploited in at least two ways:

a) through the introduction of interactions between P_1 and P_2 only when cond does not hold;

b) by activating P_1 and P_2 when cond holds and forcing P_i to terminate as soon as $x_i \notin S_{ii}$. In the case that x_1 and x_2 belong to $S_{12}=S_{21}$, requests from U_1 and U_2 are served sequentially by P.

Notice that in solution a) the program of processes P_1 and P_2 is more complex since a process should always be ready to interact with the other and it is not known in advance when $x_i \notin S_{ii}$. On the other side, the disadvantage of solution b) is that the time interval between the termination of one process and that of the other is potentially unbounded, and hence the interactions implemented by the terminated P_i might never have place. This is possible also in the sequential solution when fairness cannot be assumed.

Solutions a) and b) are always possible when we can determine, for each variable x_i, a convex subset of its range, CSR_i, such that when each x_i belongs to CSR_i then some commands of the process can be concurrently executed. This may be seen as an extension of Bernstein's conditions in order to be able to exploit process activation and termination. As a matter of fact, Bernstein's conditions require CSR_i to be equal to the whole range of x_i.

Another possible solution to concurrently execute some operations is to choose two values α and β and to activate processes $P\alpha$ and $P\beta$,similar to P_1 and P_2 when the difference (x_1-x_2) is equal to $\gamma=\alpha+\beta$. $P\alpha$ is active till the value of x_1 has not been decreased by α, while $P\beta$ terminates when x_2 has been increased by β. Notice that, in the worst case, only γ messages are received by $P\alpha$ and $P\beta$: hence γ should be chosen *so that to compensate* the overhead due to the activation and termination of $P\alpha$ and $P\beta$.

It is possible to reduce the amount of synchronizations provided that we accept the presence of some *inconsistencies* and are able to *detect* and *recover* them before they can affect the system in a permanent way. In other words, we could adopt an "optimistic" point of view on synchronization. This point of view is based upon the fact that in most cases a low cost synchronization is sufficient but, to be able to guarantee consistency even in the worst possible cases, we might be forced to adopt high cost synchronizations.

If the worst cases have a very low probability, the computation will be consistent most of the time even when adopting a simpler synchronization policy, and thus it may be cheaper to detect and recover inconsistencies instead of preventing them. Of course, the feasibility of defining a recovery requires, in general, some knowledge of the semantics of the computation.

Consider again process P of fig. 1 and assume that it implements the scheduling policy for a resource R encapsulated by another process: by receiving a message $c_i(...)$, P allows the sender to execute an operation on R. In this case when the invariant $x_1 \geq x_2$ is violated, this means that an operation has been executed on R when it was forbidden by the scheduling. If we know how to recover such an erroneous execution, then it is possible to reduce the amount of interactions required by a parallel implementation of process P.

Let us analyze the processes P_1, P_2 and Cons in fig. 2 and assume that they are used to replace process P ($Buffer_1$ and $Buffer_2$ just implement asynchronous communications from Cons to P_1 and P_2 in order to avoid deadlock).

In this version, a request from U_1 (or U_2) is accepted immediately by P_1 (or P_2) provided that $l_1 \leq x_1 \leq h_1$ ($l_2 \leq x_2 \leq h_2$). Then the condition $x_1 \geq x_2$ is checked by Cons, that may execute the recovery and allows the involved P_i to continue its execution only if no inconsistency has been detected. Notice that

a) the checks are executed only after a request has been accepted and, at least potentially, concurrently with the execution of the operation on R;

b) a P_i does not have to wait for the permission to continue its execution (assignment to dec_i and message go ( )) when the value of x_i is outside range(x_1) $\cap$ range (x_2), that is to say cond holds.

The solution is based upon the adoption of copies, cx_1 and cx_2, of the variables x_1 and x_2; these copies are used only to evaluate the condition $x_1 \geq x_2$. Since x_i and cx_i are not always equal , we have to be able to recover errors that may arise.

Though very simple, this example shows the central point of our methodology, that is to say the *transformation of a nondeterministic behaviour into a concurrent one*.

As a matter of fact, when several alternatives may be chosen and one does not interfere with the others, then nondeterminism is equivalent to a sequential emulation of parallelism.

Hence, when the tools of the programming environment are able to recognize such an emulation, and when it is convenient from the point of view of overhead reduction, the emulation may be transformed into real concurrency,

The approach of increasing concurrency at the expence of recovering inconsistencies has already been proposed by several authors [22,23,31] mainly with reference to the "multiple copy update" problem. In these approaches the detection and recovery of inconsistencies are executed by the language *run time support* through the adoption of timestamps or virtual

```
P1:: ...; dec1:=true;
    * [ x1<h1, U1?c1(...) -> Cons! c1( ); x1:=x1+1; ...;
     □  dec1, x1>l1, U1? c2(...) -> Cons!c2(); x1:=x1-1;
                                          if x1≤ h2 then dec1:=false; ...
     □  Buffer1? go ( )  -> dec1:=true;
     ]

P2:: ...; dec2:=true;
       *[ dec2,   x1<h2, U2? c3 (...) -> Cons! c3 ( ); x2:=x2+1;
                                    if x2≥ l1 then dec2:=false; ...
        □ x1>l2, U2?c4 (...) -> Cons! c4(); x2:=x2-1;
        □ Buffer2? go ( ) -> dec2:=true
        ]
Cons :: ...; stopP1:=stopP2:=false;
      *[ P1?c1 ( ) -> cx1:=cx1+1; if  cx1=cx2+1 then begin
                                            if stopP1  then Buffer1! go ( );
                                            if stopP2  then Buffer2! go ( );
                                          stopP1:=stopP2:=false
                                            end
       □ P1?c2  ( ) -> cx1:= cx1-1; if cx1<cx2 then <recovery>; stopP1:=true;
                                 else if  cx1  >h2      then Buffer1! go ( )
       □ P2?c3 ( ) -> cx2:=cx2+1; if cx1<cx2 then <recovery>; stopP2:=true
                              else if cx2 ≥ h1      then Buffer2! go ( )
       □ P2?c4  ( ) -> cx2:=cx2-1;  if  cx1=cx2+1 then begin
                                         if stopP1 then Buffer1! go ( );
                                         if stopP2 then Buffer2! go ( );
                                          stopP1:=stopP2:=false;
                                                 end
       ]
```

Fig.2. A parallel implementation of the resource manager of fig.1.

time [18], and hence independently of the semantics of the computation. As an example, when adopting timestamps as defined in [22], each time a process receives a message M_1 with a timestamp lower than the one associated to a message M_2 that has already been received, then the situation preceding the reception of M_2 is restored, M_1 is inserted into the input queue of the process and then the execution of the process is resumed. In several cases, the recovery is not required: this cannot be exploited by the support since it requires information about the semantics of the operations.

A further advantage of our solution is that the checks introduced to detect inconsistencies due to the absence of some synchronizations might be exploited *also to discover hardware or software faults*. Provided that the recovery action is appropriate, often there is no need of distinguishing whether an inconsistency is due to concurrency or to a fault.

5. THE ECSP LANGUAGE AND ITS PROGRAMMING ENVIRONMENT

As an example of a programming language satisfying most of requirements stated in the previous sections, we present ECSP, a message passing concurrent language developed and implemented by the authors [1-6]. Some tools of the ECSP programming environment will also be discussed, mainly in their relation to the topics discussed in the paper.

5.1. The ECSP Programming Language

ECSP will be presented mainly in terms of the adopted extension to the CSP model [9,14,15,16]; the sequential part, which is Pascal-like, will not be described.

5.1.1. Communication

ECSP processes interact by means of input/ output (i/o) commands. The communications take place through typed channels, each one identified uniquely by the triple (source process, destination process, message type).

The communication is in general asynchronous, i.e. a channel contains a constant amount of FIFO ordered buffers. The synchronous communication with rendez-vous may be obtained as a particular case. The set of channels defined by an ECSP program, and the buffers of a channel, are derived by a static analysis of the i/o commands and of declarations [3]. The declaration for the buffer amount is:

buffer from <name> *pattern* (<constructor >, <type of var>) *length* <number of buffers>.

Channels are not shared objects in ECSP. Instead, channels are private data structures of the destination process. This results in the uniformity between the communication and protection mechanisms (e.g. there are no explicit capabilities), and supports very strong checks, both static and dynamic, on interactions.

ECSP distinguishes between static and dynamic channels, according to the name of the partner process is given by a constant or a variable value respectively.

Using *dynamic channels,* the name of the partner (source or destination) of a process P is given by the value of a *processname variable*, local to P, whose range is given by the names of the processes "visible" to P [4] and by the undefined value Ø. The following operations are defined on a processname variable x (they can be executed only by the process declaring x):

connect (x, name) <-> x:=name
detach(x) <-> x:=Ø
is(x) <-> *if* x=Ø *then* false *else* true
eq(x, name) <-> *if* x=name *then* true *else* false

Dynamic channels are the main ECSP mechanism to achieve process isolation and reconfiguration, as well as rapid error detection and confinement.

The termination conditions of an i/o command are:

a) *with success*: for an output command this means that the message values has been copied into a channel buffer; for an input command, that the contents of a channel buffer have been assigned to the targed variable;

b) *with failure because of the partner termination*;

c) *with failure because the (dynamic) channel has been disconnected*:in the case of an output command this means that the destination revoked the channel access rights to the source; in the case of an input command the source disconnected the destination;

d) *with failure because of the unability to communicate with the node where the partner process is allocated*: this failure depends on the physical communication media, or on decisions of the communication protocols in the language run-time support.

The failure of an i/o command can be handled by means of the *onfail* clause:

<i/o command> *onfail begin*
partner terminated : CL1
disconnected channel : CL2
transmission fault : CL3
end
else CL4; / any CLi is optional /

We have chosen to not introduce the termination of a command due to a "time out" specified by the process. Besides being not a general solution, the time-out value could be very difficult to compute and of scarce significance, in particular when the system is nondeterministic in its specifications (and not only because of physical distribution) [23].

However, a time-out mechanism can be easily emulated using nondeterministic constructs. Thus the user can choose the solution most fitting to its problem.

5.1.2. Control of Nondeterminism

The ECSP constructs for nondeterminism control are essentially the CSP guarded commands, i.e. alternative and repetitive commands.

Each guard may have associated, besides a boolean component, a *priority* expressed by an integer variable, in order to drive some nondeterministic choices by program.Priority guards are an essential mechanism to express several scheduling and real-time decisions directly (e.g. a non blocking receive can be implemented by an alternative command containing a true guard with the lowest priority).

Only input guards are allowed in ECSP. The behaviours achievable by means of generalized (i/o) guards may be emulated at the cost of extra communications (asynchronous channels have in general to be used to avoid mutual blocks). The cost of this emulation is in general lower than the one due to the increase of complexity in the run time support to implement generalized guards. As shown in [7], in the case of generalized guard the support should include a deadlock prevention policy. We believe that this policy should be expressed in the program.

The termination conditions of guarded commands are similar to those of CSP. The failure of an alternative command may be handled explicitly by the onfail clause.

5.1.3. Process Structuring

ECSP programs use extensively the *nesting of parallel commands*.

A parallel command [P1 || ... || Pn] causes the simultaneous activation of P1, ..., Pn; the activating process is suspended during their execution. The command terminates if and when all the activated processes end (by the command *terminate(fail/succ)*). If one or more processes failed, the parallel command fails. The failure can be handled by the onfail clause, where a distinct command list may be executed for distinct set of failed processes.

The visibility rule of process names in a nested structure is the following: Pi has visibility of Pj if Pi and Pj belong to the same parallel command or an "ancestor" of Pi has visibility of Pj. The relation "ancestor" is the closure of the transitive relation "activate": Pa activates Pb if Pa executes a parallel command including Pb.

A model to implement nested processes in a distributed system according to the ECSP semantics is shown in [4].

Another feature of process nesting in ECSP is given by the *import / export* (I/E) *lists* to express communications between a process and the processes it activates. I/E lists support a by value communication from the process executing a parallel command to the activated processes and vice-versa.

When a process P activates a set of processes P1, ..., Pn, it can specify an export list given by a set of variables whose values have to be transmitted to P1, ..., Pn as well as an import list including the variables that will be assigned the values received from the Pi's. Each Pi in turn includes an import and an export list which specify, respectively, the variables that receive the values from, and those whose values are to be transmitted to, the father. The value of a variable in an export list is assigned to the variable in the import list with the same name. To avoid ambiguities, the output lists of the activated processes must be disjoint. As an example, in the command

```
P:: ...; out (x,y,z)
        [ P1 :: in (x) ... out (t)
        || P2 :: in (x,y,z) ... out (z)
        ] in (z,t);
```

at the beginning of the parallel command the value of x is assigned to the corresponding variable in P1 and P2, while the values of y, z are assigned to the variables y, z in P2. When the parallel command ends, the values of t in P1 and of z in P2 are transmitted to P.

The implementation of the parallel command should guarantee that the crash of a processor may be transformed into the termination with failure of all the processes allocated to the processor. When instead, a process P allocated to the crashed node is suspended because of the execution of a parallel command, the crash should be masked till the termination of the command itself. Hence no centralization point in the processor of P should be introduced by the implementation of the parallel command.

5.2. The ECSP Programming Environment

The main tools of the environment are the type checker, the channel generator, the interface checker and the deadlock checker.

The *type checker* is applied to a single process. The analysis of types is based upon nominal equivalence; hence two variables have the same type only when their types have the same name. This is a very strong notion of equivalence and it has been adopted to increase the detection of possibly erroneous statement. The only exception to nominal equivalence is for operation on variable with type subrange.

The type checker employs flow analysis to check that a variable at the right of an assignement has been previously assigned a value.

The *channel generator* (CG) analyzes the consistency of the interface of a single process. When applied to a process P, CG derives the set of input channels of P and the dynamic channels associated with any processname variable of P. After this, CG verifies the feasibility of sequential ambiguities among the channels. We have a *sequential ambiguity* when, as a consequence of an assignement to a processname variable, two processes are connected by two channels with the same message type.

Consider, as an example the following process:

```
P:: ... ; Q?c(x); ...; pr1?c(x); ... ;pr2?c(x); ...
```

A sequential ambiguity arises when the value Q is assigned to pr1 or pr2 and when pr1 and pr2 are equal. This situation is considered a potential error since it could reveal an inconsistency in protection policies. As a matter of fact, when Q is connected to a channel of P, it has the right to invoke a given operation, hence a sequential ambiguity reveals that Q has been granted an access right it already has.

The existence of sequential ambiguities has to be checked on each update of a processname variable. This requires that each channel associated with the variable is compared against the other channels of the process. To reduce the amount of comparisons each dynamic channel is associated with a set PC of possible collisions. PC includes all and only the channels that could generate an ambiguity with respect to the considered channel. For a dynamic channel Ci=<sender, Pi, Ti>, PC(Ci) includes all the channels Cj such that Tj=Ti. In this way, a dynamic channel has to be compared only against the channels in its PC.

CG analyzes also the output commands of P to determine the input channels that have to be defined by the partners of P. This information will be used by the interface checker and by the deadlock checker.

The *interface checker* (IC) analyzes (a subset of) the processes of a program using the output of CG and a tree describing the structure of the program (*activation tree*, AT). This analysis can be logically divided into two phases.

In the first phase, IC derives the set of channels of a process P by extending the set of channels defined by the program of P with those defined by its descendants since they are considered as *inherited* from P. This phase is necessary since ECSP does not require these channels to be defined by P as well. This analysis includes the detection of concurrent ambiguities. A *concurrent ambiguity* is produced when two or more processes, that can be executed concurrently, inherit the same channel from a common ancestor. As an example, the following program fragment

```
[Q || P :: ...; [ P1 :: x : integer; ...; Q?c(x); ...;
                 ||P2 :: y : integer; ...; Q?c(y); ...;
                 ]; ....;
```

produces a concurrent ambiguity since both P1 and P2 inherit the channel (Q, P, <c, integer>). A concurrent ambiguity can be produced also at run time by assignement to processname variables.

The presence of a concurrent ambiguity, or its feasibility because of updates to processname variables, is considered as a static error. As a matter of fact, a concurrent ambiguity is a source of nondeterminism and of time dependent behaviour but this situation is not pointed out by an appropriate language construct as in the case of guarded commands. In the case of an ambiguity produced by updates to processname variables, we have not adopted run time checks since the variables belong to distinct processes, hence the controls should be implemented in the run time support at the expence of efficiency.

The second phases of the analysis implemented by IC verifies the mutual consistency of process interfaces. For each channel C defined by a process, IC searches for a channel defined by a partner that corresponds to C, or that could correspond after a proper assignement to a processname variable. If such a channel does not exist, an error is signaled. This phase heavily exploits naming in process communication and typed messages. Nominal equivalence between types is adopted.

The two phases of the analysis are by now interleaved in a bottom-up visit of the AT.

The deadlock checker tries to determine whether a program can enter a deadlock state since a circular chain of processes waiting for a communication has been produced. By now this tool does not insert run time checks in the output code of processes, and so it is used only to assist the programmer in program design.

6. INTEGRATING RECOVERY AND CONCURRENCY

We show here how ECSP may express forward/backward recovery policies without sensibly reducing available concurrency. An example integrating the recovery of faults and of inconsistencies due to parallelism is then presented, together with some quantitative evaluations of the increase in performance supported by the proposed methodology.

6.1. Forward Recovery

To discuss forward recovery in ECSP we will refer to a typical example:a resource management subsystem where several users cooperate through a single resource implemented by a further process.

In this example, nondeterministic commands are employed to concisely express the choice among several requests from distinct partners. The requests correspond to one or more operations invoked to the considered instance of an abstract data type.

Let us consider a computation consisting of a shared resource, R, and several user processes, U1, ..., Un. Two operations, op1 and op2, can be executed on the shared resource.

The simplest way to structure R is by means of a repetitive command as shown in fig. 3 where each Ui is connected to R through static channels with types op1, op2 to invoke operations and with types res1 and res2 to receive results. Let s be the data structure encoding the shared resource state.

The onfail clause associated with the output command allows R to detect anomalous

```
R :: ...;
   *[  priority(pr1), U1? ...
    □ priority(pri),  Ui ?op1(par1)  → Ui ! resi(op1(par1,s) onfail  <recovery>;
                                       s:=nextstate(op1, par1, s)
    □  priority(pri),  Ui ?op2(par1)  → Ui ! resi(op2(par2,s) onfail  <recovery>;
                                       s:=nextstate(op2, par2, s)
          . . .
    □  priority(prn), Un? ...
    ]; ...
```

Fig. 3. First version of Resource Manager.

terminations/crashes of the users after an invocation is accepted, and to fire suitable recovery actions without affecting the resource availability.

However the nondeterministic command, where several channels from distinct processes are lissen to simultaneously, forces R to consider the global situation in terms of the user requests, and therefore it reduces the amount of cooperation during fault treatment. In fact, the spontaneous termination of a single user is not necessarily an error and it is detected only when and if all the users end. In some cases greater granularity in users control is required, as the user termination may depend on node/system faults.

Furthermore, in this solution any checks on the parameters of a request is executed sequentially with respect to the operation of R.

A solution able to overcome both the drawbacks may be obtained by transforming nondeterminism into concurrency as shown in fig. 4.

The repetitive command is replaced by a parallel command activating a set {Ri} of processes. Each of them contains a nondeterministic command that controls only the communications from a subset of users characterized by a homogeneous behaviour and/or with similar rights to access the resource. Fig.4 refers to the case where an Ri is associated with a single Ui.

Each Ri acts as an "intelligent channel", that controls the access rights and the correct behaviour of Ui: it handles situation like inconsistent parameters, anomalous terminations,

```
R ::  . . . ; [ R1 || ... || Ri || ... ||  Rn  || S ] onfail  <. . .> ;

where for each  i in {1..n}

Ri :: ...;  *[ Ui ? op1(par1) -> S!getstate(op1, par1) onfail <. . .>;
                                  S?s onfail < . . . >;
                                  Ui ! res1(op1,  (par1,s)) onfail < . . .>;
          □  Ui ?op2(par1)  -> < . . .>
           ];
          < handling of Ui termination>; ....;
```

Fig. 4. Parallel transformation of Resource Manager.

```
R :: . . .;
    [ R1 :: . . . ; [ RM1 || RC1] ...
    || . . .
    ...
    || Ri :: . . . ; [ RMi  || RCi ] ...
    ...
    || Rn :: . . . ; [ RMn || RCn]  ...
    || S  :: . . . ; [ < multiple copies>]
    ] onfail  < . . . >
```

Fig. 5. Final version of Resource Manager.

"suspected" communications, and so on. Notice that, also in the example discussed in sect.4, P1 and P2 might be considered as intelligent channels that also execute a part of the computation. In fact, the introduction of intelligent channel is essential when a nondeterministic choice cannot be avoided in order to be able to reduce the complexity of each alternative .

The resource state s is managed by one or more distinct processes, activated by R, as S in fig. 4. Notice that:

i) all the communications with S may be controlled by the onfail clause;

ii) to avoid that S becomes a bottleneck for system performance, it can be further decomposed according to a parallel and /or pipeline style;

iii) to avoid that S becomes a critical component for system reliability, it can be further decomposed according to a multiple copy style. In this case that several copies of the process managing S are activated by a parallel command distinct from the one of the user, and hence the redundancy is hidden from the user and completely solved within the parallel command of S;

iv) the termination condition of the parallel command guarantees that the termination of a certain Ri does not force the behaviour of the other processes activated by R.

A solution that matches the results of sect. 4 and of this section is shown in fig. 5. Here the interactions between each Ri and the corresponding Ui (or a homogeneous subset of users) are performed by means of dynamic channels to allow each Ri/Ui to establish new conversations with different user/resource processes in the case of (suspected) faults and therefore to reconfigure the system. A limited number of additional communications channels has to be inserted for this purpose.

Every Ri may be further decompsed into a "connection manager" (RMi) and a "controller" (RCi), working in parallel and, in their turn, cooperating to achieve a stronger control on the user behaviour [5,11].

6.2. Backward Recovery

The main mechanism to express backward recovery in ECSP is the parallel command with I/E lists. Since variables in the input list of the process P executing a parallel command are assigned only if the parallel command ends successfully, the state of P is unaffected and hence, through the onfail list, another execution of the same computation may be attempted. Since the failure of a single process produces that of the whole command, the assignment is conditioned by the consensus of all the activated processes.

The ability of exploiting I/E lists for backward recovery, paired with the one of nesting parallel commands, supports the definition of recovery actions with distinct granularity and hence distinct costs. The resulting structure of the program is similar to the one obtained by adopting ***nested atomic actions*** [27,28]. Notice the similarity between the process P executing a parallel command and the "coordinator" of a distributed atomic action: P receives the outputs of the activated processes and then decides the result of the whole computation.

Despite the similarity previously described, a parallel command with I/E lists is not atomic in general since the activated processes may communicate with processes outside the parallel command and these communications are not revoked after the failure of the parallel command [5]. Thus the idempotency of the actions executed in the parallel command is lost. To obtain atomicity it is sufficient to guarantee the idempotency of communications outside the parallel command itself. Notice that the classical implementation of atomic actions guarantees idempotency by preventing communications among processes not belonging to the same atomic action. In ECSP, instead, it is possible to distinguish the allowed communication from those that should be forbidden. This is a typical advantage allowed by the implementation of atomic actions in terms of simpler constructs.

An ECSP mechanism that can easily be exploited to achieve idempotency in communications is the *dynamic channel*. Since a dynamic channel dc is reinitialized when the corresponding processname is updated, it is possible to "undo" the effects of the communications through dc. Another application of dynamic channels is *when an atomic action includes processes beloging to distinct parallel commands :* since these processes cannot refer each other, the failure of processes in a parallel command might not be detected by processes in another command. If after the failure of a command, the dynamic channels used by processes of the command are detached, the next i/o commands of the other processes of the action will fail thus conveying the information of the anomalous termination of the partners.

As an example of the various recovery policies that can be defined in ECSP we will refer to the following problem.

Given two data structures IS1 and IS2, produce the streams S1 and S2, where Si depends on ISi only, and then produce the stream S3 where S3j=f(h(S1j),S2j) (Sij is the j -th element of the i-th stream).

Two functions, f1 and f2, are then to be applied to S3, f1 requires the knowledge of all elements of S3, while f2 may be applied to one element at the time. Let us focus on the computation and the trasmission of S3 to the processes that compute f1 and f2.

A solution in terms of atomic actions, as implemented in a network system, is shown in fig. 6. In this case the process Rstream computes S3 by an atomic action implemented by the parallel command activating P1, ..., P4. Since none of these processes communicate with a process outside the parallel command, the atomicity of the command is guaranteed. For the sake of simplicity, we have assumed that we are interested in recovering only faults of the interconnection structure. Function f2 is implemented by process Other2 that receives the elements of S3 only after all the stream has been computed. This is necessary for being able to avoid communications between Other2 and a process of the parallel command.

Suppose now that function h may be used also by other processes, and hence we implement it in a process Functions, activated by the same parallel command of Rstream. To increase concurrency, communications between Rstream and Functions are asynchronous. To guarantee idempotency of communications between P3 and Functions we can introduce a unique identifier for each pair of messages for invoking f and receiving the result. This unique identifier allows P3 to recognize a result corresponding to an invocation that had place before a termination with failure of the parallel command. This solution is shown in fig.7.

To further increase the degree of concurrency, suppose that we decide to transmit each

```
Program :: [ Rstream || Other1 || Other2 ]

Rstream :: ... ;
            Other1?IS1; Other2?IS2; nret:=0;
            repeat
              done:=true;
              out(IS1,IS2) [P1 || P2 || P3 || P4 ] in(S3) on fail begin
                                                                nret:=nret+1;
                                                                done:=false
                                                              end;
                                      until done or nret >max;
          if done then
                        Other1! S3;
                        while not empty(S3) do begin
                                                     <x,S3>:=<first(S3),rest(S3)>;
                                                     Other2!x
                                                   end;
                        Other2!end();
             else ...;

Pi [i:1..2] :: in (ISi)
              ...;
              while < cond_i>do
                   begin
                        x:= ...(ISi , ... );
                        Pi+2! x
                   end
              ...;

P3 :: ... ;    *[ P1?y -> P4 ! h ( y) ]

P4 :: ... ;*[  P3 ? t -> P2 ? g ; append(S3, f(t,g))
            □ P2 ? g -> P3 ? t ; append(S3, f(t,g))
            ]
       out (S3)
```

Fig. 6 . Example of "classical" atomic actions.

element of S3 to Other2 as soon as it has been computed. The problem now is to guarantee that, regardless of failures of the parallel command, each element of S2 is transmitted exactly once. Assume that we know that S3 is a strictly increasing sequence: in this case the problem may be easily solved by introducing a further process that filters the values produced by any activation of P4 to eliminate out-of-sequence values. By nesting this process into Rstream, as shown in fig.8, its presence is hidden to the environment and hence the two versions of Rstream in fig. 7. and in fig. 8 are equivalent. Notice that

a) the requirement that S3 is an increasing sequence is not very restrictive, since it is always possible to build a sequence S3' so that S3'j= <S3j, tj> where tj is a timestamp and the ordering takes into account the second element of the pair only;

b) if the parallel command activating P1, ..., P4 cannot be successfully completed, then Bufferout will not be able to transmit the whole sequence. In this case a larger recovery, eventually involving also Other1 and Other2, is needed. This recovery

```
Program :: [ Rstream || Functions || Other1 || Other2 ]

Rstream :: ... ;
          Other1?IS1; Other2?IS2; nret:=0;
          repeat
            done:=true;
            out (IS1,IS2) [P1 || P2 || P3 || P4 ] in (S3) onfail begin
                                                           nret:=nret+1;
                                                           done:=false
                                                         end;
                              until done or nret >max;
          if done then
                         Other1! S3;
                         while not ( empty(S3)) do begin
                                          <x,S3>:=<first(S3),rest(S3)>;
                                           Other2!x
                                         end;
                         Other2!end();
          else ...;

Pi [i:1..2] :: in (ISi)
           ...;
           while <cond_i>do begin
                             x:= ...(ISi , ... );
                             Pi+2! x
                           end
           ... ;

P3 :: ... ;buffer from Function type (type(z), integer) length h;
         s:=unique();
         P1?y; Function ! (y, s); ls:=s; s:=unique();
         *[ P1?y -> Function ! ( y, s);
                    repeat
                      Function ? (z, t);
                    until t=ls;
                    P4 ! z; ls:=s; s:=unique();
          ];
         repeat Function ? (z,t) until t=ls; P4 ! z;


P4 :: ... ; *[ P3 ? t -> P2 ? g ; append(S3, f(t,g))
           □ P2 ? g -> P3 ? t ; append(S3, f(t,g))
           ]
       out (S3)
```

Fig. 7. Asynchronous communications outside the atomic action .

action will also take care of values that have already been transmitted;

c) Bufferout does not have to be modified when more complex actions, such as the execution of a distinct parallel command, are defined by the *onfail* list associated with the parallel command.

A last version of the program is shown in fig. 9 where a further process, Buffercrash, has been introduced to recover a failure of Rstream1 after the successfull termination of the

```
Rstream :: [ Rstream1 || Bufferout ]

 Rstream1 ::  < same as Rstream of fig.7  >;
              if  done then   Other1 ! S3
              else  begin .... end;

 P1, P2, P3  < same as fig. 7  but each one communicates its termination by end() >

 P4 ::  ... ;
          S3:=0; ends:=false
         repeat
           [   P3 ? t -> P2 ? g; x:= f(t, g); append( S3,x); Bufferout ! x
           □   P2 ? g -> P3 ? t ; x:= f(t, g); append(S3, x); Bufferout ! x
           □   P2 ? end() - > P3 ? end(); ends:=true
           ];
        until  ends;
         Bufferout ! end();

Bufferout :: ... ; buffer from Rstream1 type  integer length  k;
              *[  Rstream1 ? out  -> if  out > out1 then begin
                                                  Other2 ! out;  out1:=out
                                                  end
               □ Rstream1 ? end() -> Other2 ! end(); terminate(succ);
               ]
```

Fig. 8. Asynchronous transmission of the result of the atomic action.

```
Rstream :: [ Rstream2 || Bufferout || Buffercrash ]


 Rstream2::  < same as Rstream of fig.7  >;
                                    onfail begin
                                       done := false;nret:=nret+1; Buffercrash ! reset()
                                         end;
             until  done or  nret >max ;
             if  done then   Other1 ! S3 ; Buffercrash ! end ()
             else  begin  .... end;

 P1, P2, P3  < as in fig. 8  >

 P4 ::   ... ; S3:=0; ends:=false
         repeat
           [   P3 ? t -> P2 ? g; x:= f(t, g); append( S3,x); Bufferout ! x; Buffercrash ! x
           □   P2 ? g -> P3 ? t ; x:= f(t, g); append(S3, x); Bufferout ! x; Buffercrash ! x
           □   P2 ? end() -> P3 ? end(); ends:=true
           ];
        until  ends;
         Bufferout ! end(); Buffercrash ! end()

Buffercrash ::  . .. ; S4:=0;
             *[  Rstream2 ? el  ->  append(S4,el)
              □  Rstream2 ? reset() -> S4:=0
              □  Rstream2 ? end()  -> Rstream2 ? end() onfail  Other1! rec(S4) onfail  skip;
               ];
```

Fig. 9. Recovery of the process executing the parallel command.

parallel command and before S3 has been sent to Other1. The failure of the input command in Buffercrash signals that Rstream might have been affected by a fault and hence Buffercrash will send S2 to Other1; if this output command fails, the failure of Rstream1 has not prevented the communication between Rstream1 and Other1. Distinct message types are exploited in the communications from Rstream1 to Other1 and from Buffercrash to Other1 in order to inform Other1 of the occurence of a fault. The introduction of Buffercrash is a typical example of the implementation of stable storage through concurrent processes.

6.3. Recovering from faults and inconsistencies

To show a case where both faults and inconsistencies due to parallel activities are taken into account, we present a solution to the "airline reservation problem" as defined in [10].

The problem can be summed up as follows: a computer system handles seat reservation on K flights. Reservations are made by N users, who can also ask whether a given number of places is available on a flight. For the sake of simplicity, each flight is closed when no more places are available.

Our solution, shown in fig 10, is structured as follows: at the higher level the program includes K+N+H processes: one for each flight, FL[i] (i=1..k), one for each user, U[h] (h=1..N), and H spares copies, CF[m] (m=1..H), of the FL[i]'s.

A process U[h] acts as an interface between the user and the system. U[h] tries to reserve rp places on a flight by a message *reserve* (rp) or asks whether ap places are available by a message *avail* (ap).

A process FL[i] is structured as follows: until M places are available on the flight, it activates a set of processes SFL[i, j] (j=1..M). SFL[i,j] serves requests from a partition upart[j] of the users and manages fp[j] places. The initial value of fp[j] is received through I lists and it depends upon Σ_x E(x, FL[i]), for each x beloging to upart[j] and where E(x, FL[i]) is the average amount of places requested by user x on the i-flight.

On receiving a message *reserve*(rp), SFL[i, j] checks whether rp $\leq$ fp[j] and in this case reserves the places by updating fp [j] and replies *yes*( ) to the user. Otherwise, it terminates successfully and transmits the request to FL[i]. The termination of SFL [i, j] induces those of both SFL[i, j-1] and SF [i, j+1] and so on. Each SFL[i, j] transmits to FL[i], by E lists, the amount of its places still available.

When FL[i] is restarded, it determines the global amount of free places and replies to pending requests. This is done by activating a set of processes, one for each request. After this, FL[i] partitions the places still available among the various SFL[i,j] and activates them again.

```
FL[i] :: ...;repeat
            <assign fp >;
            out (upart, fp) [ SFL[i,1] || . . . || SFL[i, M]] in (fp, failreq, sflstate)
< sflstate[j]=req    => SFL[i,j] has not been able to satisfy a request;
  sflstate[j]=noreq=> termination of SFL[i,j] has been induced by the one of a partner;
  failreq[j] contains information about the request not satisfied by SFL[i,j] >
            onfail  [ ( || t :1..N)  U[t]!error() ]
<this parallel command broadcasts that an error has occurred; its failure is a disaster>
            else  begin  Requesthandling; Commit end;
< this command list is executed only if the parallel command terminates successfully>
          until  free > M; ...
```

Fig. 10.1 Process managing places for the i-th fligth.

```
SFL[i,j] :: in (upart[j], fp[j])
          buffer from  SFL[i,j-1], SFL[i,j+1] type  end length  1;
*[  (u : {upart[j]}) u ? reserve(rp) -> if  rp < fp[j] then begin  fp[j]:=fp[j]-rp; u !yes() end
                                                          else  begin
                                   failreq[j].pl:=rp;  sflstate[j]:=req; failreq[j].type:=req; exit
                                                               end
 □  (u : {upart[j]}) u ? avail(ap)  -> if  ap < fp[j] then  u !yes() else begin
                                   failreq[j].pl:=ap;  sflstate[j]:=req; failreq[j].type:=info; exit
                                                                                  end
 □  (u : { SFL[i,j-1], SFL[i,j+1]})  u ? end()-> sflstate[j]:=noreq; exit
 ];
if  sflstate[j]=req then begin  connect (failreq[j].name, u);
                                SFL[i,j-1]! end() onfail skip;
                                SFL[i,j+1]! end() onfail skip;
                  end
else  if  eq (u, SFL[i,j-1])  then   SFL[i,j+1] ! end()  onfail  skip
                             else    SFL[i,j -1] ! end()  onfail skip
out ( fp[j], sflstate[j], failreq[j])
```

Fig. 10.2. Process managing the j-th subfligth

```
Requesthandling = free:=Ø; asspl:=Ø; for  h:=1 to  M do  free:=free+fp[h];
                    for  h:= 1 to   M do
                      if  sflstate[h]=req then begin
                                  connect(name[h], failreq[h].name);
                                  if  free-asspl>failreq[h].pl then begin
                                                                   answ[h]:=yes;
                                       if  failreq[h].type=req then  asspl:=asspl+failreq[h].pl
                                                                  end
                                                           else  answ[h]:=no;
                                            end  else  answ[h]:=quit;
                    out  (answ, name)  [ ( || h : 1..M)  in  ( answ[h], name[h])
                                         case  ans[h] of
                                           quit  :  skip ;
                                           yes   :  name[h]! yes() onfail  answ[h]:=error
                                           no    :  name[h]! no()  onfail  answ[h]:=error
                                         endcase
                                       ] onfail  [ ( || h :1..N) U[h]! error()]
                       else  for   h:=1 to  M do
                                 if  answ[h]=error then  asspl:=asspl-failreq[h].pl;
                      free:=free-asspl;
```

Fig 10.3. Handling of requests not satisfied by the subfligths

```
Commit = repeat
            spare ! update(free); onfail begin <set up a new spare >; done:=false end
                                  else done:=true;
         until done; [ (|| h : 1..N) U[h] ! commit () onfail skip ];
```

Fig. 10.4. Update of the number of places reserved on the i-th flight.

The command *(u :{<set>}) u? ...* denotes an asymmetric communication from any process belonging to *<set>*.

To describe recovery actions, let us consider the use of redundant information. Assume that CF[m] is the process that has to replace FL[i] after a crash.A checkpoint of the number of free places on the i-th flight is maintained in CF[m] and it is updated on each termination of the parallel command activating SFL[i, j]. After this update, each U[h] is informed that its reservations are permanent. Assume that each U[h] records the amount of places reserved on a flight and not yet permanent. On the occurrence of a crash of FL[i], U[h] can recover, by means of just one message to CF[m], all reservations that have been lost. FL[i] can be affected by a crash of the CE where it is executed or of a CE executing an SFL[i, j]. A crash affecting a SFL[i, j] can be recovered by FL[i] by communicating to the U[h]'s that they have to redo their reservations, and by distributing the users and the free places among the SFL [i, j]'s which are still working. Notice that in this case, the variables in the E list of FL[i] are not modified by the parallel command and are a valid checkpoint .

Assume now that a *fault affects the CE executing FL[i]*. The fault will be masked until any parallel command executed by FL[i] is terminated and it is detected only when the execution of FL[i] is resumed. From now on, all the i/o commands referring to FL[i] fail and hence any U[h] can detect the fault and ask that the switching to the spare copy has place. Any U[h] has now to redo all non permanent reservations.

For the sake of simplicity, only the program of FL[i] is shown in the figure.

The performance of the concurrent solution (PCONC) versus the sequential one (PSEQ) has been evaluated by simulation. The main assumptions are :

- a square mesh topology;
- each node executes one process;
- the node structure includes two Transputer-like processors [17], one for executing the process and the other for the run time support.

The results are summarized as follows :

i) the concurrent solution has a good scalability (s = PCONC/PSEQ) for a parallelism degree (pd) less or equal to five: in particular for pd = 5 we have $4 < s < 4.5$, when the system utilization factor is equal or greater to one;

ii) the number of operations performed in recovery actions is low with respect to the total amount of operations, about 10%;

iii) the previous results are not sensibly affected by the allocation of processes to nodes, showing that the nested structure of ECSP program exploits a good communication locality.

The discussed problem exemplifies a situation where available resources are to be distributed among concurrent requests. In term of a DGOS, the adopted solution may be interpreted as follows: resources should be distributed among various instances of the operating system (an SFL[i,j] in the example) and each instance can manage its resources autonomously except when a request cannot be satisfied by resources controlled by a single instance. In this case a global decision should be taken, eventually leading to a new distribution of resources among instances. A main advantage of this approach is that it can exploit any available information on the amount of requests received by an instance to reduce the probability that a request cannot be satisfied and that a new distribution is necessary.

7. CONCLUSION

We have described a programming methodology for achieving high concurrency in DGOS. It has been shown that the main point is the ability to decrease the degree of coupling of cooperating instances of abstract data type, while keeping the number of processes as high as possible and their size as small as possible. This requires that fault tolerance, a fundamental aspect of any distributed system, is integrated with concurrency as regards the cooperation mechanisms, the management policies and the programming methodology. Both forward and backward recovery should be taken into account in the design.

Emphasis has been placed on the definition of a concurrent language, able to express the required features. In fact, the definition of ECSP has been driven by the desire of integrating powerful mechanisms for concurrency and fault tolerance, and, at the same time, of introducing a minimum amount of congruent constructs.

Of course, our methodology may be adopted as a guideline for defining or using a different language. As an example, it would be possible to program in Ada, although some features (e.g. I/E lists, asynchronous communications, dynamic channels) cannot always be easily emulated.

REFERENCES

1. F. Baiardi, A. Fantechi, M. Vanneschi, "Language Constructs for a Robust Distributed Environment", Int. Rep., Dept. of Comp. Science S-81-9, Univ. of Pisa, May 1981.

2. F. Baiardi, A. Fantechi, A. Tomasi, M. Vanneschi, "Mechanisms for a Robust Multiprocessing Environment in the MuTEAM Kernel", Proc. of 11th Fault Tolerant Computing Symp., Portland (USA), June 1981, pp. 20-24.

3. F. Baiardi, L. Ricci, M. Vanneschi, "Static Checking of Interprocess Communication in ECSP", ACM SIGPLAN Symposium on Compiler Construction, Montreal, June 1984.

4. F. Baiardi, A. Fantechi, A. Tomasi, M. Vanneschi, "Distributed Implementation of Nested Communicating Processes and Termination', 13th Int. Conf. on Parallel Processing, Aug. 1984.

5. F. Baiardi, L. Ricci, A. Tomasi, M. Vanneschi, "Structuring Processes for a Cooperative Approach to Fault-Tolerant Distributed Software", Proc. of 4th Symp. on Reliability in Distributed Software and Database Systems, Oct. 1984.

6. F. Baiardi, N. De Francesco, G. Vaglini, "Development of a Debugger for a Concurrent Language". IEEE TSE, April 1986.

7. A. J. Bernstein, : "Output Guards and Nondeterminism in Communicating Sequential Processes", TOPLAS, vol. n. 2, pp. 234-238, April 1980.

8. D. Bjørner, "Formal Development of Compilers and Interpreters", Int. Comp. Symposium '77, North Holland, pp.1-21.

9. S.D. Brookes, C.A.R. Hoare and A.W. Roscoe: "A Theory of Communicating Sequential Processes", JACM, vol. 31, n. 3, pp. 560-599, July 1984.

10 . R.E.Bryant, J.B. Dennis "Concurrent Programming", MIT Report, 1978.

11. P. J. Denning ,"Fault tolerant operating systems", ACM Computing Surveys, vol. 8, n.4, Dec. 1976, pp. 359-389.

12. DOD , "Reference Manual for the Ada Programming Language", ANSI MIL-STD 1815A, 1983.

13. J.A. Feldmann "High Level Programming Language for Distributed Computing", CACM, vol.22, n.6, June 1979, pp. 353-368.

14. N. Francez, C.A.R. Hoare, D. J. Lehmann, and W.P. de Roever, "Semantics of Nondeterminism, Concurrency, and Communication", JCSS, vol. 19, 1979, pp.290-308.

15. C.A.R. Hoare, "Communicating Sequential Processes", CACM, vol. 21, n. 8, Aug. 1978, pp. 666-677.

16. C.A.R. Hoare, "A Calculus for Total Correctness of Communicating Processes", Science of Computer Programming, vol. 1, pp. 49-72, 1981.

17. Inmos Ldt., "Occam Reference Manual", Prentice Hall , 1984.

18. D. Jeffrey, "Virtual Time", ACM TOPLAS, vol. 7, n.3, July 1985, pp. 404-425.

19. E.D. Jensen, "Distributed Control" in "Distributed Systems: an Advanced Course", (B.W.Lampson ed.), Lect.Notes in Comp. Science, Springer & Verlang, 1981.

20. E.D. Jensen, "Hardware-Software Relationships in Distributed Systems" in "Distributed Systems: an Advanced Course", (B.W.Lampson ed.), Lect.Notes in Comp. Science, Springer & Verlang, 1981.

21. E.D. Jensen, L. Sha, R.F. Rashid, J.D. Northcutt, "Distributed Cooperating Processes and Transactions', ACM SIGCOMM Symp.,1983.

22. L. Lamport, "Time, Clocks, and the Ordering of Events in a Distributed Systems". CACM, vol. 21, n. 7, pp. 558-565, July 1978.

23. L.Lamport. "Using Time Instead of Timeout for Fault-Tolerant Distributed Systems". ACM TOPLAS, vol. 6, n.2, April 1984.

24. B.W. Lampson, H.E. Sturgis, "Crash Recovery in a Distributed Data Storage System", Xerox Palo Alto Res. Center, Apr. 1979.

25. G. Levi et al., "Programming Environments: Deriving Language Dependent Tools from Structured Denotational Semantics", Int. Comp. Symposium '83, Nurberg, March 1983.

26. B. Liskov, S.N. Zilles, "Programming with Abstract Data Types", ACM SIGPLAN Notices, vol.9, n.4, April 1974, pp. 50-59.

27. B. Liskov and R. Scheifler, "Guardians and Actions: Linguistic Support for Robust, Distributed Programs". TOPLAS, vol. 5, n. 3, pp. 381-404, July 1983.

28. J.E. Moss, "Nested Transactions and Reliable Distribued Computing", 2nd Symp. on Reliability in Dist. Software and Database Systems, 1981.

29. D.L. Parnas, "On the Criteria to Be Used in Decomposing Systems Into Modules", CACM, vol.15, n.12, Dec. 1972, pp. 1053-1058.

30. B. Randell, P.A. Lee. P.C. Treleaven, "Reliability Issues in Computer System Design", ACM Comp. Surveys, vol. 10, n.2, June 1978, pp. 123-165.

31. D.P. Reed, "Naming and Synchronization in a Decentralized Computer System", MIT Technical Rep., TR-205, Sept. 1978.

32. C.L. Seitz, "Concurrent VLSI architectures", IEEE TC, Vol. C-33, n. 12, Dec. 1984.

33. J. Wensley et al., "SIFT: Design and Analisys of a Fault-Tolerant Computer for Aircraft Control", Proc. IEEE, vol. 66, n.10, Oct. 1978, pp. 1240-1254.

Communication Models for Distributed Computation

Notes for the Advanced Study Institute, August 1986
Izmir, Turkey

David K. Gifford

This paper presents a short survey of contemporary work in communication models for distributed computer systems, and then discusses in detail the *Remote Pipe and Procedure Model.* The survey portion of the paper discusses two classes of models for distributed communication: message based models and remote procedure call models. The advantages and disadvantages of both approaches are outlined.

After introducing the two major classes of communication models, we consider in detail the Remote Pipe and Procedure Model. The Remote Pipe and Procedure Model is a new communications model for distributed systems that combines the advantages of remote procedure call with the efficient transfer of bulk data and the ability to return incremental results. Three ideas form the basis of this model. First, remote procedures are first-class values which can be freely exchanged among nodes, thus enabling a greater variety of protocols to be directly implemented in a remote procedure call framework. Second, a new type of abstract object called a *pipe* allows bulk data and incremental results to be efficiently transported in a type safe manner. Unlike procedure calls, pipe calls do not return values and do not block a caller. Data sent down a pipe is processed by the pipe's sink node in strict FIFO order. Third, the relative sequencing of pipes and procedures can be controlled by combining them into *channel groups.* A channel group provides a FIFO sequencing invariant over a collection of channels. Application experience with the Remote Pipe and Procedure Model is reported.

NATO ASI Series, Vol. F28
Distributed Operating Systems. Theory and Practice
Edited by Y. Paker et al.

Table of Contents

1. Communication Models for Distributed Systems

A distributed computing system is a confederation of cooperating computers, called *nodes*, that work together on a single task or set of tasks. An essential part of any distributed computing system is a means for the nodes to communicate with one another. The flexibility and performance of the communication system used to interconnect nodes determines to a large extent the types of tasks that the nodes can successfully process.

Our discussion of communication in a distributed system will focus on *communication models*. A communication model describes an abstract set of operations which a programmer can directly use to communicate with other nodes, and a methodology for using these operations to create distributed programs. An important property of communication models is that they provide a powerful way of thinking about communication that is abstracted away from the details of how bits are actually transmitted from node to node. Although we will describe the implementation of one model in terms of datagrams, discussions of communication hardware (such as Ethernets and Rings), or layered protocols (such as the ISO Reference Model) are beyond the scope of this paper.

We shall dicuss two types of communication models which have been developed for distributed systems:

- *Message Based Models* Message based communication models assume a prexisting collection of cooperating processes that communicate by sending messages to one another via **Send** and **Receive** primitives. **Send** is reliable and will keep retransmitting a message until it is successfully received by its destination node. Because **Send** does not block waiting for a response message, message based models do not limit inter-process communication to pairs of request and response messages. In message based models messages are sent to *ports* instead of being sent directly to remote nodes. Ports allow messages to be automatically demultiplexed into independent streams of related data at a receiving node. Process creation and recovery are accomplished outside of the scope of the communication model. Some message based models provide a facility that will generate code to assemble and disassemble messages based on programmer supplied message specifications. Examples of message based models include Accent [Rashid81] and the V System [Cheriton85].

- *Remote Procedure Call Based Models* Remote procedure call based communication models provide programmers with the ability to call a procedure at a remote node in the same manner in which a local procedure is called. Remote procedure call models are limited to request-response applications because a remote procedure call blocks the calling process until the call is complete and a reply has been received. A single remote procedure call results in:

- the automatic assembly of the parameters to the call into a request message,
- the transmission of the request message to the remote node,
- the creation of a process at the remote node to execute the desired procedure,
- the creation of a reply message,
- the transmission of the reply message to the calling node,
- and the automatic unpacking of the reply message at the call site.

An advantage of a remote procedure call model is that the interface of a remote service can be easily documented as a set of procedures with certain parameter and result types. From such interface specifications, code that hides all of the details of messages from the application programmer is automatically generated. Thus, a remote procedure call model imposes a simplifying structure that hides messages, but at the cost of reducing the range of communication options available to the applications programmer.

The advantage of a message based model is that it provides flexibility not found in a remote procedure call framework. However, as we have already observed, this flexibility comes at a cost. It is difficult to precisely document the behavior of a message based interface as the number and relative sequencing of component messages can vary from operation to operation. On the other hand, the interface of a remote procedure call system provides a uniform and easily understood abstraction.

Both message and remote procedure call models require a *binding* mechanism to establish and maintain appropriate logical connections between nodes in a distributed system. In a message based system, a node that wishes to print a file at a remote printer node must have an appropriate port with which to communicate with the remote printer node. In a remote procedure call system, a node that wishes to print a file at a remote printer node must have an appropriate remote procedure value that will result in communication with the remote printer node.

Establishing appropriate logical connections between parts of a distributed system is usually accomplished via a set of well-known nodes that operate as *name servers.* In response to a query about a particular kind of remote node, a name server will return an appropriate set of ports or remote procedures (depending on the communication model in use). These ports or remote procedures can then be used to directly contact the remote server of interest.

The following sections of this paper describe an example communication model, the *Remote Pipe and Procedure Communication Model* in detail.

2. The Remote Pipe and Procedure Communication Model

Remote procedure call is now a widely-accepted standard method for communication in distributed computer systems [White76, Gifford81, Nelson81, Liskov83, Birrell84]. This popularity can be attributed to three advantages provided by remote procedure call. First, remote procedure call uses a widely-accepted, used, and understood abstraction, the procedure call, as the sole mechanism for access to remote services. Second, remote procedure call allows remote interfaces to be specified as a set of named operations with certain type signatures. Such specifications enable remote interfaces to be precisely documented, and distributed programs to be statically checked for type errors. Third, since interfaces can be precisely specified, the communication code for an application can be automatically generated, by either a compiler or a specialized stub generator.

The wider use of remote procedure call systems has led to an understanding of their disadvantages as well as their advantages. Based on our recent application experience [Gifford85], we have have discovered three major problem areas in standard remote procedure call systems: protocol flexibility, incremental results, and bulk data transport.

1. *Protocol Flexibility* Certain communication protocols are impossible to implement if a remote procedure call system does not allow remote procedure values to be exchanged freely between nodes. For example, imagine that a client node wishes to provide a server node with a procedure for use in certain circumstances, and the server node then wishes to pass this procedure on to another server. Unless remote procedures are first-class objects that can be passed from node to node this protocol can not be expressed in a remote procedure call framework.

2. *Incremental Results* Consider a server that is computing a result on behalf of a client and wishes to communicate incremental results to the client as they are computed. In present remote procedure call systems this would be

accomplished by having the client ask the server to compute the first incremental result, then the second, and so forth until all of the results have been computed. The problem with this approach is that it forces a single computation to be decomposed into a series of distinct remote procedure calls. This decomposition reduces the performance of the server since it is inactive between client procedure calls unless it creates a sophisticated process structure upon the client's first incremental result request. Sophisticated process structures are undesirable because they substantially complicate a program.

3. *Bulk Data Transport* Remote procedure call mechanisms are optimized for both low call-return latency and the transmission of limited amounts of data (usually less than 10^3 bytes). These optimizations for the normal case seriously affect the ability of remote procedure call mechanisms to transport large amounts of data efficiently. Since only one remote procedure call can be in transit at a given time between a single process client and a server, the communication bandwidth between them is limited. For example, if we assume that a program transmits 10^3 bytes per remote procedure call and the network has a 50 millisecond round trip latency, the maximum bandwidth that can be achieved is 20 KBytes/second. Furthermore, to achieve even this performance, the client must combine data values as they are produced into 10^3 byte blocks before a remote procedure call is made. If a remote procedure call was made whenever data was available to be sent, e.g. for each character to be displayed on a remote screen, communication performance could drop to 20 bytes/second.

As a direct result of our experience with these limitations we have developed a new communication model called the *Remote Pipe and Procedure Model* that extends remote procedure call in three directions and address the three disadvantages discussed above. First, we permit remote procedures to be first-class values which can be freely passed between nodes. Second, we introduce a new abstraction called a *pipe* that allows bulk data and incremental results to be efficiently transported. Third, we introduce *channel groups* which control the relative sequencing of calls on pipes and procedures.

Elements of the Remote Pipe and Procedure Model have been present in previous work although these elements have not been combined into a single consistent framework. The idea of transmitting remote procedure values is discussed by Nelson [Nelson81], and is also present in ARGUS [Liskov83] as handlers. However neither of these proposals allow remote procedures to be created in nested scopes which limits the generality of remote procedures. The notion of a pipe is similar in some respects to Nelson's immediate return procedures [Nelson81], and the unidirectional messages of

Matchmaker [Jones85]. Nelson however rejected immediate return procedures for his communication model because they were inconsistent with procedure call semantics. Our solution to the consistency problem is the creation of a new type of abstract object with well defined properties. In Matchmaker remote procedures are not first-class values and unidirectional message sends are not optimized for bulk data transmission. None of the above systems include an idea similar to a channel group.

The remainder of this paper is organized into three sections: Semantics (Section 2), Pragmatics (Section 3), and Practical Experience and Conclusions (Section 4).

3. Semantics

We discuss in this section

- how remote pipes and procedures are typed,
- how remote pipes and procedures are created and used,
- stable channels that survive crashes,
- channel call ordering,
- how channel groups provide inter-channel synchronization,
- secure channels for secrecy and authentication,
- and failure semantics.

A *node* is an abstract computer. A physical computer can implement one or more nodes; the precise size and scope of a node will depend on application requirements. All of the nodes in a system are interconnected by a network.

Remote procedures and pipes are defined as follows:

- *Procedures* A *remote procedure value* provides the capability to call a procedure on a remote node, and is used as is a local procedure value. A *remote procedure call* blocks the caller until the remote procedure has finished execution and a response has been received from the remote node. In the event that a remote procedure call fails, a distinguished error value is returned as the value of the call.

- *Pipes* A *pipe value* provides the capability to send bulk data to a remote node. A pipe is used as is a remote procedure. However, unlike a remote procedure call, a *pipe call* does not block the caller and does not return a result. Since a pipe call does not block its caller a pipe call implicitly initiates concurrent activity at the sink's remote *sink* node. The caller continues execution as soon as the call to the sink is queued for transmission. The data values sent down a pipe by a given process are processed by the pipe's sink node in strict FIFO order. Processed means that the sink receives the data in order and performs some computation on the data. This computation could process the data to completion or simply schedule the data for later processing.

Both remote procedures and pipes provide a communication path to a remote node, and thus we call them *channels.* A channel represents the ability to perform a specific remote operation at a remote node. Channels are first-class values. In particular, channels can be freely passed to remote procedures or pipes as parameters, or returned as the result of a remote procedure. Connections are implicitly established as necessary when channels are used as described in Section 3.

3.1. Channels and interfaces have static types

Every channel has a statically known type. A channel's type describes the channel's input values and the channel's result values. For example a pipe value might have type

```
pipe-a: pipe[string]
```

indicating that the pipe is a string pipe, while a remote procedure might have type

```
proc-a: proc[string] returns [sequence[byte]]
```

indicating that the remote procedure takes a string and returns a sequence of bytes.

Local procedures have type `subr` instead of type `proc`. We restrict `pipe` and `proc` types so that they can not include `subr` types as parameters or results. Thus, a local procedure must be converted to a remote procedure before it can be used with a channel. This conversion is implicitly performed as we will describe in a moment.

We assume in our model that nodes have disjoint address spaces and thus call by value semantics must be used for channel calls. One consequence of the lack of a shared address space is that remote and local procedure calls can not provide the same semantics for mutable objects.

The semantics of remote and local calls are rationalized in our model by insisting that channel parameters and results be instances of *immutable types.* Instances of immutable types cannot be modified; this allows remote and local calls to have consistent semantics. In order to ease the burden on the programmer (who will often be working with mutable types) implicit conversions between mutable and immutable types are performed at a remote procedure or pipe call site as necessary.

A *remote interface* consists of a set of named channels and can be represented in our model by combining a set of channels into an aggregate structure such as a *package.* The following is an example of a package containing two channels.

```
r: package[print: pipe[string],
           read: proc[string] returns[sequence[byte]]]
```

Channel values can be selected from packages in the same manner as values are selected from records. For example, `r.print` could be used to select the print pipe from the package `r`. New packages can be composed by assembling an arbitrary set of channels, including channels which have been selected from existing packages.

Other aggregate structures (such as records or arrays) can also be used to combine channels. However packages are attractive because their type compatibility rules present the programmer with more flexibility than standard aggregate types. One package is compatible with another package even if the first package contains extra fields or a set of fields which is not in the same order.

Packages by virtue of their type declarations contain enough information to permit a stub generator to automatically generate code to implement the details of a communications protocol. Once an interface is specified an application programmer can deal with pipes and procedures, and not be concerned with how information is encoded and transmitted over a wire.

3.2. Channels are used and created like procedures

A remote procedure value is used in the same manner as is a local procedure value. Thus to call the procedure **proc-a** declared above, the source expression

```
my-sequence := proc-a("myfile.txt");
```

could be used. This expression would result in a call message to the node that implements **proc-a**, the execution of **proc-a** with the string parameter "myfile.txt", a reply message containing the sequence of bytes computed by **proc-a**, and the assignment of this sequence of bytes to **my-sequence**.

A new remote procedure value is created by providing a local procedure (a **subr**) where a remote procedure (a **proc**) is expected. In the following example a remote procedure value will be implicitly created from **local-proc-a**:

```
t: int := 0;
local-proc-a = subr[x: int]
   t := x + t;
   end;
% remote-proc-a (which is at a remote node)
% can call local-proc-a during its execution
result := remote-proc-a(local-proc-a);
```

Note that **local-proc-a** is a closure and is able to access variables in its environment. All local and remote calls to **local-proc-a** will update the same variable **t**.

A remote procedure value can also be created by returning a local procedure as the value of a remote procedure call.

```
remote-proc-b = subr[] returns [proc[int]]
  return(local-proc-a);
  end;
```

In this example a program that calls **remote-proc-b** will receive a remote procedure value which will enable the program to call **local-proc-a**.

The actual creation of the remote procedure value that corresponds to **local-proc-a** in both of these examples is performed implicitly as a conversion between objects of type **subr** (local procedures) and objects of type **proc** (remote procedures). No conversion needs to be performed in the opposite direction. Remote procedures are compatible with local procedures, and remote procedures can be provided where a local procedure is expected.

A pipe value is used in precisely the same way as a procedure value is used except that pipes do not return result values. The following expressions send the values "first" and "second" down **pipe-a**:

```
pipe-a("first");
pipe-a("second");
```

The values "first" and "second" are guaranteed to be processed by the sink of **pipe-a** in order (because the two pipe calls shown above are performed by the same process). No processing order is defined for pipe calls that are made by separate processes.

Since pipe calls do not return values and are processed asynchronously, a *synchronize* operation is provided. When a *synchronize* operation is applied by a source process to a pipe, the pipe's sink is forced to process all outstanding data sent down the pipe from the source process, after which the synchronize operation returns. If the pipe has broken for some reason (e.g. the sink node has crashed) then synchronize will return a distinguished error value and reset the pipe so that it can be used again.

```
pipe-a("mit-cls:/usr/smith/rpp.imp")
pipe-a("mit-db:/usr/gifford/545.tmp")
code := synchronize(pipe-a);
```

A pipe value is created through the provision of a local procedure called a *pipe sink procedure*, that will process data received over the pipe. As data arrives through a pipe its corresponding sink procedure is applied to each datum in FIFO order. A pipe's sink procedure must return before it will be applied to the next datum sent down the pipe from the same source process. A pipe can be declared as follows:

```
total: int := 0;
pipe-b = pipe[val: int]
  total := total + val;
  end;
remote-proc-d(pipe-b);
% remote-proc-d synchronizes pipe-a before it returns
% thus, we know that total is the sum of all pipe calls
% made by remote-proc-d
```

We have assumed that remote procedures will be implicitly created from local procedures when necessary, and that language support is provided for pipe declaration. The Remote Pipe and Procedure Model can be used in a language environment without making these assumptions by introducing the primitives **make-pipe** and **make-proc**. The primitive **make-pipe** creates a new pipe value when supplied with a local pipe sink procedure, and the primitive **make-proc** creates a remote procedure when provided with a local procedure for remote export. In the example below **make-pipe** and **make-proc** are used to create a remote procedure and a pipe.

```
proc-b := make-proc(local-proc-b);
pipe-c := make-pipe(local-proc-c);
```

An alternate model for the sink end of a pipe is to allow a program to create a pipe that has no sink procedure. The following primitives are used by a sink node to obtain values which have been sent down a pipe that has no sink procedure. The following primitives will return a distinguished error value if they are not applied at a pipe's sink node.

- `pipe-value` returns the next value from a pipe. If no value is available `pipe-value` blocks until a value arrives. `pipe-value` does not remove a value from a pipe. Successive applications of `pipe-value` to a pipe will return the same result unless `pipe-accept` has been called.

- `pipe-accept` states that the last datum read with `pipe-value` has been accepted and the datum may be removed from the pipe. `pipe-accept` blocks its caller if no data has arrived for the pipe. Once `pipe-accept` discards the present value of a pipe, it does not block its caller waiting for the next pipe value.

- `pipe-get` gets and accepts the next value from a pipe. Thus this operation is equivalent to combining `pipe-value` with `pipe-accept`.

- `pipe-ready` is a predicate that returns true if a pipe has data available and false if no data has arrived down the pipe.

A simple example of how a pipe can be serviced follows.

```
total: int := 0;
pipe-d: pipe[int] := pipe-create();
remote-proc-e(pipe-d);      % pass the new pipe to remote source
val: int := pipe-get(pipe-d);
while val#0 do              % remote source will terminate with 0
  total := val + total;
  val := pipe-get(pipe-d);
  endloop;
```

We call pipes which are connected to a procedure *procedure serviced*, and pipes which are polled *explicitly serviced.* We expect that both procedure serviced and explicitly serviced pipes will find application.

When program starts it will need to obtain appropriate channels in order to communicate with other nodes. This is accomplished by providing a program with a system supplied channel to a clearinghouse service. The program can use the clearinghouse service to obtain other channels of interest and to make channels that it creates known to other nodes.

3.3. Stable channels survive crashes

The above examples have shown how both remote procedures and pipes can be dynamically created, but their lifetimes have not been discussed. The desired lifetime of a channel depends upon its application. Thus in our model a *dynamic channel* will exist until it is explicitly destroyed by a program or until the channel's sink node crashes. An attempt to call a remote procedure which has been destroyed will result in a distinguished error value, and an attempt to call a pipe which has been destroyed will result in a distinguished error value from `synchronize`.

Channels which can survive node failures are useful for stable services that are registered with a clearinghouse. We call a channel that can survive a node failure a *stable channel.* The state of a stable channel and its associated procedure must be recorded in stable storage to permit recovery of the channel upon node restart. The details of how stable channels are created will depend on the host language environment.

3.4. Calls on a channel by a single process are ordered

Our communication model guarantees that if a process makes two separate calls on the same channel then the calls will be processed at the sink in the order in which they were made by the process. Processed means that the second call is not processed at the sink until the procedure invoked by the first call has returned. In the case of explicitly serviced pipes processed means that the second call will not be processed until a process has accepted the first call's datum by executing `pipe-accept`.

The ordering of channel calls not covered by the above invariant is undefined. Thus, a single channel can be invoked simultaneously by different source processes. We assume that monitors [Redell80] or a similar mechanism is used to ensure the proper operation of remote procedures and pipes in the presence of concurrent invocations.

3.5. Channel Groups provide inter-channel FIFO timing invariants

In our present model the ordering of calls on separate channels is undefined. However at times it is desirable to provide a timing invariant across channels. For example, imagine that we model a remote color display as a package with two channels: `set-color` and `put-character`. `set-color` sets the color of subsequent characters and returns the previous color setting of the display, while `put-character` is used to write characters on the display.

```
display-a: package[set-color: proc[Color] returns[Color],
                   put-character: pipe[char]]
```

In our present model there is no way to specify that calls on `set-color` and `put-character` must be performed in the order in which they were made. Thus if we used `display-a` characters could be displayed in the wrong color.

When timing invariants must be preserved between a set of channels the channels can be collected into a *channel group*. A channel group value is a collection of pipes and procedures that all have the same sink node and that observe FIFO ordering constraints with respect to a source process. A channel group value has a distinguished type. For example the following group is identical to `display-a`, except that the group guarantees that calls made by a single process will be performed in the order in which they were made:

```
display-b: group[set-color: proc[Color] returns[Color],
                 put-character: pipe[char]]
```

The type compatibility rules for groups permit extra fields, out of order fields, and for a group value to be provided where a package value is expected. Thus, a package may in fact be a channel group. The type `group` is provided to allow the static enforcement of FIFO sequencing where desired.

A group constructor is used to create a channel group value. A group constructor assembles a set of procedure and/or pipe values into a single composite channel group. All of the members of a group must reside at the same sink node. If they do not the group constructor will return a distinguished error value. We could have used the expression

```
display-b := group[set-color: display-a.set-color,
                   put-character: display-a.put-character];
```

to create the group value `display-b`.

A group constructor copies the values of its component channels, creates a new unique *sequencing stamp*, adds this new stamp to each of the channel copies, and constructs a group value out of the stamped copies. The sequencing stamp added to each channel is used to identify its membership in the newly created group. In addition to the sequencing stamps obtained by group membership, upon creation each channel is assigned a unique sequencing stamp.

The individual components of a channel group can be selected in the same manner as can the components of a record. Once a channel is selected from a group the channel can be used. For example, in order to display a character one could issue the call:

```
display-b.put-character["d"];
```

It is possible that a channel which is selected from a channel group will be included in another group. In this case the resulting channel will have more than two sequencing stamps (one unique stamp, and two or more group stamps). If desired, one could prohibit selection on group values in order to limit a channel to a single group sequencing stamp. We will not place this restriction on group values.

Because channels can be selected from groups it is possible to create a package that includes channels that are members of a group. Consider the following package that implements a terminal consisting of a color display and a keyboard:

```
terminal := package[set-color: display-b.set-color,
                    put-character: display-b.put-character,
                    get-character: get-char];
```

`set-color` and `put-character` calls will be performed in the order in which they are made, but `get-character` calls are not ordered with respect to the display calls. This allows characters to be independently displayed and read on a remote terminal.

The channel timing invariant provided by the communication model can now be succinctly stated:

Channel Timing Invariant If a process makes two separate calls on channels that (1) are at the same sink node, and (2) have a sequencing stamp in common, then the calls will be processed at the sink in the order in which they were made by the process. Processed means that the second call is not processed at the sink until the procedure invoked by the first call has returned. In the case of explicitly serviced pipes, processed means that the second call will not be processed until a process has accepted the first call's datum by executing `pipe-accept`.

The channel timing invariant implies the invariant for calls on a single channel (because a channel will always be at the same sink node as itself and will have a sequencing stamp in common with itself). The channel timing invariant describes all of the ordering provided by the Remote Pipe and Procedure Model. The ordering of channel calls not covered explicitly by the channel timing invariant is undefined. Table 1 shows some of the implications of the channel timing invariant.

3.6. Secure Channels for Secrecy and Authentication

In order to provide secrecy and authentication in our communication model we introduce the idea of a *secure channel.* A secure channel has the same type as does a normal channel and is used in the same manner. Secure channels however, provide additional secrecy and authentication guarantees. These guarantees are provided with cryptographic techniques.

Secure channels can be created only with the assistance of an *authentication service.* An authentication service is a trusted entity which is charged with establishing secure conversations between *principals* in a system [Voydock83]. Principals are the unit of authorization in our model of communication. Each principal has an associated secret key. The keys that are possessed by a node define its principals.

The first step in establishing a two-way authenticated secure conversation is to obtain a *conversation* [Birrell85] from an authentication server. A conversation can be obtained from an authentication server by using an unprotected remote procedure call. For example:

```
conversation := as.two-way[source-principal, sink-principal];
```

A conversation includes a conversation key that is encrypted under the source principal's secret key. Once a conversation is obtained no further interaction with an authentication server is necessary.

One or more secure channels can be created from a single conversation. `secure` creates a secure channel given a channel. For example:

```
secure-chan := secure(proc-a, conversation);
```

`secure` can be used to secure a single channel, a package of channels, or a channel group.

The following three invariants are guaranteed for secure channels which have been created with a two-way authenticated conversation.

- *Secrecy* Information sent over `secure-chan` will be kept secret from all principals except `source-principal` and `sink-principal`.
- *Source Authentication* During a call on `secure-chan` the sink can use the primitive `SourcePrincipal` to obtain the authenticated principal identifier of the process that made the call. Channel calls from a given principal are protected against modification and replay.
- *Sink Authentication* Results that are returned from `secure-chan` are guaranteed to have come from a node that is authenticated as `sink-principal`.

One-way authenticated conversations are also possible within this framework. Needham and Schroeder [Needham78] discuss one way authenticated conversations and other possible extensions.

3.7. Failures complicate channel semantics

Our communication model guarantees that a remote operation (a pipe or a procedure call) will be performed precisely once in the absence of failures. In the presence of failures the semantics of remote operations are more complicated. Many kinds of distributed system failures (e.g. node crashes, network partitions) can cause a source node to wait for a reply which will never arrive. In such cases it is impossible to tell if the corresponding remote operation was ever attempted or completed.

In the presence of failures *at-most-once* semantics can be provided for remote calls. At-most-once semantics guarantees that a remote operation either will be performed exactly once, or will have been performed at most once if a failure has occurred. For procedure calls the occurrence of a failure causes a distinguished *failure* value to be returned as the result of the call. For pipe calls the occurrence of a failure causes a distinguished *failure* value to be returned as the result of `synchronize`. When a failure occurs it is impossible to determine whether a remote operation was completed, never started, or only partially completed. Thus *at-most-once* semantics present a serious challenge to the application programmer who wishes to cope gracefully with failure.

One technique used in several practical systems accepts the limitations of at-most-once semantics and insists that procedure calls that mutate stable storage be idempotent. With this restriction a remote procedure call that returns *failure* can be repeated safely until the call completes without failing.

Exactly-once semantics is an alternative to at-most-once semantics. Exactly-once semantics guarantees that a remote operation will be performed exactly once or not at all. Exactly-once semantics is implemented by protecting the actions of a remote operation with a transaction. If a remote operation returns *failure* the operation's corresponding transaction is aborted. The transaction abort will undo the effects of the failed remote operation and the failed operation will appear to never have happened. The failed operation can then be retried (if desired) with a new transaction.

Exactly-once semantics can be achieved through the combination of communication with transactions in one of two ways. One approach as suggested by ARGUS's innovative design [Liskov83] is to integrate transactions into the communication model such that each remote operation has an implicit associated transaction. A second approach is to keep the communication model and transactions separate by explicitly specifying transactions where they are required [Brown85].

4. Pragmatics

We discuss in this section

- a model implementation,
- and performance elaborations.

4.1. A model implementation is possible

In order to demonstrate that our communication model can be effectively realized we present a model implementation. The model implementation describes the key algorithms that are necessary to implement the Remote Pipe and Procedure Model. The implementation describes the format of messages and channel values, how calls are generated and sequenced, message retransmission and timeout, incoming call processing, and crash recovery. The section following the model implementation considers performance optimizations.

We assume that the message system may lose, reorder, and duplicate messages. In addition when a message is delivered we assume that it has not been damaged in transmission. This ideal can be realized with high probability in practice if messages with incorrect checksums are discarded.

We also assume that typed values can be converted to byte strings and back again via encode and decode operations [Herlihy82]. We consider neither a particular type space or exception handling.

Finally we assume that when a node crashes it loses all of its volatile state. The entire state of the following implementation is stored in volatile storage, except for the state necessary for global unique id generation.

A channel value consists of the channel's sink node address, the channel's unique *channel id*, the type of the channel (pipe or procedure), and the channel's set of sequencing stamps. A channel has one unique sequencing stamp for each group membership, along with a sequencing stamp which is a copy of the channel id.

```
channel = record[sink: Address,
                 channel-id: GlobalUniqueID,
                 type: (pipe, proc),
                 stmps: Stamps];
```

When a channel is called the procedure `SourceCall` is invoked. `SourceCall` is passed the channel being called and its encoded parameters. We assume that an encoding algorithm such as Herlihy's [Herlihy82] is used to convert the actual parameter values to a format for transmission in a message.

`SourceCall` constructs a call message that includes the sink and source addresses, the *generation id* of the source and sink, a unique request id, the process id of the calling process, a *sequence vector*, the channel called, and the data for the channel. A node's generation id is the value of the node's unique id generator at the time of the node's last recovery from a crash.

```
message = record[sink, source: Address,
                 sink-generation: GlobalUniqueID,
                 source-generation: GlobalUniqueID,
                 type: (call, return),
                 request-id, process-id: GlobalUniqueID,
                 sequence: SequenceVector,
                 channel-id: GlobalUniqueID, data: any];
```

Channel calls are ordered with sequence vectors. A sequence vector is a set of pairs of the form <sequence stamp, integer>. Two sequence vectors are ordered if and only if they have a sequence stamp in common. The comparison of two ordered sequence vectors is accomplished by comparing the integers associated with common sequencing stamps. The larger sequence vector will have larger integers associated with all of the common stamps (because of the way sequence vectors are generated).

`SourceCall` generates a unique sequence vector for each call by calling the procedure `GetNextSequence`. Each process has its own independent counter for each sequence stamp. `GetNextSequence` takes as input both the id of the process making the call and the sequence stamps that are to be used for this call. `GetNextSequence` increments the per-process counters associated with the input sequence stamps, and returns the new counter values along with their stamps as the next sequence vector.

```
SourceCall = subr[c: channel, data: any] returns [any]
  m := message$create[sink: c.sink,
                      source: GetMyAddress[],
                      source-generation: GetMyGeneration[],
                      sink-generation: GetGeneration[c.sink],
                      request-id: GetMonotoneUniqueID[],
                      process-id: GetMyProcessID[],
                      sequence: GetNextSequence[c.stmps,
                                                GetMyProcessID[]],
                      channel-id: c.channel-id,
                      data: data];
  RegisterOutgoing[m, c.type];
  Send[m];
  if c.type=pipe then return[nil]
    else return[WaitForResult[m]];
  end;
```

Each request message includes both source and sink generation ids. A sink must reject any message that specifies an obsolete sink generation (because the message was destined for a previous incarnation of the sink) and must also reject any message that specifies an obsolete source generation (because the message originated from a previous incarnation of the source node).

The set of remote generation id's held by a node comprises its connection state. As shown **GetGeneration** returns a node's cached copy of a remote node's generation id. If the generation id of a remote node is not cached **GetGeneration** must send a message to the remote node requesting its generation id.

The source repeats a call message if the call's corresponding reply has not been received after a predetermined interval. This is accomplished by registering all outgoing call messages with the procedure **RegisterOutgoing**. A retransmission process periodically retransmits the set of registered calls. Note that both pipe calls and procedure calls are retransmitted.

Incoming messages to a node are demultiplexed into call and reply messages. This is accomplished by the following loop that receives incoming messages and dispatches call messages to **SinkCall**, and reply messages to **ProcessReply**.

```
while true do
  m := receive[];
  if m.type = call
    then SinkCall[m]
    else ProcessReply[m];
  end;
```

ProcessReply looks up the **request-id** of an incoming message in the set of outstanding calls maintained by **RegisterOutgoing**. If the outstanding call corresponding to an incoming message is not found the incoming message is discarded. If a corresponding outstanding call is found the call is taken out of the outstanding call set. If the incoming message is a reply to a procedure call **m.data** is returned to the calling process that is waiting inside of **WaitForResult**. If the incoming message is a reply to a pipe call, all other outstanding calls with smaller request ids, which are in the outgoing call set for this pipe and process, are removed. These calls are removed because we know, based on the channel timing invariant maintained by the server, that the calls must have been processed previously.

If a reply to a call in the outstanding call set is not received within a predefined interval, the process that retransmits messages will eventually force the call to terminate. The retransmission process accomplishes this by providing **ProcessReply** with a fake reply message for calls with a distinguished *failure* value for **m.data**.

After a sink crash the source must resynchronize with the sink node. This is accomplished by querying the sink for its generation id when the sink fails to respond to a call message. If the sink replies with a generation id value different from that cached by the source, then the sink has crashed and restarted. In this case all of the source's sequence counters for sequence stamps associated with the sink are reset to 0, and the cached copy of the sink's generation id is updated.

`SinkCall` processes incoming call request messages. `SinkCall` first determines if the received message was generated by a previous incarnation of the source node. The message is ignored if the message's source generation field is less than the sink's copy of the source's generation. If the message's source generation field is greater than the sink's copy of the source's generation then the source has crashed, and the sink must update its copy of the source's generation id, abort any calls in progress from the previous generation of the source, as well as garbage collect sequencing state and held results associated with the previous generation of the source node.

```
SinkCall = subr[m: message]
  g := GetGeneration[m.source];
  if m.source-generation < g then return[];
  if m.source-generation > g then
    UpdateGeneration[m.source, m.source-generation];
  % invariant: m sent from current incarnation of source
  if m.sink-generation # GetMyGeneration[] then return[];
  % invariant: m sent to current incarnation of sink
  channel := LookupSinkChannel[m.channel];
  if channel=nil then begin
     UnknownChannelReply[m];
     return[];
     end;
  % see if we have the result
  if HaveResult[m] then begin
     SendResult[m, GetResult[m], channel];
     return[];
     end;
  if not NextInSequence[channel, m]
    then return[];
  FORK DoCall[channel, m];
  end;
```

After `SinkCall` ensures that `m` is a contemporary message `m.channel-id` is looked up by `LookupSinkChannel`. If the channel does not exist a distinguished response is returned to the source. If the channel does exist the sink checks to see if it has already computed the result for `m`. The sink will have a held result if `m` is the last procedure call processed from the source process, or if `m` is a pipe call with an old sequence vector. Pipe calls with obsolete sequence vectors have already been processed by the sink and thus can simply be acknowledged. If `SinkCall` can return a response immediately it does so.

If **SinkCall** cannot immediately create a response for the incoming message, **NextInSequence** checks the per-process sequence counters to ensure that **m.sequence** is the next operation to be scheduled for the channel, and that the operation is not already in progress. If either of these conditions is not met **NextInSequence** returns false and the message is ignored. Otherwise **NextInSequence** increments the per-process counters, notes that the operation is in progress, and returns true.

DoCall is forked by **SinkCall** to actually perform the computation requested by the source node. After the processing is complete **Finished** is called to update the per-process sequence stamp counters for **m.process-id**, and indicate that the current call is finished. **DoCall** then uses **SendResult** to send a result message back to the source. **SendResult** also remembers the most recent procedure call result computed by each process.

```
DoCall = subr[c: sink-channel, m: message]
   result  := c.procedure[m.data];
   Finished[m.process-id, m.sequence];
   SendResult[m, result, c];
end;
```

synchronize can be added to our model implementation by sending a distinguished synchronize operation to a pipe and waiting for the sink to respond. The synchronize operation will be processed after all other outstanding pipe calls have been processed by virtue of the sink's normal message sequencing mechanism. When the sink acknowledges the synchronize operation **synchronize** returns a value signifying normal completion. If the synchronize operation is not acknowledged within a certain time **synchronize** returns a distinguished error value.

The **secure** primitive for creating secure channels creates a channel value that includes both a regular channel value and a conversation. A detailed treatment of the implementation of secure one-way and two-way authenticated communication is discussed in [Needham78]. A complete system that uses this information for a two-way authenticated remote procedure call mechanism is described in [Birrell85].

4.2. The performance of the model implementation can be improved

The model implementation we have described is intended only to be suggestive; a practical implementation of the Remote Pipe and Procedure Model would require performance optimizations. Important optimizations include:

- *Buffer pipe calls* Multiple pipe calls destined for the same sink node can be buffered at a source and transmitted as a single message in order to reduce message handling overhead and improve network throughput. The amount of time that a pipe call is buffered before it is sent presents a tradeoff between low pipe latency and efficient bulk communication. A moving window flow control algorithm can be employed [Postel79] to manage the transfer of buffered pipe calls between a source and a sink.

- *Combine pipe calls with procedure calls* A procedure call message will always be transmitted immediately, and any buffered pipe calls to the same sink should be prepended to the procedure call message whenever possible.

- *Preallocate Processes* Processes can be preallocated into a process pool at node startup so that performance of a FORK operation for each incoming remote call is not required. Eliminating FORK overhead on is especially important for a collection of pipe calls that arrive in a single message, because the overhead per pipe call is limited to approximately the cost of a procedure call, as opposed to a process creation. A process allocated from a pool would return itself to the pool when the process had finished processing its assigned call message.

- *Explicitly Acknowledge Messages* At times both call and return messages should be explicitly acknowledged in order to improve performance. A call message should be explicitly acknowledged by a sink when the sink has been processing a call for a predetermined interval without a result having been produced. This acknowledgment informs the source that the call has been successfully received, and that the source does not need to retransmit the call message. A procedure return message from a sink should be explicitly acknowledged by a source when the same source process does not make a subsequent procedure call to the sink within a predetermined interval. This informs the sink that the return message has been received by the source, and that the sink can discard the result contained in the return message.

- *Factor Packages and Groups* In order to save space, information that is common to all of the channels in a package or group value need only be represented once.

5. Practical Experience and Conclusions

We conclude with

- experience with an application of the Remote Pipe and Procedure Model that has proven certain of its elements practical,

• and discussion about general application of the model.

5.1. The elements of the model have been proven practical

In order to gain experience with the Remote Pipe and Procedure Model we have used it to implement a distributed database system. The database system we implemented provides query based access to the full-text of documents and newspaper articles, and is presently in use by a community of users. The database system is divided into a user interface portion called Walter that runs on a user's local node, and a confederation of remote database servers which are accessed by Walter via the DARPA Internet. Walter employs a query routing algorithm to determine which server contains the information required for processing of a given user query.

The protocol that Walter uses to communicate with a database server can be abstracted as follows:

```
server: group[establish-query: proc[string],
              count-matching-records: proc[] returns [int, bool],
              fetch-summaries: proc[Range, pipe[Summary]],
              fetch-record: proc[Range, pipe[Line]]]
```

When a user supplies a query the procedure `establish-query` is called. `establish-query` initiates processing of a query at a server and then returns immediately to Walter. The server procedure `fetch-summaries`, which computes the summaries for a range of articles matching the current query is then called. As the summaries are computed they are sent down the pipe supplied in the `fetch-summaries` call. The pipe sink procedure that receives the summaries displays them as they arrive. All of the summaries generated by `fetch-summaries` are guaranteed to arrive before `fetch-summaries` returns. In order to view an entire database record the server procedure `fetch-record` is used in precisely the same manner as `fetch-summaries` is used.

A second process is conceptually running concurrently with the information which is arriving down a pipe and being displayed. This process checks for the abort user request, which aborts the query in progress. If such a keyboard request is received, a primitive is used to abort the `fetch-summaries` or `fetch-record` operation in progress.

The use of pipes in this database application has provided two distinct advantages over remote procedures. First, pipes permit both `fetch-summaries` and `fetch-record` to send variable amounts of bulk data to Walter simply. Second, since pipe calls do not block a server can continue computing after it has sent a datum. If a procedure instead of a pipe were used to return data the server process would suspend processing while waiting for a response from Walter. The concurrency provided by pipes has proven to be important to Walter's performance in practice.

5.2. The Remote Pipe and Procedure Model has many advantages

We have proposed three major ideas:

- *Channel values* Channels should be first-class values which can be freely transmitted between nodes. If a communication model does not not permit channel values to be transmitted between nodes, then its application will be limited to a restricted set of protocols. An application of channel values is the return of incremental results from a service to a client.

- *Pipes* A new abstraction called a pipe should be provided in the communications model. A pipe permits bulk data and incremental results to be transmitted in a type safe manner in a remote procedure call framework. Existing remote procedure call models do not address the requirements of bulk data transfer, or the need to return incremental results.

- *Channel groups* A new sequencing technique, the channel group, is important in order to permit proper sequencing of channel calls. A channel group is used to enforce serial sequencing on its members with respect to a single source process.

As we have explained these three ideas form the basis for the Remote Pipe and Procedure Model. We expect that this model will find a wide variety of applications in distributed systems.

Acknowledgments The ideas in this paper benefited from meetings with fellow MIT Common System Project members Toby Bloom, Dave Clark, Joel Emer, Barbara Liskov, Bob Scheifler, Karen Sollins, and Bill Weihl. I am especially indebted to Bob Scheifler for posing a question that resulted in the notion of a channel group. Barbara Liskov, John Lucassen, Bob Scheifler, Mark Sheldon, Bill Weihl, and Heidi Wyle commented on drafts of the paper.

6. References

[Birrell84] Birrell, A., and Nelson, B., Implementing Remote Procedure Calls, ACM Trans. on Computer Systems 2, 1 (February 1984), pp. 39-59.

[Birrell85] Birrell, A., Secure Communication Using Remote Procedure Calls, ACM Trans. on Computer Systems 3, 1 (February 1985), pp. 1-14.

[Brown85] Brown, M., et. al., The Alpine File System, ACM Trans. on Computer Systems 3, 4 (November 1985), pp. 261-293.

[Cheriton85] Cheriton, D., and Zwaenepoel, W., Distributed Process Groups in the V Kernel, ACM Trans. on Comp. Systems 3, 2 (May 1985), pp. 77-107.

[Gifford81] Gifford, D., Information Storage in a Decentralized Computer System, Report CSL-81-8, Xerox Palo Alto Research Center, Palo Alto, CA.

[Gifford85] Gifford, D. et. al., An Architecture for Large Scale Information Systems, Proc. of the Tenth ACM Symposium on Operating Systems Principles, ACM Ops. Sys. Review 19, 5, pp. 161-170.

[Herlihy82] Herlihy, M., and Liskov, B., A Value Transmission Method for Abstract Data Types, ACM Trans. on Programming Languages and Systems 4, 4 (October 1982), pp. 527-551.

[Jones85] Jones, M., et. al., Matchmaker: An Interface Specification Language for Distributed Processing, Proc. of the 12th Annual ACM Symp. on Princ. of Prog. Languages, January 1985, pp. 225-235.

[Liskov83] Liskov, B., and Scheifler, R., Guardians and Actions: Linguistic Support for Robust, Distributed Programs, ACM Trans. on Prog. Lang. and Sys. 5, 3 (July 1983), pp. 381-404.

[Needham78] Needham, R., and Schroeder, M., Using Encryption for Authentication in Large Networks of Computers, Comm. ACM 21, 12 (December 1978), pp. 993-998.

[Nelson81] Nelson, B., Remote Procedure Call, Report CSL-81-9, Xerox Palo Alto Research Center, May 1981.

[Postel79] Postel, J., Internetwork Protocols, IEEE Trans. on Comm. COM-28, 4, pp. 604-611.

[Rashid81] Rashid, R., and Robertson, G., Accent: A communication oriented network operating system kernel, Proc. of the Eighth Symposium on Operating System

Principles, Pacific Grove, CA, Dec. 1981, pp. 164-175.

[Redell80] Experience with Processes and Monitors in Mesa, Comm. ACM 23, 2 (February 1980), pp. 105-117.

[Voydock83] Voydock, V., and Kent, S., Security Mechanisms in High-Level Network Protocols, Comp. Surveys 15, 2 (June 1983), pp. 135-171.

[White76] White, J., A high-level framework for network-based resource sharing, Proc. Nat. Comp. Conf. 1976, AFIPS Press, pp. 561-570.

NEW CONCEPTS
FOR
DISTRIBUTED SYSTEM STRUCTURING.

Jean-Pierre BANATRE

IRISA/INSA and INRIA Rennes

Campus de Beaulieu

35042-RENNES-Cedex

FRANCE

Abstract

Distributed systems and data base applications tend to put forward the need of new structuring concepts. These concepts allow the grouping of several computations into logical entities called process groups,activities,teams... This paper reviews some recent proposals and presents a program structure, called multi-function, which generalizes the well known concept of function in order to describe parallel computations.

Prepared for the NATO Advance Study Institute: Distributed Operating System: Theory and practice. Izmir, 18-29 August 1986.

NATO ASI Series, Vol. F28
Distributed Operating Systems. Theory and Practice
Edited by Y. Paker et al.

1-Introduction

Several abstraction mechanisms have been incorporated into modern programming languages. These mechanisms are concerned in particular with control abstraction (conditional, loops etc.), data abstraction (classes, abstract data types etc.) and communication abstraction (parameter passing mechanisms, communication mechanisms etc.).

As far as distributed systems are concerned the basic control abstractions are procedures and processes. The associate control abstractions are procedure call with parameter passing mechanisms and process activation with message passing mechanisms. These two control structures were already used in the design of centralized operating systems, the only novelty stands into a new implementation technique for the procedure call when the caller and the callee are not situated on the same site, this new technique is called Remote Procedure Call [BIRR-84].

Distributed systems and data base applications tend to put forwards the need of new concepts allowing the grouping of "processes" into logical entities, called process group, activities, transactions, teams etc. So the basic building block of the system is no more the process but a new abstraction encapsulating the behaviour of a set of cooperating processes. This new abstraction should behave as a whole, that is to say, should be able to receive data, to transform this data and to send a result.

This paper is divided into two main parts:

(i) a review of few proposals aiming at incorporating such abstractions in ' programming languages,

(ii) a presentation of a program structure called multi-function. This program structure generalizes the concept of function as it allows for concurrent execution of several sequential programs(functions) which may be nested in a very general fashion [BANA-86].

2-Recent proposals.

This section reviews some recent proposals aiming at providing tools for distributed program construction. Subsection 1 describes the language ARGUS [LISK-84] which incorporate such notions as remote procedure call and atomic actions. Some aspects of the V-kernel[CHER-85] are introduced in subsection 2, in particular the notion of process group is presented. Finally, a recent model developed in the MCC project LEONARDO is briefly described.

2.1.The ARGUS approach.

ARGUS is a programming system based on the concepts of guardian and atomic action. It is an extension of the abstract data type based language CLU [LISK-77].

2.1.1.Guardians.

In ARGUS, a program is made out ot processes grouped into some kind of classes, called guardians. Within a guardian, processes may access directly some common data, but communication between guardians is done only by handler calls. Handlers may be seen as procedures. Handlers calls may be viewed as remote procedure calls. The caller process provides the name of the handler and the list of its arguments. Arguments are passed by value, so that a guardian can keep all of its own data under control (protection property). When the handler terminates, the calling process gets its results and resumes its execution.

The implementation of an application consists of defining a set of guardians . Guardians are created dynamically. The programmer must specify on what site a guardian should be implemented.

The state of a guardian is made out of two types of objects : volatile objects and stable objects. Stable objects are saved periodically on a so-called stable storage [LAMP-76] which ensures among other properties, the non-volatibility of information. When a site supporting a guardian happens to fail, volatile data and the current execution state of the process are lost. However stable objects are still available, and when a restart is attempted the state of lost objects is recreated from stable objects.

2.1.2.Atomic actions.

Although a distributed application might be made out of a unique guardian, it is more generally compound of several guardians residing on different sites. Of course, the state of the system is also distributed. This state must remain coherent even in presence of faults (hardware or software), this explains why ARGUS introduces the notion of "atomic action".

In ARGUS, an action should result in changing the state of certain (shared) objects. This change should appear as "atomic" to the outside world, i.e., the change occurs normally or no side effect should be visible. In other words, no intermediate state should be visible. Such actions are called "atomic actions".

Atomic actions may also be nested at any level thus providing a very powerful tool for the construction of distributed applications.

As a conclusion on ARGUS, let us mention the structure of a guardian :

name = **guardian**[parameter_decls] **is** create_names[**handlers** handler name]

#here are defined : the name of the guardian, the types of its parameter, the name of its creation operation and the names of the handlers it offers to the outside .#

{[stable] variable_decls_and_units}

#variable declaration list...some variables may be declared as stable, by default they are considered as volatile#

[**recover** body **end**]

#instructions executed when restarting after a failure. The body section should only use stable objects. #

[**background** body **end**]

#periodical tasks accomplished by the guardian#

{handler definitions}

end name

Atomic actions are defined by using the prefix **enter**, for example :

enter action body **end** implies the execution of body as an atomic action. Such a body may terminate in two ways : abort or commit.

Of course, several atomic actions may be run in parallel, this is done with the construct **coenter**, which may be examplified as follows :

coenter

    action foreach db : db_copy **in** all copies

                db : write(...)

end

Where a write operation is executed concurrently on all copies of a replicated database.

Further details on ARGUS language and system may be found in [LISK-84].

2.2. V-Kernel process groups [CHER-85].

In a majority of distributed systems, the concept of process is still the key concept. However, some designers are recognizing the fact that often it would be useful -and closer to reality- to group processes according to certain logical properties and to use these groups as basic entities. This notion is used in the V-kernel and also in a similar way in systems such as ENCHERE and GOTHIC to be presented later.

2.2.1. Process groups.

A process group is set of processes located possibly on different machines. A process group is identified by a unique name or group_id.

Three main operations allow for group handling :

(i) dynamic creation of a group.

group_id = **create_group**(initial pid, type)

which returns a unique group identifier with the process (initial Pid) being the first member of the group. So initially, a group has only one member.

(ii) joining a group.

Join_group(group_id, pid)

which makes the process pid join the group group_id. Notice that a process may belong to more than one group.

(iii) leaving a group.

leave_group(group_id, pid) which makes the process pid leave the group group_id. A group is considered as "dead" when the last member leaves it.

Process groups communicate by message transactions. This communication method is very similar to the well-known RPC [BIRR-84]. Some caution is taken in order to ensure a minimal reliability for communication facilities. In the same way, protection mechanisms have been studied in order to solve to three following issues :

- who may send to a group,
- who may determine or need to know the numbership of a group,
- who may join a group (and therefore reply messages sent to the group).

These issues are dealt with by using techniques such as message encryption, a group having its own secret key (more details in [CHER-85]).

2.2.2.Some comments.

This proposal is a first step towards a generalization of the concept of process, but it is not yet clear whether process group or process is the key entity in the V-kernel. Of course, process groups have been isolated, but it is still possible to manipulate processes as such. The next step would probably be to get rid of the notion of process and to stick to this interesting and innovative notion of process group. Protection and security matters have been addressed in the V-kernel, but no special attention has been -purposely- given to reliability aspects. For example, it should be interesting to study the notion of atomic process group ... and it is far from clear that this notion could be adapted easily to the very dynamic nature of process groups -which posseses a variable number of elements.

2.3. The RADDLE approach [FORM-86].

The RADDLE model is developed within the context of the LEONARDO project at

MCC. RADDLE has two main goals:

(i) to facilitate the description of distributed systems,

(ii) to enable the hierarchical description of distributed systems.

RADDLE introduces an abstraction mechanism -the team- which captures the concept of group of coordinated entities. These entities cooperate by using a communication tool called interaction. Let us give a more precise description of these concepts through an example:

2.3.1.RADDLE description of a bounded buffer.

```
team Bounded_buffer

new(size)
        bound:=size;
        current:=0;
        bqueue:=nil;
        previous:=nil;
end new

role producer(pstuff)
        rule
                iproducer[ ] ---> return nil;
end producer

marked role buffer
        var bqueue, bound, current, stuff, previous;
        rule current < bound & iproducer [ stuff:=pstuff ] --->
                if stuff <> previous --->
                  bqueue:=appendl(bqueue,stuff);
                  current:=current+1;
                  previous:=stuff;
                | stuff=previous --->
                  skip;
                fi
        rule current <> 0 &
                iconsumer [ bqueue:=cdr(bqueue),current:=current-1]
                  ---> skip;
```

```
end buffer

role consumer
        var cstuff;
        rule iconsumer [ cstuff:=car(bqueue)] ---> return cstuff;
end consumer

end Bounded_buffer
```

The team Bounded_buffer contains three roles:

1-the role producer which is able to transmit the information pstuff to an interacting role, i.e., a role referring to iproducer. Such an unmarked role can be seen as a process accessible from outside the team.

2-the marked role buffer which implements the communication between producers and consumers. Buffer cannot be accessed from outside the team.

3-the role consumer which picks up an element from the buffer and stores it into its local variable cstuff.

A role is composed of rules which may be seen as guarded commands of the form: rule predicate & box ---> command list . A box denotes an interaction (e.g., iconsumer, iproducer) . An interaction takes place when all intervening roles are ready. So instead of a 2-party interaction as usual(rendez-vous), RADDLE offers a N-party interaction. all parters which may participate in an interaction are known at compile-time. When an interaction occurs, the sequence of instructions associated with it is executed (this sequence is between brackets) and the command list following the guard is executed.

2.3.2.Discussion

RADDLE is a very interesting model which integrates concepts from object-oriented programming and concepts from parallel programming. Actually, an object may be seen as a set of interacting roles sharing some common data.

Another interesting feature of RADDLE is the relationship between this model and Petri-nets. Actually an interaction possesses the same semantics as the transitions in Petri-nets: no interaction begins until all partners are ready and the interaction is complete only when all partners have terminated.

In the same vein as RADDLE, another model called SCRIPT [FRAN-85] is being developed. The SCRIPT abstraction is similar to the RADDLE team and is used to describe patterns of communications. A script is composed of a set of roles (formal processes) in which actual processes enroll in order to communicate.

Next section introduces another model for distributed computing based on the concept of multi-function.

3. Multi-functions:definition, use and implementation.

The present section describes a program structure currently investigated in the GOTHIC project [BANA-86b]. This structure generalizes the concept of procedure as it allows for concurrent execution of several sequential programs which may possibly be nested in a very general fashion.

First, we describe the background of this research. The basic structuring facilities of GOTHIC are then described, in particular we introduce the concept of multi-function as the primary means of describing operational behaviour and communications. Several examples illustrating multi-functions are then exhibited. We conclude with some implementation considerations.

3.1. Background.

GOTHIC is assumed to be a general purpose distributed operating system designed by generalizing concepts previously implemented in the application-oriented distributed system ENCHERE [BANA-84, BANA-86a]. We think it is worthwhile to recall some salient contributions of ENCHERE as far as distributed program structuring is concerned.

The essential structuring facility of ENCHERE is the activity. An activity is a set of "cooperating processes" whose interactions define the dynamic structure of the application. Activities can be nested at any level, thus an application is represented by a tree of activities.

Two nested activities (mother and daughter) can communicate only via parameter passing (when the mother "creates" the daughter) and via result transmission (when the daughter terminates).

An activity may also possess the property of atomicity:

-Indivisibility: its intermediate states are hidden to other activities,

-Recoverability: any object currently being modified can be restored to its initial state in case of failure.

The design and implementation of nested atomic activities is the major achievement of the ENCHERE project. Two aspects have to be emphasized:

-this is one of the few actual distributed implementations of nested activities.

-an original stable storage facility was designed and built. Its use was determinant in the implementation of atomic activities.

However, due to the specificity of the application, some simplifications in the implementation of nested activities and of atomicity were considered as reasonable. The concept of activity, although very useful, was not fully investigated and further studies were considered as necessary.

3.2. The concept of multi-function.

A well-known structuring concept for classical operating systems and even for distributed operating systems is the procedure or function. The procedure is an abstraction of the notion of block with strict rules for communication with the environment (parameter and result passing mechanisms). Furthermore, procedures offer the possibility of nested computation through "recursive" calls.

Our purpose was to discover a somewhat similar concept allowing for:

-simultaneous processing of different components,

-parameter/result communication mechanisms,

-general nesting facilities.

3.2.1.Block and parallel clauses.

A block may be represented as (D;F) where D stands for declarations and F a sequence of instructions.

Given two blocks, B_1: $(D_1; F_{11}; F_{12})$ and B_2: $(D_2; F_2)$,

B_2 "nested within" B1 may be represented as:

(1) $(D_1; F_{11}; (D_2; F_2); F_{12})$, with the following properties:

D_1 and F_{11} are the first executed, then block B_1 is interrupted. D_2 and F_2 are executed and B_1 is resumed thus allowing the execution of F_{12}; Visibility rules are such that F_2 "sees" D_2 and D_1, F_{11} and F_{12} "see" D_1.

A parallel clause may be described as:

$((D_1; F_1)//(D_2; F_2)// \dots //(D_n; F_n))$

Components $(D_i; F_i)$ may be run in parallel. Several languages allow the following structure:

(2) $(D_0; F_0; ((D_1; F_1) // \dots // (D_n; F_n)); F_{n+1})$

where D_0 and F_0 are first executed, then $(D_i; F_i)$'s are executed and finally F_{n+1} is executed. Visibility rules are such that F_{n+1} "sees" D_0.

Procedural nesting (1) is qualified of 1-1 nesting (one caller, one callee), and parallel clause nesting is qualified of 1-p nesting (one caller, p callees). This last form of nesting is the one generally found in distributed systems where such concepts as nested actions or nested activities are implemented [LISK-84, MUEL-83, MOSS-81]. Let us now describe a more general form of nesting as introduced in GOTHIC.

3.2.2.A general form of nesting.

The nesting of a parallel clause within another parallel clause may be visualized as follows:

cobegin

$(A_{11}/$		$/A_{12})$
$(A_{21}/$	(B_1)	$/A_{22})$
.	(B_2)	.
.	.	.
.	(B_p)	.
.	.	.
$(A_{n1}/$		$/A_{n2})$

coend

Where the parallel clause $((B_1)// \ldots //(B_p))$ is nested within the parallel clause $((A_{11}/A_{12})//\ldots//(A_{n1}/A_{n2}))$. The execution of this structure can be described as follows:

A_{i1}'s sequences of instructions are initiated, and when they have all reached their "/", B_j's are executed. Upon termination of all B_j's A_{i2}'s are resumed with the property that A_{i2} may access the context defined in A_{i1}.

This form of nesting is the most general (n-callers, p-callees) and one can realize that 1-1 and 1-p nesting are particular cases of this n-p nesting [BANA-80]. After this informal description of nested parallel clause, let us introduce their logical properties.

3.2.3.Logical properties of nested parallel clauses.

These logical properties are expressed with a formalism introduced in [LAMP-84] and known as Generalized Hoare Logic (GHL).

In order to describe control information, GHL uses the following predicates:

at(π)≡"control resides at entry point of program fragment π".
in(π)≡"control resides inside π".
after(π)≡"control resides at a point following immediately π".

Let us first describe the logical properties of nested blocks. Consider the fragment program π defined as:

π: (π1 : α;
π2:β;
π3:γ)

If α, β and γ are characterized by their pre and post conditions as follows: {P}α{Q}, {R}β{s} and {T}γ{U}. For simplicity sake, α, β and γ are considered as atomic (or indivisible), so (at(α)≡in(α), at(β)≡in(β), at(γ)≡in(γ)). Block nesting control properties may be described as follows in terms of predicate at and after:

(I1)	$at(\pi_1) \Rightarrow P$	(I_2)	$after\ (\pi_1) \Rightarrow Q$
(I3)	$at(\pi_2) \Rightarrow R$	(I_4)	$after\ (\pi_2) \Rightarrow S$
(I5)	$at(\pi_3) \Rightarrow T$	(I_6)	$after\ (\pi_3) \Rightarrow U$

The invariant which characterizes the behavior of π is $\mathbf{I} \equiv (\bigwedge^{6}_{i=1} \mathbf{I}_i)$, where **I** is the pre-condition of π, (i.e., at(π)⇒**I**). Furthermore, the following relationships are true:

(1)	$at(\pi)$	$\Rightarrow$	$at(\pi_1)$
(2)	$after(\pi_1)$	$\Rightarrow$	$at(\pi_2)$
(3)	$after(\pi_2)$	$\Rightarrow$	$at(\pi_3)$
(4)	$after(\pi)$	$\Rightarrow$	$after(\pi_3)$

They are derived from the properties of the sequentiality (;) operator. We can generalize these properties in order to deal with nested parallel clauses:

π: **cobegin**

$$\begin{array}{lll} (\pi_{11}:A_{11}/ & & /\pi_{12}:A_{12}) \\ (\pi_{21}:A_{21}/ & \pi'_1:(B_1) & /\pi_{22}:A_{22}) \\ \dots & \pi'_2:(B_2) & \dots \\ & \dots & \\ & \pi'_k:(B_k) & \\ (\pi_{n1}:A_{n1}/ & & /\pi_{n2}:A_{n2}) \end{array}$$

coend

As above, A_{ij},($i\in[1,n]$, $j\in[1,2]$) and B_j, $j\in[1,k]$, are considered as atomic.

If A_{ij}'s are characterized in Hoare's notation, by $\{P_{ij}\}A_{ij}\{Q_{ij}\}$ and B_j's by $\{R_j\}B_j\{S_j\}$, then we have the following relations in terms of predicates at and after:

(I1) $\Lambda^n_{i=1}at(\pi_{i1})\Rightarrow\Lambda^n_{i=1}P_{i1}$ (I2) $\Lambda^n_{i=1}after(\pi_{i1})\Rightarrow\Lambda_{ni}=1Q_{i1}$

(I3) $\Lambda^k_{i=1}at(\pi'_i)\Rightarrow\Lambda^k_{i=1}R_i$ (I3) $\Lambda^k_{i=1}after(\pi'_i)\Rightarrow\Lambda^k_{i=1}S_i$

(I4) $\Lambda^n_{i=1}(\pi_{i2})\Rightarrow\Lambda^n_{i=1}P_{i2}$ (I6) $\Lambda^n_{i=1}after(\pi_{i2})\Rightarrow\Lambda^n_{i=1}Q_{i2}$

The invariant which characterizes the behaviour of π is $\mathbf{I}\equiv(\Lambda^6_{i=1}\mathbf{I}_i)$, where **I** is the precondition of π. The following hold:

(1') $at(\pi)\Rightarrow\Lambda^n_{j=1}at(\pi_{j1})$

(2') $\Lambda^n_{i=1}after(\pi_{i1})\Rightarrow\Lambda^k_{j=1}at(\pi'_j)$

(3') $\Lambda^k_{j=1}after(B_j)\Rightarrow\Lambda^n_{i=1}at(\pi_{i2})$

(4') $after(\pi)\equiv\Lambda^n_{i=1}after(\pi_{i2})$

These formulae describe the synchronization rules governing the nesting of parallel clauses. Used in conjunction with GHL, they would allow to prove properties of programs involving nested parallel clauses.

3.2.4. General form of multi-functions

In the same way as procedure are abstraction of blocks we can define a computational model, the **multi-function**, which may be seen as the abstraction of the parallel clause. It is possible to call a multi-function from a procedure but also from another multi-function, thus providing a general form of nesting.

The description of multi-functions can be seen as a generalization of PASCAL functions.

For example, here is the definition of a multi-function called "mf":

```
muti-function mf;
        (x, y, z:integerl): (u, v, w:integer);

        var
         <declarations>

        cobegin
              (x,y)u: begin    ...    return u end //          (1)
              (z)v: begin      ...    return v end //          (2)
              (y,z)w: begin    ...     return w end            (3)
        coend;
```

This multi-function is made out of three components. Component (1) deals with input parameters (x,y) and delivers the output u, component (2) deals with input parameter z and delivers v and finally (3) deals with input parameters (y,z) and delivers w. Let us describe the usual multi-fonction call (or 1-p call).

a) 1-p multi-function call.

The statement (l,m,n) := mf(a,b,c) describes a statement where input parameters are (a,b,c) and the final result of the call will be assigned to variables l, m, n. The execution of this multi-function call may be depicted as follows:

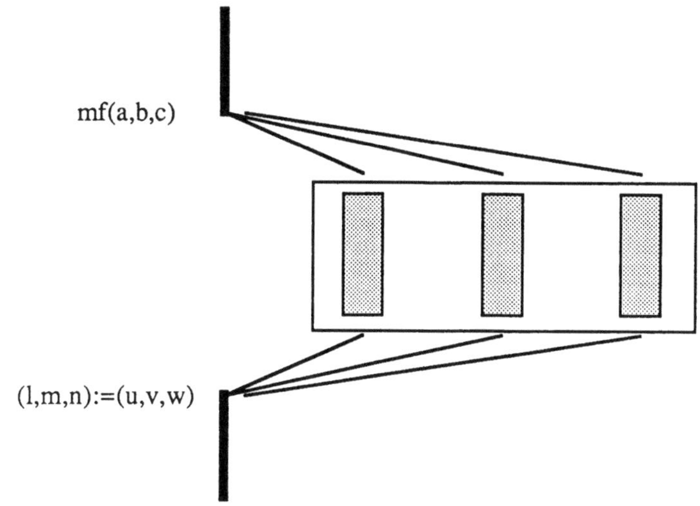

Figure 1: 1-3 call

Where the call mf(a,b,c) results in:

-distribution of input parameters to components of the instance of the multi-function mf created according to the call,

-parallel execution of the components,

-synchronization for result construction and transmission,

-resumption of the caller.

This execution scheme can be seen as a generalization of the usual procedure call (1-1 to 1-3).

b) Coordinated multi-function call (or n-p call).

Let us now introduce the most general multi-function call, the coordinated call (or n-p call). Assuming the multi-function mf previously defined, consider the following program skeleton:

```
    cobegin
(1)     (integer a, k, l; ... ; (k,l):=mf (x<-a).(u,v); ... ) //
(2)     (integer b, c, m; ... ; m:=mf(y<-b,z<-c).v; ...   ) //
(3)     (integer n;  ... ; n:=mf().w;  ... )
    coend
```

The execution of the call to mf can pictured as follows:

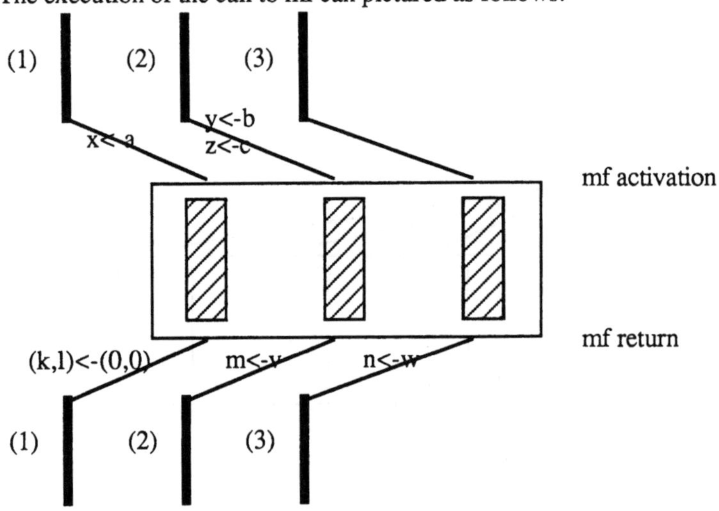

Figure 2: 3-3 call

where this coordinated call results in:

-coordination of components (1), (2) and (3) of the calling parallel clause for input parameter transmission. Notice that component (3) gets coordinated without providing any input parameter,

-distribution of the input parameters to the components,

-parallel execution of the components,

-synchronization of the components for result construction and transmission,

-distribution of the result to the components of the calling parallel clause. For example, notation n:=mf().w means that this component is involved in the coordinated call without providing any input parameter, but, after the processing of the call receives the w part of the result which is assigned to n.

3.2.5. Multi-functions and atomicity.

Our experience with ENCHERE convinced us that the atomicity property is fundamental in the construction of reliable distributed systems. So, in the same way as ENCHERE activities had to be atomic, we require multi-function calls and execution to be atomic. This atomicity ensures that:

i)-either appropriate parameters are transmitted to every component of the multi-function or a failure is reported to the caller.

ii)-in case of failure of a component of the callee, a failure is reported to the caller and the effects of this tentative call are undone.

iii)-all the results, elaborated independently by the components of the callee should be transmitted to the caller. This means that in case of failure during result transmission, this operation is re-attempted till it is successful.

The implementation of points (i) and (ii) makes necessary the design of protocols for distributed agreement. These aspects are currently under investigation.

3.3. Applications of multi-functions.

In this section we describe some potential uses of multi-functions.

a)-Generalized rendez-vous.

The use of nested multi-functions provide a possible mean to implement communications between components of a multi-function. as illustrated by the following example:

```
begin

        multi-function rdv;
                (input: integer): (output: integer);
                cobegin
                        (input): output:
                                begin
                                output:= input
                                end
                coend; #rdv#

        multi-function com;
                cobegin
(1)                     begin
                        ...
                        rdv(input<-9);
                        ...
                        end //

(2)                     begin
                        y:integer;
                        ...
                        y:=rdv.output;
                        ...
                        end //
                coend #com#;

        ...
        #com invocation#
        com
        ...

end.
```

Component (1) of the multi-function com sends the value 9 to the component (2) by calling the muti-function rdv. This nested call implements a generalized form of Rendez-vous [HOAR-78].

One can remark that this use of nested multi-functions may involves too many coordinated calls and, because of the over-synchronization of the execution of components, may become inefficient. Moreover, the logical structure of the multi-function tends to be destroyed. This reason led us to propose that components of multi-functions could communicate through a common shared context, which is described in the header of the multi-function declaration. We do not describe this feature in more details here.

b)-Cooperation between groups of processes.

As an example, imagine the situation where a common agreement must be reached by two groups of people, G1 and G2. The following communication scheme may be taken:

Group G1 has a meeting and makes a proposal which is sent to group G2 for approval or modification, eventually G1 takes the final decision. Notice that this is a group to group communication and that a member of a group cannot be distinguished.

If we model the behaviour of a group by the execution of a multi-function where a component represents a member of the group, control flow governing the above decision taking algorithm may be pictured as follows (fig. 3).

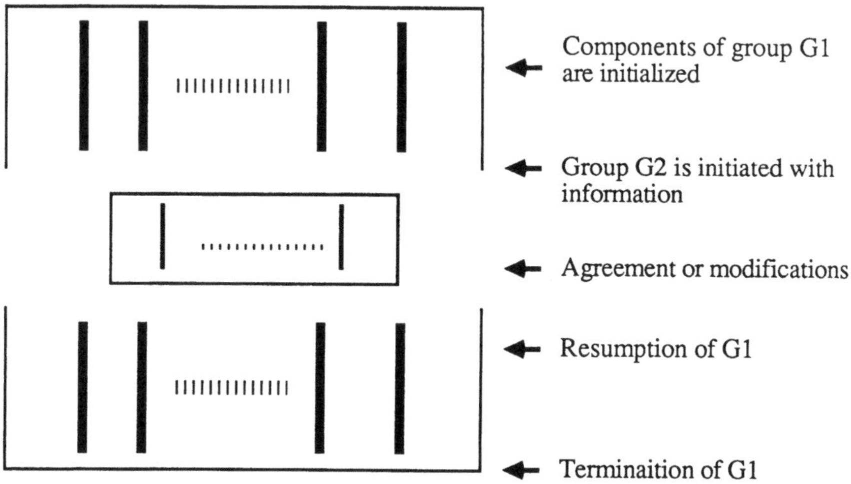

Figure 3: Cooperation between G1 and G2.

Of course, G2 is nested within G1. One can imagine that multi-functions provide a highly structured tool for describing this type of control. In this view, multi-functions may be seen as the abstraction of V-kernel process group [CHER-85].

c)-Global virtual memory.

Let us consider the problem of implementing a global virtual memory over a network as described in [LEAC-83]. In the most general case, an object is made out of a number of pages which may be located on different nodes.

Imagine that we want to allocate a number of pages (say pages) for a new object O. This will be achieve in three steps:

(i) A multi-function ("allocate-pages") is called. A component of allocate-pages runs on each node S_i of the network and determines for each S_i the number (ap_Si) of pages potentially available on node S_i.

(ii) The different numbers ap_Si are determined by a coordinated call to another multi-function "available-pages". Available-pages receives as input the number of pages request for the object, the number (fp_Si) of free pages of each Si and determines for each site the number of pages which can be allocated to the object.

(iii) The execution of the multi-function allocate-pages is resumed and actual allocation takes place on each node by updating local data structures (page lists).

Figure 4 visualizes control and information transfers occuring during this distributed page allocation algorithm:

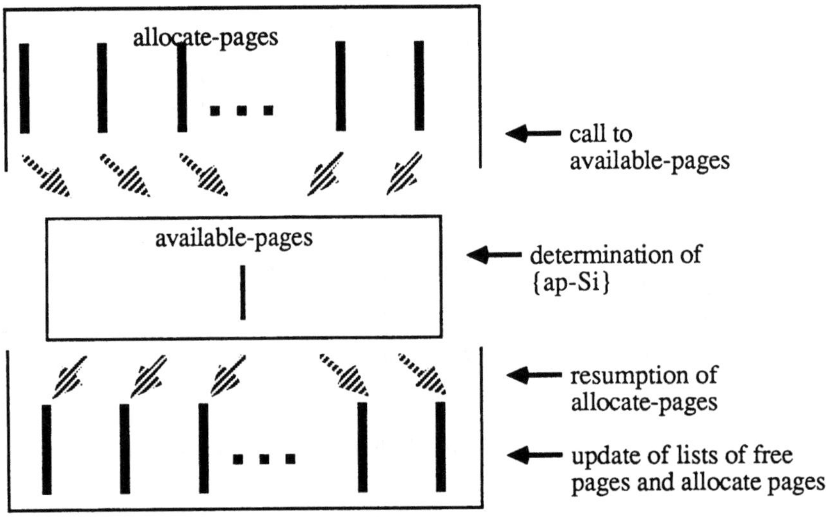

Figure 4: pages-allocation

Now we give a detailed program of the global virtual memory example.

We assume the availability of the type **list** with three operations:

add:**list⊕list→list**, which concatenates two lists.

remove:**N⊕list→list**, which removes the n first elements of a list and creates a new list with these elements.

card:**list→ N**, which delivers the cardinality of a list.

Let us define the two following types:

type site_memory: **record**(allocated-pages, free-pages:**list**)

type obj-repr: **record**(S1_pages, S2_pages: **list**)

Actually, we restrict our problem where only two sites are available. Dealing with the problem in its full generality would lead us to manage list of sites or multisets of sites, thus making the solution less clear. So pages allocated for the representation of an object belong either to S1 or to S2.

The following program represents a possible solution:

```
begin
...
S1, S2 : site_memory;
Obj : obj_repr; #lists of pages#
...
multi-function available_pages;
      (nb_pages, fp_S1, fp_S2 : integer): (ap_S1, ap_S2: integer);

      cobegin
      (nb_pages,fp_S1,fp_S2):(ap_S1,ap_S2):
            var np: integer;

            begin
            if fp_S1≥nb_pages
                  then
                  ap_S1:=nb_pages;
                  ap_S2:=0
                  else
                  np:=nb_pages-fp_S1;
                  if np>fp_S2
                        then
                        #error#
                        ap_S1:=ap_S2:=0;
                        else
                        ap_S1:=fp_S1;
                        ap_S2:=np
                  fi
            fi;
            return (ap_S1,ap_S2)
            end

      coend #available_pages#

multi-function allocate_pages;
      (pages: integer): O: obj_repr;

      cobegin
      (pages):(O.S1_pages):
            var v_ap_S1: integer;
            begin
            v_ap_S1:=available_pages(nb_pages<-pages,
                                          fp_S1<-card(S1.free_pages)).ap_S1;
```

```
            if v_ap_S1≠0
                  then
                  O.S1_pages=remove(v_ap_S1,S1.free_pages);
                  S1.allocated_pages:=
                        append(S1.allocated_pages,O.S1_pages)
                  else
                  O.S1_pages:= nil;
            fi;
            return O.S1_pages
            end  //

      (pages):(O.S2_pages):
            var v_ap_S2: integer;
            begin
            v_ap_S2:=available_pages(nb_pages<-pages,
                                    fp_S2<-card(S2.free_pages)).ap_S2;

            if v_ap_S2≠0
                  then
                  O.S2_pages=remove(v_ap_S2,S2.free_pages);
                  S2.allocated_pages:=
                        append(S2.allocated_pages,O.S2_pages)
                  else
                  O.S2_pages:= nil;
            fi;
            return O.S2_pages
            end

      coend #allocate-pages#

...
Obj:=allocate_pages(pages<-10).O;
...

end.
```

From these examples, it is clear that multi-functions are well suited to program distributed problems. Generally, the treatment of such problems involves three steps:

i)-Invocation of a multi-function each component of which is dedicated to the processing of a particular data fragment. In the last example, the set of pages can be considered as a fragmented data distributed over the set of sites. Each search for free pages is performed by a component of the multi-function.

ii)-common agreement between components. Of course, this phase can be expressed with a nested multi-function.

iii)-termination of the multi-function execution and delivery of the result.

Other distributed problems may be expressed in a very elegant fashion using this high level concept: updating a replicated object or maintaining a distributed naming server are examples.

3.4. Implementation aspects.

A prototype implementation of multi-functions has been developed under UNIX BSD 4.2 on a SUN workstation [LECL-86]. UNIX BSD 4.2 offers two kinds of facilities: (i) inter-machine communications and (ii) Remote Procedure Call.

The execution of a multi-function is made according the following steps:

- Synchronisation of the caller multi-function by the system process,
- Creation of a process for each component of the callee multi-function and t ransmission of parameters,
- Execution of the components of the multi-function,
- Transmission of the results to the system process,
- Resumption of the caller components and result transmission.

All communications are managed by using the Remote Procedure Call facilities.

A second implementation is currently under development as the basic control structure of the GOTHIC system. The implementation machine is a network of two 3-processor machines (called SPS7 [BULL-85]), the basic processor being the M68020.

4.Concluding remarks.

This paper has introduced some new approaches in distributed system structuring and has developed a proposal which extends the classical notion of function to that of multi-function. This concept is used as the basic structuring facility of a distributed operating system currently under development. Multi-functions have proved to be very useful when dealing with replicated or partitioned objects. Furthe experience is still needed in order to fully evaluate the possibilities offered by this new concept.

References:

[BANA-80] BANATRE J.P.
Contribution à l'étude de méthodes et d'outils de construction de programmes parallèles et fiables.
Thèse d'Etat, Université de Rennes 1, december. 1980.

[BANA-84] BANATRE M.
Le Système ENCHERE: une Expérience dans la Conception et la Réalisation d'un Système Réparti.
Thèse d'Etat, Université de Rennes 1, March 1984.

[BANA-86a]
BANATRE J.P., BANATRE M., LAPALME G., PLOYETTE Fl.
The Design and Building of ENCHERE, a Distributed Electronic Marketing System.
Com. of the ACM, Vol 29, n°1, January 1986. pp.19-29.

[BANA-86b] BANATRE J.-P., BANATRE M., PLOYETTE F.
An overview of the GOTHIC distributed operating system.
INRIA Research Report, 504, March 86.

[BANA-86c] BANATRE J-.P., BANATRE M., PLOYETTE F.
The concept of multi-function: a general structuring tool for distributed computing systems.
Proc. of the 6th DCS,Cambridge MA,May 86,pp 478-485.

[BIRR-84] BIRRELL A., NELSON B.
Implementing Remote Procedure Calls.
ACM TOCS, Vol 2, n°1, Feb. 1984, pp. 39-59.

[BULL-85] BULL Cie
Structure générale du SPS7. Manuel de présentation.
BULL Documentation, Jan 85.

[CHER-85] CHERITON D.P., ZWAENEPOEL W.
Distributed Process Group in the V Kernel.
ACM TOCS, Vol. 3, N°2, May 1985, pp. 77-107.

[FORM-86] FORMAN I.R.
Raddle, an informal introduction.
MCC publication, Feb. 86.

[FRAN-85] FRANCEZ N., HAILPERN B., TAUBENFELD G.
Script: A communication abstraction mechanism and its verification.
In NATO ASI Series, Vol. F13, K. Apt Ed., 1985.

[HOAR-78] HOARE C.A.R.
Communicating Sequential Processes.
Com. ACM 21,8, Aug.1978, pp.666-677.

[LAMP-84] LAMPORT L., SCHNEIDER F.
Formal Foundation for Specification and Verification.
LNCS 190, 1984, pp. 203-270.

[LAMP-76] LAMPSON B., STURGIS H.
Crash recovery in distributed data storage systems.
Working paper, XEROX PARC, Nov. 1976.

[LEAC-83] LEACH P.J., LEVINE P.H. DOUROS B.P., HAMILTON J.A., NELSON D.L., STUMPF B.L.
The architecture of an Integrated Local Network.
IEEE Journal on selected areas in comm.,Nov. 1983, pp.842-856.

[LECL-86] LECLER P.
Mise en oeuvre des multi-fonctions sur UNIX BSD 4.2.
DEA Report, University of Rennes, June 1986.

[LISK-77] LISKOV B., SNYDER A., ATKINSON R., SCHAFFERT C.
Abstraction mechanisms in CLU.
CACM 20(8), August 1977, pp. 564-576.

[LISK-84] LISKOV B.
The Argus Language and System.
*LNCS 190,*1984, pp. 343-430.

[MOSS-81] MOSS J.E.B.
Nested Transactions: an Approach to Reliable Distributed Computing.
MIT/LCS/TR-260, M.I.T. LCS, Cambridge, Ma., 1981.

[MUEL-83] MUELLER E., MOORE J., POPEK G.
A Nested Transaction System for LOCUS.
Proc of 9th *SOSP*, Bretton Woods, N.H., Oct. 10-13.

[SHRI-82] SHRIVASTAVA S., PANZIERI F.
The Design of a Reliable Remote Procedure Call Mechanism.
IEEE Trans. on Computer, vol C-31, n°37, July 1982, pp. 692-697

Part 3

Hardware Support for Distributed Computing Systems

DISTRIBUTED COMPUTING SYSTEM ARCHITECTURES:HARDWARE

Presented at NATO Advanced Study Institute, August 86
Izmir, Turkey

M. Bozyigit*

Department of Computer Engineering
Middle East Technical University
Ankara, Turkey

Abstract

Distributed Computing System(DCS) architectures have taken various forms through a considerably short development stage. In a DCS the underlying hardware characteristics are to be transparent to the application level processing. This transparency is regarded to be the function of the operating systems. The standardization efforts in communication protocols and layered approach in the analysis of DCSs has contributed to the advances in distributed control, thus the distributed operating systems.

Fortunately, most distributed architectures are of one of several kinds: computer communication networks, local area networks, and various multicomputer systems (often merged with the first two). The tightly coupled multiprocessor systems, associative processors, data flow machines, and similar parallel architectures are strictly excluded from our discussion of the DCSs.

In this presentation the emphasis is given to computer networks, local area networks, and the channel sharing mechanisms such as point-to-point and multi-point connections which have been basis of the communication medium in many DCSs.

Keywords: Distributed Computing Systems(DCS), DCS Architectures, Distributed Operating System, Computer Communication Network, Local Area Network, Multicomputer System , Communication Channel, Point-to-point and multipoint connections.

* Presently with College of Computer Science & Engineering UPM, Dhahran 31261, Saudi Arabia; on leave from METU

NATO ASI Series, Vol. F28
Distributed Operating Systems. Theory and Practice
Edited by Y. Paker et al.

DISTRIBUTED COMPUTING SYSTEM ARCHITECTURES: HARDWARE

1. INTRODUCTION

Distributed computing systems, can be viewed in terms of three main functional components (or layers):

1. Applications.

2. Operating system and support system software.

3. Hardware.

In fact, computer networks have been the pioneers of DCSs. The standardization efforts on the communication protocols of computer networks have also had considerable effect on the design of distributed computer systems. After all, communication has been one of the main objectives of DCSs. The seven layers (application, presentation, session, transport, network, data link, and physical layers [7]) specified by ISO as OSI model for computer networks are dispersed among the above three main components.

Despite the structuring attempts, sharp boundaries between the consecutive layers are not expected. Even the standardization attempts allow some discrepancies, especially at higher layers. The interface between the operating system layer and the hardware is comparatively well defined. This is because hardware/firmware concepts are often developed by the teams that can work quite independent of the teams that develop complex software systems. The hardware layer of a DCS architecture consists of the following main components:

a. Hosts (or application environment).

b. Communication interfaces, including communication processors and their interfaces with the hosts and the communication lines.

c. Communication Channels including cables, modems, line drivers, multiplexers, concentrators, etc.

In this presentation we will first discuss representative DCS architectures. Next, some common channel sharing mechanisms that are often employed in DCS architectures are presented.

2. TYPES OF DCS ARCHITECTURES

The first systems that have utilized device-computer/

computer-device interconnection were timesharing computer systems where a large number of users can access a computing facility, via terminals. Obviously, such systems are not to be regarded as distributed. The next class of systems close to our view of distributed computing systems are multiprocessor computer systems, where tightly coupled processors share memory and I/O devices using hardware/firmware features. There are cases where it is hard to tell if a multiprocessor system is to be regarded as DCS or not. The architectures such as array processors, and data flow machines also fall outside the scope of the distributed computing system architectures. On the other hand, the architectures that share memory only for communication purposes and those that can operate in loosely coupled as well as tightly coupled mode can be considered as DCS.

The case study examples for such systems are C.mmp [1], Cm* [2], Pluribus [27], and many others[11]. Figures 1,2,and 3 show the block diagram of these three examples. The common property is that the processors involved have their local memory as well as shared global memory. In fact, these are early examples. Despite the fact that the memory is shared, they are regarded as distributed systems as the nodes are able to do local processing and the global memory can be used mainly for communication purposes.

The term multicomputer systems, here, is used for systems in which the processors do not share global memory at all. They can still be rather tightly coupled. The structures such as VTM [6] are multicomputer type of distributed architectures. Figure 4 shows a block diagram of a two-node VTM architecture.

The contemporary distributed computing system architectures fall into one of two main classes:

a. Computer networks, also known as computer communication networks or long haul networks.

b. Local area networks.

2.1 Computer Networks

The real interest in distributed systems has been inspired by the availability of separate computers and devices with possibility of their interconnection. Two important objectives behind the fast developments were resource sharing and need for digital communication. The first operational computer networks have emerged as early as 1970, although, they were then merely research tools [3,5]. ARPA should be singled out being a pioneer in the networking field [3]. The success of these attempts has lead to many other computer networks. Some other known or well documented computer networks have been EPSS (U.K's Experimental Packet Switching System, now converged into operational PSS-Packet Switching System), ALOHA (radio based computer network covering Hawaii islands) [22], CYCLADE [4], TRANSPAC [23], EURONET [24]. The carrier companies have long joined the wagon providing the networking services, Tymnet and Telenet being popular in USA. The computer manifacturers have also been able to provide network architectures which include large software developments. The main architectures are SNA (System Network Architecture) by IBM, DECNET by Digital, BNA (Burroughs Network Architecture) by Burroughs, DSA (Distributed System Architecture) of Honeywell, DCA (Distributed Communication Architectrure) of Univac, and TRANSDATA of Siemens [25]. This list does not cover military and private computer networks.

The layered structure of the ISO's OSI model has clarified the communication mechanisms in computer networks. Even if the networks do not completely obey OSI model there is a loose functional correspondance for each layer specified in the model. It is also a functional structuring requirement, if not necessity, to view a computer network in the form of a communication subsystem and the hosts connected to it. It will then be the responsibility of the communication subsystem to ensure end-to-end reliable communication, i.e., transport services. The distributed operating system should thus utilize this service in user transparent manner, like its IPC- Inter Process Communication- service.

The physical level line connections are normally in the form of point-to-point (see Section 3.1).

2.2 Local Area Networks

The local area networks appear to be the most commonly used systems regarding the DCS architectures. Their communication medium does not extend out of private boundries, and are within several hundred meters to several kilometers. Their geographic locality require them to behave as integrated wholes with all their hardware and software, so the need for distributed operating systems.

The rapid advances in microelectronics and the communication technology, both hardware and software, have accelerated the widespread emergence of local area networks. The operational examples are so large in number that it is not practical to name them here. However, it is possible to classify them according to criteria such as topology and communication mechanisms and then present them in that context. Topologically the local area networks can be classified into four main groups:

1. Connected topology (ad-hoc or irregularly connected).
2. Star topology.
3. Bus topology.
4. Ring topology.

Connected

The early examples of local area networks in which several minicomputer and/or mainframe computers are interconnected has been in an ad hoc manner. The transmission is normally store-and-forward as is the case in computer networks. The interconnection medium is point-to-point. The speed of the communication channels depends on the physical channel access protocol. Obviously higher speeds, in the order of mega bits per second, can be achieved compared to long haul computer networks where speed has generaly been around 50K bits per second or so. Figure 5a shows a connected topology. It has already been stated that the long haul networks are also of connected type.

Star

The star-connected topology is a special case of the connected topology. The switching is done by a central node, break down of which is devastating to the network (see Figure 5b). Such a centralization could also be a source of a bottleneck in handling the traffic flow. There is no elaborate routing problem in star networks. The connected type topology intermixed with star-connected sub topologies form tree shape or hierarchical type topology layouts, in which case routing techniques become important and more involved. The communication mechanism is normally store-and-forward as in the connected topologies. The reliability of the communication can be achieved by node-to-node and/or end-to-end protocols as in the long-haul computer networks.

Bus

Bus type topology allows computers to share a communication medium called a bus. The bus can be parallel as well as serial, but the parallel bus is not very common [26]. Coaxial cable based bus architectures are the most common types. These are also of two basic types: (1) baseband type allows transmission of single digital signal in half-duplex mode, (2) broadband type utilizes frequency modulation technique as in the cable television.

The baseband bus architecture, as a LAN architecture, was first documented by Metcalf as Ethernet [9] (see Figure 5c). Since then it has been accepted as de facto bus type local area network architecture, albeit with different communication mechanisms (or protocols).

The channel access protocol of Ethernet is CSMA/CD (Carrier Sense Multiple Access/ Collision Detection). The principles of CSMA/CD are as follows:

A station on the bus transmits only if the channel is free. There may be more than one station that finds the channel free and starts transmission. The collision of data packets is inescapable. Therefore, each transmitting station listens the Ethernet to see that what it sees is what it is transmitting. Note that a collision can happen only during the time slice equal to twice the time it takes for a bit to propagate from one end of the bus segment to the other end. If no collision is detected than the transmission will continue to the completion. If collision does happen then the collision detecting stations will defer for a randomly determined time interval before transmitting again (see IEEE 802 CSMA/CD standard) [12]. Different algorithms of deference are possible. An algorithm may take the successive collisions into consideration.

Another bus architecture is based on token passing technique. In this technique the stations form a logical ring on the bus. A station can transmit only if it is in possession of the token. The token is put on the bus after the completion of a particular data transmission to be captured by the next station on the logical ring (see IEEE 802 Token Bus standard [13]).

Because of the easy handling and the availability of components at low cost, the bus architectures have been quite common among research organizations and the commercial world. Though, the channel access protocols are not limited to those above.

Ring Type Architectures

The ring type DCS architectures have always been attractive because of implementation advantages, such as simpler protocols and thus simpler interfacing. The common principle of ring type architectures is that the data transmission is one way on the ring shape channel (see Figure 5d).

There have been various studies on ring. Some are known as Pierce Ring [15], Farmer and Newhall Ring [8], Farber Ring [16], Spider Ring [17], DLCN (Distributed Loop Computer Network [10], DDLCN (Distributed Double-Loop Computer Network) [10], IBM Token Ring [28], and Cambridge Ring [19]. Some of the ring type architectures use slotted ring access method, some use register insertion, some are controlled by a supervisory station, and some utilize token technique. IEEE has drawn the specifications for standard Token Ring Access method [14].

The Cambridge Ring (CR) is probably the most publicised ring type network. The CR uses slotted ring access method. The ring is configured to allocate a fixed number of slots, also known as ring packets. A station transmits only if it captures an empty slot. A full slot is freed only by its source. Return of a packet at the originator serves as an acknowledgement for the correct delivery or a negative acknowledgement for unaccepted, or incorrect delivery at the destination. The starvation of certain stations is avoided by allowing the stations to transmit in every second empty slot. The slots in early implementations of CR are 38 bit long each, 16 bits of which are allocated to data only. The CR has also gone under various changes, regarding the slot size, speed, and gateways [29,30].

The token ring access method, like token bus method allows a station to transmit only if it is in possession of the token. The token is forwarded down the cannel following a transmission, allowing round-robin fashion for the right of transmission. Token management is the part of the communication protocol.

These rather lower layer communication protocols can be enhanced and are enhanced further by higher layer protocols. Note that the distributed operating systems have to take the communication protocols into consideration, at least to the extend of drawing the specification of the interfaces of the layers involved.

3. CHANNEL SHARING MECHANISMS

The DCSs that fall outside the particular LANs mentioned above can be considered in two groups. Those of the first group are dedicated type utilising any organization that the present level of hardware and the software allow to perform a particular distributed application or a set of specific distributed applications (see Manner in this book). The second group contains those systems that use rather commonly known interconnection mediums and communication mechanisms that meet their requirements.

The second group utilizes one of the following channels.

1. Point-to-point.
2. Multidrop.

Each of these connections allows various sharing mechanisms.

3.1 Point-to-point

The point-to-point channel is the basic commonly used channel, interconnecting two units directly. This technique has been in use ever since the computers have been interconnected. In fact, the networking started with point-to-point interconnection. The examples are terminal-to-computer and computer-to-computer connections. The connected type of distributed computing sytems in general (LANs and geographically distributed long haul computer networks) fall into this category.

Several point-to-point channels form links (physical or logical circuits) that connect the units indirectly. Common carrier circuits (for transmission of data over the telephone system) and ISO's X.21 physical layer protocol, and V24 (or RS232-C or RS422) interfaces all implement point-to-point channels. These interfaces specify appropriate handshaking mechanisms whereby the senders and receivers can establish communication[7]. The point-to-point channels are multiplexed between a number of users in networking environment.

The communication medium that is used for point-to-point channel can be twisted pairs of wires, coaxial cables, fiber optics cables, and radio tranmission/reception medium (satellite communication).

3.2 Multi-point Channels

Multi-point channel allows more than two stations (computers or devices) to share a channel as in the bus and ring type LAN topologies. The multi-point channel can be used in various modes. The Ethernet employs one such mechanism over the multi-point channel. In fact, ring type connections are also of this type. Multi-point channels can provide a broadcast mode communication, i.e., a station can communicate a message to a set of other stations aligned on the channel, simultaneously. Note that both ring and bus type LANs are appropriate for this type of broadcast mode operation.

The multi-point channel connections can provide three main modes of operations:

1. Reservation.
2. Selection.
3. Random access.

Reservation

In this method the channel can be allocated to a number of stations using FDM- Frequency Division Multiplexing- (in case of broad band) and TDM- Time Division Multiplexing- (in case of baseband). These methods are normally static, i.e., the assignment is done before the actual operation, independent of the upper layer communication protocols. Dynamic time slot (TDM) assignment is also possible.

Selection

The term selection is used to indicate the selection of the station to access the channel, while others wait for their turn. Otherwise, selection is a channel allocation technique. There has been three main allocation techniques in use:

1. Daisy chaining.
2. Polling.
3. Independent request for channel access.

Each of above techniques can be implemented in either centralized or decentralized mode. The physical (and/or logical) configuration for each mode will obviously be different.

In decentralized daisy chain mode a station has to wait for the channel available signal to arrive so that it can acquire the channel. The station forwards the channel available signal after completion of its current transmission, if any, or passes the signal on if it is not in need of the channel. The daisy chain allocation works in a round-robin fashion.

In decentralized polling technique, the polling station broadcasts the address of the station to be polled and signals the channel as available- the use of separate lines for polling is an implementation detail. The polled device will then set the channel to busy state and hold on to the channel for the duration of the unit communication.

The decentralized request method allows each station to put request for the allocation of the channel. The station that has the right (highest) priority will acquire the channel by setting the channel as busy and release it upon completion of the transmission. The priority can be fixed. Alternatively, the priority is recomputed after each use.

Random Access mode (or Contention)

The random techniques are common in radio communication (electromagnetic medium), coaxial cables, and fiber optics. As the name suggests, the channel access attempt is made whenever there is a need for it. In this method the collision is inescapable. There has been several approaches to resolve the collision in random access methods (refer to bus type LANs in Section 2).

Pure Aloha technique allows the stations to transmit whenever there is a need to do so. The stations will then wait for the acknowledgement. If the reception is not acknowledged retransmission takes place. The channel utilization for this technique can be as low as 18% at average. In slotted Aloha technique the time is divided into slots, each slot being as long as a packet. The channel utilization is doubled as the stations can not access the channel at any time. They have to wait for the begining of the slot.

In CSMA-Carrier Sense Multiple Access- technique, another variation of random access, the stations listen to the channel and transmit only if it is free. The collisions still happen; the acknowledgement and the retransmissions are still in effect. The CSMA/CD technique implements a collision detection mechanism and a retransmission mechanism to complement it, as discussed in Section 2.2. The channel utilization can exceed 90%, under favourable conditions [9].

4. CONCLUSION

With the concept of distributed computing systems architectures various systems are put under the same umbrella. What have so far been known as multicomputers, local area networks, and computer networks comply well with DCSs. Fortunately, the standardization attempts in computer communication protocols, especially at low levels, has freed the designers of distributed systems from the burden of the communication hardware/firmware, allowing them to think more on innovative architectural designs for distributed processing and also mechanisms of distributed control. The standardization in communication protocols is also aimed to provide the integration of the heterogeneous systems. The heterogeneity allows vendor independent but application oriented growth of the DCSs. After all, the world is heterogeneous.

On the other hand, homogeneity (or uniformity) in DCSs hardware and software would naturally allow higher cost effectiveness compared to heterogeneous systems, especially at the design and development stages. However, in a real life environment there is place for both.

In the final analysis, regarding which path to follow in acquiring a DCS environment, it will be the objectives of the DCS, the application requirements, and the total cost that would count.

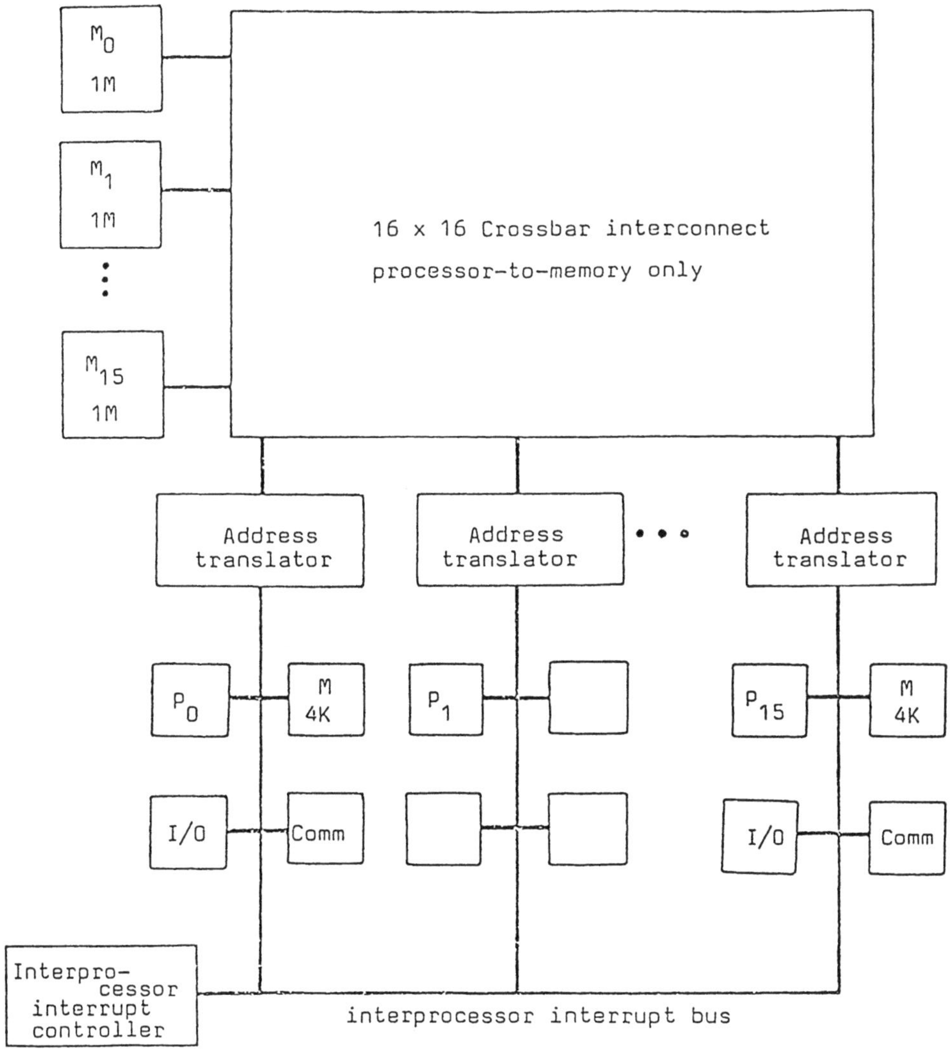

Figure 1. C.mmp: Carnegie Mellon's Multi-mini-processor

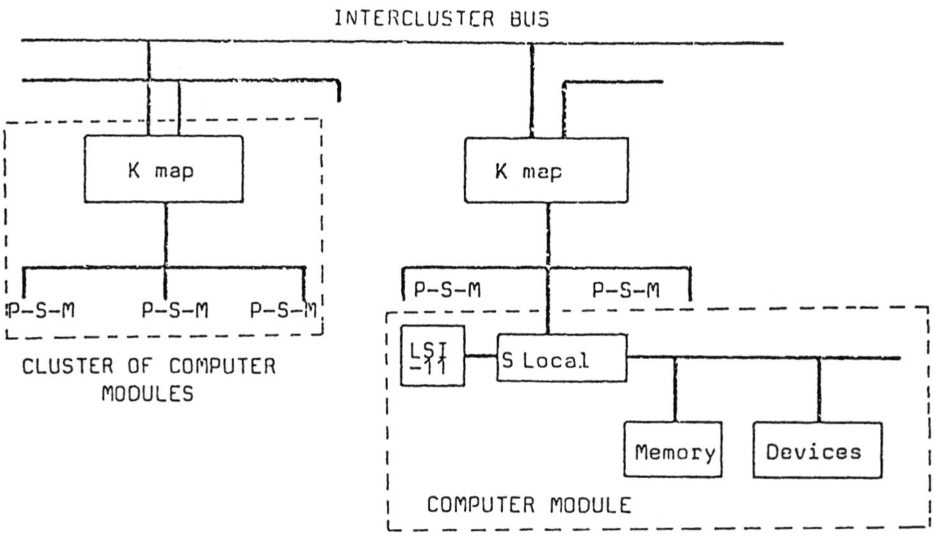

Figure 2. Two-cluster Cm* of Carnegie Mellon University.

DISTRIBUTED COMPUTING SYSTEM ARCHITECTURES: HARDWARE

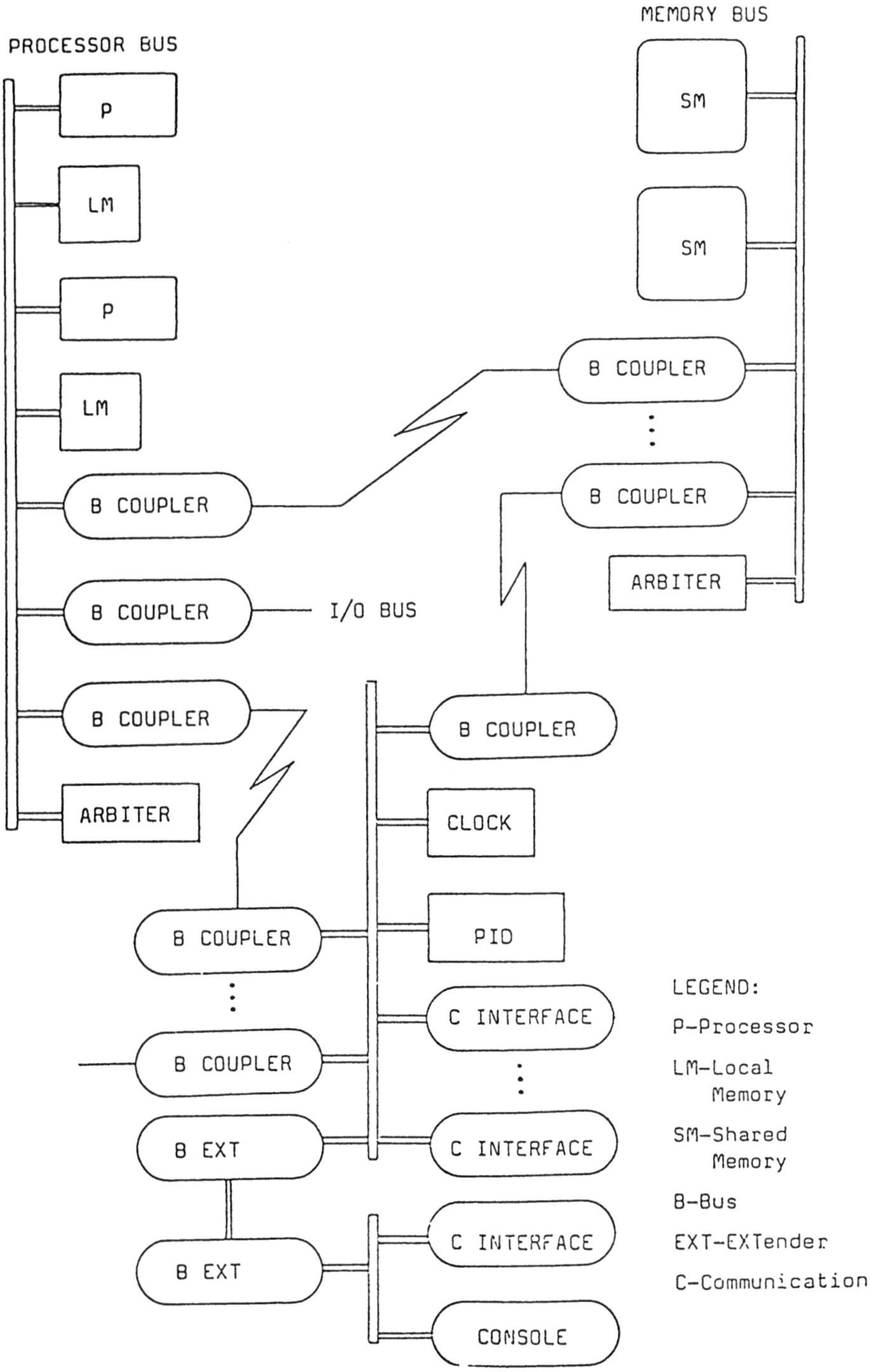

Figure 3. Pluribus Multiprocessor System for ARPA IMP.

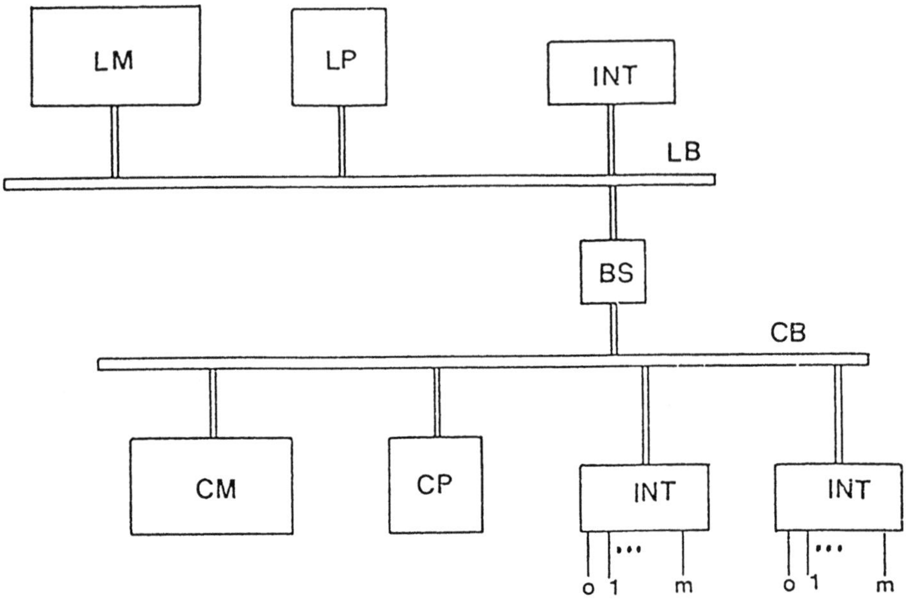

Legend:

LC - Local computer comprising

LP - Local Processor

LM - Local Memory

LB - Local Bus

INT - I/O interface

CC - Communication computer comprizing

CP - Communication Processor

CM - Communication Memory

CB - Communication Bus

INT- I/O Interface to other nodes

BS- Bus Switch

Figure 4. A node in VTM-Variable Topology Multicomputer Architecture.

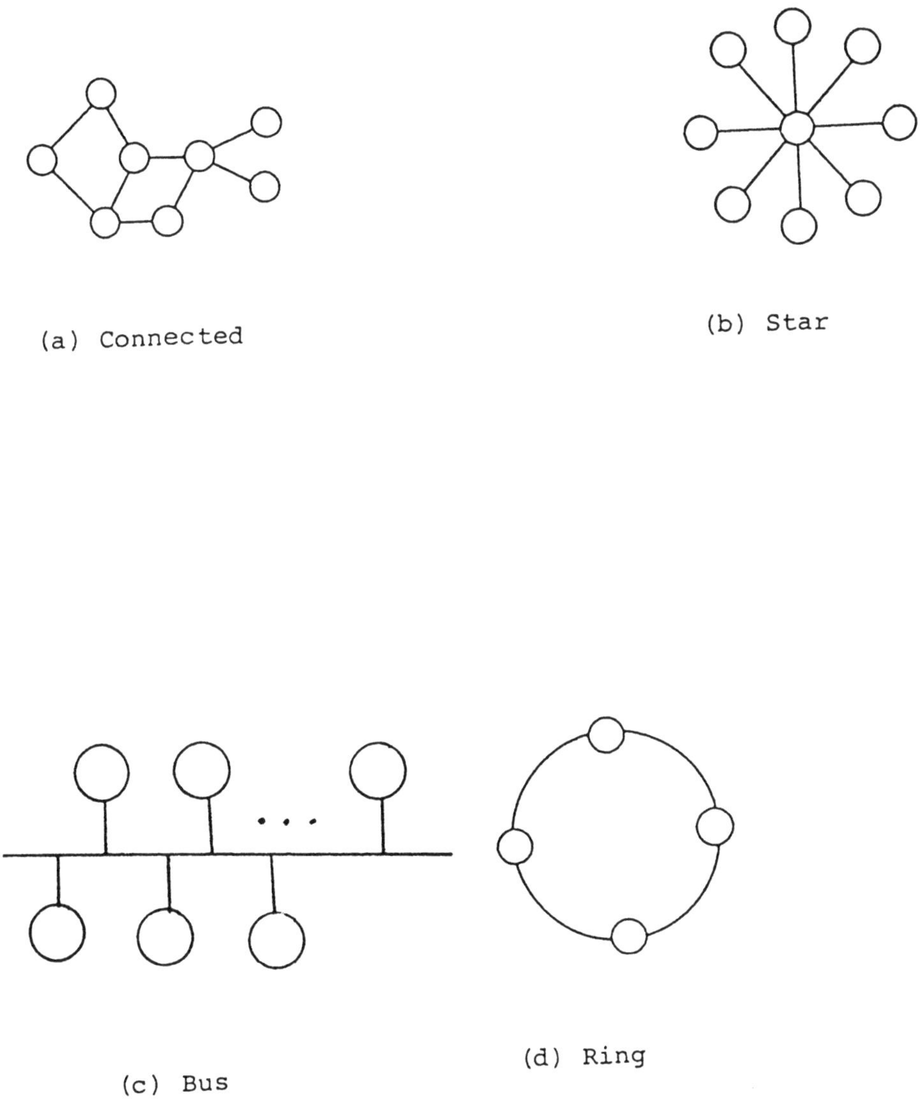

Figure 5. Topological representations for LANs

5. REFERENCES

1. W.A. WULF, C.G. BALL, "C.mmp- a multi mini processor",AFIPS Conf Proc Vol.41, Pt.2, 1972.

2. R.J. SWAN, S.H. FULLER, D.P. SIEWIOREK, "Cm*- A modular multiprocessor", AFIPS Conf Proc Vol.46, 1977.

3. J.McQUILLAN, D.C. WALDEN, "The ARPA design decisions', Computer Networks, Vol.1, Aug 1977.

4. L. POUZIN, "Presentation and major design aspects of the CYCLADE computer network ," Proceedings of 3rd ACM Data Comm Conf., Nov. 1972.

5. D.L.A. BARBER, "Operating experience with NPL networks", Proc of ACM Symp on Computer Networks, IRIA, 1972.

6. M. BOZYIGIT, A Dense Variable Topology Multicomputer System: Specifications and Performance Analysis; Report, PCL, London 1979.

7. A.S. TANENBAUM, Computer Networks; Printice-Hall Inc., 1983.

8. D.J. FARBER, "The distributed computer system", Proc. 7th Annual IEEE Comp. Soc. Int. Conf. 1973.

9. R.M. METCALF, D. BOGGS, "Ethernet: Distributed packet switching for local computer networks", Comm ACM,Vol.19,1976.

10. D. TSAY, M.T. LIU, "MIKE: A network operating system for the distributed double-loop computer network", IEEE Trans SE, Vol.SE-9, No.2, March 1983.

11. L.D. WITTIE, A.M.V. TILBORG, "MICROS,A distributed operating system for MICRONET, a reconfigurable network computer", IEEE Trans SE, Vol.C-29, No.12, Dec 1980.

12. ANSI/IEEE Standars for Local Area Networks, "Carrier sence multiple- access with collission detection (CSMA/CD) access methods and physical layer specifications, 802.3", May 1985.

13. ANSI/IEEE Standars for Local Area Networks, "Token-passing bus access method and physical layer specifications, 802.4", May 1985.

14. ANSI/IEEE Standards for Local Area Networks, "Token ring access method and physical layer specifications, 802.5", May

15. J.R.PIERCE, "Network for block switching of data", Bell Sys Tech Journal 51, NO.6, july 1972.

16. D.J. FARBER, "A ring network", Datamation 21, Feb 1975.

17. A.G. FRASER, "SPIDER-a data communication experiment", Tech Report 23 , Bell Lab, 1974.

18. Joint Network Team, Cambridge 82 protocol specification, Computer Board and Research Council, Dept of Education and Science, 1982.

19. M.W. WILKES, D.J. WHEELER, "The cambridge digital communication ring", Proc Local Area Communication Network Symp., MITRE and NBS, Boston, May 1979.

20. CORNAFION, Distributed Computing System, Elsevier Science Publ , 1985.

21. B.W. LAMPSON, M. PAUL, H.J. SIEGERT, (ed.), Distributed Systems: Architecture and Implementation, Springer-Verlag, 1981.

22. N. ABRAMSON, "The ALOHA system", in Computer Communication Networks, (Eds. Abramson, Kuo), Prentice Hall, 1973.

23. A.DANET, R. DESPRES, A. LE REST, G.PICHON,"The French public packet switching service: The TRANSPAC network", Proc 3rd ICCC, 1976.

24. P. JEGU, "The Euronet Network", Proc. Regional Seminar on Computer Networks, (Ed. M. Bozyigit), METU, Ankara, 1980.

25. A. MEIJER, P.PEETERS, Computer Network Architectures, Computer Sicence Press, 1982.

26. Y. PAKER, H. ENGLISH, M. BOZYIGIT, "NPL multicomputer ring modelling and simulation", in Ring Technology Local Area Network, (Eds. Dallas, Spratt), North-Holland, 1984.

27. D.P. SIEWIOREK, C.G. BELL, A. NEWELL, Computer Structures: Principles and Examples, McGraw-Hill, 1982.

28. W. BUX, F. CLOSS, P.A. JANSON, K. KUMMERLE, H.R. MULLER, E.H. ROTHAUSER, "A local are communication network based on a reliable token ring system", Proc IFIP TC6 Symp on LANs, (Eds. Ravasio, Hopkin, Naffah), North-holland, 1982.

29. W.P. SHARP, A.R. CASH, Cambridge Ring 82 Interface Specifications, Report, UK SERC, Joint Network Team, Sep. 1982.

30. S. TEMPLE, The Design of a Ring Communication Network, Report# 53, University of Cambridge Computer Lab., Jan. 1984.

HARDWARE SUPPORT FOR THE DISTRIBUTED OPERATING SYSTEM OF THE HEIDELBERG POLYP PROCESSOR

R. Männer
Physical Institute
University of Heidelberg
Heidelberg, F.R. Germany

Abstract

A multiprocessor consisting of independent processing elements with local memory and local system and application software is a special case of a distributed computer system (DCS). This paper describes such a system, the Heidelberg Polyp polyprocessor [1], its distributed operating system (DOS), and hardware support for distributed resource sharing. Current versions use 30 clusters with one or a few 32 bit microprocessors each [2,3]. Depending on the configuration, clusters may be general purpose or specialized servers. Clusters offering the same server functions can be grouped into pools of identical resources. Clusters using specialized hardware set up static pools. General purpose processor clusters can be specialized by software and can be assigned to pools dynamically. Hardware support is provided for handling pools independent of their sizes. Thus, adding new members to pools for speed up or shut-down of faulty members can be done software transparently. All processing clusters are interconnected by multiple buses for data transfers and interrupts. The system is managed decentrally by a DOS. A copy of this DOS is stored locally in each cluster. DOS requests may be executed in parallel and operate on common, but distributed system tables. The basic function of the DOS is to assign tasks with certain requirements to clusters supplying these functions and to establish communication between them. Some of the DOS functions may be time critical for certain applications. For that, hardware support is offered, e.g. for setting up an optimal dynamic load distribution within a heterogeneous DCS [4]. Pool-size independent system management as well as hardware scheduling is done via two resource sharing interconnection networks (RSIN) [5]. One of them, the Polybus system [6] allows to address pools as a whole and to request random selection of a member by hardware. The other RSIN, the Syncbus, allows to distribute priority queues of waiting tasks and uses a nonempty queue status as a distributed programmed interrupt to a certain pool. Application of boths RSINs is discussed in detail.

NATO ASI Series, Vol. F28
Distributed Operating Systems. Theory and Practice
Edited by Y. Paker et al.

1. Introduction

Originally, multiprocessor systems were characterized by multiple processor units operating on a common memory. Distributed computing systems, on the other hand, consisted of autonomous computers located in considerable distances and linked via networks. These architectural differences were reflected in the communication structure. Communication between processors in a multiprocessor system was usually done via shared variables, whereas computers in a distributed computing environment communicated via messages.

This sharp distinction between multiprocessors and distributed computing systems could not be maintained during the last years. The first multiprocessors were limited in system size by the speed of the common memory or the bus system connecting the processors with it [7]. These bottlenecks were partly avoided by usage of local cache memories. Dropping memory costs allowed soon to provide each processor with local memory for instructions and private data like task stacks. The resulting two-level communication structure allowed for very high transfer rates between spatially close neighbors units, e.g. processor and local memory, and for moderate transfer rates between units with distances of up to meters. Consequently, multi-level architectures were designed, e.g. were several processor-memory pairs form a cluster. Here the coupling within a pair is very tight but spatially very restricted, the coupling within a cluster moderate but more extended, and eventually the coupling between clusters loose.

Distributed computing systems evolved in the other direction. Starting from individual computers linked via the telephone net, the coupling was strengthened by usage of high speed data links. Spatially closer coupling became reality with widespread installation of workstations and powerful microcomputers. For efficiency reasons such systems are now sharing common resources like disks or printers. An even stronger coupling is required for sharing of data processing resources like special purpose processors or highly intelligent devices like data base managers. Today, many computers of a distributed system consist itself of multiple processors. Such systems are architecturally comparable to the clustered parallel processors mentioned above.

On each level of parallelism, system resources have to be managed. On the cluster level, the system resources are computers and possibly the links between them. Within clusters, resources may be general purpose or specialized processors, memories, all types of peripherals, and buses connecting them. Still one level deeper are the usual resources of single-processor systems. All resources have to be managed, i.e. tasks with specific processing requirements have to be assigned to appropriate resources. This is usually done by operating system software. This software can consist of a single operating system, multiple copies of an operating system, or different operating systems. Only small parallel processors can be managed by a single operating system; this case is not considered here. Large-scale parallel processors as well as distributed systems are managed by cooperating operating systems, also called a distributed operating system. Its main function is to provide primitives like task synchronization and communication, but also to set up an assignment between tasks and resources with an efficiency as high as possible. The cooperation between several operating systems requires unique information about the status of all system resources. If this information is stored centrally, it has to be accessed by all operating systems and possibly represents a bottleneck. If multiple copies are stored to avoid access conflicts, data cohrenece has to be maintained by an updating policy which also restricts the number of participants. Whether these restrictions are important or not depends on the granularity of the application software. Coarse granularity means relatively large tasks with few communication and synchronization overhead. Such software can be executed with high efficiency on smaller systems. Fine granularity allows for higher parallelism and is therefore better suited for large-scale systems. This is, however, only true, when the operating system overhead for task scheduling, resource management, and communication and synchronization is still negligible compared to application program execution. In many cases, the efficiency is limited by access to common tables and operating system execution times [8]. To overcome this limitation, one can support critical operating system functions by hardware.

This paper describes the Heidelberg Polyp system, a multi-level parallel processor. On the outermost level, it can be regarded as a distributed computing system consisting of cooperating clusters. Whereas in principle any number of clusters with arbitrary and possibly different specialization can be used, only a small number of different clusters is usually present. Clusters of the same specialization are regarded as a pool. Pool members can be considered as system resources of the pool type. System management then requires to assign tasks to these resources in an efficient way. This is done by a distributed operating system. It consists of one operating system for one cluster each. All operate on common system tables containing uniquely the status of the whole system. To reduce system overheads generated by execution of operating system requests and by delays due to access to the cluster interconnection network or to common system tables, the distributed operating system is supported by hardware.

Hardware support is offered for access to system resources in a synchronous and an asynchronous mode. In both cases, only the required type of resource is specified by a requestor. The actual selection of a resource of the requested type is done by resource-sharing interconnection networks. The operation of these networks is very general and can be used for management of any kind of resource. In the Polyp system, however, it is used for pool-size independent management of the processor system and for setting up an optimal dynamic load distribution.

The next section gives an overview over the processor architecture. This is followed by a description of the two resource-sharing interconnection networks and their cooperation with the distributed operating system.

2. Overview of the Heidelberg Polyp system

The Heidelberg Polyp system was designed as a general purpose parallel computer, supporting large and medium grain applications. Performance figures were taken from two special problems, real-time filtering of data from nuclear physics experiments and higher level image processing. These applications called for a computing power of up to 100 MIPS (million instructions per second) and 100 MFLOPS (million floating-point instructions per second). Today this can most efficiently be achieved by an assembly of 32-bit microprocessors. With a typical speed of 1 - 3 MIPS per processor and 0.3 MFLOPS per floating-point coprocessor, approximately 30 - 100 microprocessors are required to provide the requested computing power. Application dependent, it may be advantageous to cluster a few of these processors to form a very powerful processing cluster. One example in the Polyp system is a cluster consisting of a 68000 CPU and a combination of a 68020 CPU and a 68881 floating-point coprocessor. The clusters themselves have to be interconnected for transferring data into or out of the system (I/O), for communication between clusters, and for access to common system resources, e.g. a common memory. The required inter-cluster bandwidth is highly application dependent. The current applications mentioned above require bandwidths between 10 to 100 MBytes/s. This bandwidth is provided by an interconnection network.

The total computing power of a Polyp system depends on the number of processors respective clusters used. In the simplest case, all clusters are of the same type, so that all of them constitute a pool of identical resources. If there are clusters of different type, the Polyp system consists of several pools. The pool size, i.e. the number of members within a pool, is a system parameter which can be adjusted according to the application needs. This allows to balance the system for highest efficiency. An arbitrary distribution of tasks over a pool of identical resources is, however, only possible, when all pool members are identical not only in their function, but also in their interconnection topology. This requires an homogeneous interconnection network for linkage of clusters. The Polyp system uses a multiple bus system, the Polybus, for that. Each bus is comparable to modern microprocessor buses like VME or P896. The Polybus system consists of any number of 32-bit buses operating independently and in parallel. Each two clusters may be connected by each bus. The Polybus system can therefore be considered as a pool of buses. The total bandwidth of this system increases linearly with the number of buses used. The general structure of such a Polyp system is shown in fig. 1. Pool-organized distributed systems can easily be managed, so that faulty members of a pool are bypassed automatically. In this case, the system performance is only degraded, but the system keeps running. Graceful degradation is especially important for large-scale systems, because the probability for totally error-free operation decreases exponentially with the system size. The Polyp system uses therefore Hamming-coded addresses and data for storage and during transfers via the Polybus system.

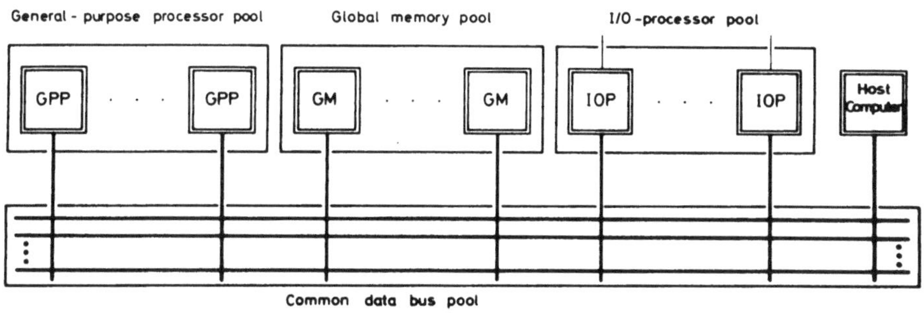

Fig. 1: General structure of a Polyp system with pools of specialized clusters and the data bus pool

Each cluster of a Polyp system makes available a certain set of server functions. These may be trivial, e.g. storage of data, or complex, e.g. the parallel execution of a set of tasks. Besides of their specialized features, all clusters have some common functions. One is active or passive participation on Polybus transfers including bus arbitration, protocol handling and address decoding. Another one is support of fault-tolerance including bit correction, rerun of failed transfers etc. The presence of local memory is still another feature common to all clusters. Clusters providing processing functions use one or more processing units, possibly with different specializations. For that reason, clusters have a modular structure. Fig. 2 shows the internal structure of a cluster, in this case a processor module. It consists of several units connected by a single bus. There are two processor units, one with an additional cache memory for speedup. These processors operate with instructions and on data stored in multiple local memory units. Fault-tolerant operation is supported by an error-correction unit. The cluster-internal bus is connected to the Polybus system via multiple busswitch units. Clusters with other specialization can easily be assembled mainly from such units. Global memory clusters are obtained by omitting processor and cache memory units. Clusters specialized for

I/O use DMA controllers instead of processor units etc.

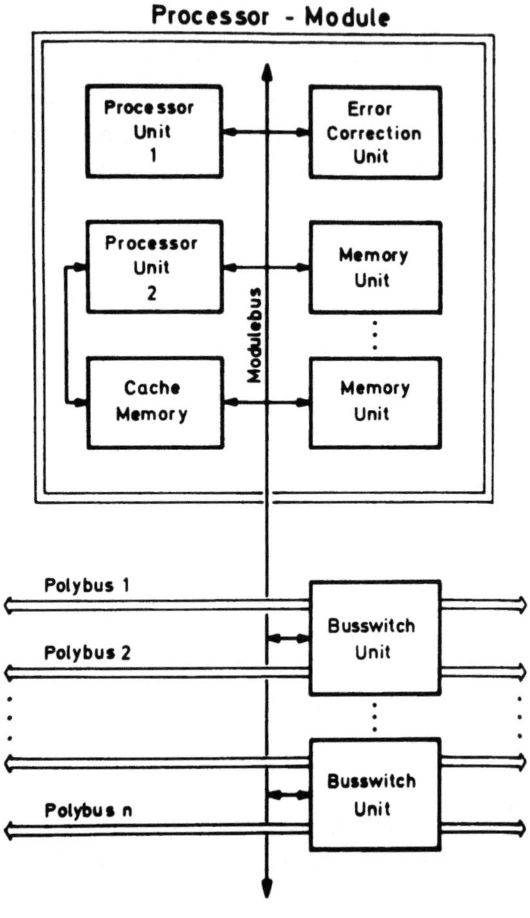

Fig. 2: Internal structure of a cluster, here a processor module

The Polybus system connecting all clusters is a two-stage interconnection net with a multiple common data bus structure. It is the communication path used for all transfers, e.g. messages. All buses work asynchronously and independently of each other. The multiple bus structure is transparent to connected clusters. Circuit switching through the bus system is managed by a decentralized arbiter which allows prioritized access as well as fair treatment of requests. Random assignment of buses to requesting clusters enables automatic bypassing of faulty paths by re-try. A snapshot of a Polybus operation is given in fig. 3. Shown are modules with their respective module-internal bus. All modules are connected by a pool of buses which are used for transfers and optionally by a special bus controlling priority access to the bus system. The figure shows an established communication path from one module to another one via two busswitches. Also shown is a path which is directed to a busy module and is therefore only routed up to the second busswitch, where the access conflict is resolved by the arbitration. The assignment of free buses as well as conflict resolution is done via a decentral arbitration. It is based on rotating tokens signalling available buses. The arbitration is expandable in the number of clusters connected as well as in the number of buses used.

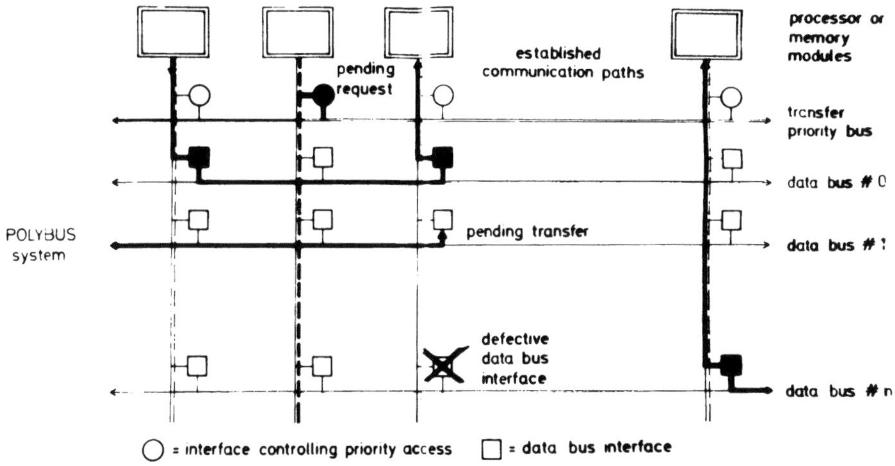

Fig. 3: Snapshot of a Polybus operation

The pool of buses could in principle be managed by software. In most cases, however, software handling would cause delays much higher than individual transfers and is therefore not acceptable. Hardware management of the bus pool is moreover very simple. A cluster requesting a communication path asserts this request to the whole bus system. Free buses are characterized by rotation of their respective token. A bus is therefore reserved for exclusive usage by stopping its token. Because all buses work asynchronously, there is a chance of stopping more than one token for a single request. In this case, a second token is used to uniquely mark one of the reserved buses. This simple kind of pool management is used in the Polyp system also for handling pools of resources of other type.

3. Resource-sharing with the Polybus system

A pool is a set of identical resources. In the case of clusters, identical means the same set of functions. This set can be sugessted by a certain hardware structure. A cluster containing not only an integer microprocessor, but additionally a floating-point coprocessor is better suited for scientific computation tasks than without coprocessor. But even clusters identical from the hardware point of view can have different function sets if assigned so by software. Depending on the application, it might even be advantageous to dynamically change the assignment of clusters to pools. To allow this, all clusters of a Polyp system not only have a unique address for direct access, but additionally a freely programmable pool address. This pool address may be used by an arbitrary number of modules. All clusters having the same pool address constitute the respective pool. By loading a new pool address, pool membership can at any time be changed arbitrarily.

The Polyp system provides several modes to access clusters via their pool address. One of them is a broadcast mode, where a write transfer is executed to all members of the addressed pool in parallel. More often required is, however, to access any cluster of a pool with a certain function set. Here the selection can be done in two different ways. On one hand, the requestor is responsible for selection of a proper cluster. In this case, it can use the pool identification to route a path through the interconnection network. Such methods have been proposed by Rathi et al. [9] and Jenevein et al. [10]. They show the usual disadvantage of centralized solutions, i.e. deficient extendability and susceptivity to faults. On the other hand, it can be ceded to the interconnection network itself to select one of the requested clusters. Destination address is here not a certain cluster, but the pool with the needed function set. Networks with such a selection feature are called resource-sharing interconnection nets [11]. Wah investigated a certain type of such networks. There, the availability status of the requested type of resource is transmitted to all requestors before path routing to the resource is actually done. This is to avoid blocking of the network in the case where no cluster of the requested type is available at all. In the Polyp system, a slightly different approach was taken.

Assignment of a resource to a requestor is done in a two-step process. The requestor first asserts the pool address to the network and informs all clusters about the intended selection operation. After that it creates a token which propagates along the bus until it is stopped by a cluster. This cluster is then selected and gets assigned to perform the required function. Presupposition for stopping the token is, of course, a match between the asserted pool address and the pool address of the cluster. A second supposition can be specified by the requestor. Depending of the transfer type chosen, all clusters of the addressed pool will try to stop the token or only those which are currently not busy. In case a nonexisting pool is addressed or all clusters of the requested pool are busy, the token is passed on from cluster to cluster cyclically. Because the busy status can change during this time or because pool membership can change dynamically, it is possible to get a resource assignment within a reasonable time. Otherwise, the request is aborted with an error after timeout.

This kind of pool management can be used when the execution of certain tasks is necessary immediately, i.e. where the requestor has to wait for the assignment of the appropriate resource. In other context, this is called a synchronous operation.

4. Resource-sharing with the Syncbus system

The described method to handle pools of resources is however only applicable, when the averaged waiting time between a request and the assignment of the resource is short. Otherwise it may block buses of the Polybus system and may therefore degrade the transfer bandwidth considerably. This situation can arise, if resources are requested with priorities. An example is a program requesting low priority output of data to disk. Here it is not necessary to get an immediate response from the assigned resource. Instead the requested task will be put into a queue. The queue elements are then distributed over the appropriate pool according to a certain scheduling policy. Such scheduling functions are traditionally performed by operating systems. Many resources, e.g. a disk drive, can only be started to execute a certain function. Thereafter, they remain uninterruptable until completion. Other resources allow to interrupt the execution of certain functions, to start another one, and to complete the interrupted one later. The most well-known example of resources of this type are processors in a prioritized multi-tasking environment.

To achieve here an optimal assignment of m tasks to n processor clusters (m > n), two steps are necessary, the selection of n tasks according to their priority and the assignment to specific clusters. In case there are pools with different function sets, this selection has to be done for each pool separately.

Task selection and assignment are required only at specific instants, and that whenever the number of tasks or their priority distribution is modified. This happens as a result of status changes of tasks caused by operating system requests. In the Polyp system, each cluster runs an operating system. All of them work on common system tables stored in common memory. This memory can be realized as a separate cluster. However, it can also be distributed over several or all clusters as discussed later. The system tables describe the status of all tasks and all processor clusters. In case there is only one pool, the cluster status is described sufficiently by stating the priority of the currently assigned task.

Tasks may be in one of three states:

- Suspended
  Such tasks are not executable due to any kind of waiting condition.

- Waiting
  Such tasks are executable, but currently not assigned to any processor cluster due to their low priority. Waiting tasks are put into a queue according to their priority. As soon as a processor cluster becomes available, the first element of the queue of highest priority gets assigned to this cluster.

- Active
  Such tasks are assigned to a processor cluster and are executed.

Between these states, transitions are possible. They request different actions by the operating system. Possible transitions are:

- Suspended to suspended
  This transition happens, whenever the priority of a suspended task is changed. It does not require any further action.

- Waiting to suspended
  This transition happens, whenever a condition occurs which forbids the execution of a waiting task. This task has therefore to be dequeued.

- Active to suspended
  This transition happens, whenever a task currently being executed has to be stopped temporarily. The interruption makes a processor cluster available. The operating system has to assign it to one of the waiting tasks of highest priority.

- Suspended to waiting
  This transition happens, as soon as all suspension conditions of a task are raised and it becomes executable. This task has to be entered into the queue of proper priority. In this instant it can occur that the priority of the new task is higher than the lowest priority of all tasks currently in execution. Optimal scheduling requires then to interrupt one of these tasks and to assign its processor cluster to the new task. The interrupted task has

to be enqueued according to its priority.

- Waiting to waiting
  This transition happens, whenever the priority of a waiting task is changed. It is required to dequeue this task and to enqueue it again according to the new priority.

- Active to active
  This transition only happens, when the priority of a task is changed which is currently executed. An increase in priority requires no further actions. After a decrease other tasks with higher priorities might be waiting. In this case, a new assignment of tasks to processor clusters is necessary.

All other transitions can not be requested directly, but might happen only as a consequence of a preceeding state transition. The actions of the operating system after state transitions can be condensed into

- management of task pools
- management of processor cluster pools.

Both pools are further partitioned into subpools of different priority. For all these pools, the number of pool members can change dynamically. In the case of task pools, this happens as a result of the state transitions discussed above, but also during creation or termination of tasks. The size of processor cluster pools changes with each new assignment. Management of these pools may constitute a system bottleneck. It is caused by access conflicts to common system tables. This is the case for software with fine granularity. A certain improvement can be achieved by distributing these system tables over all clusters and by providing parallel access to the individual pieces. In the Polyp system, this is possible via an address mapping mechanism [6] and the multiple independent buses of the Polybus system. Such an improvement, however, can not remove this bottleneck.

This is possible by also using a resource-sharing interconnection network for management of task pools and processor cluster pools. Such a network has to determine, whether a new assignment of tasks to processor clusters is necessary. In this case, it has to select one member of both pools each. In the Polyp system, this is done with a second bus system, the Syncbus. The Syncbus system connects all processing resources as shown in fig. 4. If there is only one kind of processor cluster, the Syncbus consists only of a single bus. Otherwise, it is assembled of one bus per pool. For a discussion of its principle of operation it is assumed for the present that only a single pool exists.

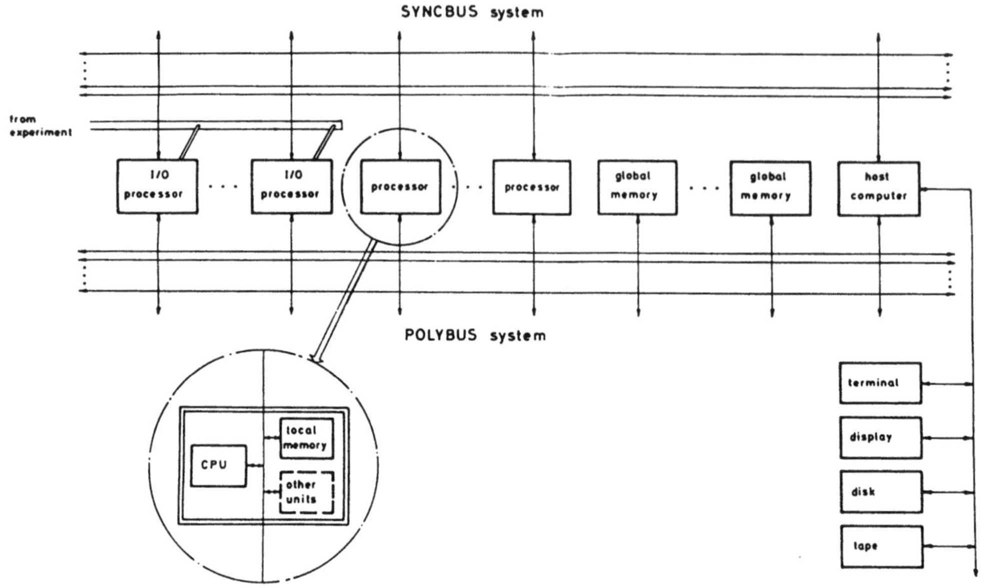

Fig. 4: A Polyp system including the Syncbus

Under this presumption, each processor cluster contains an interface unit which connects it with the Syncbus system. As shown in fig. 5, it consists of three rather independent sections. The transmitter section manages local waiting tasks according to their priority in the whole system. The receiver section manages the own processor cluster according to its priority in the whole system. The comparator section determines, whether a task reassignment is necesary. To discuss the interface's operation, one proceeds from a situation where only active and suspended tasks exist, i.e. where no task is waiting. The priority distribution of these tasks may be arbitrary. Tasks of the same priority are allowed. All processor clusters operate with the priority of the task assigned to them. If there is a cluster without any task, it waits at a priority lower than all possible task priorities.

The priority of a processor cluster is stored in a register in the receiver section of the Syncbus interface (task priority register). It is updated after each priority change by the local operating system. The n bits of the processor cluster priority are now decoded and put onto a set of 2^n Syncbus lines. There is one line for each priority. These lines are realized in open-collector technology. This means that any number of interfaces can assert their bit states at the same time, at which all bits of the same priority are ORed together. This set of Syncbus lines therefore carries the information, what processor cluster priorities exist at each instant in

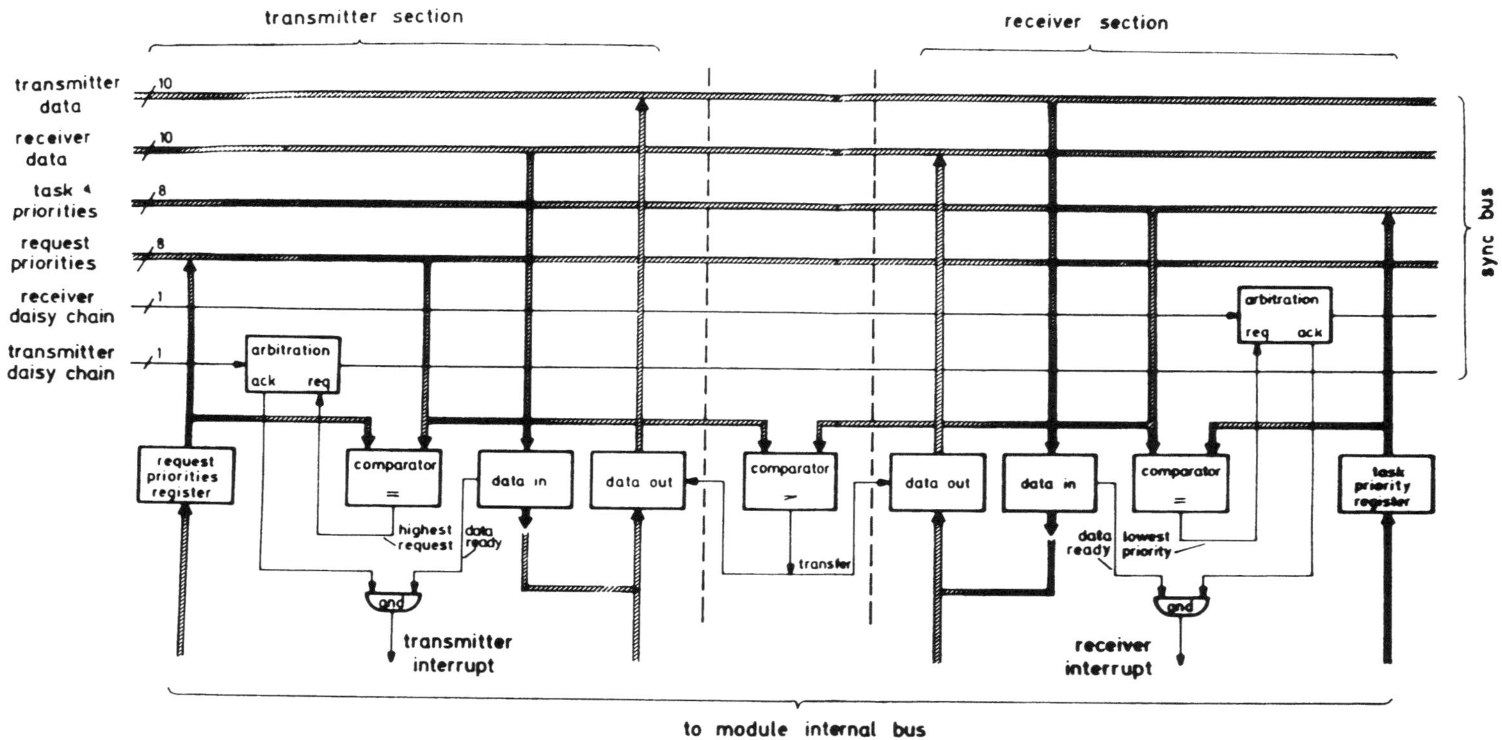

Fig. 5: Internal structure of a Syncbus interface

the whole system. A task reassignment has to be done at the very instant when a task becomes executable, whose priority is higher than the priority of the processor clusters with currently lowest priority. The membership in the subpool of all processor clusters with lowest priority can now easily be determined by the help of the discussed processor prioriоty lines of the Syncbus. Each interface reads back these lines, decodes the lowest priority existing system-wide, and compares it with the priority of the own cluster. Only if both are equal, it is possible to assign this cluster a new task. The selection which member of this subpool to take is arbitrary. It is done in analogy to the management of the Polybus pool. On the Syncbus exists a token, which can only be stopped by members of this subpool. Because there is at least one processor cluster of lowest priority at each instant, one of the clusters is usually keeping the token. This selection is updated automatically in case of a modified priority distribution.

This can happen as a result of a state transition of a task. Such a transition is caused by a modification of system queues during execution of local operating system requests. By application of the Syncbus system, these queues can be decentralized. Each processor cluster stores locally queues of such tasks, which are put into the waiting state by the local operating system. There is, as before, one queue for each priority. Whether there is any need for a task reassignment or not depends on whether the individual queues contain elements or not. These nonempty queue states are represented by hardware with a bit of a second register (request priority register) in the transmitter section of the Syncbus interface. This register is put onto another set of Syncbus lines in analogy to the priority of the processor cluster. These lines carry the information, what queues in the whole system are nonempty.

In case of a task-processor reassignment, a task of currently highest priority will be assigned to a processor cluster of currently lowest priority. The selection of this task is done exactly like described above. All task priorities are read back by each interface, but now the highest one is decoded. In case the local task queue of this priority is nonempty, this processor cluster has queued a task which might be the next one to be executed. The final selection of a single task is again done by a rotating token which can be stopped by only those clusters.

Eventually it remains to decide, whether a reassignment is actually necessary. This can easily be done with the local knowledge of the task queue states and processor cluster priorities. It is necessary exactly when the highest priority of all nonempty queues exceeds the lowest priority of all processor clusters. This is determined in the comparator section of the Syncbus interface. If so, information is exchanged between both selected clusters, and interrupts to the processor units are generated. One processor dequeues the accepted task locally. The other one interrupts the execution of its current task, puts it into its local task queue, and starts execution of the new task.

The selection of clusters via a rotating token is independent of the number of pool members actually present. It therefore still works correctly, if only a single member exists, like in a single-processor system. In this situation, the only cluster creates requests for execution of tasks and accepts them according to its priority. This is possible, because all three sections of the Syncbus interface work independently of each other. Speed advantages result from determination of a required reassignment by hardware.

This method of a decentralized hardware supported task and processor cluster scheduling can easily be extended for the case, where more pools exist. Here, one pool management, i.e. one Syncbus, is used per pool. In this situation it has to be distinguished what pool a certain task can run on and what task a certain processor cluster can execute. Generally, any processor cluster can create requests for execution of arbitrary tasks. It therefore has to be connected via one transmitter section of a Syncbus interface with all existing Syncbuses. On the other hand, a processor cluster can only execute tasks, for whose execution it is suited. It is therefore connected via a receiver section of a Syncbus interface only with the Syncbus belonging to its own pool. This is shown in fig. 6.

The Syncbus system is superior to software pool management for several reasons:

- It decentralizes task queues and reduces therefore access conflicts at common system tables. Access to local queues can take place with arbitrary parallelism.

- It makes superfluous system tables describing the state of all processor clusters. This additionally reduces access conflicts.

- It allows to execute the time-critical part of the scheduling process completely within the Syncbus system, without any interruption of processors. Such interruptions take place only when a reassignment is actually necessary. After an interrupt, the scheduling process is already finished.

Compared to resource-sharing with the Polybus system, the Syncbus operates asynchronously. Requests may be created at any time. After creation, the requesting taskcontinues execution. The request may be granted at any time later. The requesting task is notified of that.

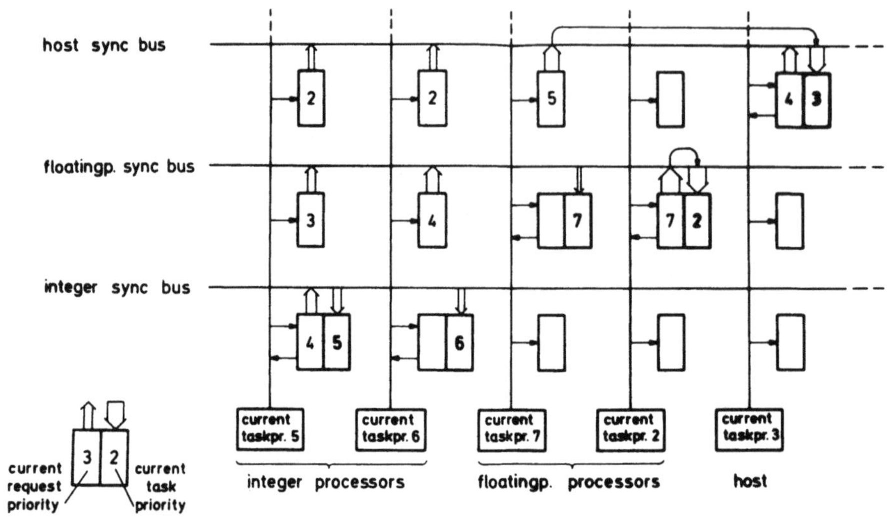

Fig. 6: Snapshot of a multiple Syncbus operation

5. Conclusions

The Polyp system uses two types of resource-sharing interconnection networks. The Polybus system can be used to manage pools of identical resources synchronously. The Syncbus system undertakes preemptive scheduling of tasks and processor clusters in a distributed system consisting of identical or different clusters. It also can be used to manage system resources other than processors. It has been shown perviously [4] that this method allows to increase the efficiency of certain application program executions by up to two orders of magnitude.

Several Polyp systems were set up until now. Fig. 7 shows a 30-processor Polyp system used at an experiment in nuclear physics in Heidelberg.

Fig. 7: A 30-processor Polyp system

References:

[1] Männer R., Deluigi B., Saaler W., Sauer T., v. Walter P.: Design and Realization of the Large-Scale Multi-Microprocessor System "Heidelberg Polyp"; Proc. 1st Int'l Conference on Computers and Applications, Beijing, China (1984) 264 - 270

[2] Bartels P. H., Männer R., Shoemaker R. L., Paplanus S., Graham A.: Computer Configurations for the Processing of Diagnostic Imagery in Histopathology; in: Uhr L. et al., eds.: Evaluation of Multicomputers for Image Processing; Acad. Press, New York, N.Y. (1986)

[3] Griswold W. G., Bartels P. H., Shoemaker R. L., Bartels H. G., Männer R., Hillman D.: Multiprocessor Computer System for Medical Image Processing; in: Duff M. J. B. et al., eds.: Intermediate Level Image Processing: Bonas Workshop on Languages, Architectures, and Algorithms for Image Processing; Acad. Press, New York, N.Y. (1986)

[4] Männer R.: Hardware Task/Processor Scheduling in a Polyprocessor Environment; IEEE Trans. Comp. **C-33**, 7 (1984) 626 - 636

[5] Wah B. W.: A Comparative Study of Distributed Resource Sharing on Multiprocessors; IEEE Trans. Comp. **C-33**, 8 (1984) 700 - 711

[6] Männer R., Deluigi B., Saaler W., Sauer T., v. Walter P.: The Polybus - A Flexible and Fault-Tolerant Multiprocessor Interconnection; Interfaces in Computing **2**, 1 (1984) 45 - 68

[7] McGehearty P. F.: Performance Evaluation of a Multiprocessor Under Interactive Workloads; Rep. CMU-CS-80-137, Carnegie Mellon Univ., Pittsburgh (1980)

[8] Vaughan R. F., Anastas M. S.: Limiting Multiprocessor Performance Analysis; Proc. Int'l Conference on Parallel Processing (1979) 55 - 64

[9] Rathi B. D., Tripathi A. R., Lipovski G. J.: Hardwired Resource Allocators for Reconfigurable Architectures; Proc. 1980 Int'l Conference on Parallel Processing (1980) 109 - 117

[10] Jenevein R., Degroot D., Lipovski G. J.: A Hardware Support Mechanism for

Scheduling Resources in a Parallel Machine Environment; Proc. 8th Annual Symposium on Computer Architecture (1981) 57 - 66

[11] Wah B. W., Hicks A.: Distributed Scheduling of Resources on Interconnection Networks; Proc. NCC (1982) 697 - 709

Part 4

Case Studies

The Apollo DOMAIN Distributed File System

Paul H. Levine
Apollo Computer Incorporated
Chelmsford, Massachusetts 01824
USA

Abstract

The Apollo DOMAIN® system is a fully operational distributed computing environment for a network of personal workstations and network servers. When it was first developed in 1980, its distributed system focus was on a file system that provided users of autonomous workstations with the same ease of file sharing they enjoyed with central time-sharing systems. While the DOMAIN system has since been extended to provide a stronger base for additional distributed system facilities, this examination of the Apollo DOMAIN system will deal primarily with the design and implementation of the DOMAIN distributed file system.

Introduction

The principle motivation for the development of a distributed file system is the need to provide information sharing. While new technology has reduced the need to share processing power, the need to share information among co-workers is intrinsic and permanent. Speed and convenience of sharing are most important when computer users work in close-knit teams. The introduction of high-performance personal workstations placed a local area network (LAN) between the computer user and the bulk of the data generated and used by his or her team members.

The ease with which the team members can exchange their designs, data, images, and documentation contributes in large part to the ease with which those people can share their ideas. This, in turn, determines the productivity of an individual as a member of a team. These team members use their workstations to design, prototype, simulate and document their project. Their ability to simply and efficiently share the computing system's data also greatly affects the kinds of tools that can and will be developed to run on LAN-based computing systems, both by the end-users of the system and ap-

NATO ASI Series, Vol. F28
Distributed Operating Systems. Theory and Practice
Edited by Y. Paker et al.

plication software developers that cater to specific engineering, scientific and business markets.

The basic file system data sharing requirements of a team using a network of workstations can be stated simply. These team members need the complete freedom and flexibility to use the project data files safely. They share their files constantly and at a minimum need a file system model that provides the same degree of data-sharing transparency that their old time-sharing machine provided. Such a model provides data consistency (the instant a file is changed, all other users see the change), naming consistency (every team member can always access a file by giving the same name), authentication consistency (all workstations are bound by a common mechanism for access control), and performance (one team member shouldn't have to fight to get some piece of data kept on a local disk so that his or her job will run acceptably). These requirements formed the basic design goals of the Apollo DOMAIN distributed file system.

The remainder of this paper provides an in-depth examination of the design and implementation of the DOMAIN distributed file system. The first section provides context by briefly introducing the Apollo DOMAIN workstation environment. The second section examines the design goals in more detail. The third section presents a framework for considering file system design, and it is followed by several sections that present the DOMAIN system architecture within that framework. The final section reviews the original implementation decisions in light of new experience and discusses alternatives we have more recently considered.

Apollo DOMAIN Workstation Environment

A DOMAIN system consists of a collection of powerful personal workstations and server computers (generically, nodes) interconnected by a high speed local network [NELS-84]. Users interact with their personal nodes via a display subsystem, which includes a high resolution raster graphics display, a keyboard, and a locating device (mouse, touch pad, or tablet). A typical display has 1024 by 1280 pixels, and "bit BLT" (bit block transfer) hardware to move arbitrary rectangular areas at high speed. Server nodes have no display, and are controlled over the network.

While there are several models of both personal and server nodes, all run essentially the same operating system software (different only to account for the vagaries of hardware implementation). Each node offers memory management unit (MMU) support for 128 processes; each process is able to address as much as 256 megabytes of demand-paged virtual memory. All nodes are able to support connections to hard disks, floppy disks and tape, although no disk storage is required for a node to operate. Server nodes support standard peripheral buses and, when configured as file servers, can have 500 to 1000 megabytes of disk storage; those configured as peripheral servers can have printers, magnetic tape drives, plotters, and so forth.

Each node is equipped with network connection hardware. The network originally designed by Apollo is a 12 megabit per second baseband token passing ring [LEAC-83]. (Other ring implementations are described in [WILK-79] and [GORD-80]. Saltzer has described reasons for preferring a ring network in [SALT-79] and [SALT-81].) Each node's ring controller provides the node with a unique node ID, which is assigned at the factory and is contained in the controller's microcode PROMs. The maximum packet size is 2048 bytes. The ring hardware controller has both broadcast and simple multicast capabilities. We will not discuss the network further here; for purposes of the file system, all that is required is that it deliver messages with high probability and low CPU overhead.

Distributed File System Design Goals

This section identifies the basic file system design goals peculiar to the development of a *distributed* file system. These goals formed the foundation of the DOMAIN file system.

Location transparency - A user or system administrator should be able to move file system objects from one network node to another without having to find and alter all name and program references to that object. The human-readable name for an object, therefore, must not bind the specified object to a particular network node.

Data consistency - A computing installation (usually) exists to produce and to use data; consequently the integrity of that data must be guaranteed by the file system. Users unknowingly competing for simultaneous yet logically conflicting access to a file (such as two people trying to edit a file at the same time) must be protected by some form of version or concurrency control. Even a single user can cause cross-machine sharing by running part of an application on a workstation and the rest on a computation server elsewhere in the network. Changes to files must never be lost for any reason other than complete catastrophe. It is certainly unacceptable to allow damage to files because of timing windows or poor cache managment. One can never accept "fast" at the expense of "right". The sharing issues for data files and the cross-machine consistency guarantee is crucial to correct operation.

Consistent naming - Consistent naming means that every program, script, and person in the network uses exactly the same name text for a file system object regardless of where it (or he or she) runs. An important metric for measuring the success of an implementation against this design goal is the strength of the guarantee that a given name will access a particular file from anywhere in the network. The system must *guarantee* consistent naming rather than depend on the cooperative actions of individual users.

Consistent authentication - Consistent authentication means your identity needs to be both recognizable by others in the network with whom you interact (e.g. file servers), and inheritable by those you ask to do work on your behalf (e.g. computation servers). Further, consistent authentication allows each user to retain his or her identity, context and privileges, regardless of which workstation he or she happens to log into on any particular day.

In addition, there are three important considerations that cross all of these design goals. First, and most importantly, the distributed file system must be a full-function file system. No compromises in the file system facility may be made in the interests of simplifying the distributed aspect of the mechanism.

A second important concern is performance. File system operations are often the bottle-necks for long and complicated computations. None of those applications can afford a large loss in the speed of file access just because the file happens to be accessible only through a LAN. Successful network-wide file systems will meet the basic design goals without sacrificing performance. (See [CHER-83] and [LAZO-84] for discussions about the performance of distributed systems.)

The final consideration is ease of administration. Here we mean that a system is somehow "better" if the system administrator has fewer tasks to perform when a new network node, more file storage, or a new user is added to the network.

The components of a file system

The architecture of any file system can be separated into five rough functional components: (1) an object storage system, (2) a data access facility, (3) a concurrency control facility, (4) a naming facility, and (5) a user authentication facility. This section outlines the working definitions and responsibilities of these file system components.

An object storage system (OSS) is responsible for the management of all objects contained in or controlled by the file system. (We say *objects* rather than files to emphasize that a "file system" actually supports entities in addition to disk files, such as interprocess communication facilities, communication ports, magnetic tape drives, and display pixel maps. However, this paper deals primarily with the distributed system aspects of sharing disk files.) These management responsibilities include creation, deletion, storage, user access control, and locating file system objects based on some form of internal name. The OSS is also the file system component that is responsible for accepting data from and returning data to users of the file system data access facility.

A data access facility defines the interfaces and mechanisms by which users and their applications gain access to the OSS file system data. The most common user-level data access facility interfaces are *open, close, read* and *write*.

A concurrency control facility provides a single locus of control for regulating simultaneous access to an object by multiple users. Such a facility is responsible for implementing whatever sharing policies the system is built to provide.

A naming facility manages human-readable names and their translation into the internal names that are meaningful to the OSS. The storage policy and translation rules are logically separate from the underlying facility that manages the objects that the names represent.

A user authentication facility assigns a single identifier for each human user of the system and supports some form of object protection keyed to these identifiers. A distributed system has the additional requirement of protecting remote objects as strongly and with the same mechanisms as local objects.

The DOMAIN object storage system

The DOMAIN object storage system provides a completely flat space of location independent objects identified by 64-bit unique identifiers (UIDs). Associated with each object is the UID of an access control list object and an object type ID (also a UID). The OSS also stamps each object with a last date-time modified (DTM) field whose use is described below.

DOMAIN UIDs consist of a 36-bit creation time, a 20-bit node ID, and an 8-bit reserved field which is currently unused (see figure). They derive their uniqueness from the concatenation of an Apollo unique node ID manufactured into every Apollo machine and the time-of-day data from a monotonically increasing hardware clock. (For other examples of UID-based OSS's see [SWIN-79] and [REDE-80].)

object creation time	unused	creating node node id
36 bits	8 bits	20 bits

Anatomy of a UID

UIDs of this form have several advantages in a distributed file system over other forms of internal name. UIDs are completely location independent. Without any associated location context, each UID unambiguously identifies a single file system object. They may always be passed from process to process and from node to node safely, without having to be examined and transformed at each step. While the UID *does* contain a network node ID, that ID is necessary only to guarantee uniqueness and not for locating the object in the network.

Internal names of this form benefit both distributed file system clients and servers. The internal IDs for a file system object must be short and fixed length so that copying, passing, and comparing them is easy and fast. The IDs must be unique so that once a client starts to use an ID, there will never be any doubt about the file to which it refers. This is especially important in the face of network failures and partitions. The lifetime of a DOMAIN UID and the lifetime of the object it names are one and the same. An example of a common internal name that was discarded are UNIX-style "inode" numbers [THOM-78], which are only unique within a particular disk volume and are reused upon file deletion. A more complete discussion of the use of UIDs in the DOMAIN system can be found in [LEAC-82].

The primary programming interface exported by the DOMAIN OSS is based completely on object UID; all clients of the OSS reference their target objects via object UIDs. The operations supported by this interface include creating, deleting, and locating existing objects, getting and setting object attributes, and reading or writing object data pages. OSS clients are completely insulated from the home location of the objects; it is the responsibility of the distributed OSS to find the specified objects and to make file system objects stored at each node equally available throughout the network (see diagram). When the target object is local, the OSS performs the necessary disk I/O. When the object is found to be remote, the OSS uses a "problem-oriented" protocol [LEAC-83] to send the appropriate network request message to the object's home node.

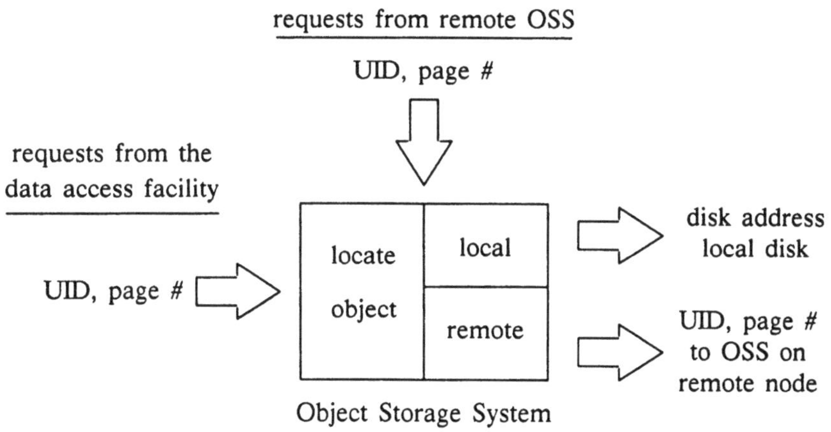

The object storage system (OSS) locates an object specified by UID in the network.
If the object is local, the OSS performs the necessary disk I/O;
otherwise, a request is sent to the OSS on the object's home node.

The DOMAIN OSS employs a searching algorithm to find objects given only their UID. This algorithm and the data base on which it relies has undergone several revisions [LEAC-82]. The current technique depends on receiving a list of likely locations from a facility referred to as the *hint manager*. The hint manager categorizes UIDs by the node at which they were created. For each category, the hint manager data base contains a list of nodes at which UIDs of that category have been found before. Any time a system software component has any form of location information, it passes that data to the hint manager. A particularly good source of hints is the naming facility (described later) which suggests to the hint manager that an object may be co-located with the directory in which its name is catalogued. To perform its seach for a particular UID, the OSS retrieves the appropriate node list from the hint manager and iterates through it until it finds the object.

This algorithm works because in practice objects infrequently move from the node at which they were created. When they do move, it is most often on some form of removable media and so a large number of UIDs created at one node all move simultaneously to one other node. Finally, the hints supplied by the naming facility are almost always correct. Extensions to allow either network broadcast or user-supplied hint data have proven, so far, to be unnecessary.

When the time to make a disk access for a particular system facility is barely acceptable, the wait for a network transaction is completely unacceptable. To meet the file system performance goals, the OSS implements very aggressive caching for both file attributes and data. The OSS stores the results of both local and remote operations and reuses them when needed if it can ascertain that they are still valid.

The caching strategy is built around the notion of *active* (recently used) objects. For each active object, the OSS stores a full set of object attributes and the most recently used data pages of that object. The attributes of active objects are kept in system managed tables. However, the cache area for active object data pages is all of physical memory. Since the OSS provides the *only* form of access to file system objects, every in-use disk block is necessarily part of some OSS object. A disk page whose contents are currently in physical memory is merely being cached by the OSS as part of an active object. (For a more detailed description of the use of physical memory as an OSS cache see [LEAC-85]). When an OSS client references an object that is not active, the OSS *activates* that object by first locating the object, looking on a local disk (if the object was found to be local) or otherwise asking the OSS server agent on the object's home node to provide the required information, and then storing the data in the appropriate local caches.

For the most part, the active object data cache is a "write-back" cache. That is, the modified data is *not* immediately passed through to the data's home node. As part of its normal operation, the OSS periodically writes modifications to cached data back to their appropriate home nodes. However, the OSS also supports a per-object *purify* operation which searches the active object caches for modifications to the structure or data of a particular object and writes all of those modification back to that object's home node all at once. We will see later that the *purify* operation is essential to the proper cooperation between the concurrency control facility and the OSS. The figure shows the form of the basic operations exported by the OSS.

Object management operations	Data management operations
locate_object (uid, home_node)	read_attributes (uid, attributes)
purify_object (uid)	write_attributes (uid, attributes)
validate_cache (uid, dtm)	read_page (uid, page_#, data)
create_object (home_node, uid)	write_page (uid, page_#, data)
delete_object (uid)	

Basic Object Storage System (OSS) operations

To insure the validity of cached data over time, the OSS stamps all cached data with the last date-time modified (DTM) of the underlying object. The DTM is maintained by the OSS at the object's home node. It is guaranteed to be of sufficient resolution to capture *every* modification to the object, and as a result the DTM of an object acts safely as that object's version number. Active object cache validation, then, consists of getting the most recent DTM of the target object from the object's home node and comparing that value with the DTM stamp in the cache. If they match, the cache data is valid because the object has not been modified since the data was entered into the cache. If they differ, the object *has* been modified and so the cached data must be discarded.

In the discussion of concurrency control below, we shall see that by using the OSS's object version and cache content control facilites, the DOMAIN concurrency control facility can effectively guarantee distributed cache consistency for all clients who obey the system locking rules.

The DOMAIN data access facility

The data access facility sits above the OSS level and defines the means by which applications reference OSS data. The most familiar data access facility interfaces support explicit file I/O and can be represented generically by the operations *open, close, read* and *write*. While the DOMAIN file system supports this level of interface, the entire data access facilty is built on a set of mechanisms and primitives referred to as a network-wide *single level store* (SLS). (Multics [ORGA-72] and the IBM System/38 [FREN-78] are examples of a single level store for a centralized system.)

With the SLS, a program accesses a file system object by presenting its UID and asking for some portion of that object to be *mapped* into the program's address space. The DOMAIN SLS facility partitions every file system object into object *segments* which (currently) consist of 32 1024–byte pages. Each mapping request adds entries to the per process *mapped segment table* (MST) which records the association of virtual addresses with parts of the object. Once the MST entry is made, the object is *mapped* (i.e. the mapping is recorded) and the program may use the corresponding virtual addresses to access the underlying objects. The system users virtual memory demand paging to actually fetch data from and return data to the OSS. A corresponding *unmap* operation breaks the association between virtual address and object by deleting entries from the MST. (See [REDE–80] for a discussion on the desirability of mapping in distributed systems.)

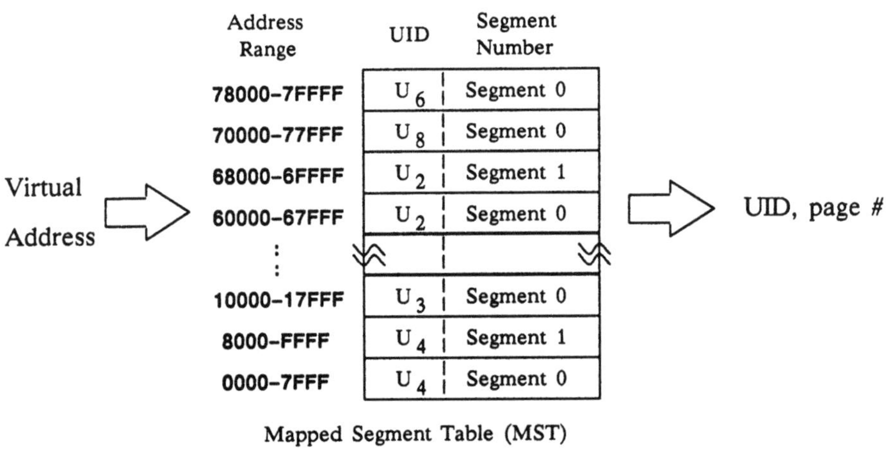

The Single Level Store (SLS) maps program generated virtual addresses into (UID, page number) pairs for the OSS.

Our implementation of SLS has many aspects in common with typical virtual memory systems. Main memory is divided into 1024–byte page frames each of which holds one object page. Physical main memory is managed as a write–back cache and memory management unit (MMU) hardware allows references to encached pages at main memory speeds. If a machine instruction references a page of an object that is not in main memory, the MMU hardware causes a page fault, and supplies the faulting virtual address and the ID of the faulting process to software. The SLS page fault handler looks in the MST to find the mapping of the faulting address to a file system object, and hands the appropriate UID and object page number to the OSS. The OSS finds a physical memory frame and reads the object page (whether from local disk or remote node) into the allocated frame. The SLS updates the MMU related information to show that the page is now main memory resident and restarts or continues the faulting instruction.

The DOMAIN concurrency control facility

The mechanisms and interfaces that provide concurrency control in the DOMAIN system are referred to as the DOMAIN distributed *lock manager*. The lock manager offers the means by which a process may obtain access to and control over an object so as to block other processes that wish to use the object in an incompatible way.

The primary operation that the lock manager exports is the *lock* operation. This operation allows the specification of both a *locking mode* and an *access mode*. The locking mode specifies the concurrency rules that the requesting process wishes applied to the indicated object during its use of that object. The access mode indicates the specific intent (i.e. read, write, or read with intent to write later [GIFF-79]) that the process has for this object.

The DOMAIN concurrency control facility supports two locking modes for objects. The more familar is the "many readers or single writer" lock mode (nR-xor-1W) [HOAR-74]. This mode allows *either* any number of reading processes from any number of nodes to simultaneously access a single file *or* exactly one writing process from a single node to access the file. The other locking mode is the *co-writers* (co-located writers) lock mode which makes no restrictions on the number of simultaneous readers and writers, but demands that they be co-located at a single network node. This mode allows the use of shared memory semantics, but only among processes located at the same node.

Other operations include *unlock* (to unlock a locked object), *relock* (to change one type of lock to another without unlocking) and the operations necessary to inquire about a particular lock or list all of the objects currently locked at a particular node.

An instance of the lock manager exists on every network node and each lock manager serves as the single locus of concurrency control for the objects local to it. Each lock manager keeps its own lock data base that records all locks on local objects and all locks held by local processes. Lock and unlock requests for remote objects are always sent to the home node of the object involved, and cause both the requesting node lock manager and the home node lock manager to update their respective data bases.

The lock manager enforces compatible use of an object by refusing to grant conflicting lock requests. Locks are either granted immediately or refused; processes never wait for locks to become available, so there is no possibility of deadlock (but indefinite postponement is of course possible). This kind of locking is not meant for distributed database types of transactions, or for providing atomicity in the face of node failures, but for human time span locking uses such as file editing. For this same reason, locks are not timed out, since realistic time outs would be unreasonably long.

Besides concurrency control, the DOMAIN lock managers are also responsible for the management of the caches kept by the OSS. The two supported lock modes ensure that the simultaneous users of a particular file are either all readers (in the case of nR–xor–1W) in which case the data they cache is identical, or all processes running on the same node (in the case of co–writers) in which case the main memory cache they see is the same as in a single centralized system. All other simultaneous uses of a file system object are (currently) unsupported by the DOMAIN file system. However, *serial* users of an object must correctly see all changes made to the file by earlier users.

The lock managers use the two cache management operations exported by the OSS (*validate_cache* and *purify_object*) in combination with the supported lock modes to guarantee cache correctness. The logic for cache control is split evenly between the *lock* and *unlock* lock manager operations.

At *lock* time, the client lock manager requests the appropriate lock from the lock manager running at the home node of the target object. If the lock is granted, the client lock manager requests the current version number (DTM) of the object, and passes that DTM along with the UID of the target object in to the OSS through the OSS *validate_cache* operation. The OSS examines its caches for data pertaining to the target object and any data not stamped with the current DTM is discarded. Thereafter under this lock, all cached data is known to be valid because the lock manager prohibits conflicting use.

At *unlock* time the client lock manager demands that the local OSS write–back all cached data modifications to the home node of the object through the OSS *purify_object* operation. This guarantees that the copy of the object at the home node is completely up–to–date, and that the DTM of the object will not change again as a result of modifications occurring under this lock. As a result, at unlock time, both the client

OSS cache and the object data at its home node are stamped with the same DTM. When the object is locked again by this same client, the latest DTM is requested from the home node and any data remaining in the cache can be verified.

To demonstrate the need for this level of cache verification, consider an object O that resides on disk storage physically connected to network node 1 and whose initial DTM is D_0. Network node 2 is granted a writers lock for O, modifies the file and then unlocks it. The unlock operation does two things. First, it sends (via OSS *purify_object*) all modifications that node 2 made to O back to node 1, establishing a new DTM value for O of D_1. Second, it unlocks O, releasing it for use by other nodes. These two steps leave the data from O cached at node 2 stamped as being from version D_1. At this point, node 3 locks O for writing, modifies it, sends its changes back to O's home node and unlocks it. The modifications made by node 3 result in O's being stamped with a new DTM, D_2. If Node 2 now wants to reuse object O, its lock manager acquires the necessary lock, discovers the now current DTM is D_2, and calls the node 2 OSS *validate_cache* operation to purge the D_1 version cached data.

The DOMAIN naming facility

The DOMAIN naming facility provides human-readable text string names for objects through a directory subsystem referred to as the DOMAIN *naming server*. The principle function of the naming server is to store the association between these human-readable names and their UIDs. The DOMAIN naming server manages a hierarchical naming tree, like Multics [ORGA-72] or UNIX(TM) [RITC-74], with directories at the nodes and other objects at the leaves.

Each directory is a regular OSS object whose object type happens to be "directory" and which primarily contains a list of pairs which associate "component names" (strings) and object UIDs for that level of the naming hierarchy. An object's *pathname* is an ordered list of component names all but the last of which are necessarily names of directories. The naming server iterates through the levels of the pathname, translating components into UIDs until the end of the pathname is reached. The resulting UID is the UID of the named object. The naming server accesses directories via the mapping primitive of the SLS layer. Consequently, the naming server operates on its directories without knowledge of their location in the network. (See the discussion of the naming server in the section titled "Lessons" below.)

The unique aspect of the DOMAIN distributed naming server is its ability to support an "absolute pathname" for every file system object. The naming server supports a replicated network-wide naming tree *root* directory (described below) for every process on every network node. An "absolute" pathname, then, is a pathname whose leading component is to be looked up in the network root directory. A pathname of this form leads to the same object UID regardless of the node on which the lookup runs, or (because of SLS) where the directories that participate in the target object's name exist. In these ways, a pathname whose translation starts at the root directory is just like a UID; it is equally valid when issued from any node in the network and always identifies exactly one object.

Since absolute pathnames are potentially very long and cumbersome, the naming server defines a context-relative form of pathname in addition to the absolute form. The supported context options include "working directory" relative and local node boot-volume-relative names. The relative naming context can always be represented as an absolute pathname prefix, and so relative pathnames are all expandable to absolute pathnames through the concatenation of the context pathname text to the relative path name itself.

The network-wide naming root directory is implemented as a replicated distributed data base with data base servers running at the site of each replica. Special root data base management commands are provided to allow system administrators to create and delete data base replicas and to add entries to and delete entries from this data base. The data base servers respond to root directory lookup requests and system administrator commands, and support an automatic mechanism used to bring the replicas into agreement after node failure or network partitioning. To minimize dependence on the sites of the root directory replicas, every network node implements a very large and long-lived cache of most recently used root directory entries. When the cache data proves insufficient, the requesting node broadcasts through the LAN to find an operational root directory data base server process.

The DOMAIN user authentication facility

The DOMAIN system supports a network-wide user registry. Like the replicated network naming root, the network registry is a replicated data base. The system administrator plans the locations of the network registry replicas and each network node is given a list of valid registry locations. At login time, the system consults an available registry site to determine if the login name and password supplied by the human user match. (When no valid site is available, the system consuls a local cache of recently successful logins.) When the name and password do match, the login subsystem returns an identifier which will represent that user in all subsequent authentication transactions.

Each logged-in DOMAIN user is represented by a four-component user identifier. The components are: Person ID, Project ID, Organization ID, and Node ID (PPON). Each component has a unique text name that is paired with a UID. When a person logs in, the login subsystem uses the registry data base to lookup the PPO portion of the identifier and appends the node ID of the login node to form the full user identifier (see figure).

person identifier	project identifier	organization identifier	login node node id
uid	uid	uid	network node id

Anatomy of a user identifier

The human readable text of a typical PPON might be:

levine, os-development, engineering, 01824

to indicate that the person *levine* working on the *os-development* project works for the *engineering* organization and is currently logged into the node whose node ID is *01824*. Each file system object is associated with an *access control list* (ACL) object which contains a list of the PPONs that should be granted access to the object and rights that should be granted to each. These ACL entries support wild card matching to allow granting of specific rights to like users. Typical forms of access control entry include:

PPON	RIGHTS	MEANING
%.%.%.06251	---	users from node 06251 are denied access
levine.%.%.%	rwx	grant user levine all access
%.os-development.%.%	rwx	grant os developers all access
%.%.marketing.%	r--	grant members of marketing read access

For more information about DOMAIN ACLs, see [APOL-01] and [APOL-02].

By choosing a UID for the internal representation of each field of the textual user identity, the system guarantees that two separately created registries will have no internal identifier conflict. The system, therefore, does not need to prevent a malicious user from withdrawing a node from participation in the network registry system and creating his or her own version of a registry. The internal identifers (UIDs) created in this new registry will be necessarily different from those present in the original registry. As a result, access control list entries which grant rights to participants in the original registry will never accept new registry assigned identities.

In addition, the registry data base also stores configuration information about the user community. An example of a particularly useful piece of information is the user's default working directory. Because the registry supplies access to this user context toe-hold, the login subsystem at every node is able to construct the same personalized context for a user, even if that user has never logged in to that particular node before.

The most important aspect of the DOMAIN user authentication system is that it *guarantees* that a DOMAIN user is always identified with the same PPO fields regardless of the location of login. In addition, should it be desired for geography related security considerations, the current login location is separately available for use in access control decisions.

Lessons

The first implementation of the DOMAIN system was completed in March of 1981. In the intervening five years we have accumulated a wealth of experience about DOMAIN in particular and insights into distributed systems in general. This experience has validated (and in some cases vindicated) many of our choices and has also suggested alternative implementations for some facets of the system.

The overall design of the DOMAIN OSS has been very successful. It was relatively simple to implement, put a firm boundary around the location-dependent aspects of object usage, and provided a single memory utilization caching strategy for both local and remote file access.

Several modifications have been made to the OSS since its original implementation. For example, the *read_page* operation has been extended to take a number of pages to be read. While the unit of caching has remained the same, the SLS layer is now able to "read-ahead" several pages of the object to minimize the costs of disk and network I/O and to amortize the cost of invoking the OSS across more data.

The object DTM had to be of sufficient resolution to guarantee that the system would catch every modification sequence (lock–modify–unlock). This guarantee remains essential to the OSS cache data validation algorithms. We found our original DTM resolution of 256 milliseconds far too coarse and have since increased the resolution to 32 milliseconds with provision to reduce it still further to 2 milliseconds.

The OSS has ended up caching essentially all of the attributes of active objects. We had originally hoped to minimize table space by caching only frequently used attributes. Analysis has shown this method to be false economy.

Our original implementation strategy was to layer absolutely every system facility directly on top of the single level store. The characteristics of network location transparency and a low penalty for remote transparent access combine to make the "map–it, use–it, unmap–it" approach to object manipulation terrifically attractive. However, we have learned that there are sometimes compelling practical reasons for avoiding the allure of network transparency at the SLS level and instead using explicit message–passing protocols for some object managers that want to provide a higher level of abstraction.

One example of such an object manager is the naming server, which was originally designed to map and operate on directories without regard to their location in the network. The naming server, then, did not, in fact could not, distinguish between directories on local disks and those on remote disks. As a result, the server was straightforward to implement, and as soon as it worked on local directories, it worked on remote directories, too.

The problem with this implementation strategy for the naming server was that the storage system (naturally) provided no layer of abstraction for the notion of directory. The SLS provided access to the raw bits of a directory to each naming server that wanted to manipulate that directory. This was fine as long as each naming server in the network could operate on directories of the same format. In practice, however, the naming servers are *not* the same on every node in the network (generally due to software updates occuring at different times) and the older naming servers are unable to handle constructs added to directories by newer naming servers running on other nodes.

Directories are an important example for a system like DOMAIN. They are permanent (stored on disk), heavily shared by multiple nodes, and most transactions on them take very little time. Also, they are likely candidates for extensions and improvements. Because we can never demand simultaneous update of software on every node in a network, and because we want very much to offer cross-release compatibility, we have found ourselves somewhat constrained by our original implementation.

Nonetheless, we have implemented partial support for a message-passing based naming server. This change demanded that the naming server learn the difference between local and remote directories and increased the naming server's complexity. However, we have found that the time it takes to do a naming server tree-walk has decreased by asking the node that owned the target directory do the lookup work itself rather than sending pages of the directory over to the requesting node.

The concurrency control and data cache management that the lock manager provided has proven to be essential to the success of the DOMAIN system. The importance of coordinated sharing becomes increasingly more evident in very large (greater than 1000 nodes) networks. Further, because cached data is always validated before use, file data very often stays in the OSS caches long enough to be reused. This reuse contributes greatly to the overall performance of the distributed file system.

Summary

The DOMAIN distributed file systm fulfills the objectives of allowing easy sharing and cooperation among large groups of workstation users. Five years of experience have shown the design goals described in this paper to be both individually necessary and altogether sufficient as the basis for a viable distributed file system. The DOMAIN distributed file system meets these design goals. In our design we encountered problems that required us to invent and develop many new facilities and techniques, including: unique identifiers (UIDs) for file system objects, object locating strategies, distributed file lock managers, trans-network file data caching, a replicated user registry and ACL facility, and a singly-rooted hierarchical network name space.

The Apollo DOMAIN system has been in full commercial production since the middle of 1981. It has an installed base of thousands of networks and over 20,000 workstation and server nodes. The current, largest, single network is at Apollo corporate headquarters which at last count consisted of over 1300 nodes and over 1000 disk drives to form a single distributed file system containing over sixty gigabytes of disk storage.

Acknowledgements

Besides myself, responsibility for the design and original implementation of the DOMAIN distributed system belongs to James Hamilton, Paul Leach, and Bernard Stumpf. Over the years, an ever growing number of Apollo engineers have made important suggestions and implemented substantial improvements. I would like to thank Randi Levine for her patience, Lisa Zahn for her usual meticulous editting, and Nathaniel Mishkin for his coments on the form and content of this paper.

References

[APOL-01] **Administering Your DOMAIN System**, Apollo Computer Incorporated, Chelmsford, MA, 1985

[APOL-02] **DOMAIN System Command Reference**, Apollo Computer Incorporated, Chelmsford, MA, 1985

[CHER-83] D. R. Cheriton, W. Zwaenepoel, "The Distributed V Kernel and its Performance for Diskless Workstations," in *Proceedings of the Ninth Symposium on Operating System Principles*, October 1983, pp. 128–139.

[FREN-78] R. E. French, R. W. Collins, L. W. Loew, "System/38 Machine Storage Management," *IBM System/38 Technical Developments*, IBM General Systems Division, 1978, pp.63–66.

[GIFF-79] D. K. Gifford, "Weighted Voting for Replicated Data," *Proceedings of the Seventh Symposium on Operating Systems Principles*, December 1979, pp. 150–162.

[GORD-80] R.L. Gordon, W. Farr, and P.H. Levine, "Ringnet: A packet switched local network with decentralized control," *Computer Networks*, vol. 3, North Holland, New York, NY, 1980, pp. 373-379.

[HOAR-74] C. A. R. Hoare, "Monitors: An Operating System Structuring Concept," *Communications of the ACM*, 17, 10 October 1974, pp. 549–557.

[LAZO-84] E. D. Lazowska, J. Zahorjan, D. R. Cheriton, W. Zwaenepoel, "File Access Performance of Diskless Workstations," *Technical Report 84–06–01*, Department of Computer Science, University of Washington, Seattle, WA, June 1984.

[LEAC-82] P.J. Leach, B.L. Stumpf, J.A. Hamilton, and P.H. Levine, "UID's as internal names in a distributed file system," in *Proceedings 1st Symposium on the Principles of Distribributed Computing*, Ottawa, Ont., Canada, August 1982.

[LEAC-83] P.J. Leach, P.H. Levine, B.P. Douros, J.A. Hamilton, D.L. Nelson, and B.L. Stumpf, "The architecture of an intergrated local network," IEEE Journal on Selected Areas in Communications, vol. SAC-1, no. 5, November 1983.

[LEAC-85] P.J. Leach, B.L. Stumpf, J.A. Hamilton, and P.H. Levine, "The File System of an Integrated Local Network," in *Proceedings ACM Computer Science Conference,* New Orleans, LA, March 13–15, 1985.

[NELS-84] D.L. Nelson and P.J. Leach, "The architecture and applications of the Apollo Domain," IEEE Computer Graphics and Applications, April 1984.

[ORGA-72] E.I. Organick, *The Multics System: An Examination of Its Structure*. M.I.T Press, Cambridge, MA, 1972.

[REDE–80] D. D. Redell, Y. K. Dalal, T. R. Horsley, H. C. Lauer, W. C. Lynch, P. R. McJones, H. G. Murray, S. C. Purcell, "Pilot: an Operating System for a Personal Computer," *Communications of the ACM*, 23, 2, February 1980, pp. 81–91.

[RITC-74] D.M. Ritchie and K. Thomson, "The UNIX time-sharing system," *Communications of the Association for Computing Machinery*, vol. 17, pp. 365-375, July 1974.

[SALT-79] J.H. Saltzer, "A star-shaped ring network with high maintainability," in *Proceedings of the Local Area Communicaions Network Symposium,* MITRE Corp., May 1979, pp. 179-190.

[SALT-81] J.H. Saltzer, D.D. Clark, and K.T. Pogran, "Why a ring," in *Proceedings of the 7th Data Communications Symposium*, October 1981, pp. 211-217.

[SWIN–79] D. Swinehart, G. McDaniel, D. Boggs, "WFS: A Simple Shared File System for a Distributed Environment," *Proceedings of the Seventh Symposium on Operating Systems Principles*, December 1979, pp. 9–17.

[THOM-78] K. Thomson, "UNIX implementation," *Bell System Technical Journal*, vol. 57, pp. 1931-1946, July-August 1978.

[WILK-79] M.V. Wilkes and D.J. Wheeler, "The Cambridge Digital Communication Ring," *Proceedings of the Local Area Communications Network Symposium.*, May 1979, pp. 47-61.

The CHORUS Distributed Operating System: Some Design Issues

Marc Rozier†, *José Legatheaux Martins*††

Institut National de Recherche en Informatique et en Automatique
B.P. 105, 78153 Le Chesnay Cedex, France.
Tel. (1) 39 63 52 94, Telex: 697 033 F

ABSTRACT

CHORUS ™ is a portable, open, message-based, distributed operating system. Since 1980, start time of the CHORUS project at INRIA, several versions of the system have been designed and implemented. The current version, CHORUS-V2, offers a full UNIX ™ compatibility at the user level, while providing control of distribution by relying on a powerful IPC facility, based on ports and messages, as the heart of its architecture.

This paper first includes an overview of the CHORUS system, and second discusses some issues of our work: ports and port groups, IPC, naming and binding, and distributed execution control.

1. Introduction

CHORUS is the main result of a research project initiated at INRIA in 1980. It is a distributed operating system, running on a set of interconnected computers. It is designed for applications that can take advantage of distribution for dynamic reconfiguration, improved performance, better resource utilization and fault tolerance, in a transparent manner.

A prototype of the CHORUS system was written in Pascal under the Pascal-UCSD system on Intel 8086 processors. A first *real* version (CHORUS-V1) was implemented in Pascal on SM90™ computers (a 680x0 based multi-processor), interconnected with a local area network (Ethernet). This version has a proprietary interface both at the programming and at the command language levels. A second version has been designed and implemented, and is now available. One of the major extensions that can be found in this version is a UNIX interface: UNIX (System V)

† the authors list ordering reflects the responsibility engaged during the CHORUS presentation at the NATO ASI.

†† José Legatheaux Martins is with the Computer Science Departement of Universidade Nova de Lisboa - Quinta da Torre, 2825 MONTE da CAPARICA, Portugal - he is currently on leave at INRIA. Its leave has been partially supported by the Fundaçao Calouste Gulbenkian, Lisbon.

- CHORUS is a registered trademark of INRIA.
- UNIX is a registered trademark of AT&T in USA and other countries.
- SM90 is a registered trademark of CNET.

NATO ASI Series, Vol. F28
Distributed Operating Systems. Theory and Practice
Edited by Y. Paker et al.

system calls are part of the CHORUS-V2 interface, accessible to application programs. This version allows standard UNIX applications to run transparently in a distributed environment. It also provides powerful tools allowing the user to write new applications which take the real advantages of distribution.

Although CHORUS-V2 can be seen as an extended distributed UNIX system [Armand 86], its structure is very different from a standard UNIX system structure. It is based on a small message-passing kernel, and a distributed set of system processes - called **actors** - providing standard Operating System services.

In section 2, we overview the fundamentals of the CHORUS architecture. We also describe the operating system very briefly. A full description can be found in [Guillemont 86].

In CHORUS, a distributed application is a set of autonomous processes, basically clients and servers, interacting with each other by message passing. When designing such a system, the following issues are fundamental:

- defining server access points: in CHORUS, ports and port groups play this role;
- defining how clients address these access points: CHORUS offers a powerful IPC for this purpose;
- defining how are the resources named in the system: CHORUS offers several naming layers allowing location-transparent naming;
- defining how are processes and distributed protocols structured: we introduced on top of the CHORUS architecture a powerful structuring tool, the activity concept.

The discussion of these four issues is the essential purpose of this paper (sections 3 to 6 respectively).

2. System Overview

2.1. Basic concepts

In the **CHORUS basic architecture,** [Zimmermann 81, 84], a system comprises a set of autonomous entities, called **actors,** distributed across a network of computers. An actor resembles a sequential process. It has its own code, data and a context and it communicates with the outside world only by receiving and sending **messages** through **ports** which it owns. These ports have global names which are independent both of the name of the owning actor and its location.

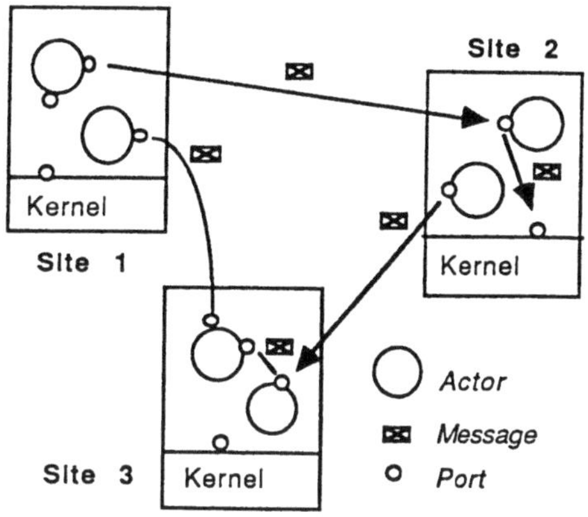

Figure 1 : CHORUS Basic Concepts

2.2. Message driven execution

One of the distinctive features of CHORUS is its message-driven model of computation. An actor operates as a sequence of execution granules, called **processing-steps.** Each message received by an actor triggers the execution of a processing step (basically a procedure) that ends in the sending of zero or several messages: each actor processes only one message at a time and its operation appears as a succession of processing-steps.

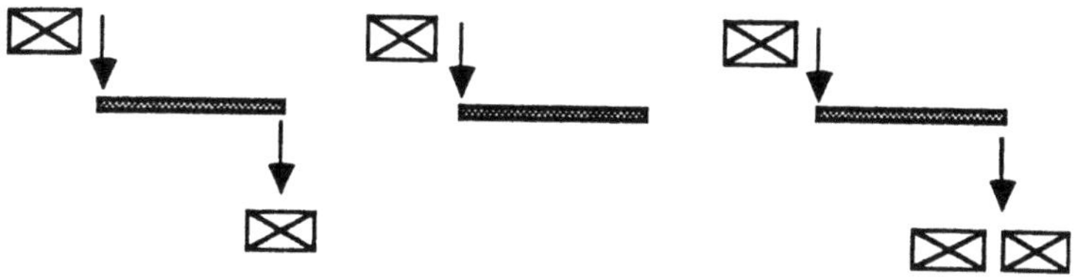

Figure 2 : Message driven execution

CHORUS distinguishes clearly between an actor's processing and communication phases: in the course of a processing-step an actor can not communicate with the outside; messages resulting from the processing-step are sent all together at the end of this step. The actor can then process the next message. This clear structure eases the design of fault-tolerant mechanisms, because checkpoints may be naturally placed at the beginning of processing-steps [Banino 82, 85a].

The succession of processing-steps carried out by an actor depends, on the one hand, on the messages it receives at its ports and, on the other hand, on the **selections** defined by the actor; a selection is a list of connections consisting each of a source port and a local destination port; only a message received through one of these connections may trigger the following processing-step. In addition, message selection relies on the priority of ports and the arrival order of messages.

So, as ports can be dynamically associated with processing-steps, an actor is structured as some kind of an ***active monitor*** where ports are the access points to the monitor procedures, and operations on the data of the monitor are processing-steps.

2.3. Operating System Overview

The **CHORUS operating system** [Guillemont 82] consists of a kernel and a set of system actors. Located at each CHORUS site are the CHORUS kernel and at least those system actors which manage the local resources. The kernel implements the logical CHORUS machine. It schedules execution of processing-steps by actors, and handles their local communications. Moreover it entirely hides the physical machine by transforming exceptions, such as interrupts and errors, into messages addressed to ports. The kernel is small, all the system resources being handled by the system actors. Basic CHORUS system actors manage devices, communication links, files, actors, ports, names, etc.

For programming convenience, interactions with such system actors are embedded into synchronous system calls, in a system interface library. This set of system calls includes the entire UNIX system V interface. Actors may be created and destroyed both dynamically and remotely, using the standard UNIX calls (fork, exec, exit, kill, etc.). CHORUS offers a distributed file system. Location-transparent file access is done through the standard UNIX calls (open, read, write, close, etc.). The specific CHORUS facilities (ports, groups, IPC, naming, execution control, etc.) are available though additional calls. Some of them will be presented in the next sections.

3. Ports and Groups in CHORUS

In message oriented systems, messages are sent to some sort of "message receptacles". The different ways these receptacles are bound to processes introduce different message addressing methods. The most common ones are: direct addressing, or process-to-process addressing (V-Kernel [Cheriton 84] for example), and port-to-port or functional addressing (Accent [Rashid 81] for example).

In CHORUS, messages are exchanged through ports. An actor may own more than one port. A port designates an access point to a *service*, or to an *operation*, and not necessarily a *server*. Particularly, in CHORUS, ports can exist independently of actors and the same port may be, successively and dynamically, associated to different actors. This method allows dynamic reconfiguration (achieved by keeping a stable port interface while changing the actors) and makes the synchronization and the server structuring easier.

Logically, a port is a message queue which may be in one of the following states:

closed the port is idle: the queue is empty; it can not be used for message exchange; messages sent to a closed port are lost.

open the port is active: it can receive and send messages; only one actor, the one which opened the port, may consume messages sent to that port.

When it is created, an actor owns some open ports. In addition, an actor can *create* other ports. In order to use a port to send and receive messages, an actor must *open* it, and when the actor doesn't need the port any more, it may *close* it. A port can be created by an actor and successively opened/closed by others, although it can be opened by only one actor at a time, i. e., by its current owner.

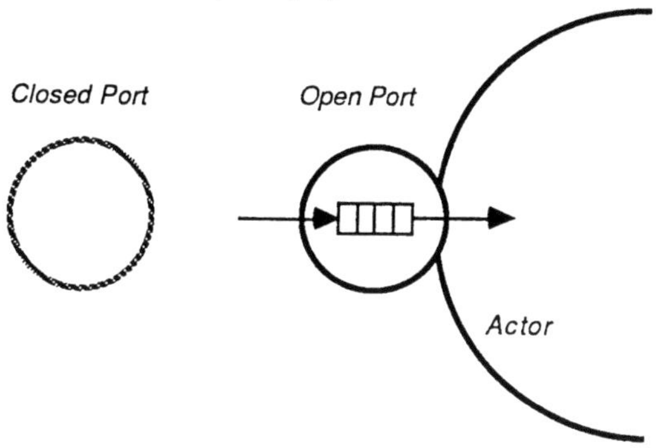

Figure 3 : Port States

In order to achieve symmetrical designation of senders and receivers, messages are also (logically) sent through opened ports: a message flows from a source port to a destination port, and not from a source actor to a destination port. As a consequence, the only communication environment of an actor is a set of ports.

In addition, ports may be associated into **port groups.** This concept, which allows broadcasting and functional addressing of services with several equivalent access points, is discussed in detail in the next sections.

3.1. Port Management

We overview here the system calls provided for port management. Within an actor, ports are designated by **contextual names** (ranging from 0 to n). These contextual names are referenced below as *pgd* (for Port or Group Descriptor). Port naming will be discussed in detail in section 5. The system call:

creatport → pgd

creates a new port in the closed state and returns a *pgd* for that port. In order to use a port, an actor must open it:

openport (pgd, priority)

opens the port designated by *pgd*; the priority of an opened port sets the priority of the processing of messages received on it. Once opened, a port may be used by the actor in order to send or to receive messages.

closeport (pgd)

closes the port designated by *pgd*; only the owner of a port can close it. Messages received at that port and not yet processed by the actor are destroyed. The port returns to the closed state and can be opened by another actor. In this way, *receive rights* on ports may be transfered from actor to actor (an actor having the *receive right* on a port is the owner of that port).

dlport (pgd)

deletes the port designated by *pgd*; that port must be in the closed state.

An alternative for deleting ports is to create them with the *self-destruction* attribute: when an actor is destroyed, all its opened ports are closed and those which have this attribute set are also automatically destroyed. This feature allows the cleaning up of ports that are not used for dynamic reconfiguration.

For an actor, there is no difference between local and distant communication. When an actor closes a port, another actor can open it, possibly at another site. In this case, the port migrates, but this fact is completely transparent to other actors (in particular, the port will continue to belong to the same groups - see 3.5). The system deals dynamically with its new location (see 5.2).

3.2. Our Experience in using Ports

Basically, the CHORUS system itself is built using the same set of mechanisms as used by applications. Most system services are implemented by actors, outside the kernel: the network server, the port/group server, the file server, the actor server, several driver servers, etc.

These servers use ports in different ways: one port by operation, one port by set of operations of the same priority, one port by set of related operations, one port by group of servers with which a dialogue is set up, etc. In each case, we found that the use of different ports, by the same server, and the dynamic association of ports to processing-steps, are very helpful and powerful facilities for server structuring and synchronization.

For instance, let us illustrate the case of dynamic association of ports to actors and port migration facilities, by an example taken from the CHORUS process management strategy. In CHORUS, an actor can call the function *exec* (like in the UNIX system), even remotely. After this call, all the ports of the actor are associated with another code and context, possibly on another site. Among the ports of an actor, a special one (hidden to the code of the actor) identifies it: the *signal port*. UNIX signals are transformed into *signal messages* sent to the *signal port* of the receiver of the signal. If an actor performs a *remote exec*, its *signal port* will migrate to another site and it will continue to receive signals sent by its partners; for them, migration is transparent. It has also been shown [Banino 82] that port migration may be used to build replicated servers which are dynamically reconfigured, when faults occur, in a transparent way to their clients.

In the next sections we illustrate the port grouping feature.

3.3. The role of Groups in Distributed Systems

There are many cases where it is desirable to address a group of entities. For example, in UNIX, a signal sent to a process group allows a user to destroy all the processes belonging to a *pipe line* in one operation. In a distributed system, message *broadcasting* - or generic addressing (one-to-N addressing) - and the possibility to materialize the logical concept of *distributed service* with several equivalent access points are critical issues. We illustrate these ideas by three examples.

For instance, if a client wants to open a file F and does not know which server manages it, it can broadcast an "open" request to all the servers; only the server that knows the file will answer to the client. This is a one-to-N request protocol with only one reply.

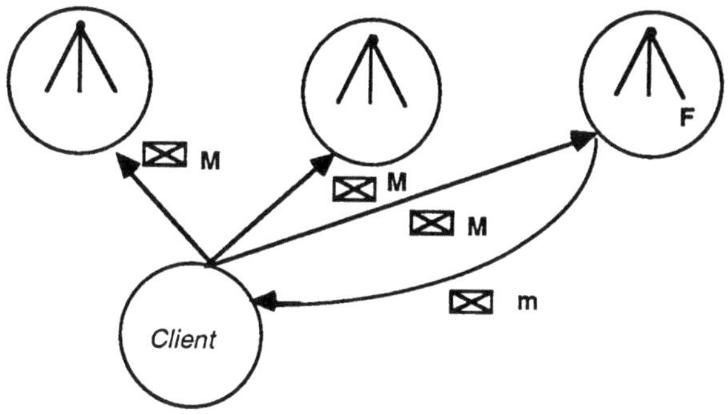

Figure 4 : File F localization using Generic Addressing

Message broadcasting is also useful to implement replication. If the file F is replicated in several servers, the client can also broadcast an "open" request to all servers, execute a majority voting on the received replies, and choose one server among those wich manage the most recent version of F. This is a one-to-N request with M replies protocol.

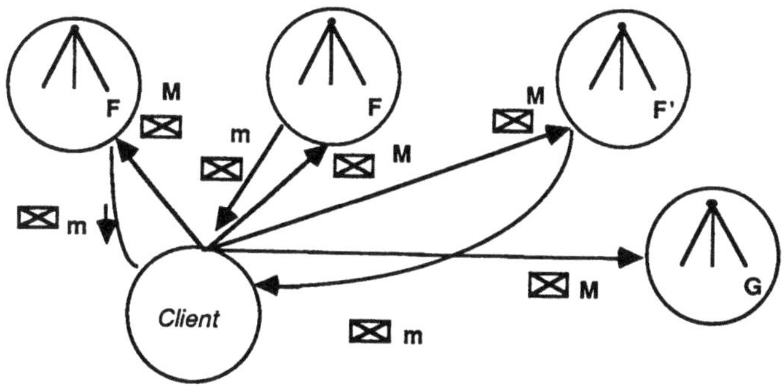

Figure 5 : Majority Voting to Open the replicated file F

Finally, a client may request a service and be unaware of which server performs it. For instance, the client wants to print a file without being aware of which printer is used. We call this form of addressing, functional addressing or "one-to-(one-among-N) addressing".

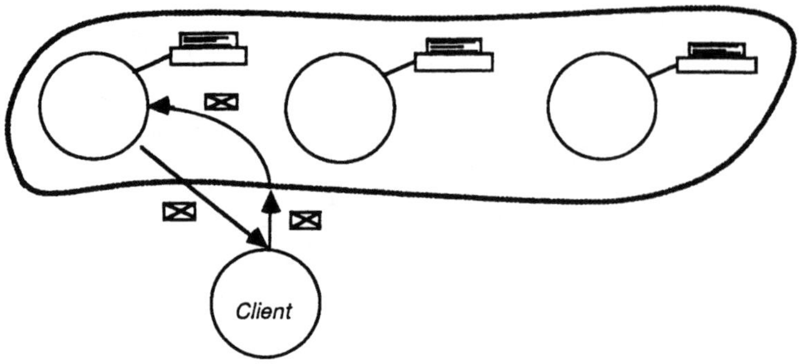

Figure 6 : Printing a file using "one-to-(one-among-N)" Addressing

In summary, group addressing provides more functionality than one-to-one addressing (port-to-port addressing for example) because clients need not know the actual membership of the group or they are not able (or they do not want) to choose a member of the group. Moreover, broadcasting is cheap in local area networks.

The most natural way to introduce the group concept in CHORUS is to support port grouping.

3.4. Groups of Ports in CHORUS

A group of ports is an arbitrary set of ports: it may be empty or it may include opened or closed ports; the ports of a group may be located on any site. A port may belong to zero or more groups, but a group may not belong to another group (in order to avoid cycles). Within an actor, groups are designated by **contextual names,** exactly like ports (*pgds*, see 3.1).

This relationship between ports of a group has only a communication significance. The life of a port is not related to the life of the group (or groups) it belongs to. Mainly, the role of port groups is to allow more powerful communications and addressing than deterministic one-to-one port addressing.

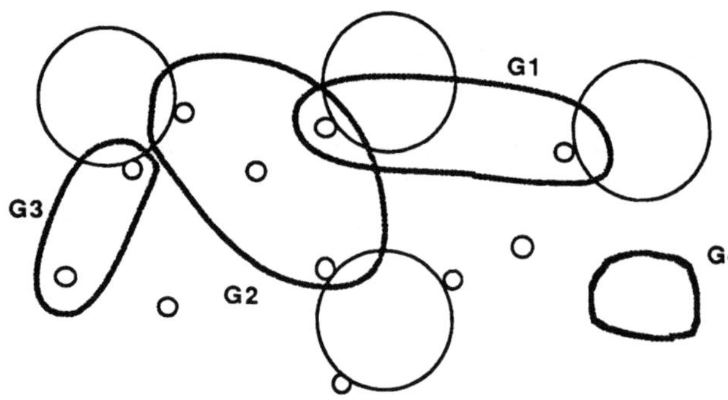

Figure 7 : Ports and Groups of Ports

3.5. Group Management

Groups may be created and destroyed; ports may be inserted or removed from a group. The operations available on groups are detailed in this section.

creatgroup → pgd

creates a new empty group and returns a *pgd* for that group.

dlgroup (pgd)

deletes the group named by *pgd*. An alternative for deleting groups is to create them with the *self-destruction* attribute: when such a group becomes empty, it is automatically destroyed and, conversely, it is the only way to destroy such a group.

So, in CHORUS, users can choose the way a group is destroyed. If a group is a set of ports belonging to an application, it is natural to destroy it automatically when the application ends. However, if the group represents a set of ports of a distributed service S, it must continue to exist even if it becomes empty; in fact, later, another server belonging to S may become active. Here our options are different from those taken by systems that systematically destroy the empty groups: UNIX and the V-System [Cheriton 85] process groups for example.

The last operations on groups control the group membership:

portinsert (port pgd, group pgd)

portremove (port pgd, group pgd)

portisin (port pgd, group pgd) → { yes, no }

respectively insert *port* in *group*, remove *port* from *group* and check whether *port* belongs to *group*. Even if the state of a port changes (open, close), or if the port migrates, it remains in the same groups.

Finally, the system offers some pre-defined groups [Legatheaux 86]: pre-defined groups are neither created nor destroyed, they always exist. The system provides for each user a set of pre-defined groups.

Groups of ports play an essential role in the system. We will discuss our experience on groups use after the presentation of the communication primitives of CHORUS.

4. The CHORUS Inter-Process Communication Facility

A message is a sequence of bytes of arbitrary length; the structure of a message is left to the application level. Messages are exchanged among actors through ports and groups. There is no a priori connection between ports: a message may flow from any source port to any destination port or group, provided that the sender knows a contextual name of the port or the group. The communication mode is the *datagram* or connection-less: once a message is sent, there is no guarantee of eventual delivery.

A message in transit has the following components:

Pe, Pr, Ns, Data

where Pe designates the source port, Pr the destination port or group and Ns the **sequence number** of the message; the sequence number is a global and unique (not reused) stamp that identifies the message forever. The receiver of a message has read-only access to these components of its header, through specific system calls.

We review below two types of communications disciplines: synchronous and asynchronous, and two point of views: the sender and the receiver ones.

4.1. Sender point of view: Asynchronous Communication

putmsg (message, source pgd, destination pgd, addressing mode)

places *message* in the actors transmit queue; the effective transmission of the message is delayed until the end of the current processing-step (see 2.2). The message will be sent from the *source* port (which must be an open port of the actor) to the *destination* port or group.

If the destination is a group, the *addressing mode* parameter is considered. Basically, two values are available:

- **broadcasting**: the message will be sent to all the ports in the group (even if it belongs to the group, the *source* port will never receive a copy of the message);
- **functional**: the message will be sent to only one port in the group, this port being selected in an arbitrary way (the *source* port will never be selected even if it belongs to the group).

If a message M = { Pe, Gr, Ns, Data } is sent to a group (Gr), each receiving port (Pr) receives the message { Pe, Pr, Ns, Data } i. e., groups and addressing modes are transparent to receivers.

4.2. Sender point of view: Synchronous Communication

call (message1, source pgd, destination pgd, addressing mode, delay)
→ message2

performs a request/reply protocol: *message1* is sent from the *source* port to the *destination* port or group; the *addressing mode* must be such that the message is sent to only one port, i. e., *mode* must be the *functional* one if *destination* is a group. The call returns in one of these cases:

- the reply message has been received (*message2*) - i. e., a message with the same *sequence-number* as the request message (see below);
- *delay* has elapsed and the expected message has not been received.

4.3. Receiver point of view

CHORUS does not provide any primitive for message receiving. When a processing-step ends, the actor implicitly enters in the *receiving state*. The next processing-step will be invoked automatically whenever the next message is selected. This state is blocking, a **time-out** mechanism being used to prevent an endless blocking.

The receiver of a message can send it using the *putmsg* call but, if it is involved in a request/reply protocol, it often uses one of the two following calls:

putfwd (message, destination pgd)

forwards the message, i. e., it has the same effect as *putmsg* except that the source port of *message* is not changed, and

putreply (message)

that will reply *message* to its original sender; this is equivalent to a *putmsg* of *message* where source and destination of the message are swapped.

The *sequence-number* of the message is not modified by these calls and, therefore, this number is like a request/reply transaction identifier.

4.4. Our Experience in using the CHORUS IPC and Port Groups

In systems based on the client/server paradigm, as CHORUS, the request/reply protocol is a very powerful facility. *Call* represents the point of view of the client in such an exchange, *putfwd* and *putreply* represent the point of view of the server in the same protocol. Basically, all the system interface procedures (stub procedures) transform their calls in a request/reply protocol with the server concerned by the system function.

Asynchronous send is mainly used by clients that wish to trigger an asynchronous event, or by multiplexed servers engaged in more complex protocols (see section 6).

CHORUS port/group and file servers use broadcasting to locate migrating or duplicated entities. Even when broadcasting is not reliable, our experience confirms that broadcasting is the simplest way to locate such entities. Moreover, more reliable broadcasting protocols can be easily built upon these simple mechanisms (as proposed in [Cheriton 85]).

UNIX process groups are easily implemented with CHORUS port groups. A group of actors G is implemented as a group of *signal ports* (see 3.2). A signal sent to G is then a *signal message* broadcasted on this port group. In the same way, the system builds the group of all the children of an actor, the group of all the actors attached to the same terminal, etc. These groups are all fully distributed.

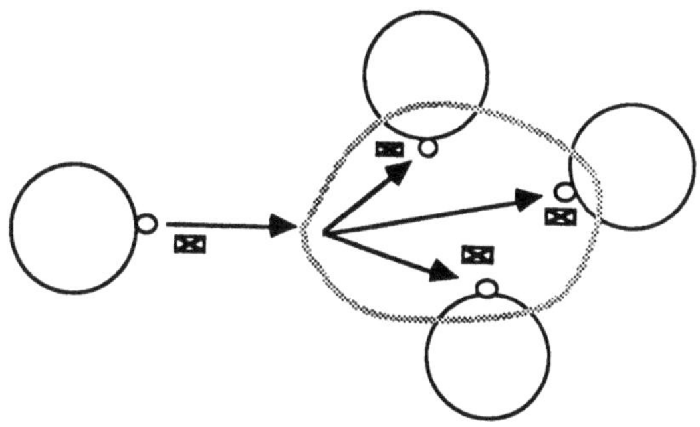

Figure 8 : Signal Broadcasting upon a Group of Actors

Further useful examples of functional addressing use are:

- **Load Balancing:** in CHORUS, load balancing among several equivalent servers can be implemented in the following way: the service is represented by a group of ports (one for each server). The clients address that group in the *functional addressing mode.* Each time a server is selected and receives a message, it removes its port from the group, processes the client's request, replies and re-inserts its port in the group.
- **Binding:** a client wishing to establish a continuous dialogue with any server among a set of equivalent servers first calls the servers group in the *functional mode* and, in the next calls, uses the source port of the first reply.

So, port groups and the *functional addressing mode*, taken together, provide a concept allowing the implementation of communication paths with N senders and M alternating receivers.

5. Naming and Binding

Having presented ports and groups and discussed their use, we show, in this section, how these entities are named and how actors acquire their names.

Generally, operating systems use two kinds of names: symbolic names or user-level names (character strings such as file path-names, user names, etc.) and low-level or internal names (such as process numbers, file descriptor numbers or file internal numbers, etc.). Concerning names, distribution introduces some new requirements:

- naming must be transparent to location; in particular, the rules for structuring the user-level name space must be enforced by administrative and not by location constraints;
- it must be possible for an entity to migrate or be replicated while keeping its name;
- the relationship between a name and the entity it denotes must remain constant even in the presence of faults;
- the naming system must allow the simultaneous use of several sites by one application;

These requirements lead distributed operating systems to build the naming system on top of *global and unique names*, known as UIDs (for Unique IDentifiers), see [Leach 82] for example.

5.1. Naming Layers in CHORUS

CHORUS uses UIDs to designate, at low level, ports and groups. These names have the following structure:

Creation site name	Type	Unique stamp within the site

Figure 9 : The CHORUS UID Structure

Names of sites are statically allocated and are unique within a CHORUS network. The stamp denotes the logical creation time of the entity and is unique within the creation site. These names are globally unique both:

- in space: a given UID always references the same entity even if this entity migrates,
- in time: if an entity is destroyed or lost, its UID will never be re-used to designate another entity even in presence of faults.

In earlier versions of CHORUS, UIDs were directly available to clients. As CHORUS became a full distributed development and execution environment, portability, protection and binding requirements (see [Legatheaux 86]) led us to hide the UIDs behind contextual names. In the current version of the system, actors only know contextual names of ports and groups. UIDs are hidden and only known by the system (kernel and system servers). This contextual address space is protected and typed as the message addressing spaces of Accent [Rashid 81] or DEMOS/MP [Powell 83]. The naming layers present in the system are those of figure 10.

User-level Layer - Symbolic Names
Contextual low-level Layer - Contextual Names (PGD)
Global low-level Names - Global and Unique Identifiers (UID)
Network Addresses

Figure 10 : Naming Layers in CHORUS

In CHORUS, four layers of naming co-exist: network addresses and UID within the system, contextual names within actors and symbolic names at the user level; the system is able to compute all the mappings between names from user level names to network addresses (see the following sections).

5.2. Port Localization Algorithm

For performance and implementation reasons, the dynamic binding to ports and groups representing system services (system servers or kernel services) is achieved by using *static global names* for those ports and groups, i.e. names with stamps known at compile-time. Interface procedures and system servers can compute system port UIDs from their pre-defined stamps and the name of the site where they reside. As these ports never migrate, static port UIDs always contain their current location. This property is essential to avoid recursion in the following algorithm.

In every site a port/group server manages ports and groups. Each of these servers knows the current location of each port that has been created on its site and has migrated. When a network server, or another port server, needs to locate a remote port, it asks the port server that has created the port for its actual location. In order to speed up port addressing, each network server maintains a cache of the location of the last referenced remote ports. Finally, when a site crashes, broadcasting is used to locate the ports it has created.

The protocols used to update the location tables and to request for port location are based on the use of static ports and groups. Moreover, these protocols are very simple because the system considers location information as hints (as a "last solution", broadcast is always available to localize a port).

5.3. Contextual Names, Protection and Binding

Within an actor, **contextual names** reference ports owned by the actor, ports owned by other actors, closed ports and groups. At the same time, two different contextual names known by the same actor always reference two different entities However, as these names can be dynamically acquired or released, the same contextual name may successively reference two different entities. Basically, these names are entries in a table of the actor's context, the message addressing context, that maps contextual names (*pgd*) into global and unique names (UID).

The use of contextual names involves two issues: protection and binding (name exchange). We present below how these two issues are addressed by CHORUS.

Protection, in CHORUS, is based on the following scheme: each actor in the system runs in charge of a given user (generally the user who loaded it); every passive entity (port, group, file, etc.) belongs to an user (generally the user who created it); each entity is associated, at creation time, with a set of protection attributes which specify who may perform which operation on the entity.

Namely, at creation time, a port receives a set of protection attributes which indicate which actors may *open* or *destroy* that port; and a group receives a set of protection attributes which specify which actors may *modify* the group (insert or remove any port and destroy the group) or *self-modify* the group (insert or remove only its own ports).

These protection attributes and the *auto-destruction* attribute are implicitly specified by a contextual *mask* that the actor may set and that is associated with the subsequent created ports or groups.

A CHORUS contextual name differs from a *capability*: its knowledge is required, but not sufficient, to manipulate the entity it denotes. It only shares the properties of a capability under the point of view of the *message sending right*: the knowledge of a contextual name of a port is sufficient to send messages to that port. However, to get the *receiving right* upon one port, an actor must have the right to open it; and to get the *receiveing right* upon a group, an actor must have the right to belong to the group. Port and groups protection attributes are static and can not be acquired or released dynamically.

Let us now examine the binding and exchange of contextual names. In systems with typed messages, as Accent [Rashid 81] for example, this typing may be used to exchange contextual names among processes. In this case, name exchange and binding does not require special facilities. Clients use this general mechanism to implement their own policies.

In CHORUS, messages are not typed but the system offers some facilities for inheritance and dynamic acquisition of contextual names. We present now these facilities:

1) Automatic Sender Identification

The system records in each message header the UID of the sender. The operation:

msgsrc (message) → pgd

allows an application actor to get a contextual name that designates the source port of *message*.

2) Inheritance of Contextual Names

When an actor is created, it inherits the contextual names known by its parent. The system allows the parent to hide some of these names to its children. This facility, taken together with the possibility for the parent actor to create ports that its children will open, may be used to load and bind together the members of a distributed application; this scheme is, in some way, analogous to the scheme used by the UNIX command interpreter (the *shell*) to load pipe-line commands if pipes are replaced by ports and pipe-lines by nets of actors (see [Legatheaux 86] for details and illustrative examples).

3) Dynamic Binding using Symbolic Names

CHORUS file servers have been extended to support an elementary name service. Ports and groups may be associated with symbolic names through special nodes of the file tree which are called *port/group nodes*. A port or a group may be thought of as representing a service and the associated symbolic name is the user level name of that service.

For instance, the actor in charge of managing a laser printer has a port which receives the message requests for printing; that port may be named */printers/laser*. When this actor starts its operation, it associates that port with this user level name by calling:

setname ("/printers/laser", pgd)

A client of the laser printer may get a contextual name of the same port by calling:

getname ("/printers/laser") → pgd

The association between a port or a group and a symbolic name is independent of the state of the port or the group: for example, an actor may get a *pgd* of a closed port and open it. It is the client's responsibility to ensure the consistency of names.

To sum up, binding can be the result of communication, of inheritance, or of the use of a name service.

The name service is integrated with the file service; which we shall now discuss.

5.4. Distributed Interpretation of Symbolic Names

As we have stated before, distribution requires a naming system with location transparency (i. e., global names) and freedom to structure the user level name space by administrative decisions, independent of location constraints. These requirements are satisfied by systems that offer an unique name space, as for example an unique name tree (Grapevine [Birrell 82], LOCUS [Popek 81]).

Building such a name space requires replication of directories and/or files. To avoid such complication, many systems offer name spaces that are built by interconnecting (i.e. by introducing some kind of special link among) "local" name spaces. The most popular approaches are known as the "network root" approach (Apollo/DOMAIN [Leach 83] for instance) and the "remote mount" approach (NFS [Sandberg 85] for instance). These intermediate approaches are more or less suitable; this depends mainly on the context of use of these systems.

CHORUS also takes an intermediate approach, but is open to evolution: the CHORUS file and naming system is a collection of interconnected local UNIX-like (extended) file systems. In addition to traditional "local" file access, CHORUS offers new facilities which are a sound basis on the way to an *integrated* distributed file and naming system. These facilities are based on two extensions in the UNIX-like "local" file systems: port/group nodes and distributed interpretation of path names based on symbolic forwarding.

As we have already said, port/group nodes allow the registration in the file tree of an access point to a server. When a file server interprets the path-name contained in a client's request message, each time it encounters a port/group node (which needs not be the final name of the path), it replaces the initial path-name by the yet uninterpreted part of it and forwards the client's request message (using *putfwd*, see 4.3) to the corresponding port or group (if the node represents a group, the addressing mode is the *functional* one). If the message is forwarded to another file server, the name interpretation continues in that server and, when finally the path-name is exhausted, the concerned server may execute the client's request and reply (using *putreply*, see 4.3).

One of the results of this distributed name interpretation is to allow the introduction of arbitrary links between a leaf node of a file server and the root node of another one. This is approximatly the function of a "remote mount". This facility is used to interconnect the several "local" naming trees of a CHORUS system in the CHORUS naming forest.

5.5. Naming Conventions of the CHORUS naming forest

This section shows how the above protocol has been used in CHORUS to build a distributed file system allowing access transparency (access to "local" and "remote" files is equivalent), naming transparency ("local", "remote", as well as "global" file names are syntactically equivalent) and providing network-global names for resources. This is achieved through an access method based on the use of ports to interface file servers as well as some precise naming conventions and the replication of directories.

Every request concerning an open file (read, write, etc.) or a named resource (open, creat, getname, etc.) is, in CHORUS, sent to a file server port. For this access, actors always know the file servers ports associated with their root, current directory or open files [Armand 86]. This access method allows an actor to have its root, current directory and open files managed by different file servers ("local" or "remote"). It also allows, for example, that child actors, even remotly created, share root, current directory and open files with their parents.

In order to allow an actor to access every file, managed by any server, each file server tree contains a directory */fs* (for "file servers") which gathers the identifications of all file servers in the system; these directories are identical in all servers and their leaf nodes are port/group nodes which reference the *root port* , i. e., the port able to interpret path-names starting with "/", in each file server. Therefore, each path-name which begins by */fs* is a network-global path-name: the interpretation of such a path-name will be automatically forwarded to the same server (see the above paragraph), whatever the server which begins the path-name interpretation is, and the path-name will always designate the same entity.

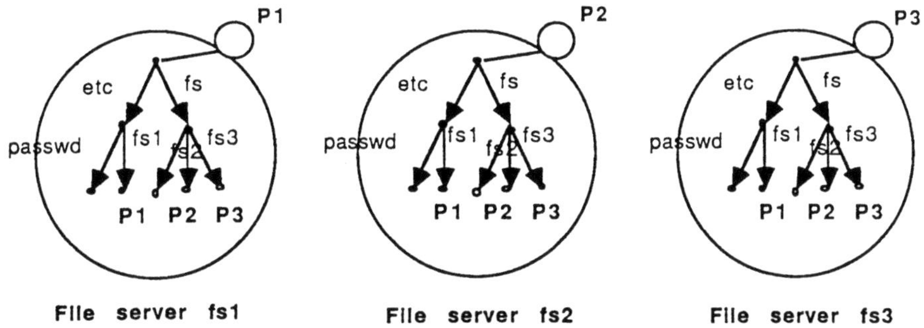

Figure 11 : Configuration of the CHORUS Naming Forest

This forest configuration may be interpreted in two dual ways:

1/ The */fs* directory in each tree contains the directories where other file system tree roots are *mounted remotely*; however, these mounts are automatic and reflect the integrated aspect of CHORUS.

2/ All the naming trees are interconnected through a kind of *network root, /fs* (introduced with no syntactic exception);

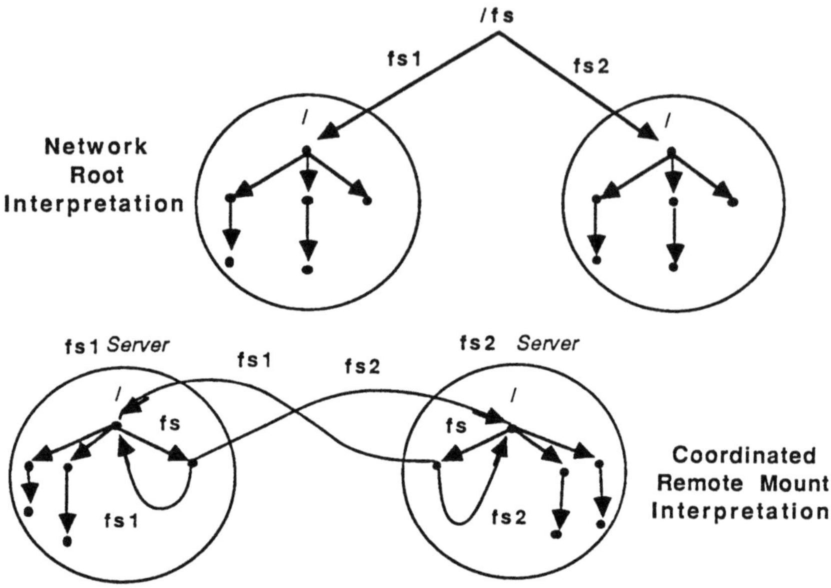

Figure 12 : The dual interpretations of the CHORUS Naming Conventions

This configuration allows the mapping of network-global symbolic names to the name of the port of the server being able to interpret them. Why did we choose it? Because it is rather open to evolution on the way to a truly unique name space (showing an unique name tree). In fact, this scheme is compatible with the introduction of more sophisticated facilities to locate (replicated) named resources as we show below.

Let's name ***s-absolute*** (absolute for a server) a path-name beginning by "/"; the interpretation of that path-name begins at the root of the tree managed by the file server which interprets it. Two identical s-absolute path-names do not necessarily designate the same entity; they do if they are interpreted by the same server or if the entities referenced by that path-name in two servers are identical, i.e. duplicated. Thus, a s-absolute path-name does not designate one entity but a class of entities with, possibly, several different instances in different servers. By the moment, the equivalence of the different instances is the client's responsibility. However, the client is able to distinguish between the different instances.

For example, in a three sites system (as illustrated on figure 11), the file */etc/passwd* is present in every file server tree. The s-absolute path-name */etc/passwd* designates the class of the files which define the users of the system; this class gathers three instances of the file, respectively designated by */fs/fsm1/etc/passwd, /fs/fsm2/etc/passwd* and */fs/fsm3/etc/passwd.* On the other hand, */fs/fsm1/etc/passwd* always designates the same file whatever the server which begins its interpretation is.

So, our naming conventions support the evolution to full replication of files and currently they also enable clients to manage (manually) their own duplication or back-up facilities. Moreover, the use of symbolic links (which have also been introduced in the CHORUS file servers) and network-global names allow clients to rely on a "s-global vision" of names, rather independent of the servers really used. We are also planning to introduce some special-tailored facilities to help the management of "read-only" replicated files as "/etc/passwd" for example.

The conventions introduced may be summarized as follows:

- a path-name beginning with */fs* is a global path-name;
- a path-name beginning with "/" but not with */fs* is a s-absolute path-name, i.e. relative to the server which interprets it;
- every s-absolute path-name of a replicated entity is also a global path-name for the entity; in particular, all the names of the form */fs/server* are global because of their replication.

This ends our discussion on some issues which concern directly the design of the current version of the CHORUS system. The last section of this paper is more dedicated to an experiment that was run on top of the system. This work was stimulated by some expression problems that our experience in distributed system programming has pointed out. Its result is the design - and implementation - of a new structuring concept for CHORUS: the **activity** [Rozier 86, Banino 85].

6. Distributed Control: The Activity Concept

6.1. Definitions

In a system like CHORUS, a distributed application is basically a set of autonomous processes, with separate address spaces, interacting with each other by message passing. Generally, a complex application is structured into layers of *distributed services*. A distributed service involves a set of *servers* and two kinds of *protocols*. The servers are distributed among the system and manage the *resources* of the service. The two kinds of protocols are the following:

- *access protocols*: the service provides a number of *functions* to the outside world; to each of these functions is associated an access protocol, i.e. the way in which the function is invoked. Such protocols are very simple, and are often "Request/Reply" protocols: the client sends a request to an access point of the service (a port or a group), and waits for an answer. For programming convenience, such protocols are generally embedded into standard procedures, or *stub* procedures (as for the CHORUS system calls - see 2.3).
- *function protocols*: the execution of a function of a distributed service involves the cooperation of different servers. These servers provide the *basic operations* on the resources. The way in which these basic operations are combined to execute the functions is defined by protocols which can be very complex, and are called here *function protocols.*

Let us take the example of our distributed file system. The *resource* is here a set of file trees, distributed over some set of sites. On each site, a local tree is managed by a *file server.* The *functions* offered by this distributed service are for example: open a file, read n bytes from a file, etc. They can be applied to any file in the network. Each of these functions is invoked by a Request/Reply protocol: the *open* system call embeds the sending of an open request to a server (the server which manages its current root or the server which manages its current directory, depending on the structure of the name) and the waiting for an answer. This answer is not necessarily sent by the same server. In fact, the opening of a remote file needs the cooperation of several file servers (see 5). The *basic operations* provided by a file server can be seen as: look if a file - defined by a pathname - is local, open a local file, etc. The *open function protocol* includes the forwarding of the request message by the different servers.

In that case, the function protocol is rather simple. But such protocols can be very complex; for example, they generally include some parallelism; they often involve heterogeneous servers. In the next sections, we focus on the problem of the expression and execution of such protocols.

6.2. Problems and Objectives

Our experience in the design of several distributed services in the CHORUS system led us to point out three general problems:

- the communication primitives found in existing systems are not powerful enough for many parallel protocols. Let us take the example of a client which needs to invoke several operations in different servers. For efficiency reasons, the invocations may be done in parallel. The different answers must be collected. Moreover, because we are in a distributed system, the client must cope with particular situations: a message may be lost, a server may crash or take a very long time to answer, etc. The client must decide when it stops to wait for answers; it will also have to cope with answers which return after this resuming point. In CHORUS and other systems, the communication primitives are too basic for a good description of such behaviors.
- the description of a function protocol is scattered into the different servers involved in the function. For example, in the distributed file system, the protocol which defines the open function is described in the code of all the file servers, and eventually other servers (name servers,...). When a modification must be done on the protocol, existing servers must be modified and replaced. Moreover, the description of the protocol is a part of the description of the basic operations: these a priori independent descriptions may be affected by the modification. Finally, modification is difficult because the protocol is not globally documented.
- at run time, the execution context of the protocol is scattered into the contexts of all the servers. When we need to trace the progress of the protocol, we need to trace all the servers, and then to modify them.

Our approach to solve these problems is the following: a function protocol must be represented as a new type of system entity, which we call an **activity.** An activity is described as a separate algorithm. This description is independent from the description of the basic operations in the servers. Moreover, the tools used for this description must be adapted to parallelism. An activity instance owns its own context, defining the progress of the protocol. The activity appears at run time as a *process* which migrates in the distributed system to invoke the basic operations in the servers.

In the next section, we show how the activity concept has been introduced into the CHORUS system. The architecture of the system has not been modified at all.

6.3. Activities in CHORUS

6.3.1. Notes on CHORUS

In CHORUS, an **activity** appears naturally: it is a graph of processing-steps executed by actors. The *basic operations* introduced above appear explicitly in the actors programs, as processing-steps. In CHORUS, a processing-step is always triggered by a message. Message-passing is the only control tool offered by the CHORUS architecture. The messages are identified, can be very large and have long lives: a given message can be reused during the different phases of a protocol.

The main idea of our experiment derives from these remarks, and consists of implementing the activity as a message, called the activity message.

6.3.2. The Activity Message

Our approach consists of providing a programming method for the activity and mechanisms for the control of its execution. The description of the activity is made in terms of a program, the activity template. We will see later the formalism used to program activities. At run-time, an activity is represented by a message: the activity message. This message holds the description of the computation, i.e. the path of processing steps to be performed, and its current context. The activity message is transmitted from actor to actor, triggering in each of them a processing-step of the activity. When all of the processing-steps required by the activity has been completed, it terminates.

Logically, an activity message has three distinct parts: control, context and data. The control part contains the description of the path of processing-steps to be executed. The context part holds the information representing the identity of the activity message and the current state of its progress. The data part is the only part of the message which can be seen by the various processing-steps which will be executed in the activity (see below).

6.3.3. Execution Model

When an activity message is received on a port, the actor executes a processing-step, as it does for any message received. The activity message is seen as a normal message: the actor accesses only the part of the data of the activity message which has been structured as a normal message. At the end of the processing-step, the actor only *replies* the activity message. When the message is an activity message, the *PutReply* system call updates the context part of the message and determines the next processing-step of the activity from the control part (*Putmsg* or *Putfwd* has no effect on the activity message). It then forces the activity message to be sent to the corresponding port in the system. This processing (the "interpretation step") is done automatically by the system, and the code of the actor does not have to be modified. This mechanism is shown on Figure 13.

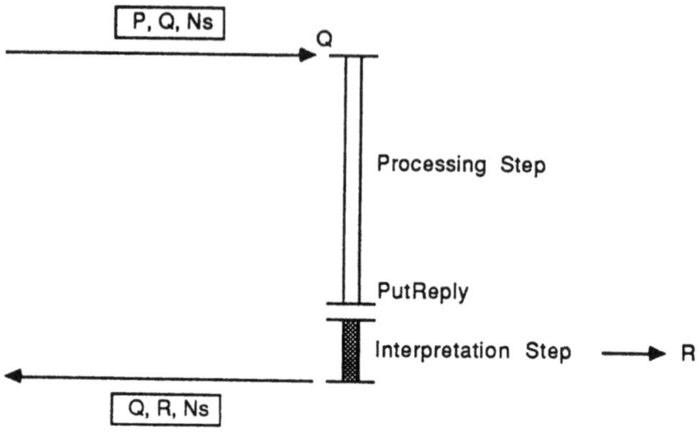

Figure 13 : Activity message processing

6.3.4. Expression Formalism

In the actual implementation, activity templates are written in high level languages (just as are actors). A few specific control structures are added to the language to express activities (see [Rozier 86] for details).

The first additional structure is the basic control structure, the sequential operator. This operator expresses the invocation of a basic operation, i. e., the migration of the activity message to a given port in the system. Its primitive form is the following:

Forward_m (port_name, parameters). This interface procedure causes the activity message to be sent to the "port_name" port in order to trigger the next processing-step of the activity.

Three other control structures, CALL, SPLIT and JOIN are used for the **composition** of activities. They are required to express more complex graphs of processing-steps.

Call (activity_model, parameters) is used to nest activities (the semantics of this construction are similar to a procedure call of another activity).

Split (M, D)
is used to transform an activity into several parallel activities. The syntax of the use of the SPLIT procedure is illustrated on Figure 14.

```
SPLIT (M, Delay) IN
 sub-activity_1 //
 sub-activity_2 //
     ...
 sub-activity_N
ENDSPLIT ;
```

Figure 14 : The SPLIT construction

By the SPLIT construction, the "N" sub-activities are processed in parallel. **JOIN** is used to merge the results of the parallel activities. When a JOIN appears in the code of a sub-activity, the corresponding activity JOINs the main activity. The presence of a JOIN call in the sub-activity programs is optional: some of the sub-activities may have no need to join. In the parameters of the SPLIT call, the programmer gives the minimum number (M) of sub-activities that must JOIN before the main activity resumes and also specifies a delay (Delay) for the success of the "JOIN"s. When all the expected sub-activities have JOINed or when the time-out occurs, the original activity continues its progress. The sub-activities which join after the main activity has resumed are discarded. The structure is associated with a two-way interface scheme: at the SPLIT, the main activity can give some parameters to the sub-activities; when JOINing, a sub-activity may return some results to the main activity.

This SPLIT/JOIN mechanism can be compared to a UNIX fork where the number of children is not limited to one, and where children can communicate some results to the father when terminating. It is a convenient tool for expressing parallel protocols [Rozier 86].

6.3.5. Implementation

An Activity message is implemented as an executable program enclosed in a message. The control part of the message is composed of the code itself. The context part of the message is a subset of the static data of the program and the data part contains the rest of the data for the program. The starting of an activity message consists of the initialization of a message from a compiled activity template.

The current version is implemented in compiled PASCAL. In this implementation, all the features of PASCAL are available to express the control of an activity.

The activity messages are managed in the system by new system actors (these actors perform the creations of activity messages, the split and join operations, etc.). A very important result of our implementation is that the CHORUS system is not affected: the kernel sees activity messages like ordinary messages; activity messages respect the protection rules in CHORUS.

6.4. Conclusion

The activity concept described above provides the system designer with a convenient mechanism for building distributed services. Its most important feature is the two-fold way of expressing a distributed service: on one hand the description of static basic operation in actors, and, on the other hand, the description of the functions as dynamic activities that will invoke these services. The function protocols are described globally as activity templates. The access protocols to the services have a standard form - initialization of an activity message and waiting for the return of this message - embedded into stub procedures. This methodology improves the legibility and flexibility of the distributed applications. It is in particular convenient for programming fault-tolerant applications [Rozier 86, Banino 85a], where complex protocols are added to the functional code of the applications.

In this experiment, we stand up for the idea that a distributed protocol must be described globally (this idea can also be found in [Betourne 85], for example), and be implemented as an active entity in a distributed system. We have exploited the qualities of CHORUS, which offers a clear distinction between processing and communications, and which have proved to be open enough to allow new execution schemes to be defined on its top. Moreover, the implementation is efficient enough to validate the concepts and allow their use for the design of real applications.

Our future work will include a full experimentation of the mechanisms on large applications. We will also focus on the design of higher level formalisms, where actors programming and activities programming would be more homogeneous. Finally, we think that our implementation principle - "intelligent messages" - can be exploited in other fields, like mailing systems or command languages for networks systems.

7. Summary

The main guide-line of the CHORUS design has been to achieve generality with simplicity. A simple message-based architecture led to the design of a complete distributed system which is simple, modular and open to evolution. Moreover, the performances of CHORUS-V2 validate this approach: on a single-processor, they are comparable to those of a native UNIX.

In this paper, we tried to show that our solutions are simple. In fact they are sometimes too simple, leaving some work to the user. But, as we have emphasized, they are rather open to the development of more specific and user-oriented mechanisms. For example, the study of programming formalisms really suited for distribution, initiated with the "activity" experiment, will be a major issue of our future works.

The CHORUS research work is now mature. It is now becoming an industrial product, supported by CHORUS SYSTEMES, an independent company, which will port the system on several machines, enhance it according to the results of standardization and research results and promote it as a basis for the increasing need of interconnection and distribution of homogeneous and heterogeneous computers.

Acknowledgements

Hubert Zimmermann brought many of the original ideas behind CHORUS. Jean-Serge Banino directed the project at INRIA and gave it much inspiration; Gérard Morisset brought the first CHORUS (Version 1) nucleus to real life.

The current version of the system is the result of a cooperative work where individual contributions are intimately mixed. The CHORUS team includes: François Armand, Bruno Deslandes, Michel Gien, Frédéric Hermann, Pierre Léonard, Azzedine Mzouri, Mario Papageorgiou, the authors of this paper, and is directed by Marc Guillemont.

Bibliography

[Armand 86] F. Armand, M. Gien, M. Guillemont, P. Léonard
Towards a Distributed UNIX System - The Chorus Approach
EUUG, Autumn'86. Manchester, (September 1986)

[Banino 82] J.S. Banino, J.C. Fabre
Distributed Coupled Actors: A CHORUS proposal for Reliability
3rd International Conference on Distributed Computing Systems, Miami/FT Lauderdale, Florida, (October 18-22, 1982)

[Banino 85] J.S. Banino, G. Morisset, M. Rozier
Controlling Distributed Processing with CHORUS Activity Messages.
18th Hawaii International Conference on System Science, (January 1985)

[Banino 85a] J.S. Banino, M. Guillemont, J.C Fabre, G. Morisset, M. Rozier
Some Fault-Tolerant Aspects of the Chorus Distributed System
5th IEEE International Conference on Distributed Computing Systems, Denver, Colorado, USA, (May 1985)

[Betourne 85] C. Betourne, M. Filali, G. Padiou, A. Saya
Distributed Control through task migration via abstract networks
5th International Conference on Distributed Computing Systems
Denver, Colorado (May 1985)

[Birrell 82] A.D. Birrell, R. Levin, R.M. Needham, M.D. Schroeder
Grapevine : An Exercise in Distributed Computing
Communications of the ACM, Vol 25, 4, (April 1982)

[Cheriton 84] D.R. Cheriton
The V-Kernel: a software base for distributed systems
Research report, Computer Science Department, Standford University, (April 1984)

[Cheriton 85] D.R. Cheriton, W. Zwaenepoel
Distributed process groups in the V kernel
ACM Transactions on Computer Systems, Vol. 3, No. 2, (May 1985)

[Guillemont 82] M. Guillemont
The CHORUS distributed operating system : design and implementation
International Symposium on Local Computer Networks, Florence, Italy, (April 1982)

[Guillemont 86] M. Guillemont, J. Legatheaux Martins
CHORUS: a new UNIX for the distribution age
Paper submitted for publication. Currently available from the authors at INRIA, (December 1986)

[Leach 82] P.J. Leach et al.
UIDS as Internal Names in Distributed Systems
ACM Symposium on Principles of Distributed Computing, Ottawa, Canada, (August 1982)

[Leach 83] P.J. Leach at al.
The Architecture of an Integrated Local Network
IEEE Journal of Selected Areas in Communications, Vol 1, 5, (November 1983)

[Legatheaux 86] J. Legatheaux Martins
La Désignation et l'Edition de Liens dans les Systèmes d'Exploitation Répartis
(Naming and Binding in Distributed Operating Systems)
Doctorate Thesis, Rennes University I, France (November 1986)

[Popek 81] G. Powell et al.
LOCUS : a Network Transparent, High Reliability Distributed System
8th ACM Symposium on Operating System Principles, Pacific Grove, California (December 1981)

[Powell 83] M.L. Powell, B.P. Miller
Process Migration in DEMOS/MP
9th ACM Symposium on Operating Systems Principles / OSR ACM, Vol 17, 5, (October 1983)

[Rashid 81] R.F. Rashid, G.G. Robertson
Accent : A communication oriented network operating system kernel
8th ACM Symposium on Operating System Principles, Pacific Grove, California, (December 1981)

[Rozier 86] M. Rozier
Expression et Réalisation du Contrôle d'exécution dans un Système Réparti
(Expression and Implementation of Execution Control in a Distributed System)
Doctorate Thesis, INPG, Grenoble, France (October 1986)

[Sandberg 85] R. Sandberg et al.
Design and implementation of the Sun network filesystem
Usenix, Portland (June 1985)

[Zimmermann 81] H. Zimmermann, J.S. Banino, A. Caristan, M. Guillemont, G. Morisset
Basic concepts for the support of distributed systems : the CHORUS approach.
2nd IEEE International Conference on Distributed Computing Systems, Versailles, France, (April 1981)

[Zimmerman 84] H. Zimmermann, M. Guillemont, G. Morisset, J.S. Banino
CHORUS : A communication and processing architecture for distributed systems
INRIA Research Report 328, (September 1984)

THE CONIC SUPPORT ENVIRONMENT FOR DISTRIBUTED SYSTEMS

Jeff Magee, Jeff Kramer, Morris Sloman
Department of Computing, Imperial College, London SW7 2BZ.

Abstract

The Conic environment is designed to support the construction and operation of software for distributed embedded systems. It employs a host/target approach, providing a comprehensive set of tools for program compilation, building, debugging and execution on the host, and supports distributed operation on the targets. In order to provide flexibility, the environment supports dynamic configuration, the ability to reconfigure parts of the system while the rest continues to operate.

This paper sets out the basic philosophy adopted in the construction of the environment and describes in detail its implementation structure and functionality.

1. INTRODUCTION

Distributed systems are frequently used in embedded real-time applications such as factory automation, process control and telecommunications. The reasons for a distributed approach include improved performance, lower cost, higher reliability and the intrinsically distributed nature of applications.

The computers used as distributed controllers in such an environment tend to be comparatively simple processors, often without backing store. It is impractical to use these computers for software development and so a **host/target** approach is used. All software is developed on a host computer with a general purpose operating system which supports hierarchical file stores, databases, screen editors, graphics packages, printers and the tools associated with a programming support environment. The host computer can be used for initial software testing of logical behaviour. Eventually the programs are loaded into read only memory or are down-line loaded over the network into the target computers used for real-time functions.

Support for continued communication between the host and targets in an operational system, is useful. If appropriate, a larger host can still be used by the targets to provide some of the operational facilities, such as a filing system, graphic displays and printing services for logging. Also, the host can interact with the targets to provide more comprehensive source-level debugging. Thus the hardware configuration of the eventual system can be tailored, using mixed host(s) and targets as necessary, to suit the particular application.

Although these large embedded system are essentially static in nature, reflecting the static structure of their embedded environment, there is an aspect of **dynamic change** during their lifetime. On a relatively slow timescale, they are required to evolve to incorporate new functionality and technology as application requirements change. It is not possible to predetermine the *evolutionary changes* which must take place during the long lifetime of an embedded system. On a faster timescale, these systems are required to cater for *operational change* to allow for redimensioning by adding or removing components and reorganisation to recover from failures. This requirement for flexibility is important both during the development stage to allow for prototype construction and evolution, and when the system is operational so that it can easily adapt to changes. Having a host development system connected via a network to the target system allows changes to be validated and controlled.

NATO ASI Series, Vol. F28
Distributed Operating Systems. Theory and Practice
Edited by Y. Paker et al.

The Conic Support Environment

Conic provides the support for both the building and operation of distributed embedded systems. The two basic principles discussed above - host/target (mixed) development and execution, and support for dynamic reconfiguration - are the foundations upon which the Conic system was built. The support environment includes:

i) Host software development facilities which emphasise the production of modular, reuseable components. These facilities are based on a module programming language for "programming in the small" and a configuration language for building systems from predefined modules ("programming in the large"). Together they provide language support for distribution.

ii) The Conic run-time system provides the required communication and operating system features to support distribution. The run-time support also permits the system to be reconfigured dynamically and so provides the flexibility for the system to evolve and change to meet changing requirements and conditions.

The run-time facilities on the host provide similar support for the execution of software destined for target stations, and include access to host facilities from the targets, and for access to the targets for debugging and reconfiguration.

In addition to the main principles discussed above, the construction of the Conic environment adhered to the following interrelated guidelines wherever possible:

i) The same facilities should be used for the construction of the support system and its environment as is intended for the application.

In many embedded systems, it is difficult to distinguish between the application software and that of the support system. A corollary of this is that the same tools should be appropriate for the construction and operation of both. This then provides a uniform approach for the management of both system and application, and can be the basis for the construction of an "open" system (discussed below).
With the exception of a less than 100 lines of assembly code in the kernel, **all** the software for the Conic environment is implemented in Conic. This has also permitted us to easily configure the system to suit particular hardware or application environments.

ii) The system and its environment should be "open", both in terms of user modification and access.

An "open" system should provide easy access to all its facilities by use of the appropriate interface, and also provide the means for ready modification and extension of its facilities by users. Such an approach is certainly facilitated by the use of common construction tools for system and application ie. adherence to the first guideline (above). The use of a common interface structure for component interaction will also help. In our case, components all have message passing interfaces.

iii) The underlying support system should be simple and efficient.

In order to provide support for real-time systems, it is imperative that the system constructs used are not complex, nor should they require costly (in terms of time or space) support. There should be no hidden implementation overheads in the primitives provided for accessing the services of the support envrironment. More complex facilities should be implemented 'on top' of the simpler ones where required, rather than forcing users to pay the cost even when they are not used.

The primitives available in Conic have been designed to be simple and appropriate, yet capable of an efficient implementation. Furthermore, configuration of the system permits selection of those facilities actually required.

iv) As far as possible, the logical software configuration should be independent of the physical hardware architecture.

Our description of the use of a host/target approach has assumed adoption of this guideline. It is essential if one is be able to test the logical behaviour of the software on the host, and also to retain the freedom to allocate and subsequently reconfigure the software in distributed targets. Local and remote communication should have same logical semantics so that reallocation of software does not change the logical behaviour. In addition the environment should be capable of generating software to run on a variety of types of hosts and targets.

Conic provides the same primitives for local and remote communication and is easily ported to different hardware.

The rest of this paper describes the Conic support environment. First we outline the important features of the Conic programming and configuration languages (section 2). The associated host tools for compiling and configuring systems are described in section 3. The structure of the station executive — kernel, device drivers, remote communications, and file and error handling — are then presented in section 4. A similar executive is used on both the host and targets. Finally, the support for dynamic configuration is discussed in section 5.

2. THE CONIC PROGRAMMING AND CONFIGURATION LANGUAGES.

Conic provides a language based approach to building distributed systems which clearly distinguishes between the programming of individual software components and the building of systems from these components. In this section we give an overview of these languages.

2.1 Conic Module Programming Language

The language for programming individual software components (modules) is based on Pascal which has been extended to support modularity and message passing primitives [Kramer 84]. The language allows the definition of a *task module type* which is a self-contained, sequential task (process). At configuration time, *module instances* are created from these types. Module instances exchange messages and perform a particular function such as controlling a device or managing a resource.

The Module interface is defined in terms of strongly typed ports which specify all the information required to use the module. An *exitport* denotes the interface at which message transactions can be initiated and provide a local name and type holder in place of the source name and type. An *entryport* denotes the interface at which message transactions can be received and provide a local name and typeholder in place of the source name and type. The binding of an exitport to an entryport is part of the configuration specification and cannot be performed within the task module programming language.

The Conic task module thus provides *configuration independence* in that all references are to local objects and there is no direct naming of other modules or communication entities. This means there is no configuration information embedded in the programming language and so no recompilation is needed for configuration changes ie. Conic modules are *reuseable* in many different situations.

The programming language supports communication primitives to *send* a message to an exitport or *receive* one from an entryport. The message types must correspond to the port types. There are two classes of message transactions:

i) A **notify transaction** provides unidirectional, potentially multi- destination message passing. The send operation is asynchronous and does not block the sender, although the receiver may block waiting for a message.

ii) A **Request Reply** provides bidirectional synchronous message passing. The sender is blocked until the reply is received from the responder. A fail clause allows the sender to withdraw from the transaction on expiry of a timeout or if the transaction fails. The receiver may also block waiting for a request. The receiver of a message can **forward** it via an exitport to another task as an alternative to replying.

Definitions Units are used to define constants, types, functions and procedures which are common between different modules within a system. These can be compiled independently and can be imported into a module to define a **context**. The definitions unit allows the introduction of language "extensions", such as string definitions and manipulation procedures, without modifying the compiler. The definitions unit may also define data and initialisation code and so provides a facility similar to Modula-2 [Wirth 82] modules and Ada™ [USA DOD 80] packages.

The following example of a task module which acts as scaling filter for its inputs gives the "flavour" of Conic programs.

```
task module scale(scalefactor:integer);
    entryport
          control: boolean;
          input:   real reply signaltype;
    exitport
          output: real reply signaltype;
    var
          value: real;
          active: boolean;
begin
    active := false;
    loop
          select
                receive active from control =>
          or
                when active
                receive value from input reply signal =>
                      send value/scalefactor to output wait signal;
          end
    end
end.
```

2.2 Conic Configuration Language

The Conic configuration language is used to specify both the initial system and subsequent changes [Dulay 84]. It defines the following:

Context — the set of message types (from definition units) and module types needed for the system.

Instantiation — the named module instances to be created in the system from module types. Parameters can be passed to module instances when they are created.

Interconnection between module instances — linking or binding a module exitport to a module entryport. Both type and operation compatibility are checked so an exitport can only be linked to an entryport of the same data type. One-to-one, one-to-many and many-to-one interconnection patterns are supported.

Configuration Abstraction — hierarchical structures can be represented at the configuration level by nesting configuration specifications. A group module type (ie. a subsystem) is itself a configuration specification and may consist of a collection of task modules or other group module types, instance declarations and interconnections. The group module also has an interface defined in terms of entry and exitports and so from the outside it is not possible to distinguish between a single task module or a group module.

An example of a configuration language specification which uses the task module previously defined is given below. The structure of this system is depicted in Figure 2.1.

```
group module monitor;
    use
        scale; sensor; display;
    const
        Tfactor = 10;
        Pfactor = 100;
    create
        temperature: sensor;
        pressure: sensor;
        Tscale: scale(Tfactor);
        Pscale: scale(Pfactor);
        display;
    link
        temperature.output to Tscale.input;
        pressure.output to Pscale.input;
        Tscale.output to display.temp;
        Pscale.output to display.press;
        display.control to Tscale.control, Pscale.control;
end.
```

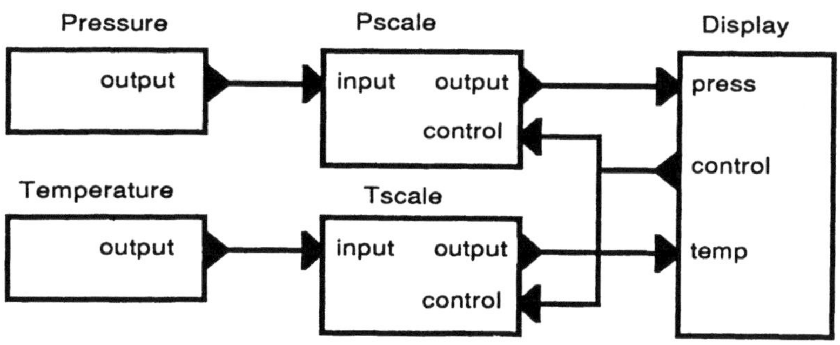

Figure 2.1 - Monitor System

3. HOST / TARGET DEVELOPMENT

The output of the Conic host program development system is a set of logical stations which form the units of configuration. A *logical station* is a collection of application task modules in a single address space together with the *executive* necessary for run-time support. These logical stations may be executed either as UNIX processes or on bare target computers with no resident operating system. This ability to execute programs on either the host or the target considerably eases the development and debugging of distributed applications. Typically, applications are tested on the host computer and then moved to the target. Communication between tasks running within the same logical station and between tasks running in different logical stations (whether target or host) is transparent to the tasks involved in the communication. Consequently, the logical behaviour of a system is independent of the hardware configuration to which it is mapped. Execution speed and communication latency will obviously depend on hardware configuration.

For example, the *monitor* system outlined in section 2 may be mapped as shown in Fig. 3.1.

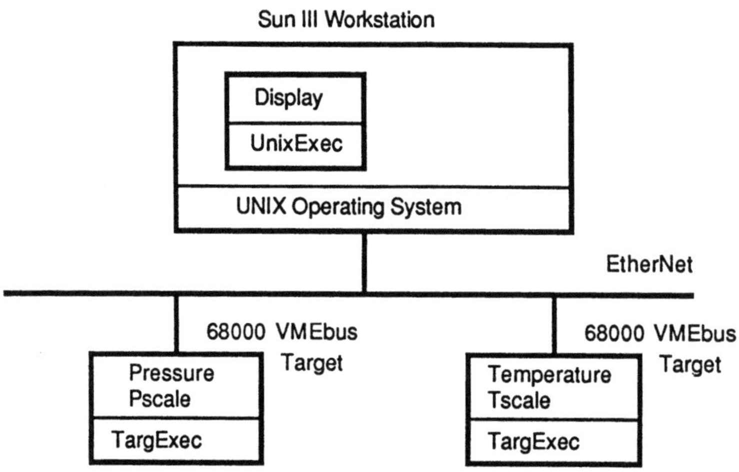

Figure 3.1 Monitor System: Hardware Configuration

3.1 Configuration Language Builder

The system of Figure 3.1, is generated on the host computer (in this case a SUN workstation) by the Configuration Builder from the following description.

```
group module monitor;
    use
        scale; sensor; display;
        UnixExec; TargExec;
    const
        Tfactor = 10;
        Pfactor = 100;
    create at node(1,"sun")
        UnixExec;
        display;
```

```
create at node(2,"t68k")
      TargExec;
      temperature:sensor;
      Tscale:scale(Tfactor);
create at node(3,"t68k")
      TargExec;
      pressure:sensor;
      Pscale:scale(Pfactor);
link
      temperature.output to Tscale.input;
      pressure.output to Pscale.input;
      Tscale.output to display.temp;
      Pscale.output to display.press;
      display.control to Tscale.control, Pscale.control;
end.
```

The executive modules *UnixExec* and *TargExec* provide the run-time support for multi-tasking and intertask communication under Unix and on a standalone target respectively. These modules are described in section 4. The output of the builder is a set of executable images *monitor1, monitor2* and *monitor3. Monitor1* can be executed directly on the host computer by invoking it as a UNIX command while *monitor2* and *monitor3* must be downloaded over the Ethernet to the target computers. The builder is essentally an intelligent linker which assembles the correct object code modules and type checks the connections between exit and entry ports. The node descriptions e.g. node(2,"t68k"), enable the builder to check that code modules are appropriate for the target processor and enables the correct run-time libraries to be incorporated into the logical station image. The connections between modules are type checked using symbol table information produced by the programming language compiler.

3.2 Programming Language Compiler

A primary objective of the Conic development system was that it should support cross-compilation to different processor types and have the capablity of being easily portable to different host computers. Consequently, we have constructed the compiler using the Amsterdam Compiler Kit (ACK) [Tanenbaum 83] running under the UNIX* operating system. ACK makes use of an intermediate code (EM) to allow compilers to generate code for more than one target machine architecture. The use of ACK has facilitated the design objective of portability allowing Conic programs to run on a range of processors. Currently, VAX, PDP11 and 68000 processors are supported.

Figure 3.2 shows the relationship between the various components of the Conic program construction system.

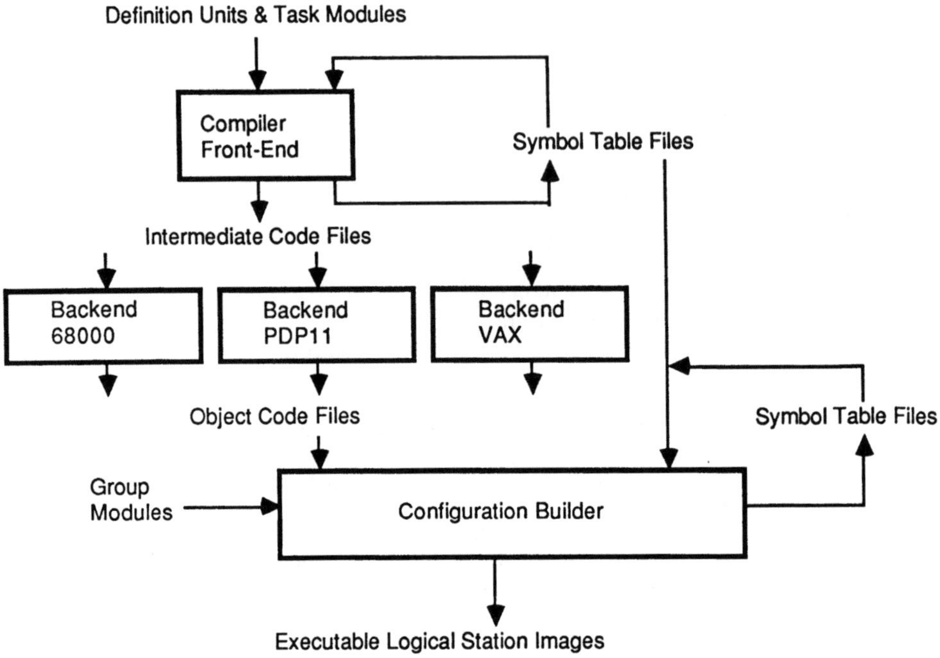

Figure 3.2 Conic Program Construction System

To simplify the maintenance of large complex systems the system includes a *makefile generator* tool. This analyses a Conic group module specification to determine dependencies and generates the required commands for the UNIX *make* utility [Feldman 83] to build a system from its source.

This section has decribed the tools for building distributed configurations. These configurations are essentially static. The facilities available for dynamically configuring systems are described in section 5.

4. STATION EXECUTIVE

The executive is the component of a Conic logical station which provides the run-time support for Conic tasks. It consists of the components shown in fig. 4.1:

Kernel:	supports multi-tasking, first-level interrupt handling, inter-task communication *within* a station;
ErrorManager:	handles error reporting and debugging;
TimeManager:	device handler for a real-time clock;
Console:	visual display terminal handler;
EtherComms:	supports inter task communication *between* stations.
FileManager:	provides Pascal file I/O facilities.

The executive is itself a Conic group module containing a set of Conic task modules. Consequently, the executive can easily be configured to deal with different hardware configurations and to provide different facilities. As outlined in the previous section, two main versions of the executive exist: *UnixExec* which provides run-time support under UNIX, allowing Conic logical stations to run as UNIX processes, and *TargExec* which provides run-time support on target machines with no native operating system. The structure of *TargExec* is described in Figure 4.1.

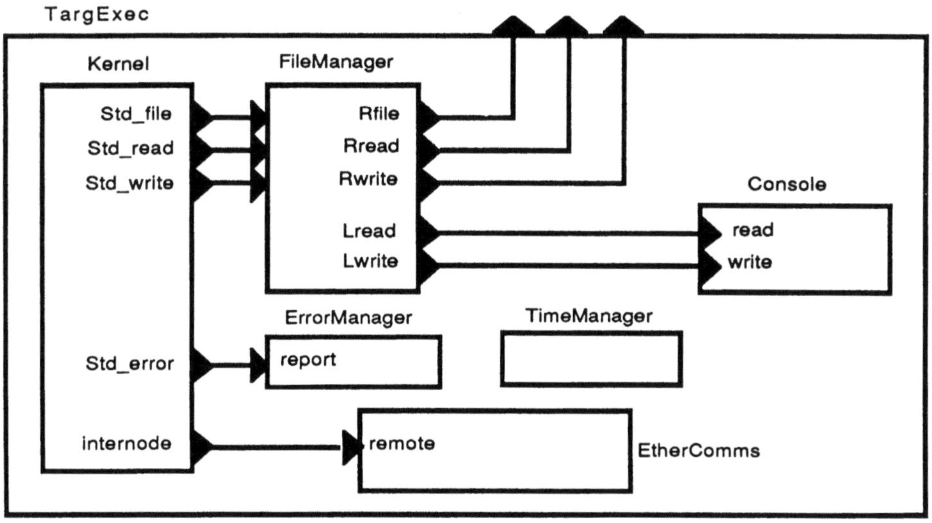

Figure 4.1 Standalone Target Executive

4.1 Kernel

The *kernel* component of the station executive creates the configuration of linked task instances within a station at station start-up time. The kernel is implemented in Conic as a task module. Unlike normal task modules, it is not scheduled but executes in response to kernel calls by other task modules. The kernel has been kept largely machine independent by isolating dependencies into a small number of routines implemented in assembler and by ensuring that devices are handled by separate task modules (see below). Currently, the assembler component of the kernel amounts to less than 100 source lines. These routines deal with context switching and first-level interrupt handling. The kernel included in *UnixExec* differs only in the details of kernel entry and the way it handles interrupts (UNIX signals).

The kernel implements the message primitives described in section 2.1, but handles only local (intra-station) intertask communication. It passes messages destined for remote stations to the communication module (in this case *EtherComms*) via its exitport *internode*. The communication module is described in more detail in section 4.3.

Currently, the kernel supports memory-only systems where the code and data for each task is permanently in main memory. Tasks are scheduled according to a priority pre-emption strategy. A task may change its priority by a kernel call. Tasks within a logical station share the same address space and so can communicate information by reference as well as by value. Communication by reference is extensively used within the executive to reduce the copying overheads associated with normal message passing. Conic logical stations are similar in this respect (shared address space) to *teams* in V-kernel [Cheriton 84] and *guardians* in Argus [Liskov 83].

4.2 Device Handlers

Device Handlers in Conic do not form part of the basic kernel but are implemented as separate task modules. Consequently, users can easily incorporate their own device modules to handle application specific input/output. The executive provides modules to handle the interrupts from a real-time clock *(TimeManager)* and a VDT device *(console).* Versions of these modules also exist in *UnixExec.* A console module is needed under UNIX to make UNIX synchronous I/O calls appear asynchronous for other Conic tasks running within the UNIX process (otherwise a *read* call from one task would suspend all tasks, waiting for the read to complete).

Initially, the interrupt handling model incorporated in Conic was similar to that incorporated in Ada[USA DOD 80] in that each interrupt was converted into a message. However, this proved too inefficient and slow for handling interrupts with a high repetition rate (e.g. 9600 baud serial lines) and consequently the method illustrated in the example below is now used. The example is a driver for sending data to a serial line device on a Q-bus based computer (e.g. LSI11/23).

```
define IOtypes: write_req; {exported type}
    type
        buffer = array [1..512] of byte;
        write_req = record
                        count:integer;
                        data:^buffer;
                    end;
end.


task module transmitter( status,vector:natural);
    use
        kercalls:setpriority,priorityT,IntMap,SendSignal;
        IOtypes:write_req;
    entryport
        input: write_req reply signaltype;
        done:signaltype;
    const
        enable = 0100#8; disable = 0;
    var
        xcsr:^natural; xbuf:^byte; request:write_req; Nsent:integer;
```

```
    procedure Handler; {Interrupt Handler}
    begin
        if Nsent = request.count then begin
            xcsr^ := disable;
            SendSignal;
        end else begin
            Nsent := Nsent+1;
            xbuf^ := request.data^[Nsent];
        end;
    end;

begin
    setpriority(highpr); {give task high priority}
    ref(xcsr,status);    {initialise xcsr to point to device status reg}
    ref(xbuf,status+2);
    IntMap(done,vector,Handler); {maps interrupt vector onto handler}
    loop
        receive request from input;
            Nsent:=0;
            xcsr:=enable; {start device - generates an immediate interrupt}
            receive signal from done;
        reply signal to input;
    end;
end.
```

The *IntMap* procedure associates an interrupt handling procedure and an entryport of type signal (*done*) with the interrupt vector. The interrupt procedure *Handler* is invoked on every interrupt but a message is only sent (using *SendSignal*) to the entryport *done* when the entire buffer has been output. This technique avoids the overhead of sending a message on every interrupt. Device drivers and their interrupt handlers are written in a high-level language and form a single configuration unit ie. a task module.

4.3 Interstation communication

Inter-station communication for targets is handled by a communication group module. A number of different communication modules are available under Conic which handle different transmission media (e.g Ethernet, Cambridge Ring) and different topologies (e.g interconnected subnets) [Sloman 86]. The internal structure of the module *EtherComms* used in Figure 4.1 is depicted in Figure 4.2.

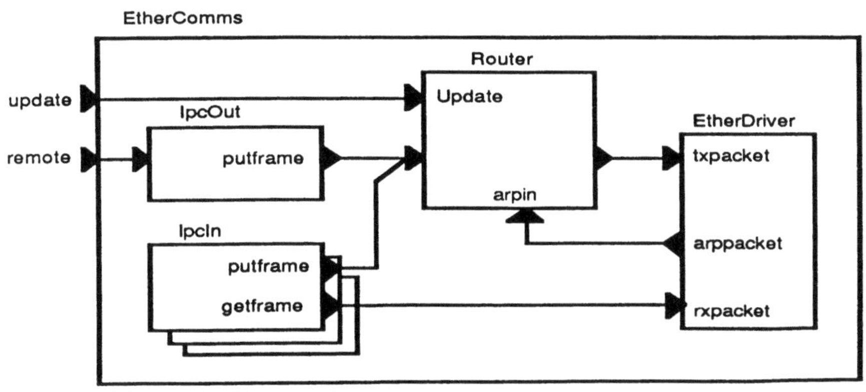

Figure 4.2 The Communications Group Module

To facilitate communication with stations running under UNIX, the communications module implements Conic port to port communication on top of the Internet UDP/IP protocol [Leffler 83, Postel 83, DOD 80] used by BSD 4.2 UNIX. Packets consequently have the following format:

Ethernet header	IP Header	UDP Header	Conic IPC header	User Data	CRC checks etc

Figure 4.3 Packet Format

A message sent to a remote station is forwarded by the kernel to the *remote* entryport of the *Ipcout* module. This module constructs a Conic IPC header which contains the address of the destination entryport and the source exitport. Conic IPC addresses are of the form:

logical station number. module instance number. port number.

Remote address information is maintained by the kernel in its port linkage data structures and obtained by *Ipcout* using privileged kernel calls not available to normal application modules.

The message is then forwarded to the *Router* module which constructs the UDP and IP headers. The *Router* module maintains a mapping table from Conic logical station numbers to the triple:

<UDP port number, Internet Address, EtherNet Address>.

The mapping (for all logical stations) to UDP port number and Internet address is given to the *Router* module at configuration time via its *Update* port. The Address Resolution Protocl (ARP) [Plummer 82] is used to translate Internet to EtherNet addresses.

Incoming messages are picked up by one of the instances of *Ipcin* from the ethernet driver module. This module strips the headers and calls a kernel operation to send the message to an entryport. The module then (in the case of request-reply communication) suspends waiting for the reply message which it transmits out of the station via the *Router* module. *Ipcin* acts as a local surrogate task for the remote sender.

A simple buffering strategy has been adopted which has proved adequate for the applications we have so far encountered. Application messages are restricted in size so that they can be contained inside one ethernet packet. The communication system contains one transmit buffer encapsulated by *Ipcout.* Messages are thus buffered by the normal message queue associated with the entryport *remote.* Receive buffers are provided by the instances of *Ipcin.* Each instance of *Ipcin* encapsulates one receive buffer. The number of instances is specified in the configuration description of *Ethercomms.*

The host executive *UnixExec* contains a similar but simpler communications module *Unixcomms*. In this module the functions of *Router* and *EtherDriver* are excluded since their functions are performed by the UNIX networking kernel. They are replaced by the module *Socdriver* which provides an interface to Berkley UNIX socket calls. The combination of *Ethercomms* and *Unixcomms* allows Conic applications to be arbitrarily distributed over multiple host computers (running UNIX) and multiple target computers connected by ethernet.

The basic design philosophy behind the communication system was that it should map the Conic IPC primitives on to a simple and efficient but unreliable datagram service. Services such as virtual circuits and message fragmentation/ re-assembly can be configured into systems, where necessary, as additional Conic modules. A more detailed description of Conic communication may be found in [Sloman 86].

4.4 File Handling

Conic is a superset of Pascal and so the run-time system must support Pascal file handling. To maintain the configuration flexibility of the executive, file handling is not supported by the kernel but is provided by a separate *Filemanager* module (fig. 4.1). Each Conic task module is given a standard set of exitports by the compiler *Std_File, Std_read, Std_write* and *Std_error.* The language run-time system turns calls to the Pascal file primitives (*rewrite, reset, write, read etc*) into message operations on the first three of these ports. The use of *Std_error* is described in the next section.

The standard ports may be linked explicitly in a Configuration description; however, usually they are linked by default by the kernel. At startup time, the kernel links all standard ports to the entryports to which its own standard ports are linked, i.e. the links from the kernel standard ports which are specified explicitly, form a template for all other standard ports.

The *FileManager* included in the target executive performs the simple task of directing read and write requests either to the local console for inter-active I/O or to the executive interface ports for disk file requests. Usually, these target executive interface ports will be linked to a file server. Conic station running on a host computer. Tasks running in a target thus have full access to the host file system. It is easy to see how *FileManager* could be modified to provide access to a local file service in addition to the remote service by giving it an extra set of exitports. A simple naming scheme would allow the manager to chose the destination for file requests. Currently, as an experiment, we are implementing an executive module to give access to Sun's Network File Service (NFS) [Sandberg 86].

The dual of *FIleManager* in *UnixExec* calls the operating system file operations directly. However, as mentioned in section 4.2, requests for interactive I/O to a console module must be forwarded by the *Filemanager.*

4.5 Error Handling / Debugging

All run-time exceptions, whether detected by the language run-time system, kernel, hardware or host operating system result in an error message being sent on the *Std_error* port of the task which was running when the error occurred. This *Std_error* port is usually linked by default to an errormanager, module although applications may chose to explicitly handle errors for recovery purposes by explicitly linking the *Std_error* ports to an application provided error handler. The *ErrorManager* included in *TargExec* displays an error message on the local console, stating the task instance in which the error occurred, the line number and type of error. This simple facility is usually sufficient, since applications are usually well debugged on the host before they are executed on a target computer. Note that it is simple to configure the system such that all errors are reported at a central error reporting station by changing the default link for *Std_error.*

Programs are usually debugged on the host by using *DebugExec* instead of *UnixExec.* This executive includes *DumpManager* which replaces *ErrorManager* and an additional module *TraceManager.*

DumpManager dumps the state of a task when an error occurs. This state can be examined using a post-mortem dump analyser (*pm*) which uses compiler symbol table information to display the state in terms of source code variable names and types. Successive dumps of a task's state can be obtained by compiling break-points into the source code.

TraceManager allows line by line tracing of a set of tasks for a specified number of steps up to the point where an error occurred. Tasks compiled with the trace option on generate trace information which is periodically dumped to file by *TraceManager*. This trace information is used by the playback utility (*pb*) to provide a display of the execution in terms of source code lines.

Both *pm* and *pb* are implemented as Conic logical stations. It is intended in the future to modify them so that they can be run on-line with the system they are examining. It is worth mentioning that while both *DumpManager* and *TraceManager* may be run in target stations, since these have access to the host file system, this is rarely done as they interfere with the real-time behaviour of an application. By the time an application is moved to a target it is usually the realtime behaviour which is of interest, logical bugs having been cured on the host.

4.6 Summary

This section has attempted to show how the run-time executives which support distributed Conic applications are provided in a simple and uniform way using the configuration and programming languages. Services are accessed through entryports and devices are encapsulated in task modules. The kernel is configured in a uniform way as a task module. A user may easily configure an executive to suit his needs by adapting one of the standard executives. System generation in Conic is the process of building a system from its configuration specification. The system is "open" in the Pilot sense [Redel 80] since users may access any executive service by linking to the appropriate entryport.

Logical stations may be run either on host computers running UNIX or standalone targets. Typically, this means that the time critical parts of a system will be run on targets and the management and display components will be run on a host computer to exploit facilities such as the SUN workstation multi-window displays.

5. DYNAMIC CONFIGURATION MANAGEMENT

The previous two sections have described the tools and run-time support for statically configured systems. The connection information which specifies the links between logical stations is built into each executable station image by the static configuration builder. Changing a statically configured system means rebuilding it from its constituent components. Static configuration is reasonable for moderately sized systems where the entire system can be built on a single host computer and where the system does not change frequently. As mentioned in the introduction, large embedded systems do not remain static, but evolve over time. The objective of dynamic configuration management is to support the modification and extension of systems on-line [Kramer 85].

The long-term aim is that it should be possible to modify systems at any level down to adding and deleting individual task modules, however, the current version of dynamic configuration management deals only with logical stations. This level was chosen since while meeting a large part of users requirements for dynamic configuration it simplified the implementation to allow early experimentation. The current version of dynamic configuration management allows the construction of systems from stations built on different host computers and allows these systems to be managed by configuration managers running on multiple hosts. Shortly, the system will support the integration of systems from stations both constructed on and executing on different types of processor (i.e heterogeneous systems).

5.1 The User View of Dynamic Configuration

To illustrate the way a user constructs and modifies a system dynamically, in the following, the Monitor system of Figure 3.1 is constructed incrementally. As discussed above, dynamic configuration deals with logical stations and consequently, the Monitor system is first partitioned into two logical station types specified as shown below.

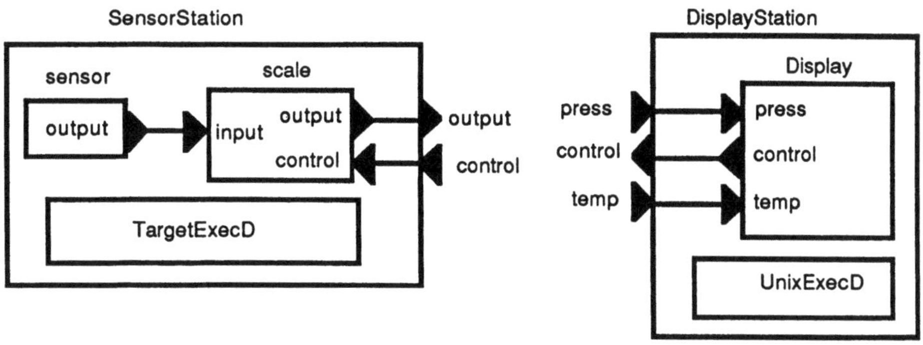

Figure 5.1 Logical Station Types

group module SensorStation(factor:integer);

> **exitport**
> > output:real **reply** signaltype;
>
> **entryport**
> > control:boolean;
>
> **use**
> > TargetExecD; scale; sensor;

```
        create
                TargetExecD;
                sensor;
                scale(factor);
        link
                sensor.output to scale.input;
                scale.output to output;
                control to scale.control;
end.


group module DisplayStation(factor:integer);
        entryport
                press,
                temp: real reply signaltype;
        exitport
                control:boolean;
        use
                UnixExecD; display;
        create
                UnixExecD;
                display;
        link
                display.control to control;
                press to display.press;
                temp to display.temp;
end.
```

These group module specifications are submitted to the static configuration builder which produces an executable image and symbol table for each group. The symbol table describes the interface to the group (or logical station). The executives, *UnixExecD* and *TargExecD*, which support dynamic configuration are described in the next section. The user proceeds to create his initial system by invoking a dynamic configuration manager through the *manage* command. The following commands submitted to a configuration manager, either interactively or from a previously prepared file, construct the system.

```
transaction monitor
        create at node( target1 ) pressure:SensorStation(100)
        create at node( sun ) display:DisplayStation
        link pressure.output to display.press
        link display.control to pressure.control
        start display
        start pressure
end monitor
```

The **transaction** command ensures that the commands bracketed between **transaction** and **end** are either all done or the effect is that none of them are done. However, if the transaction deleted a task, it's internal state information will be lost. The manager first checks that the commands of a transaction are valid by checking the logical station images are available and of the right type for the specified target and that links are made between exitports and entryports of the same type. It then attempts to execute the commands. The implementation of configuration commands is described in section 5.3. If a command fails, the commands previously executed in the transaction are undone. Created stations are deleted and links are unlinked using operations which are also available to users as the commands **delete** and **link.** This means that configuration failures do not result in half built systems and that changes leave a consistent configuration. The monitor system may be subsequently deleted by the command:

undo monitor

The **create** command instantiates a logical station but its application tasks are not executed until started by the **start** command. This means that application tasks do not send messages to stations which have not been created.

To create the rest of the monitor system, making it identical to the system of Figures 2.1 and 3.1, the following additional commands are submitted to the configuration manager.

transaction extendMonitor
  create at node(target2) temperature:SensorStation(10)
  link temperature.output **to** display.temp
  link display.control **to** temperature.control
  start temperature
end extendMonitor

The configuration manager *manage* also implements commands to display the configuration state of a system in terms of the instances of logical stations which exist and the connections between those stations.

The set of commands to construct the monitor system can be considered to be a configuration specification which describe the system in the same way as the specification of section 2.2. In this initial version of the configuration manager, each configuration language construct is treated as a command and commands are executed in the order they are submitted to the manager. However, as noted in [Kramer 85], a more intelligent manager could automatically reorder the execution of commands to minimise disruption to a running system. For example, by creating new components before deleting old ones if the change involves replacing part of a system. In that case, the configuration language specifies the desired system but does not enforce a way of creating the system on the manager.

5.2 Executive support for Dynamic Configuration

The executives described in section 4 are extended by the addition of a LocalManager module to support dynamic configuration (Figure 5.2).

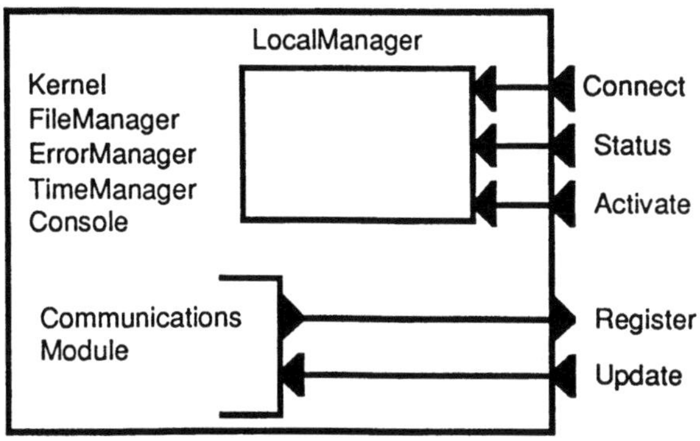

Figure 5.2 Dynamic Configuration Executive

The LocalManager module implements the executive interface to the configuration management system. The ports *Connect, Status* and *Activate* (and *Register, Update* from the

Communications System) are automatically exported by the builder to form part of the logical station interface.

The *LocalManager* links (and unlinks) station interface exitports to remote entryports in response to requests received on its *Connect* entryport. The link information, consisting of the address of the remote entryport

(logical station number . module instance number . entryport number),

is recorded in a kernel datastructure associated with the station exitport using a privileged kernel call. A dummy task module instance is created by the kernel to represent the station interface so that it does not need to deal with inter-station communication as a special case. The configuration state of a station may be queried by a configuration manager by sending a request to the *Status* entryport. The **start** command results in a request being sent to the *Activate* entryport.

As noted in Section 4.3, the *Update* entryport is used to update the mapping table from logical station number to Internet Address maintained by the communication system. The *Register* exitport is used by the communication system, when a station first starts up, to inform the dynamic configuration system of its UDP port number since this information is only available after the station starts. It is obtained from a socket call in Unix and is a constant assigned by the builder for targets. This message also confirms that the station has been successfully created.

The *LocalManager* represents only a small extension to the executives described in section 4. The other services offered by the executive are unaffected by the addition.

5.3 Dynamic Configuration Management System

The configuration system has been designed with multi-workstation host development systems in mind. The objective is that logical stations can be built and configured into a system from more than one host computer. Consequently, the implementation of configuration management must itself be distributed. The current implementation is partially distributed in that managers can be invoked on different hosts and configure stations into a system, however, there is a centralised registration server which resides on only one host computer. It is intended that this server should be replicated to avoid the reliability problems associated with the current implementation. The service was initially centralised to simplify implementation.

Dynamic configuration is implemented by two types of logical stations, *Manage*, the command interpreter and *RegServer*, the registration server which maintains information on the instances of logical stations which exist in a system. Instances of *Manage* are created whenever a user invokes dynamic configuration from UNIX via the manage command. An instance of *RegServer* must always exist. To illustrate the functions of each of these components and the relationship between them, in the following, the sequence of actions which must be performed for creation of a logical station is outlined.

Logical Station Creation Operations:

1) The manager communicates with the registration server to install the name of the logical station instance and its type in the server's tables. (The server is created with a "well known" UDP/IP address). The server checks, if the station is to be created at a target, to see if the target is already in use. The registration server replies with a new logical station number.

2) The configuration manager creates the station either by downloading it to a target or by creating a new UNIX process. The new station is created with information concerning its parameters, logical station number, internet address and the address of the registration server.

3) When the logical station starts to run it registers itself with the server via a message from its *Register* exitport. The registration server now updates the communication tables of all other stations in the system, including the manager station.

4) The manager can now communcate with the *LocalManager* module in the station to link it into the system and start it.

The configuration manager instances need not retain any information on configuration state. They obtain this from the registration server (station instances) or from local station managers (links). However, some information is cached to reduce communication overheads. The registration server is made resilient to host crashes by making it store configuration information on a disk file.

A further complication to configuration management is introduced by the needs in a multi-user system of maintaining more than one system simultaneously. Consequently, the configuration manager is invoked with the name of the system e.g.

manage monitor

This name is registered with the server when a manager is first invoked to create a new system and subsequent communications are prefixed with a system identifier allocated by the server.

The configuration manager is an example of an "autonomous" logical station. A station which can configure itself into a system. It is started with a command file instructing it how to connect itself to the registration server. The component of the manager which performs this startup connection may be configured into any station. This is useful for distributed systems with client interfaces which are invoked by users only when required e.g. a mail service.

5.4 Summary

This section has outlined the implementation of dynamic configuration management. It provides a flexible way of managing distributed systems. It has been constructed entirely using the facilities of the Conic programming and configuration languages, giving confidence in the adequacy of the features they provide for constructing distributed systems.

The current implementation is limited in its capability for handling failures. For example, if a station crashes, its link information is lost. This is partially mitigated by the fact that transactions can be re-executed to re-create the system. The configuration operations have been designed to be idempotent so it is possible to re-execute a transaction even if only part of the system it created has failed. Future work on configuration management will include the facility to attempt recovery on failure. Some early work in this area is described in [Loques 86].

6. CONCLUSION

Conic has been used by students at Imperial College, research groups at other universities and in industry. The following are the main lessons learnt from this experience of its use:

i) **On-line Host &Targets:** Host/target environments are widely used for the development of embedded systems. Our ability to test a distributed system on the Unix host, prior to down-line loading has speeded this development process. The fact that operational distributed targets can communicate with Conic Logical Stations running under Unix has obviated the development of standard facilities such as a file system or printer spooler.In addition it has allowed us to keep targets simple as the complex components of the Conic Support Envrionment can run on the host computer.

ii) **Simplicity:** The concepts embodied in the Conic toolkit, and the facilities provided by its support environment are very easy to assimilate and use. To some extent, functionality has been sacrificed for simplicity, on the assumption that simple efficient primitives can be used to provide more complex operations at a higher level. For example we have provided transactions by extending the standard facilities provided by the executive [Anido 86] rather than as base primitives as in Argus [Liskov 83], or Eden [Almes 85].

iii) **Flexibility:** The support system has been structured as a configurable set of Conic modules. For example the communication system can be configured to include a connection service, routing over interconnected subnets or drivers for different LANs. This flexibility does have some performance costs due to the overheads of message passing and task switching. However the performance has proved adequate for many real-time applications.

iv) **Open Architecture:** Users have adapted and modified the executive to support their requirements. For example GEC Research are using Conic to build a run-time environment for an object-oriented system. They have modified some of the intertask communication primitives and introduced support for manipulating capabilities.

iv) **Portability Experience:** The use of the Amsterdam compiler kit [Tanenbaum 83] as the basis of the language compiler has simplified the porting of the Conic environment to a variety of systems (PDP 11 Ultrix & BSD 2.9, VAX BSD 4.2 and Sun BSD 4.2 hosts as well as M68000 and LSI 11 targets). Structuring the executive as Conic modules has meant that the standard Conic configuration tools can be used to build the run-time system for the variety of hosts and targets. It would have been impossible to maintain and support this variety of machines any other way. The fact that device drivers and their interrupt handlers are configurable tasks rather than being part of the kernel has been a key feature in our ability to port Conic to different hardware.

The Conic environment currently supports a single programming language. This has a number of implications:

* The compiler can check messages type compatibility between messages and ports and port interconnections can be validated for type compatibility at configuration time. Therefore no run time checks are needed.

* The transformations required for transferring messages between heterogeneous computers are comparatively simple as the compiler generates similar data structure representations in different target computers.

* The communication system can be optimised to support the language communication primitives.

Future work will be aimed at supporting additional module languages eg. Prolog for implementing expert systems and knowledge bases. The Conic configuration facilities will provide the basis of integrating diverse language components with exisiting microcomputer based components for factory automation.

7. ACKNOWLEDGEMENTS

Acknowledgement is made to British Coal for a grant in aid of these studies, but the views expressed are those of the authors and not necessarily those of British Coal. This work has also been partially funded by the SERC under Grant GR/C/31440. We particularly acknowledge the contribution of our colleagues Nuranker Dulay, Kevin Twidle and Alan Dempster to the concepts described in this paper. In addition they have done a large proportion of the implementation.

8. REFERENCES

Almes 85: G. Almes et.al. 'The Eden system: a technical review', IEEE Trans. on Softwaare Eng. SE-11(1), Jan. 1985, pp. 43-59.

Anido 86: R. Anido, J. Kramer, 'Synchronised forward & backward recovery', 7th. IFAC DCCS, Germany, Sep. 1986.

Cheriton 84: D.Cheriton, 'The V-Kernel: a software base for distributed systems', IEEE Software, 1 (2), April 1984, pp. 19-43.

Dulay 84: N.Dulay, J.Kramer, J.Magee, M.Sloman, K.Twidle, 'The Conic configuration language, version 1.3', Imperial College Research Report DoC 84/20, November 1984.

DOD 80: 'DOD standard internet protocol', ACM Computer Comms. Review, 10(4), Oct. 1980, pp.12-51.

Feldman 83: S. Feldman, 'Make: a program for maintaining computer programs', Unix Prog. Manual vol. 2, Bell Telephone Labs, Holt Rinehart & Wilson, 1983, pp. 291-300.

Kramer 84: J.Kramer, J.Magee, M.Sloman, K.Twidle, N.Dulay, 'The Conic programming language, version 2.4', Imperial College Research Report DoC 84/19, October 1984.

Kramer 85: J.Kramer, J.Magee, 'Dynamic configuration for distributed systems', IEEE Transactions on Software Engineering, SE-11 (4), April 1985, pp. 424-436.

Leffler 83: S. Leffler, S FAbry, W. Joy, ' A 4.2 bsd communications primer', Computer Systems Research Group, Univ. of California, Berkley, July 1983.

Liskov 83: B.Liskov, R.Sheifler, 'Guardians and actions: linguistic support for robust distributed programs', ACM TOPLAS, 5 (3), July 1983, pp. 381-404.

Loques 86: O. Loques, J. Kramer, Flexible fault tolerance for distirbuted computer systems' to be published in IEE Proc. pt. E, 1986.

Mullender 85: S. Mullender, 'Principles of distributed operating system design', PhD Thesis, Vrije Universiteit, Mathematisch Centrum, Amsterdam, 1985.

Plummer 82: D. Plummer, 'An Address Resolution Protocol (RFC 826), Nov. 1982.

Postel 83: J. Postel, 'User Datagram Protocol (RFC 768), Information Sciences Institute, University of Southern California, 4376 Admiralty Way, Marina del Ray Calif. 90291.

Redel 80: D. Redel et. al. 'Pilot: an operating system for a personal computer' CACM 32(2), Feb. 1980, pp. 81-92.

Sandberg 86: R. Sandberg, 'The Sun network file system: design, implemention & experience' EUUG Conf. Proc., Italy, Spring 1986.

Sloman 86: M.Sloman, J.Kramer, J.Magee, K.Twidle, 'Flexible communications for distributed embedded systems', IEE Proc. Pt. E, 133(4), July 1986, pp. 201-211.

Tanenbaum 83: A.Tanenbaum, H.van Staveren, E.Keizer, J.Stevenson, 'A proctical toolkit for making portable compilers', CACM 26 (9), September 1983.

USA DOD 80: USA Department of Defense, 'Reference manual for the Ada™ programming language', Proposed Standard Document, July 1980.

Wirth 82: N.Wirth, 'Programming in Modula-2', Springer Verlag, 1982.

An Experience in Solving a Transaction Ordering Problem in a Distributed System.

Michel BANATRE
IRISA-INRIA
Campus de Beaulieu, 35042, RENNES-cedex (France)

Abstract:

This paper relates our experience about a particular problem of synchronization: the transaction ordering in the context of a distributed auction bidding system. This system must comply with the rule of fairness between sellers and buyers in order to respect the requirements of the application. This rule expects that sellers transactions be equitably interleaved and not indefinitely delayed.

Key words.

Distributed computer system, auction bidding system, fairness, transaction ordering, state machine, clocks.

NATO ASI Series, Vol. F28
Distributed Operating Systems. Theory and Practice
Edited by Y. Paker et al.

1.Introduction.

In this paper, we discuss our experience about a particular problem of synchronization related to transactions ordering in the context of a distributed auction bidding system. We show that the system must abide by the rule of fairness between sellers and buyers in order to meet the demands of the application. These rules require that sellers transactions be equitably interlaced and not indefinitely delayed. It is possible to use solutions described in the literature to provide an implementation of the fairness property[LAMP-78], [LELA-78], [RICA-81], but the assumptions used to built these solutions are too strong. We have to imagine a more efficient one, which constitutes the main topic of this paper.

In the second section we briefly present the external view of the system and its requirements. The third section is devoted to a specification of our problem, we define the events observed by user-sites and the ordering between these events. Section 4 discusses a distributed implementation of our system in terms of processes associated to a user. Each process simulates the execution of a state machine, it uses a clock to timestamp commands. We give ordering constraints that timestamps have to respect in order to implement the synchronization rules. In section 5 and 6 two distributed algorithms to build a timestamp mechanism in accordance to the abstract properties are presented. One of these algorithms is based on the use of absolute time, the second, on counters located on the seller-sites.

2. The electronic marketing: principle and requirements.

2.1. Principle of electronic transactions.

In Europe, there is a long tradition of auction transactions (or sales) for food products through a system called the "dutch clock" which can be roughly described as follows. All buyers are in one room where lots of products are presented for bidding by a sales manager representing the sellers. In front of this room there is a big clock with numbers around it representing possible prices for the lots (for example they could be numbers going from $2.00 to $0.50), the sales manager positions the arm of the clock at the starting price of the lot and the arm goes down regularly until one of the buyer in the room stops it by pushing a button in front of him; an electronic system identifies who first pushed his button and reports him to the sales manager who can then decide if he accepts this offer or not. This procedure allows a very fast pace (the transaction of a lot taking about 10 seconds).

This procedure is well accepted, and we have worked on improving it by providing the same kind of service but in distributed environment where each buyer or seller uses a workstation consisting of a microprocessor-based control unit with a small display, a "dutch clock" and keys to allow him to participate to transactions. There is also an ordinary screen display showing the result of all transactions being processed in the system.

The buyer can choose the seller he wants to deal with and can change this choice at any time. The bid from a seller is displayed on his control unit and the clock showing the starting price for the lot given by the seller: the clock starts to go down regularly and when the buyer decides that this price is good for him. He pushes a key to send his offer to the seller. He then waits for an answer from the seller telling him if he gets the lot or not. He can then receive a new offer, possibly from another seller (which is chosen by the system from the set of sellers this buyer is dealing with).

Of course, the seller sees things quite differently: he pushes a key to send his next proposition to interested buyers and waits for their offer. When all buyers have answered, the value of the best offer is displayed on his control unit; he decides either to accept or to reject this offer and transmits this decision to the buyer. He may then send his next proposition.

2.2. Requirements.

The electronic marketing context imposes by its nature severe constraints on its computer implementation.

1-Transactions order: transactions activated by a seller are carried out sequentially.

2-Fairness which can be loosely described as follows:

- buyers have an "equal chance" to buy lots proposed by the sellers,
- sellers have an "equal chance" to have their proposition seen at a given time by different sellers, no priority being defined a priori between sellers.

This property is different from the fairness one usually referred to in the distributed system literature because it must take into account the competition between the sellers and not only the absence of "starvation". This is a crucial one in our context of commercial marketing and must be enforced in all cases (normal or defective functionning). However, this has to be done while keeping the efficiency of the real-time system which can be measured in terms of availability and speed of processing. It is the direct consequence of our competitive market context in which all sellers have equal rights, i.e. their lots should be equitably interlaced and must not be indefinitely delayed; also important is the fact that the buyers must make their decisions based on the same available information. The implementation of this property is fully detailed in this paper.

Other requirements have also to be consired: reliability, extensibility, speed, distribution. Solutions to these requirements are detailed elsewhere [BANA-84], [BANA-86].

This informal presentation, useful to understand the application, is not sufficient to build its computer implementation in terms of order of transactions, fairness and reliability. We have to specify it as done in the next section.

3. Specification of the transaction ordering.

This section is not intended to be a complete specification of ENCHERE but is specifically devoted to transaction ordering.

To describe our problem, we associate the logical entity "user-site" to the human entity "user" (seller or buyer). A user-site handles user's informations (commands,...). Each user-site S is provided with his own local clock, h.S. A communication medium allows user-sites to exchange information. In order to specify the transaction ordering we assume the existence of a global observer G with a local clock, h.G.

The behaviour of a user-site is defined by the history of events it can observe. The transaction ordering can be specified by ordering events belonging to the history of users.

To reach these goals, it is necessary to define the nature of events (§3.1) and to build an ordering between local events of a user and between global events of the observer G (§3.2).

3.1.Events.

3.1.1. Definition of an event.

A local event on a site S is defined as a triple <S,d,op>, S is the site where the operation op occurs, d the time of the execution of op given by h.S.

A global event is defined in the same way, as a triple <S,d',op>, d' is the date of the execution of op given by h.G.

We make the two following assumptions.

-events are instantaneous,

-two events cannot be simultaneous.

We denote:

-EVT(S), the set of events which have occured on S,

-EVT(G), the set of events which have occured on G.

3.1.2. The operations.

Operations associated to events concern production, broadcast and receipt of values. We use the following syntax for these operations:

-production a value,

P(<value>)

-broadcasting a value,

B(<value>,{<set of receiver sites>})

-receiving a value,

R(<value>, <sender site>)

3.1.3. Event ordering.

Events belonging to EVT(S) and EVT(G) can be ordered with the relations, --S--> and --G--> which can be defined as follows:

$\forall e_1, e_2 \in EVT(S),\ e_1 \text{--S-->} e_2 \Leftrightarrow h.S.e_1 < h.S.e_2.$

$\forall e'_1, e'_2 \in EVT(G),\ e'_1 \text{--G-->} e'_2 \Leftrightarrow h.G.e'_1 < h.G.e'_2.$

We denote:

-Hist(S,d) the subset of events of EVT(S) such that $\forall e \in EVT(S)$, $e \in Hist(S,d) \Leftrightarrow h.S.e < d$,

-Hist(G,d') the subset of events of EVT(G) such that $\forall e' \in EVT(G)$, $e' \in Hist(G,d) \Leftrightarrow h.G.e' < d'$.

For each execution of ENCHERE, events belonging to EVT(G) and EVT(S) can be ordered by --G--> and --S-->. This ordering results from application specific constraints.

In the following, we detail successively,

(i)the ordering of events produced by the communication medium,

(ii)the ordering of events related to one transaction on a seller-site and a buyer-site,

(iii)the ordering of events of different transactions on a buyer-site.

3.1.4. Ordering of events associated to the communication medium operations.

The execution of the broadcast and receipt operations satisfy the three usual rules.

-A value is produced before it is broadcasted.

(1) $\langle S,d,P(val)\rangle \text{ --S--> } \langle S,d',B(val,E'(S))\rangle$, E'(S) is the set of receiver sites.

-The broadcast of a value precedes its reception on the sites of E'(S).

(2) $\langle S,d,B(val,E'(S))\rangle \text{ --G--> } \langle S',d',R(val,S)\rangle,\ S' \in E'(S)$

-Two values broadcasted by S have the same ordering when received on S'.

(3) $\langle S,d,B(val,E'(S))\rangle \text{ --G--> } \langle S,d',B(val_1,E'(S))\rangle$

$$\Rightarrow$$

$$\langle S',d_1,R(val,S)\rangle \text{ --G--> } \langle S',d'_1,R(val_1,S)\rangle$$

3.2. The transaction.

The transaction S.i, related to the lot i of the seller-site S, is charactarized by a set of events corresponding to four types of value:

-the proposal of the lot i by S, noted Pr.S.i,

-the buyer Bk's activation related to S.i, noted Ac.S.i,

-the buyer Bk's offer concerning S.i, noted Of.S.i,

-the termination of S.i, noted Te.S.i.

In the following, we note SB(S) the set of buyer-sites which are involved into transactions initiated by S.

The next diagram (figure 3.1) shows the processing of the transaction.

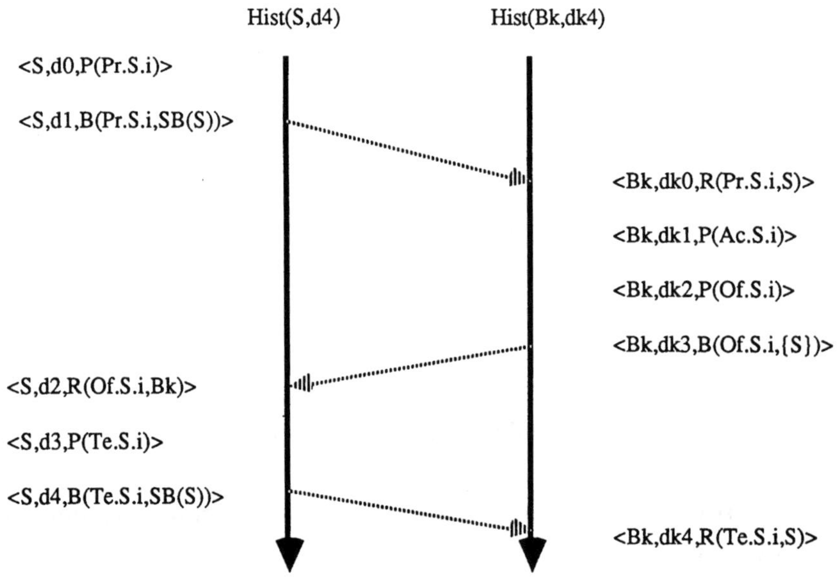

Figure 3.1: Transaction processing.

Definition:

A buyer-site B belonging to SB(S) is **active** for a transaction S.i if and only if it has produced the event <S,d,P(Ac.S.i)>.

We now have to specify local and global synchronization rules between the production of events in transactions, these rules have been introduced informally in section 2.

SR1: A seller-site cannot process two transactions simultaneously.

"init" --S--> <S,d_0,P(Pr.S.1)>

<S,d_i,B(Te.S.i,SB(S))> --S--> <S,d_{i+1},P(Pr.S.i+1)>

SR2: A buyer-site cannot be active for two transactions simultaneously.

Let SS(B) be the set of seller-sites connected to a buyer-site B,

let S,S' be two elements of SS(B),

(<B,d,P(Ac.S.i)> --B--> <B,d',P(Ac.S'.j)>

$\Rightarrow$

<B,d_1,R(Te.S.i,S)> --B--> <B,d',P(Ac.S'.j)>)

Of course, different seller-sites can initiate independent transactions. In this case, a buyer-site B, such that SS(B) > 1, could be involved in more than one transaction at a time, but following rules SR2, could not be active for more than one transaction at a time. Events of type <B,d,P(Ac.S.i)> are produced in accordance with the fairness property we define now.

3.3. The fairness property.

The ENCHERE system is fair if and only if the two following properties (FA1, FA2) are true for all executions.

FA1: Let S, S' be two seller-sites, B, B' two buyer-sites such that, S,S' belong to SS(B)$\wedge$SS(B').

Let S.i, S'.j be two transactions,

(<B,d,P(Ac.S.i)> --B--> <B,d_1,P(Ac.S'.j)>

$\Leftrightarrow$

<B',d',P(Ac.S.i)> --B'--> <B,d'_1,P(Ac.S'.j)>)

Informally, the sites B and B' are active for the transactions S.i, S'.j in the same order (figure 3.2).

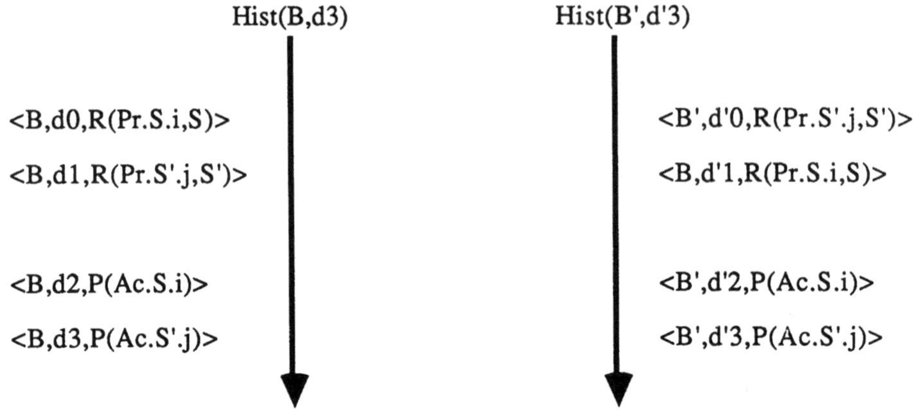

Figure 3.2: The property FA1 is verified.

FA2: Let S, S' be two seller-sites, B a buyer-site such that, S,S' belong to SS(B).
Let S.i, S'.j be two transactions,
($\exists$d, d' such that,

$$(<B,d_0,R(Pr.S.i,S)> \in Hist(B,d) \wedge <B,d_1,R(Pr.S'.j,S')> \in Hist(B,d)$$

$$\wedge$$

$$<B,d'_0,P(Ac.S.i)> \notin Hist(B,d) \wedge <B,d'_1,,P(Ac.S'.j)> \notin Hist(B,d)$$

$$\wedge$$

$$<B,d''_2,P(Ac.S.i+1)> \in Hist(B,d') \wedge <B,d''_1,P(Ac.S'.j)> \in Hist(B,d'))$$

$$\Rightarrow$$

$$(<B,d''_1,P(Ac.S'.j)> \text{ --A--> } <B,d''_2,P(Ac.S.i+1)>))$$

In other words, this rule means that the site B cannot activate the transaction S.i+1 until it has activated the transaction S'.j ready to be activated at the time d (figure 3.3).

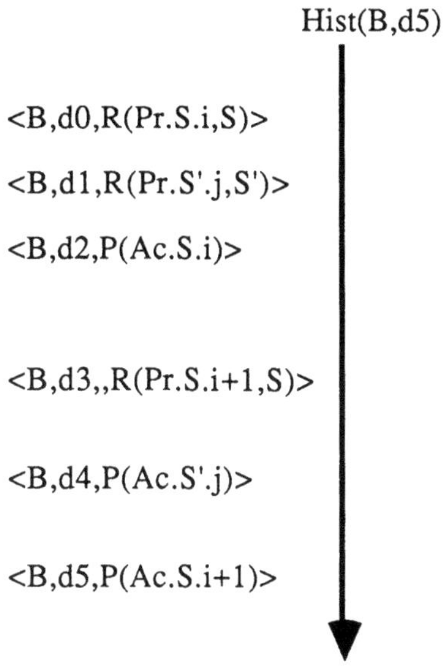

Figure 3.3: The property FA2 is verified.

This property implies the following possibilities:

i)parallel processing of transactions initiated by distinct seller-sites if the set of buyer-sites involved in these transactions are disjoint,

ii)asynchronism in the participation of the buyer-sites to transactions initiated by a seller-site.

One can remark that it is easy to explain our transaction ordering problem in terms of a ressource allocation. S.i can be considered as a distributed ressource located on different servers B, SB(S). A transaction can be considered as follows: a client S sends an allocation request concerning S.i to servers belonging to SB(S). Each server allocates its own "part of S.i" following the fairness rules.

4. State Machines associated to user-sites.

The purpose of this section is to describe a distributed implementation of our system in terms of processes associated to a user. Each process S simulates the execution of a state machine SM.S, it uses a clock to timestamped commands. Every execution of SM.S by S produces a history which verifies synchronization rules given in the previous section. We give the abstract properties that timestamps associated to commands have to respect in order to implement the synchronization rules.

4.1. The model.

The state machine SM.S associated to S is defined by a quadruple (COM.S, ST.S, COND, FT)], where:

-COM.S is the set of possible commands,

-ST.S is the set of possible states,

-COND is a function, defined as COM.SxST.S→{true,false}. COND(com.S, cs.S) is the condition to execute the command com when the current state of SM.S is cs.S.

-FT is a function defined as COM.SxST.S→ST.S, FT(com.S,cs.S) is the new current state of SM.S when COND(com,cs.S) is true.

Each command related to a transaction S.i on a site S, is defined by a triple <S,ts(S.i),op>. S is the site where the operation op is executed, ts(S.i) is the timestamp value associated to S.i.

cs.S is a set of commands which has been executed on S. A command <S,ts(S.i),op> belongs to cs.S, if and only if, it is the last command related to S.i executed by SM.S.

The following operations allow the management of cs.S, append(<S,ts(S.i),op>,cs.S), remove(<S,ts(S.i),op>,cs.S), element-of (<S,ts(S.i),op>,cs.S).

The execution of a command <S,n,op> produces an event <S,d,op>, d is the time of the execution of the command. This event belongs to Hist(S,d).

Proposition 1.

Let $<S,n_1,op_1>$, $<S,n_2,op_2>$ be two commands of COM.S, if COND($<S,n_2,op_2>$,cs.S) is element-of (<S,n1,op1>,cs.S) then $<S,d_1,op_1>$--S-->$<S,d_2,op_2>$.

The state machine associated with a user-site S models the behaviour of S if the order between events produced by the execution of commands respects the synchronization rules given in section 3. Here we describe only the state machine associated to a buyer-site, the state machine associated to a seller-site can be built easily from specifications given in the previous section.

4.2. The state machine associated to a buyer-site.

We define successively, COM.B, COND.B and FT.B.

-The set of commands COM.B:

<B,ts(S.i),R(Pr.S.i,S)>

<B,ts(S.i),P(Ac.S.i)>
<B,ts(S.i),P(Of.S.i)>
<B,ts(S.i),B(Of.S.i,{S})>
<B,ts(S.i),R(Te.S.i,S)>

-The function FT:

FT(<B,ts(S.i),R(Pr.S.i,S)>,cs.B):
(remove(<B,ts(S.i),R(Te.S.i-1,S)>,cs.S),
append(<B,ts(S.i),R(Pr.S.i,S)>,cs.S))

FT(<B,ts(S.i),P(Ac.S.i)>,cs.B):
(remove(<B,ts(S.i),R(Pr.S.i,S)>,cs.S),
append(<B,ts(S.i),P(Ac.S.i)>,cs.S))

FT(<B,ts(S.i),P(Of.S.i)>,cs.B):
(remove(<B,ts(S.i),P(Ac.S.i)>,cs.S),
append(<B,ts(S.i),P(Of.S.i)>,cs.S))

FT(<B,ts(S.i),D(Of.S.i,{S})>,cs.B):
(remove(<B,ts(S.i),P(Of.S.i)>,cs.S),
append(<B,ts(S.i),D(Of.S.i,{S})>,cs.S))

FT(<B,ts(S.i),R(Te.S.i,S)>,cs.B):
(remove(<B,ts(S.i),D(Of.S.i,{S})>,cs.S),
append(<B,ts(S.i),R(Te.S.i,S)>,cs.S))

-The function COND:

COND(<B,ts(S.i),R(Pr.S.i,S)>,cs.B):
element-of(<B,ts(S.i-1), R(Te.S.i-1,S)>,cs.B)

COND(<B,ts(S.i),P(Of.S.i)>,cs.B):
element-of(<B,ts(S.i),P(Ac.S.i)>,cs.B)

COND(<B,ts(S.i),B(Of.S.i,{S})>,cs.B):
element-of(<B,ts(S.i),P(Of.S.i)>,cs.B)

COND(<B,ts(S.i),R(Te.S.i,S)>,cs.B):
element-of(<B,ts(S.i),D(Of.S.i,{S})>,cs.B)

It is easy to verify that the order in which events are produced satisfies the synchronization rules established in section 2.

A condition to execute the command <B,ts(S.i),P(Ac.S.i)> is element-of(<B,ts(S.i),R(Pr.S.i,S)>,cs.B). Clearly, this condition is necessary but not sufficient.

We have also to consider the commands <B,ts(S'.j),P(Ac.S'.j)>, S'≠S such that element-of(<B,ts(S'.j),R(Pr.S'.j,S')>,cs.B).

4.3. A condition to execute the command <B,ts(S.i),P(Ac.S.i)>.

This condition is established from the integer values ts(S.i) associated to transactions S.i.

Let B be a buyer-site and h.B be the time given by its clock. We denote cs.B(h.B) the current state of B at the time h.B.

We define two sets:

Str(B,h.B)≡{<B,ts(S.i),R(Pr.S.i,S)>
such that <B,ts(S.i),R(Pr.S.i,S)>∈cs.B(h.B)}

Dtr(B,h.B)≡{ts(S.i) such that <B,ts(S.i),R(Pr.S.i,S)>∈Str(B,h.B)}

Dmin(B,h.B) and Dmax(B,h.B) are the minimum and maximun value of Dtr(B,h.B).

We define also a boolean function active: Str(B,h.B) → {true false}, active(B) is true if <B,ts(S.i),P(Ac.S.i)>∈cs.B(h.B).

Proposition 2:

Let's consider COND(<B,ts(S.i),P(Ac.S.i)>,cs.B(h.B)) be defined with the following expression:

(ts(S.i)=Dmin(B,h.B)∧¬ active(cs.B(h.B).

The fairness property is verified if the two following properties are assumed:

Property D1:

Let h.B the execution time of a command <B,ts(S.i),P(Ac.S.i)>,
∀dt>0, Dmin(B,h.B)< Dmin(B,h.B+dt).

In other words,the execution of a command <B,ts(S'.j),R(Pr.S'.j,S')> cannot follow the execution of a command <B,ts(S.i),R(Pr.S.i,S)> such that ts(S'.j)<ts(S.i).

Property D2:

(∀dt>0, ts(S.i)∈Dtr(B,h.B) ∧ ts(S.i+1)∈Dtr(B,h.B+dt) ∧ ts(S.i)=Dmin(B,h.B)

⇒

ts(S.i+1)>Dmax(B,h.B))

In other words, the timestamp accociated to the transaction S.i+1 must be greater than the timestamp associated to the transactions S'.j such that B has executed the command <B,ts(S'.j),R(Pr.S'.j,B')> but not yet the command <B,ts(S'.j),P(Ac.B.j)>.

A complete proof of this proposition can be found in [BANA-84].

4.4. Conclusion.

The timestamp mechanism used to implement our fairness property is similar to the one used in [LAMP-78], [RICA-81]. On a user-site, the transaction with the lowest timestamp is the next one to be active.

However our approach is somewhat different, instead of giving an algorithm to manage timestamp, we have given the properties that every sequence of timestamp has to verify in order to implement our fairness property. The two following sections are devoted to algorithms that provide a timestamp mechanism to enforce D1 and D2.

5. An implementation of timestamp mechanism using physical clocks.

We describe in this section an algorithm that provides timestamps ts(S.i) verifying the D1 and D2 properties. The algorithm uses physical clocks as proposed in [LAMP-84]. We first give some properties required for physical clocks.

5.1. Physical clock properties.

5.1.1. Notion of fuzzy time.

Let $S_1,\dots,S_i,\dots,S_n$ be n user-sites and h.Si the time given by the clock of S_i. The physical clock of $S_1,\dots,S_j,\dots S_n$ show the same fuzzy time locally to S_i if, and only if, it is possible to determine $dt.S_i$ such that $|h.S_j-h.S_i|<dt.S_i$.

$dt.S_i$ is the maximal drift between clocks of user-sites S_j, $j \neq i$, and the clock of S_i. In the following we suppose that there exist a value dt such that $dt=\max(dt.S_i)$.

In normal situations, we assume that clocks of different sites run at the same rate.

5.1.2. A sufficient condition for implementing D1 and D2.

Let d be the time execution of the command <S,ts(S.i),P(Pr.S.i)> on a seller-site S and length(S.i) the length of the transaction S.i.

Proposition.

Let's consider a transaction S.i and suppose that ts(S.i)=d and length(S.i)>2dt.

Properties D1 and D2 are verified if B and the elements of SS(B) have the same fuzzy time and Dmin(B,h.B)<h.B-dt.

Proof.

a-Proof of D1.

Sites of SS(B) and B have the same fuzzy time and Dmin(B,h.B)<h.B-dt. In that case, when we consider the execution of a command <B,ts(S'.j),R(Pr-S',S')> at the time h.B+∂t , we have the following properties:

h.B+∂t-dt<ts(S'.j),

Dmin(B,h.B)<ts(S'.j)

We have the result: Dmin(B,h.B)≤Dmin(B,h.B+∂t).

b-Proof of D2.

Let's consider a seller-site S belonging to SS(B) and a transaction S.i such that ts(S.i)=Dmin(B,h.B).

S and B have the same fuzzy time, since the length of a transaction is greater than 2dt, we can conclude that, Dmax(B,h.B)<h.B+dt and h.B+2dt-dt<ts(S.i+1)

We have the following result: Dmax(B,h.B)<ts(S.i+1).

These results are verified when the system has a normal behaviour. Now we examine how to maintain D1 and D2 when our hypothesis on clocks synchronization are not fulfilled.

5.2. Problems related to clocks desynchronization.

Let $m(S_i,S_j)$ a message sended by S_i and received by S_j, $dm(S_i,S_j)$ is its sending time. We have the two following definitions:

1-the local clock of S_j is running faster locally than the one at S_i when $dm(S_i,S_j)<h.S_j-dt$.

2-the local clock of Sj is running slower locally than the one at S_i when $dm(S_i,S_j)>h.S_j+dt$.

The reasons for clock desynchronization could be the consequence of longer transmission delays, clock period modification, complete stop of clock, ...

We now explain how to maintain D1 and D2 in the two following cases:

1-A clock of buyer-site B runs faster than a clock of a seller-site of SS(B).

2-A clock of buyer-site B runs slower than a clock of a seller-site of SS(B).

5.2.1. Study of case 1.

A buyer's clock runs faster than a seller's one. In this case, the time interval dt is "smaller" at B than the one at S.

A transaction S.i may verify one of the two following propositions:

(1) $(<B,ts(S.i),R(Pr.S.i,S)> \in Str(B,h.B+\partial t) \wedge ts(S.i)<Dmin(B,h.B))$

(2) $(<B,ts(S.i+1),R(Pr.S.i,S) \in Str(B,h.B+\partial t) \wedge ts(S.i)=Dmin(B,h.B)$
$\wedge\ ts(S.i+1)<Dmin(B,h.B))$

In the case (1), the property D1 is not verify; D2 is not verify in the case (2). The fairness property is not assumed.

To detect and correct such situations we use the following technique:

When a buyer-site B receives a message related to the command <B,ts(S.i),R(Pr.S.i,S)>, it compares the sending time, dm(S,B), of this message with its local clock value.

If $dm(S,B)<h.B-dt$, B may have performed the command <B,ts(S'.j),P(Ac.S'.j) such that $ts(S'.j)>ts(S.i)$. In order to avoid a possible deadlock, B ignores the command <B,ts(S.i),R(Pr.S.i,S)>. The termination of the transaction S.i is ensured by general recovery mechanisms provided by the system.

5.2.2. Study of case 2.

A buyer's clock runs slower than a seller's one. In this case, the time interval dt is "longer" at B than at S.

One can remark that properties D1 and D2 are verified. The only consequence is that a transaction S.j may be delayed when it should not have been.

When a buyer-site B and a site S from SS(B) have not the same fuzzy time, we have to resynchronize their clock.

5.3. Clocks resynchronization.

The principle of the algorithm is very simple: every site Sj, seeing that its clock is running late comparing to the value nt of the clock of Sj, reinitializes it with nt. It broadcasts nt to the sites linked with it.

We assume that the transmission delay is bounded with a value DT .

We must prove that if dt is greater than 2DT then, B and elements of SS(B) get eventually the same fuzzy time.

To prove this result we have to establish the following propositions:

Proposition 1.

A user-site B reinitializes its clock at most once with the value nt.

Proposition 2.

Let Si and S(Si) be the sites which communicate with Si. Let's consider Sj an element of E(Si) which reinitializes its clock with a value nt and send nt to Si. If Si does not reinitialize its clock with v then Si and Sj get the same fuzzy time.

A detailed proof of these two propositions is given in [BANA-84].

The number of sites is bounded with a value n, in this case they have reinitialized their clock with nt in a time interval bounded with nDT (proposition 1).

When all the sites have reinitialized their clocks, for each site Si, Si and E(Si) have the same fuzzy time (proposition 2).

Then we have the following result: for each site B, B and elements of SS(B) get the same fuzzy time before the time h.B+nDT.

5.4.Discussion.

The use of physical clocks to provide timestamps does not introduce extra messages to implement the properties D1 and D2. However the execution time of a command <B,ts(S.i),R(Pr.S.i,S)> is delayed: the buyer-site B cannot be active for a transaction S.i at the time h.B only if the command <B,ts(S.i),R(Pr.S.i,S)> has been executed before the time h.B-dt.

We have made two assumptions: the transmisssion time is bounded with DT and the clocks of different sites run at the same rate. When they are not met, clocks must be resynchronized and commands such that <B,ts(S.i),R(Pr.S.i,S)> can be ignored. In [BANA-84], protocols for such abnormal situations are described.

In the next section we present another implementation of the timestamp mechanism in which these assumptions are relaxed.

6. An implementation of the timestamp mechanism using counters.

To implement timestamps with counters, we associate a counter, c.S, to each seller-site S. When we perform a command <S,ts(S.i),P(Pr.S.i)>, we identify ts(S.i) with the current value of c.S. This section is devoted to algorithms running on buyer and seller-sites to manage counters c.S in order to enforce properties D1 and D2.

6.1.The description of the algorithm.

First, we describe the data structures used to implement the algorithm which is presented after.

6.1.1. Data structures.

Two kinds of data structures are defined on a seller-site S:

-a counter c.S,

-a set of estimated values Est.S, an element est(B_i).S of this set is the estimated value of c.S, given by B_i, B_i belonging to SB(S).

In the same way a set of estimated values Est.B is defined on each buyer-site B, an element est(S).B_i is the estimated value of c.S, S belong to SS(B_i).

It easy to see that est(Bi).S=est(S).B_i.

6.1.2.The algorithm.

The different steps of the algorithm are the following:

a-When a buyer-site B has performed a command <B,ts(S.i),R(Te.S.i,S)> it sends the value Dmax(B,h.B)+1 to S, it is the lower value of ts(S.i+1) in order to ensure the property D2. est(S).B is assigned with this new value.

b-When a seller-site has performed the command<S,ts(S.i),B(Te.S.i,S)>, it waits until each site Bi of SB(S) has sent to it its estimated value est(Bi).S.

When S knows all the estimated values, it can determine the current value of its counter c.S which is max(est(Bi).S).

c-When a buyer-site B has performed a command <B,ts(S'.j),R(Te.S'.j,S')>, B executes the command <B,ts(S.i),P(Ac.S.i)> such that:

(i)-ts(S.i)=Dmin(B,h.B)

(ii)-ts(S.i)<min(est(S.i).A)

If ts(S.i) does not fulfill (ii), B re-estimates the values est(Sk).B such that est(Sk).B<ts(S.i). B proceeds as follows: it sends to Sk the new value of est(Sk).B in order to ensure (ii), this value is ts(S.i)+1.

When all seller-sites have acknowledged the re-estimated requests from B, B can choose the command of type <B,ts(S.i),P(Ac.S.i)> to perform.

d-When a seller-site S receives, from B, a value nv in order to re-estimate est(B).S, assume nv this value. S assigns this value to est(B).S, moreover, if c.S is lower than nv, nv is assigns to c.S. An acknowledgment is sent to B.

One can remark that it is not necessary to update est(B).S when S has performed a command <S,ts(S.j),B(Pr.S.j,S)>, this command is the acknowlegment to the request from B.

6.1.3. Proof of the algorithm.

We have to demonstrate that properties D1 and D2 are verified by timestamps provided by counters.

Let h.B the execution time of the command<B,ts(S.i),P(Ac.S.i)>.

-the property D2 is verified:

ts(S.i)=Dmin(S,h.S)

est(S).B>Dmax(B,h.B) -step a of the algorithm-

ts(S.i+1)=max(est(B).S) -step b of the algorithm-

⇒ts(S.i+1)>Dmax(B,h.B)

-the property D1 is verified:

$Dmin(B,h.B)<min(est(S_k).B)$ -step c(ii) of the algorithm-

-for each command <B,ts(S_k.j),R(Pr.S_k.j,S)> performed at the time h.B+∂t, we have $ts(S_k.j) \geq est(S_k).B > Dmin(B,h.B)$.

So, if ts(S.i)=Dmin(B,h.B), there does not exist a transaction S_k.j such that $ts(S_k.j)<ts(S.i)$.

6.3 Abnormal situations.

We consider two situations:

-1-A seller-site does not receive all the estimated values from buyer-site. It cannot determine the new value of c.S.

This situation has no influence on the fairness property. Recovery mechanisms provided in ENCHERE handle such a situation.

-2-A seller-site does not receive the acknowlegment concerning a re-estimated request. Such a situation can lead to a deadlock. It is important such situation in order to prevent a deadlock. To avoid it, we adopt the following strategy: after a time-out period, <B,ts(S.i),P(Ac.S.i)> is performed by B such that ts(S.i)=Dmin(S,h.B). Then B discards commands <B,ts(S'.j),R(Pr.S'.j,S')> such that ts(S'.j)<ts(S.i). The termination of the transaction S'.i is ensured by recovery mechanisms provided by the system.

6.4.Remarks about efficiency.

When we compare this algorithm to the previous one, we can see that we have made no assumption about communication delay and clock period. However, it is necessary that buyer-sites send extra messages to update counters. For each transaction the minimum number of extra messages is the cardinality of SB(S), this number can increase in case of re-estimated messages.

7.Conclusion.

The aim of this paper is to relate our experience in solving the fairness problem in the context of a distributed auction bidding system. We first have specified our problem, particularly events and their ordering have been defined. We have proposed a distributed implementation of our system in terms of processes associated to a user. Each process simulates the execution of a state machine. The commands treated by processes are timestamped by a clock mechanism. Our contribution has been to express the fairness property in terms of an ordering on the timestamp values independently from a particular implementation. Once the problem has been clearly expressed two distributed algorithms have been proposed which satisfy the timestamp constraints. One of these algorithms is based on the use of absolute time, the second, on the use of counters located on the seller-sites.

Distributed mutual exclusion algorithms such as [LELA-78], [RICA-81] could have been used to solve our problem. However, our solution is more adequate and efficient in the sense that the potential parallelism of the application is preserved.

References:

[BANA-84] BANATRE M.
ENCHERE: Une Expérience dans la Conception et la Réalisation d'un Système Réparti.
Thèse de Doctorat d'Etat, Université de Rennes 1. Mars 1984.

[BANA-86] BANATRE J.P., BANATRE M., LAPALME G., PLOYETTE Fl.
The Design and Building of ENCHERE, a Distributed Electronic Marketing System.
Comm. ACM, vol 29,1 (January 1986), pp. 19-29.

[LAMP-78] LAMPORT L.
Time, Clock and the Ordering of Events in a Distributed System.
Comm.ACM 21,7 (July 1978), pp.558-565.

[LAMP-84] LAMPORT L.
Using Time Instead Timeout for Fault-Tolerant Distributed Systems.
ACM Trans. Prog. Lang. Syst. 6.2 (April 1984). pp.254-280.

[LELA-78] LE LANN G.
Algorithm for Distributed Data-sharing System which uses Tickets.
3rd Berkeley Workshop on Distributed Data Management and Computer Networks, Aug. 1978.

[RICA-81] RICARD G., AGRAWALA A.K.
An Optimal Algorithm for Mutual Exclusion in Computer Networks.
Comm. ACM, Vol. 24,1, Jan. 1981, pp. 9-17.

Distributed Transaction Processing and The Camelot System[1]

Alfred Z. Spector

Department of Computer Science
Carnegie Mellon University
Pittsburgh, Pennsylvania 15213-9998

Abstract

This paper describes distributed transaction processing, a technique used for simplifying the construction of reliable distributed systems. After introducing transaction processing, the paper presents models describing the structure of distributed systems, the transactional computations on them, and the layered software architecture that supports those computations. The software architecture model contains five layers, including an intermediate layer that provides a common set of useful functions for supporting the highly reliable operation of system services, such as data management, file management, and mail. The functions of this layer can be realized in what is termed a *distributed transaction facility*. The paper then describes one such facility — Camelot. Camelot provides flexible and high performance commit supervision, disk management, and recovery mechanisms that are useful for implementing a wide class of abstract data types, including large databases. It runs on the Unix-compatible Mach operating system and uses the standard Arpanet IP communication protocols. Presently, Camelot runs on RT PC's and Vaxes, but it should also run on other computers including shared-memory multiprocessors.

1. Introduction

Distributed computing systems are potentially reliable, because their components are redundant and fail independently. Additionally, distributed computing systems potentially offer very high throughput for applications that can use loosely-coupled multiprocessing. The major challenge is to realize these potentials efficiently, and without incurring intolerable penalties in complexity or cost. Consequently, there has been great interest in general-purpose techniques and practices for simplifying the construction of efficient and robust distributed systems.

This paper discusses a technique based on *distributed transactions* and describes a *distributed transaction facility* called Camelot that supports their use. Section 2 defines the concept of a transaction and provides a brief historical perspective on its development. Section 3 then presents three models useful for describing distributed systems that support transaction processing. Section 4 adds concreteness to this discussion by describing the goals, implementation bases, functions, structure, status of the Camelot distributed transaction facility. This paper ends with Section 5, which describes some important challenges in the area of distributed transaction processing.

---

[1]This work was supported by the Defense Advanced Research Projects Agency, ARPA Order No. 4976, monitored by the Air Force Avionics Laboratory under Contract F33615-84-K-1520, and the IBM Corporation.

The views and conclusions contained in this document are those of the author and should not be interpreted as representing the official policies, either expressed or implied, of any of the sponsoring agencies or of the United States government.

NATO ASI Series, Vol. F28
Distributed Operating Systems. Theory and Practice
Edited by Y. Paker et al.

2. Distributed Transactions

The database literature typically defines a transaction as a collection of operations bracketed by two markers: *BeginTransaction* and *EndTransaction*. A transaction has three special properties:

- Either all or none of a transaction's operations are performed. This property is called *failure atomicity*.

- If a transaction completes successfully, the results of its operations will never be lost, except in the event of catastrophes, which can be made arbitrarily improbable. This property is called *permanence*.

- Transactions are allowed to execute concurrently, but the results will be the same as if the transactions executed serially in some order. This property is usually called *serializability*.

Transactions lessen the burden on application programmers by simplifying the treatment of failures and concurrency. Failure atomicity ensures that if a transaction is interrupted by a failure, its partial results will undone. Permanence ensures that updates performed by completed transactions are not lost. Serializability ensures that other concurrently executing transactions cannot observe inconsistencies. Programmers are therefore free to cause temporary inconsistencies during the execution of a transaction knowing that their partial modifications will never be visible.

Transactions were initially developed for centralized data management systems to aid in maintaining arbitrary application-dependent *consistency constraints* on stored data. Transactions are a very useful abstraction, because these consistency constraints must typically be maintained despite failures and without unnecessarily restricting the concurrent processing of application requests. System R is an example of an early database system with good support for transactions [Astrahan et al. 76].

Extending the concept of transactions for use on distributed systems was not difficult: Distributed transactions permit operations on multiple objects that are scattered across multiple nodes. Though this concept is easily described, efficient implementations have been difficult to achieve. However, there are database systems that support distributed transactions. Berkeley's Ingres, CCA's SDD-1, and IBM's R^* [Stonebraker and Neuhold 77, Rothnie et al. 80, Williams et al. 81, Lindsay et al. 84] are three early examples, and new products have recently been announced by purveyors of commercial database software.

Supporting distributed processing is only one of the possible extensions to the transaction concept. Researchers, starting in the late 1970's, also looked for ways to increase the domain of processing in which distributed transactions could be used. One of their goals was to facilitate the construction of *highly available* applications — that is, applications that continue to work despite failures. Increasing the flexibility of transactions required extensions to the transaction model, as well as new algorithms and architectures to improved their implementation.

Perhaps, the most fundamental addition to the transaction model was the notion that programmers should be permitted invoke operations on user-defined abstract objects, rather than being restricted to using objects of a predefined type, such as relational database. *Abstract objects* are data or input/output devices, having distinct names, on which collections of *operations* have been defined. Access to an object is permitted only by these operations. A queue object having operations such as **Enqueue**, **Dequeue**, **EmptyQueue** is a typical data object, and a CRT display having operations such as **WriteLine**, and **ReadLine** is a typical I/O object. This notion of object is similar to the notions of classes in Simula [Dahl and Hoare 72] and packages in ADA [Department of Defense 82].

Gray and Lomet discussed the extended use of the transaction model in two relatively early papers [Gray 81, Lomet 77]. In other important work, Moss and Reed at MIT developed an important addition to the transaction model by defining what it means to have transactions nested within other transactions [Reed 78, Moss 81]. Briefly, nested transactions permit a transaction to spawn children which may run in parallel, but are synchronized so that the transaction system still exhibits serializability. Nested transactions also are permitted to abort without causing the loss of the entire parent transaction's work. Allchin, Herlihy, Schwarz, Weihl, and I also wrote about many other issues in the synchronization, recovery and overall structuring of abstract objects for transaction systems [Allchin 83, Herlihy 85, Schwarz 84, Schwarz and Spector 84, Spector and Schwarz 83, Weihl 84].

Related implementation work has focused on developing what I call a *distributed transaction facility* and compatible linguistic constructs for accessing it. I define a distributed transaction facility as a distributed collection of components that supports the execution of transactions and the implementation of shared abstract data objects on which operations can be performed. Although there is room for diversity in the exact functions of a distributed transaction facility, it must make it easy to begin and end transactions, to call operations on objects from within transactions, and to implement abstract objects that have correct synchronization and recovery properties. By providing a common set of synchronization and recovery mechanisms, such a facility can lead to implementations of separate abstractions that permit their combined use. For example, a computer aided design system might be built using a transactional database management system and a transactional file system.

Among the most well-known implementation work, Liskov and her group at MIT developed the Argus language and runtime system [Liskov 82, Liskov and Scheifler 83, Liskov 84]. At Georgia Tech, a group has worked on developing the Clouds operating system with support for distributed transactions [Allchin and McKendry 83]. Tandem's TMF is an example of a commercial system supporting distributed transaction processing [Helland 85]. Recent work on transactional file systems, for example at UCLA, can also support reliable and available distributed applications [Weinstein et al. 85].[2]

At Carnegie Mellon University, my colleagues and I developed TABS, which is a prototype distributed transaction facility [Spector et al. 85a, Spector et al. 85b]. We are are now developing the production-oriented Camelot (**C**arnegie **M**ellon **L**ow **O**verhead **T**ransaction) facility [Spector et al 86, CMU 87], which is described below. To reduce further the amount of effort required to construct reliable distributed systems, Herlihy and Wing and their students are developing the Avalon language facilities — a collection of constructs that will use Camelot and provide linguistic support for reliable applications [Herlihy and Wing 86]. Avalon comprises runtime libraries and extensions to C^{++}, Common Lisp, and ADA, which together

---

[2] This section contains but a partial list of related work. Due apology is made to researchers whose work has been omitted.

automatically generate the necessary calls on lower-level components [Herlihy and Wing 86]. This work on Camelot and Avalon is based upon our collective experience with TABS and Argus.

To summarize, the goal of this research and development is to simplify the construction of reliable distributed applications that access shared objects by providing facilities for supporting distributed transactions and appropriate interfaces to them. The transaction facilities need to be efficient, easily managed, and, preferably, useful on heterogeneous hardware in large network environments. The following sections should help concretize these notions.

3. Three Models

This section presents three broadly applicable models that are useful for describing distributed systems that support transaction processing: The *system model* describes underlying assumptions about the hardware, storage, and network. The *computation model* describes system operation as a collection of distributed transactions. The *architecture model* describes a five-tiered software organization for a distributed system supporting transactions.

3.1. System Model

There is substantial agreement on the underlying system model for distributed processing, which contains processing nodes and a communication network as Figure 3-1 illustrates. Processing nodes are fail-fast and include uniprocessors or shared memory multiprocessors of many types. Processing nodes are generally assumed to have independent failure modes.

Storage on processing nodes comprises volatile storage — where portions of objects reside when they are being accessed, non-volatile storage — where objects reside when they have not been accessed recently, and stable storage — memory that is assumed to retain information despite failures. The contents of volatile storage are lost after a system crash, and the contents of non-volatile storage are lost with lower frequency, but always in a detectable way. Stable storage can be implemented using two non-volatile storage units on a node or using a network service, as described in Section 4.2.3 [Daniels et al. 86].

The system model's communication network provides datagram-oriented, internetworked OSI Level 3 functions [Zimmermann 82] such as the Arpanet IP protocol [Postel 82]. In other words, the network comprises both long-haul and local components and permits processes to send datagrams having a fixed maximum size. Some local area networks may specially support multicast or broadcast, and the network protocols are assumed to support these features for reasons of efficiency. Because applications using the system may need high availability, communication networks should have sufficient redundancy to render network partitions unlikely. Network partitions can nonetheless occur, so higher levels of the system must take measures to protect themselves against the erroneous computations or inconsistencies that could result.

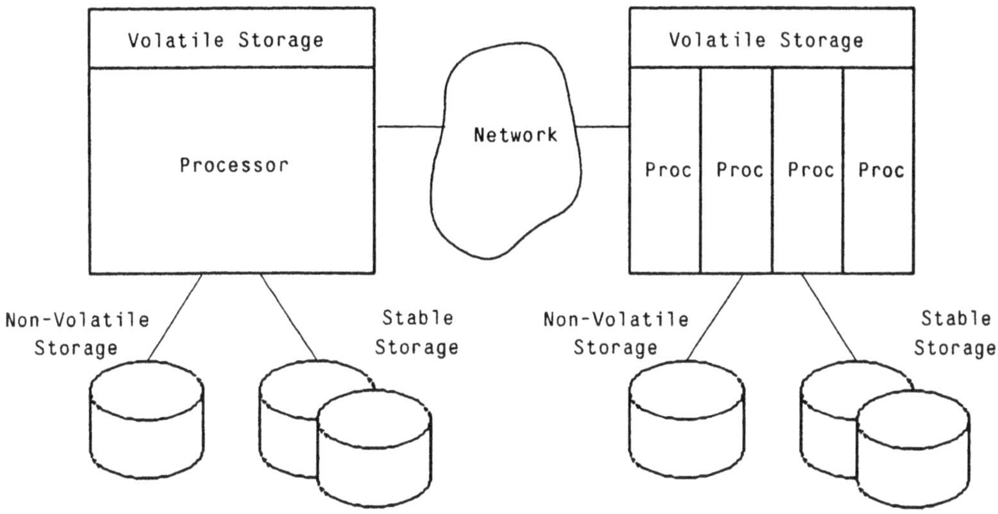

Figure 3-1: System Model

This figure shows the components of the system model. Stable storage and non-volatile storage, though pictured as disks, could be implemented with other media, such as battery backed-up memory.

3.2. Computation Model

The computation model comprises applications that perform processing by executing operations on user-defined data objects within distributed transactions. A transaction either *commits*, in which case all its updates appear to be atomically made, or it *aborts*, in which case no changes appear at all. Transactions may be nested as described above.

Data objects may be distributed across the network and are encapsulated within protection domains that (1) export only operations that make-up the defined interface and (2) guarantee that the invoker has sufficient access rights. Data objects may be nested. This computation model applies to many systems, including R^*, Argus, TABS, and Camelot.

3.3. Architecture Model

The architectural model describes how processing on a node is organized; that is, it describes how to realize the computation model on the system model. It is structured in five logical levels, as shown in Figure 3-2. As one might hope, few calls proceed from lower levels to upper levels. (The levels referred to in this model are distinct from the OSI levels, and subsume functions in OSI levels 4 to 7.)

At the base in Level 1 is the operating system kernel that implements processes, local synchronization, and local communication. Example kernels include the V and Accent kernels [Cheriton 84, Rashid and Robertson 81]. Level 2, the subject of a recent paper [Spector 86], provides session and datagram-based inter-node communication using the network support, as defined in the system model. The Mach operating system provides functions in both Levels 1 and 2 [Accetta et al. 86, Rashid 86].

Above the communication level is the distributed transaction facility, Level 3. Level 3 supports failure atomicity and permanence, and was described in Section 2. The distributed transaction facility builds upon the process, synchronization, and communication facilities of Levels 1 and 2.

Level 5: Applications
Level 4: Data Objects
Level 3: Distributed Transaction Facility
Level 2: Inter-Node Communication
Level 1: Operating System Kernel

Figure 3-2: Five Level Architecture Model

This figure illustrates the five system levels. The kernel level provides processes and inter-process communication. The communication level provides inter-node communication. The distributed transaction facility provides complete support for transaction processing on distributed objects. Shared data objects are maintained in Level 4 using system-supplied library routines or the runtime runtime support of a programming language. The applications that use the shared data objects are in Level 5.

Abstract objects may be grouped into a subsystem, and there may be multiple subsystems within the Data Object Level (Level 4). The abstract objects, such as database managers or mail systems, use the distributed transaction facility so that they may be accessed within transactions.

In Level 5, applications use the distributed transaction facility to begin, commit, and abort transactions and to execute operations on objects implemented within Level 4. Example applications include a banking terminal system and an interactive interface to a database manager.

The language support used by Levels 4 and 5 does not fit entirely within any level. Rather it naturally consists of one or more translators, which are external to this model, and runtime support that may reside in Levels 4 and 5. Of course, the language makes calls on facilities provided by the three lowest levels. For example, synchronization is typically implemented by runtime support within Level 4 objects, while the coordination of transaction commits is handled in Level 3.

This architecture, which provides a single distributed transaction facility, has two benefits over traditional architectures that may combine Levels 3, 4, and 5: First, because many of the components that support transactions are standardized and moved lower into the system hierarchy, there is the potential to implement them more efficiently. Second, the architecture provides a common notion of transactions and data objects for all objects and applications in the system. As mentioned in Section 2, this permits more uniform access to data. It allows an application, for example, to update transactionally a relational database containing indexing information, a file containing image data, and a hierarchical database containing performance records.

Having characterized the system, computational, and architectural structures of distributed transaction processing, it is now appropriate to examine a particular implementation — the Camelot distributed transaction facility.

4. Camelot

Camelot provides flexible and efficient support for distributed transactions on a wide variety of user-defined objects such as databases, files, message queues, and I/O objects. Clients of the Camelot facility encapsulate objects within server processes, which then execute operations in response to remote procedure calls. Camelot's features include the following:

- **Compatibility with standard operating systems.** Camelot runs on Mach, a Berkeley 4.3 Unix™-compatible operating system [Rashid 86]. Mach's Unix-compatibility makes Camelot easier to use and ensures that good program development tools are available. Mach's support for shared memory, message passing, and multiprocessors makes Camelot more efficient and flexible.

- **Compatibility with Arpanet protocols.** Camelot uses datagrams and Mach messages, both of which are built on the standard Arpanet IP network layer [Postel 82]. This facilitates large distributed processing experiments.

- **Machine-independent implementation.** Camelot is intended to run on all the uniprocessors and multiprocessors that Mach supports. For example, Camelot is developed on IBM RT PC's, but tested frequently on DEC MicroVaxes to ensure that no machine dependencies have been added.

- **Powerful functions.** Camelot supports functions that are sufficient for many different abstract types. For example, Camelot supports both blocking and non-blocking commit protocols, nested transactions as in Argus, and permits shared, recoverable objects to be accessed in virtual memory. (Section 4.2 describes Camelot's functions in more detail.)

- **Efficient implementation.** Camelot is designed to reduce the overhead of executing transactions. For example, shared memory reduces the use of message passing; multiple threads of control increases parallelism; and a common log reduces the number of synchronous stable storage writes. (Section 4.3 describes Camelot's implementation in more detail.)

- **Careful software engineering and documentation.** Camelot is being coded in C in conformance with careful coding standards [Thompson 86]. This increases Camelot's portability and maintainability and reduces the likelihood of bugs. The internal and external system interfaces are specified in the Camelot Interface Specification [Spector et al 86], which is then processed to generate Camelot code. A user manual based on the specification is nearly complete [CMU 87].

Figure 4-1 shows the relationship of Camelot to Avalon and Mach and describes how the components fit into the Architecture model.

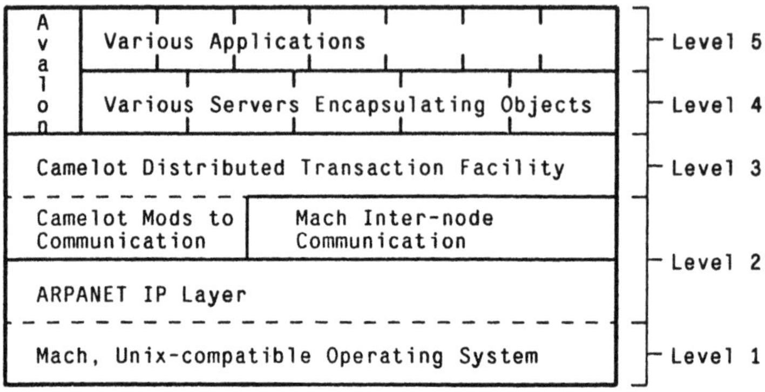

Figure 4-1: Relationship of Camelot to Other System Layers

Mach executes on uniprocessor and multiprocessor hardware and supports the functions of Level 1 of the architecture model. Level 2, or the inter-node communication level, is logically layer on top of Mach. Camelot supports distributed transaction processing (Level 3 functions) and includes several specialized additions to the communication layer. Avalon provides linguistic support for accessing Camelot and Mach, and is not a numbered level of the architecture model. Users define servers encapsulating objects (Level 4) and applications (Level 5) that use those objects. Examples of servers are mail repositories, distributed file systems, and database managers.

4.1. Background on Major Camelot Implementation Techniques

This section identifies many of the algorithms and paradigms that Camelot uses for supporting distributed transactions on abstract objects. The section focuses on issues in abstract objects, distribution, and transaction processing.

4.1.1. Abstract Objects

Many models exist for implementing the abstract objects of Level 4 in the Architecture model. In one model, objects are encapsulated in protected subsystems and accessed by protected procedure calls or capability mechanisms [Saltzer 74, Fabry 74]. Camelot uses another model, called the *client/server* model, as a basis for implementing abstract objects [Watson 81]. Servers encapsulate one or more data objects. They accept request messages that specify operations and a specific object. To implement operations, they read or modify data they directly control and invoke operations on other servers. After an operation is performed, servers send a response message containing the result. Servers that encapsulate data objects are called *Data Servers* in Camelot, *Resource Managers* in R* and *Guardians* in Argus.

Message transmission mechanisms and server organizations differ among implementations based upon the client/server model. In these aspects, Camelot is substantially influenced by the Mach operating system on which it was developed [Rashid 86]. Mach provides heavyweight processes with 32-bit virtual address spaces and supports messages addressed addressed to *ports*. Many processes may have send rights to a port, but only one has receive rights. Send rights and receive rights can be transmitted in messages along with ordinary data. Large quantities of data are efficiently conveyed between processes on the same machine via copy-on-write mapping into the address space of the recipient process. This message model differs from that of Unix 4.2 [Joy et al. 83] and the V Kernel [Cheriton 84] in that messages are typed sequences of data which can contain port capabilities, and that large messages can be transmitted with nearly constant overhead.

The programming effort associated with packing and unpacking messages is reduced in Camelot through the use of a remote procedure call facility called *Matchmaker* [Jones et al. 85]. (We use the term *remote procedure call* to apply to both intra-node and inter-node communication.) Matchmaker's input is a syntactic definition of procedure headers and its outputs are client and server stubs that pack and unpack messages, and dispatch to the appropriate procedures on the server side.

Servers that never wait while processing an operation can be organized as a loop that receives a request message, dispatches to execute the operation, and sends a response message. Unfortunately, servers may wait for many reasons: to synchronize with other operations, to execute a remote operation or system call, or to page-fault. For such servers, there must be multiple threads of control within a server, or else the server will pause or deadlock when it need not.

One implementation approach for servers is to have multiple lightweight processes within a single server process. Page-faults still cause all lightweight processes to be suspended, but a lightweight process switch can occur when a server would otherwise wait. Another approach is to allocate independently schedulable threads of control that share access to data. With this approach, a server is a class of related processes — in the Simula sense of the word "class." This technique is supported by Mach and used in Camelot [Cooper 86]. The topic of server organization has been clearly discussed by Liskov and Herlihy [Liskov and Herlihy 83].

Before leaving the topic of abstract objects, it is necessary to discuss how objects can be named. Certainly, a port to a server and a *logical object identifier* that distinguishes between the various objects implemented by that server are sufficient to name an object. The dissemination of these names can be done in many ways. A common method is for servers to register objects with a well known server process on their node, often called a *name server*, and for the name server to return one or more ports, in response to name lookup requests. Name servers can cooperate with each other to provide transparent naming across a network.

4.1.2. Distribution

Replicated and partitioned distributed objects within Level 4 of the Architecture model are feasible to implement using the client/server model. For example, there may be many servers that can respond identically to operations on a replicated object. However, servers must contain the replication or partitioning logic. The Camelot project hypothesizes that the availability of transaction support substantially simplifies the maintenance of distributed and replicated objects.

Transparent inter-node message passing can simplify access to remote servers. In the Mach environment, inter-node communication is achieved by interposing a pair of processes, called communication managers, between the sender of a message and its intended recipient on a remote node [Rashid and Robertson 81]. The communication manager supplies the sender with a local port to use for messages addressed to the remote process. Together with its counterpart at the remote node, the communication manager implements the mapping between the local port used by the sender and the corresponding remote port belonging to the target process, providing transparent communication.

4.1.3. Transactions

Camelot provides features to support all the standard notions of transactions, but does not require that objects enforce serializability, failure atomicity, or permanence. Transactions are permitted to interfere with each other and to show the effects of failure — if this is useful. That is, Camelot provides basic facilities for supporting many different types of objects and lets implementors choose how they want to use them.

Many techniques exist for synchronizing the execution of transactions. Locking, optimistic, timestamp, and many hybrid schemes are frequently discussed; many of these are surveyed by Bernstein and Goodman [Bernstein and Goodman 81]. Camelot has chosen to support two compatible types of synchronization: locking and hybrid atomicity [Date 83, Herlihy 85]. Hybrid atomicity has features of both timestamps and locking, and requires a Lamport clock facility [Lamport 78] from Camelot and substantial support from Avalon [Herlihy and Wing 86]. Since both types of synchronization are implemented primarily by servers (within Level 4), implementations can be tailored to provide the highest concurrency. For example, with *type-specific* locking, implementors can obtain increased concurrency by defining type-specific lock modes and lock protocols [Korth 83, Schwarz and Spector 84, Schwarz 84].

Both locking and hybrid atomicity may delay transaction execution, even if that delay leads to a deadlock. Some systems implement local and distributed deadlock detectors that identify and break cycles of waiting transactions [Obermarck 82, Lindsay et al. 84]. However, Camelot Release 1, like many other systems, relies on time-outs, which are explicitly set by system users [Tandem 82].

Recovery in Camelot is based upon *write-ahead logging*, rather than *shadow paging* [Lorie 77, Gray 78, Lindsay et al. 79, Gray et al. 81, Lampson 81, Haerder and Reuter 83, Schwarz 84]. It assumes the storage hierarchy defined in the system model, above.

In recovery techniques based upon write-ahead logging, stable storage contains an append-only sequence of records. These records may contain a redo component, that permits the effects of committed transactions to be redone and possibly an undo component that permits the effects of aborted transactions to be undone. Updates to data objects are made by modifying a representation of the object residing in volatile storage and by spooling one or more records to the log. Logging is called "write-ahead" because log records must be safely stored (forced) to stable storage before transactions commit, and before the volatile representation of an object is copied to non-volatile storage. Because of this strategy, there are log records in stable storage for all the changes that have been made to non-volatile storage, and for all committed transactions. Thus, the log can be used to recover from aborted transactions, system crashes and non-volatile storage failures.

The advantages of write-ahead logging over other schemes have been discussed elsewhere and include the potential for increased concurrency, reduced I/O activity at transaction commit time, and contiguous allocation of objects on secondary storage [Gray et al. 81, Traiger 82, Reuter 84]. All objects in Camelot Release 1 use one of two co-existing write-ahead logging techniques and share a common log.

The simpler technique is called *old value/new value* logging, in which the undo and redo portions of a log record contain the old and new values of an object's representation. During recovery after node or server crashes, objects are reset to their most recently committed values during a one pass scan that begins at the last log record written and proceeds backward. If this value logging algorithm is used, only one transaction at a time may modify any individually logged component of an object that is to be failure atomic and permanent.

The other technique is called *new value* logging, in which log records contain only a redo component. New value logging requires less log space but results in increased paging for long running transactions. This is because pages cannot be written back to their home location until a transaction completes. Camelot assumes that the invoker of a transaction will know if the transaction will be short and will specify that new value logging should be used.

Release 2 of Camelot will also provide another write-ahead log-based recovery technique called *operation* (or *transition*) logging. With it, data servers write log records containing the names of operations and enough information to invoke them. Operations are redone or undone, as necessary, during recovery processing to restore the correct state of objects. Operation based recovery can permit a greater degree of concurrency than the value based recovery, and may require less log space to be written. Its disadvantage is complexity.

The Camelot recovery algorithms are similar to other previously published write-ahead log-based algorithms [Gray 78, Lindsay et al. 79], in particular those of Schwarz [Schwarz 84]. However, they have been extended to support aborts of nested transactions, new value recovery, and the logging of arbitrary regions of memory.

Both value and operation logging algorithms require that periodic system *checkpoints* be taken. Checkpoints serve to reduce the amount of log data that must be available for crash recovery and shorten the time to recover after a crash [Haerder and Reuter 83]. At checkpoint time, a list of the pages currently in volatile storage and the status of currently active transactions are written to the log. Camelot also periodically forces certain pages in volatile storage to non-volatile storage and may abort long running to lessen the amount of log that must be rapidly accessible. To reduce the cost of recovering from disk failures, Camelot infrequently *dumps* the contents of non-volatile storage into an off-line archive.

Recently, researchers have begun to discuss high performance recovery implementations that integrate virtual memory management with the recovery subsystem and use higher performance stable storage devices [Traiger 82, Banatre et al. 83, Stonebraker 84, Diel et al. 84, Eppinger and Spector 85]. Camelot integrates virtual memory management with recovery and ensures that the necessary log records are written to stable storage before pages are written to their home location.

The most important component of a transaction facility not yet discussed is the one that oversees initiating, commiting, and aborting transactions. Commit algorithms vary in their efficiency and robustness [Lindsay et al. 79, Dwork and Skeen 83]. Camelot's algorithms are both instances of star-shaped star-shaped commit protocols, in which the initiator of the outermost top-level transaction serves as coordinator for all nodes in the transaction. One algorithm is based on the standard 2-phase commit protocol. It is efficient, but has failure modes in which nodes participating in a distributed transaction must restrict access to some data until other nodes recover from a crash or a network partition is eliminated. Camelot also provides a hybrid protocol, which is a cross between 3-phase and byzantine commit protocols, to reduce the likelihood that access to data will be blocked.

The increased interest in building nested abstractions using transactions has led to the investigation and implementation of facilities for supporting nesting. These facilities limit the concurrency anomalies that can occur within a single transaction that has multiple threads of control and permit portions of a transaction to abort independently. Camelot supports nested transactions as in Argus.

4.1.4. Summary of Implementation Background

The major points of this development can be tersely summarized: Camelot supports transactions on abstract objects. Objects are implemented within server processes, and operations on objects are invoked via messages with a remote procedure call facility. Inter-node communication uses both sessions and datagrams. Inter-transaction synchronization is done via locking or hybrid atomicity, with time-outs used to resolve deadlock (in Release 1). Write-ahead logging is the basis of recovery and transaction commit is done via either a blocking or non-blocking commit protocol. Camelot supports for the Argus nested transaction model.

4.2. Camelot Functions

As mentioned, the most basic building blocks for reliable distributed applications are provided by Mach, its communication facilities, and the Matchmaker RPC stub generator [Cooper 86, Jones et al. 85]. These building blocks include processes, threads of control within processes, shared memory between processes, and message passing.

Camelot provides functions for system configuration, recovery, disk management, transaction management, deadlock detection, and reliability/performance evaluation. Simple lock-based synchronization mechanisms are provided in the Camelot libraries. (Avalon's runtime support is required to use Hybrid Atomicity.) These functions are specified in the Camelot Interface Specification and Guide to the Camelot System [Spector et al 86, CMU 87]. Certain more advanced functions will be added to Camelot for Release 2.

4.2.1. Configuration Management

Camelot supports the dynamic allocation and deallocation of both new data servers and the recoverable storage in which data servers store long-lived objects. Camelot maintains configuration data so that it can restart the appropriate data servers after a crash and reattach them to their recoverable storage. These configuration data are stored in recoverable storage and updated transactionally.

4.2.2. Disk Management

Camelot provides data servers with up to 2^{48} bytes of recoverable storage. With the cooperation of Mach, Camelot permits data servers to map that storage into their address space, though data servers must call Camelot to remap their address space when they overflow 32-bit addresses. To simplify the allocation of contiguous regions of disk space, Camelot assumes that all allocation and deallocation requests space are coarse (e.g., in megabytes). Data servers are responsible for doing their own microscopic storage management.

So that operations on data in recoverable storage can be undone or redone after failures, Camelot provides data servers with logging services for recording modifications to objects. Camelot automatically coordinates paging of recoverable storage to maintain the write-ahead log invariant [Eppinger and Spector 85].

4.2.3. Recovery Management

Camelot's recovery functions include transaction abort, and server, node, and media-failure recovery. To support these functions, Camelot Release 1 provides the two forms of write-ahead value logging mentioned above.

Camelot writes log data to locally duplexed storage or to storage that is replicated on a collection of dedicated network log servers [Daniels et al. 86]. In some environments, the use of a shared network logging facility could have survivability, operational, performance, and cost advantages. Survivability is likely to be better for a replicated logging facility because it can tolerate the destruction of one or more entire processing nodes. Operational advantages accrue because it is easier to manage high volumes of log data at a small number of logging nodes, rather than at all transaction processing nodes. Performance might be better because shared facilities can have faster hardware than could be afforded for each processing node. Finally, providing a shared network logging facility would be less costly than dedicating duplexed disks to each processing node, particularly in workstation environments.

4.2.4. Transaction Management

Camelot provides facilities for beginning new top-level and nested transactions and for committing and aborting them. Two options exist for commit: *Blocking* commit may result in data that remains locked until a coordinator is restarted or a network is repaired. *Non-blocking* commit, though more expensive in the normal case, reduces the likelihood that a node's data will remain locked until another node or network partition is repaired. In addition to these standard transaction management functions, Camelot provides an inquiry facility for determining the status of a transaction. The Camelot library and Avalon use this to support lock inheritance.

4.2.5. The Camelot Library

The Camelot library packages all system interfaces and provides a simple locking mechanism. It also contains routines that perform the generic processing required of all data servers. This processing includes participating in two-phase commit, handling undo and redo requests generated after failures, responding to abort exceptions, and the like. The functions of this library are subsumed by Avalon's more ambitious linguistic support.

4.2.6. Deadlock Detection

Clients of Camelot Release 1 must depend on time-out to detect deadlocks. Release 2 will incorporate a deadlock detector and export interfaces for servers to report their local knowledge of wait-for graphs. We anticipate that implementing deadlock detection for arbitrary abstract types in a large network environment like the Arpanet will be difficult.

4.2.7. Reliability and Performance Evaluation

Camelot Release 2 will contain a facility for capturing performance data, generating and distributing workloads, and inserting (simulated) faults. These capabilities will aid in analyzing, tuning, and validating Camelot and benefit Camelot's clients as they analyze their distributed algorithms. The information returned by the facility could also be used to provide feedback for applications that dynamically tune themselves. We believe that, when properly designed, a reliability and performance evaluation facility will prove as essential for building large distributed applications as source-level debuggers are essential for traditional programming.

The reliability and performance evaluation facility has three parts. The first captures performance data and permits clients to gauge critical performance metrics, such as the number of messages, page faults, deadlocks, and transactions/second. Certain information is application-independent, but other useful information depends on the nature of the application. Therefore, the performance evaluation facility will be extensible and capture application-specific data from higher level components. Once information is obtained from various nodes on the system, the facility combines and presents it to system implementors or feeds it back to applications for use in dynamic tuning.

The second part of the performance and reliability evaluation facility permits the distribution of applications (or workloads) on the system. When many nodes are involved in a workload, this task can be very difficult unless it is possible to specify the nodes and workloads from a single node. We have built a prototype facility of this type for TABS, and we will extend it for use on Camelot.

The third part permits simulated faults to be inserted according to a pre-specified distribution. This is crucial for understanding the behavior of a system in the presence of faults. For example, the low-level communication software may be instructed to lose or reorder datagrams with a pre-specified probability. Or, a pair of nodes could greatly raise network utilization to probe the effects of contention.

4.2.8. Miscellaneous Functions

Camelot provides both a logical clock [Lamport 78] and a synchronized real-time clock. These clocks are useful not only for supporting hybrid atomicity, but other distributed algorithms, for example replication using optimistic timestamps [Bloch 86]. Camelot also extends the Mach naming service to support multiple servers with the same name. This is useful to support replicated objects.

4.3. Camelot Implementation

The major functions of Camelot and their logical relationship is illustrated in Figure 4-2. Disk management and recovery management are at the base of Camelot's functions. Both activities are local to a particular node, except that disk management and recovery may require communication with the network logging service. Deadlock detection and transaction management are distributed activities that assume underlying disk management and node recovery facilities. Specialized communication protocols (beyond those provided by Level 2) and reliability and performance evaluation are implemented within many levels of the system. The library support for data servers rests on top of these functions.

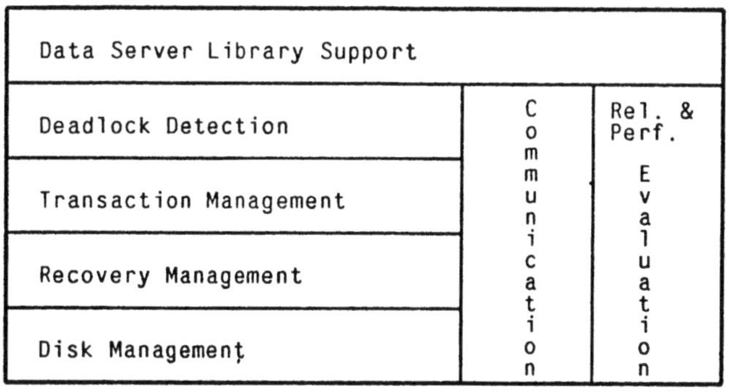

Figure 4-2: Logical Components of Camelot

This figure describes the logical structure of Camelot. Camelot is logically hierarchical, except that communication and reliability and performance evaluation functions span multiple levels.

All of Camelot, except the library routines, is implemented by a collection of Mach processes, which run on every node. Each of these processes is responsible for supporting a particular collection of functions. Processes use threads of control internally to permit parallelism. Calls to Camelot (e.g., to begin or commit a transaction), must be directed to a particular Camelot process. Some frequently called functions such as log writes are invoked by writing to memory queues that are shared between a data server and a Camelot process. Other functions are invoked using messages that are generated by Matchmaker.

Figure 4-3 shows the seven processes in Release 1 of Camelot: master control, disk manager, communication manager, recovery manager, transaction manager, node server, and node configuration application.[3]

- **Master Control.** This process restarts Camelot after a node failure.

[3] Camelot Release 2 will use additional processes to support deadlock detection and reliability and performance evaluation.

- **Disk Manager.** The disk manager allocates and deallocates recoverable storage, accepts and writes log records locally, and enforces the write-ahead log invariant. For log records that are to be written to the distributed logging service, the disk manager works with dedicated servers on the network. Additionally, the disk manager writes pages to/from the disk when Mach needs to service page faults on recoverable storage or to clean primary memory. Finally, it performs checkpoints to limit the amount of work during recovery and works closely with the recovery manager when failures are being processed.

- **Communication Manager.** The communication manager forwards inter-node Mach messages, and provides the logical and physical clock services. In addition, it knows the format of messages and keeps a list of all the nodes that are involved in a particular transaction. This information is provided to the transaction manager for use during commit or abort processing. Finally, the communication manager provides a name service that creates communication channels to named servers. (The transaction manager and distributed logging service use IP datagrams, thereby bypassing the communication manager.)

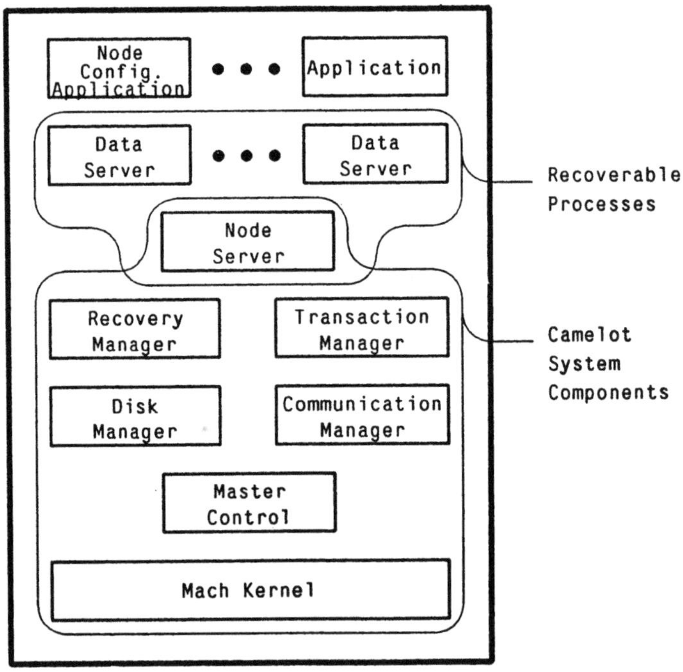

Figure 4-3: Processes in Camelot Release 1

This figure shows the Mach kernel and the processes that are needed to execute distributed transactions. The node server is both a part of Camelot, and a Camelot data server because it is the repository of essential configuration data. Other data servers and applications use the facilities of Camelot and Mach. The node configuration application permits users to exercise control over a node's configuration.

- **Recovery Manager.** The recovery manager is responsible for transaction abort, server recovery, node recovery, and media-failure recovery. Server and node recovery respectively require one and two backward passes over the log.

- **Transaction Manager.** The transaction manager coordinates the initiation, commit, and abort of local and distributed transactions. It fully supports nested transactions.

- **Node Server.** The node server is the repository of configuration data necessary for restarting the node. It stores its data in recoverable storage and is recovered before other servers.

- **Node Configuration Application.** The node configuration application permits Camelot's human users to update data in the node server and to crash and restart servers.

The organization of Camelot is similar to that of TABS and R*. Structurally, Camelot differs from TABS in the use of threads, shared memory interfaces, and the combination of logging and disk management in the same process. Many low-level algorithms and protocols have also been changed to improve performance and provide added functions. Camelot differs from R* in its greater use of message passing and support for common recovery facilities for servers. Of course, the functions of the two systems are quite different; transactions in R* are intended primarily to support a particular relational database system.

4.4. Discussion

As of January 1987, Camelot 1 was still being coded though enough (about 25,00 lines of C) was functioning to commit and abort local transactions. Though many pieces were still missing (e.g., support for stable storage and distribution), Avalon developers could begin their implementation work. Before we add to the basic set of Camelot 1 functions, others will be encouraged to port abstractions to Camelot and provide feedback on its functionality and performance.

Performance is a very important system goal. Experience with TABS and very preliminary performance numbers make us believe that we will be able to execute roughly 20 non-paging write transactions/second on an RT PC or MicroVax workstation. Perhaps, it is worthwhile to summarize why the Camelot/Mach combination should have performance that even database implementors will like:

- Mach's support for multiple threads of control per process permit efficient server organizations and the use of multiprocessors.

- Disk I/O should be efficient, because Camelot allocates recoverable storage contiguously on disk, and because Mach permits it to be mapped into a server's memory. Also, servers that know disk I/O patterns, such as database managers, can influence the page replacement algorithms by providing hints for prefetching or prewriting.

- Recovery adds little overhead to normal processing because Camelot uses write-ahead logging with a common log. Though Camelot Release 1 has only value-logging, operation-logging will be provided in Release 2.

- Camelot has an efficient, datagram-based, two-phase commit protocol in addition to its non-blocking commit protocol. Even without delaying commits to reduce log forces ("group commit"), transactions require only one log force per node per transaction. Camelot requires just three datagrams per node per transaction in its star-shaped commit protocol, because final acknowledgments are piggy-backed on future communication. Camelot also has the usual optimizations for read-only transactions.

- Camelot does not implement the synchronization needed to preserve serializability. This synchronization is left to servers (and/or Avalon), which can apply semantic knowledge to provide higher concurrency or to reduce locking overhead.

5. Challenges

Many commercial transaction processing applications already use distributed transactions. Many more algorithms and applications will benefit from them when general-purpose, high performance transaction facilities are available. For example, there have been promising applications built on both TABS and Argus that could be very useful in production environments. Also, there are a plethora of unimplemented distributed replication techniques that depend upon transactions to maintain invariants on the underlying replicas.

The challenges lie in constructing facilities that have high performance, yet are easy to use and operate within familiar computing environments. The performance challenge is clear due to the obvious complexity of implementing commit protocols, stable storage, media recovery, etc. There are also concurrency control bottlenecks that could become problematical. However, there are many good algorithms to use, and the structure of distributed transaction processing seems sufficiently well understood to permit clean implementations.

Ease of use and operational challenges are equally important. For many applications, a distributed transaction facility must run on all the nodes of a large distributed system. Thus, it should be installed along with the operating system and require minimal, if any, operator intervention. Taking dumps, managing log space, reconfiguring nodes, and adding and removing servers should be nearly automatic or at least easy to do. Programmers should also find it straightforward to use the facility. The Argus and Avalon languages, or carefully defined library support such as that in the Camelot library can substantially reduce programming complexity, but it remains to be seen how successful these efforts will be for large systems.

Camelot is intended to meet many of these challenges and to help demonstrate that transaction facilities can be sufficiently efficient and easy to use for a wide range of distributed programs. However, there are additional challenges not addressed by Camelot.

Support for heterogeneous networks and operating systems would add much to the utility of transaction processing. Even with all the standardization efforts that are underway, it would still desirable to support distributed transactions running on multiple types of systems and networks; for example, it would be useful if Camelot/Mach workstations could participate in transactions with existing data on 370/MVS mainframes. Technically, this is possible, but it is difficult to perform the needed protocol translations efficiently.

Perhaps the most important challenge is to construct the transactional abstract objects that are needed to make distributed transaction facilities really useful: mail systems, specialized databases, file systems, window managers, and queuing systems. While the availability of transactions make these objects easier to implement, they are still complex — particularly if they require replication. Reconciling the transactional semantics of new objects with the non-transactional objects that they replace is also difficult. (This could be a particularly tough problem with the Unix file system.)

In spite of these challenges, distributed transaction facilities should become more prevalent. Ongoing work in the research and commercial spheres, aided by ever-faster hardware will continue to improve their performance and usability.

Acknowledgments

I thank Jeff Eppinger, who thoroughly read and critiqued this paper, and my colleagues on the Camelot and Avalon Projects for their contributions to the systems that I have described.

References

[Accetta et al. 86] Mike Accetta, Robert Baron, William Bolosky, David Golub, Richard Rashid, Avadis Tevanian, Michael Young. Mach: A New Kernel Foundation for UNIX Development. In *Proceedings of Summer Usenix*. July, 1986.

[Allchin 83] James E. Allchin. *An Architecture for Reliable Distributed Systems*. PhD thesis, Georgia Institute of Technology, September, 1983.

[Allchin and McKendry 83] James E. Allchin, Martin S. McKendry. *Facilities for Supporting Atomicity in Operating Systems*. Technical Report GIT-CS-83/1, Georgia Institute of Technology, January, 1983.

[Astrahan et al. 76] M. M. Astrahan, M. W. Blasgen, D. D. Chamberlin, K. P. Eswaran, J. N. Gray, P. P. Griffiths, W. F. King, R. A. Lorie, P. R. McJones, J. W. Mehl, G. R. Putzolu, I. L. Traiger, B. W. Wade, and V. Watson. System R: A Relational Approach to Database Management. *ACM Transactions on Database Systems* 1(2), June, 1976.

[Banatre et al. 83] J. P. Banatre, M. Banatre, F. Ployette. Construction of a Distributed System Supporting Atomic Transactions. In *Proceedings of the Third Symposium on Reliability in Distributed Software and Database Systems*. IEEE, October, 1983.

[Bernstein and Goodman 81] Philip A. Bernstein, Nathan Goodman. Concurrency Control in Distributed Database Systems. *ACM Computing Surveys* 13(2):185-221, June, 1981.

[Bloch 86] Joshua J. Bloch. A Practical, Efficient Approach to Replication of Abstract Data Objects. November, 1986. Carnegie Mellon Thesis Proposal.

[Cheriton 84] David R. Cheriton. The V Kernel: A Software Base for Distributed Systems. *IEEE Software* 1(2):186-213, April, 1984.

[CMU 87] *The Guide to the Camelot Distributed Transaction Facility Release 0* Pittsburgh, PA, 1987. Under development.

[Cooper 86] Eric C. Cooper. C Threads. June, 1986. Carnegie Mellon Internal Memo.

[Dahl and Hoare 72] O.J. Dahl, C. A. R. Hoare. Hierarchical Program Structures. In C. A. R. Hoare (editor), *A.P.I.C. Studies in Data Processing*. Volume 8: *Structured Programming*, chapter 3, pages 175-220.Academic Press, London and New York, 1972.

[Daniels et al. 86] Dean S. Daniels, Alfred Z. Spector, Dean Thompson. *Distributed Logging for Transaction Processing*. Technical Report CMU-CS-86-106, Carnegie-Mellon University, June, 1986.

[Date 83] C. J. Date. *The System Programming Series: An Introduction to Database Systems Volume 2*. Addison-Wesley, Reading, MA, 1983.

[Department of Defense 82] *Reference Manual for the Ada Programming Language* July 1982 edition, Department of Defense, Ada Joint Program Office, Washington, DC, 1982.

[Diel et al. 84] Hans Diel, Gerald Kreissig, Norbet Lenz, Michael Scheible, Bernd Schoener. Data Management Facilities of an Operating System Kernel. In *Sigmod '84*, pages 58-69. June, 1984.

[Dwork and Skeen 83] Cynthia Dwork, Dale Skeen. The Inherent Cost of Nonblocking Commitment. In *Proceedings of the Second Annual Symposium on Principles of Distributed Computing*, pages 1-11. ACM, August, 1983.

[Eppinger and Spector 85] Jeffrey L. Eppinger, Alfred Z. Spector. *Virtual Memory Management for Recoverable Objects in the TABS Prototype*. Technical Report CMU-CS-85-163, Carnegie-Mellon University, December, 1985.

[Fabry 74] R. S. Fabry. Capability-Based Addressing. *Communications of the ACM* 17(7):403-411, July, 1974.

[Gray 78] James N. Gray. Notes on Database Operating Systems. In R. Bayer, R. M. Graham, G. Seegmuller (editors), *Lecture Notes in Computer Science.* Volume 60: *Operating Systems - An Advanced Course*, pages 393-481.Springer-Verlag, 1978. Also available as Technical Report RJ2188, IBM Research Laboratory, San Jose, California, 1978.

[Gray 81] James N. Gray. The Transaction Concept: Virtues and Limitations. In *Proceedings of the Very Large Database Conference*, pages 144-154. September, 1981.

[Gray et al. 81] James N. Gray, et al. The Recovery Manager of the System R Database Manager. *ACM Computing Surveys* 13(2):223-242, June, 1981.

[Haerder and Reuter 83] Theo Haerder, Andreas Reuter. Principles of Transaction-Oriented Database Recovery. *ACM Computing Surveys* 15(4):287-318, December, 1983.

[Helland 85] Pat Helland. Transaction Monitoring Facility. *Database Engineering* 8(2):9-18, June, 1985.

[Herlihy 85] Maurice P. Herlihy. *Availability vs. atomicity: concurrency control for replicated data.* Technical Report CMU-CS-85-108, Carnegie-Mellon University, February, 1985.

[Herlihy and Wing 86] M. P. Herlihy, J. M. Wing. *Avalon: Language Support for Reliable Distributed Systems.* Technical Report CMU-CS-86-167, Carnegie Mellon University, November, 1986.

[Jones et al. 85] Michael B. Jones, Richard F. Rashid, Mary R. Thompson. Matchmaker: An Interface Specification Language for Distributed Processing. In *Proceedings of the Twelfth Annual Symposium on Principles of Programming Languages*, pages 225-235. ACM, January, 1985.

[Joy et al. 83] William Joy, Eric Cooper, Robert Fabry, Samuel Leffler, Kirk McKusick, David Mosher. *4.2 BSD System Interface Overview.* Technical Report CSRG TR/5, University of California Berkeley, July, 1983.

[Korth 83] Henry F. Korth. Locking Primitives in a Database System. *Journal of the ACM* 30(1):55-79, January, 1983.

[Lamport 78] Leslie Lamport. Time, Clocks, and the Ordering of Events in a Distributed System. *Communications of the ACM* 21(7):558-565, July, 1978.

[Lampson 81] Butler W. Lampson. Atomic Transactions. In G. Goos and J. Hartmanis (editors), *Lecture Notes in Computer Science.* Volume 105: *Distributed Systems - Architecture and Implementation: An Advanced Course*, chapter 11, , pages 246-265.Springer-Verlag, 1981.

[Lindsay et al. 79] Bruce G. Lindsay, et al. *Notes on Distributed Databases.* Technical Report RJ2571, IBM Research Laboratory, San Jose, California, July, 1979. Also appears in Droffen and Poole (editors), *Distributed Databases*, Cambridge University Press, 1980.

[Lindsay et al. 84] Bruce G. Lindsay, Laura M. Haas, C. Mohan, Paul F. Wilms, Robert A. Yost. Computation and Communication in R*: A Distributed Database Manager. *ACM Transactions on Computer Systems* 2(1):24-38, February, 1984.

[Liskov 82] Barbara Liskov. On Linguistic Support for Distributed Programs. *IEEE Transactions on Software Engineering* SE-8(3):203-210, May, 1982.

[Liskov 84] Barbara Liskov. *Overview of the Argus Language and System.* Programming Methodology Group Memo 40, Massachusetts Institute of Technology Laboratory for Computer Science, February, 1984.

[Liskov and Herlihy 83] Barbara Liskov, Maurice Herlihy. Issues in Process and Communication Structure for Distributed Programs. In *Proceedings of the Third Symposium on Reliability in Distributed Software and Database Systems.* October, 1983.

[Liskov and Scheifler 83] Barbara H. Liskov, Robert W. Scheifler. Guardians and Actions: Linguistic Support for Robust, Distributed Programs. *ACM Transactions on Programming Languages and Systems* 5(3):381-404, July, 1983.

[Lomet 77] David B. Lomet. Process Structuring, Synchronization, and Recovery Using Atomic Actions. *ACM SIGPLAN Notices* 12(3), March, 1977.

[Lorie 77] Raymond A. Lorie. Physical Integrity in a Large Segmented Database. *ACM Transactions on Database Systems* 2(1):91-104, March, 1977.

[Moss 81] J. Eliot B. Moss. *Nested Transactions: An Approach to Reliable Distributed Computing*. PhD thesis, Massachusetts Institute of Technology, April, 1981.

[Obermarck 82] Ron Obermarck. Distributed Deadlock Detection Algorithm. *ACM Transactions on Database Systems* 7(2):187-208, June, 1982.

[Postel 82] Jonathan B. Postel. Internetwork Protocol Approaches. In Paul E. Green, Jr. (editor), *Computer Network Architectures and Protocols*, chapter 18, pages 511-526.Plenum Press, 1982.

[Rashid 86] Richard F. Rashid. Threads of a New System. *Unix Review* 4(8):37-49, August, 1986.

[Rashid and Robertson 81] Richard Rashid, George Robertson. Accent: A Communication Oriented Network Operating System Kernel. In *Proceedings of the Eighth Symposium on Operating System Principles*, pages 64-75. ACM, December, 1981.

[Reed 78] David P. Reed. *Naming and Synchronization in a Decentralized Computer System*. PhD thesis, Massachusetts Institute of Technology, September, 1978.

[Reuter 84] Andreas Reuter. Performance Analysis of Recovery Techniques. *ACM Transactions on Database Systems* 9(4):526-559, December, 1984.

[Rothnie et al. 80] J. B. Rothnie Jr., P. A. Bernstein, S. Fox, N. Goodman, M. Hammer, T. A. Landers, C. Reeve, D. W. Shipman, and E. Wong. Introduction to a System for Distributed Databases (SDD-1). *ACM Transactions on Database Systems* 5(1):1-17, March, 1980.

[Saltzer 74] Jerome H. Saltzer. Protection and the Control of Information in Multics. *Communications of the ACM* 17(7), July, 1974.

[Schwarz 84] Peter M. Schwarz. *Transactions on Typed Objects*. PhD thesis, Carnegie-Mellon University, December, 1984. Available as Technical Report CMU-CS-84-166, Carnegie-Mellon University.

[Schwarz and Spector 84] Peter M. Schwarz, Alfred Z. Spector. Synchronizing Shared Abstract Types. *ACM Transactions on Computer Systems* 2(3):223-250, August, 1984. Also available as Technical Report CMU-CS-83-163, Carnegie-Mellon University, November 1983.

[Spector 86] Alfred Z. Spector. Communication Support in Operating Systems for Distributed Transactions. In *Proc. IBM European Networking Institute 1986*. July, 1986. Also available as Technical Report CMU-CS-86-165, Carnegie-Mellon University, November 1986.

[Spector and Schwarz 83] Alfred Z. Spector, Peter M. Schwarz. Transactions: A Construct for Reliable Distributed Computing. *Operating Systems Review* 17(2):18-35, April, 1983. Also available as Technical Report CMU-CS-82-143, Carnegie-Mellon University, January 1983.

[Spector et al 86] Alfred Z. Spector, Dan Duchamp, Jeffrey L. Eppinger, Sherri G. Menees, Dean S. Thompson. The Camelot Interface Specification. September, 1986. Camelot Working Memo 2.

[Spector et al. 85a] Alfred Z. Spector, Jacob Butcher, Dean S. Daniels, Daniel J. Duchamp, Jeffrey L. Eppinger, Charles E. Fineman, Abdelsalam Heddaya, Peter M. Schwarz. Support for Distributed Transactions in the TABS Prototype. *IEEE Transactions on Software Engineering* SE-11(6):520-530, June, 1985. Also available in Proceedings of the Fourth Symposium on Reliability in Distributed Software and Database Systems, Silver Springs, Maryland, IEEE, October, 1984 and as Technical Report CMU-CS-84-132, Carnegie-Mellon University, July, 1984.

[Spector et al. 85b] Alfred Z. Spector, Dean S. Daniels, Daniel J. Duchamp, Jeffrey L. Eppinger, Randy Pausch. Distributed Transactions for Reliable Systems. In *Proceedings of the Tenth Symposium on Operating System Principles*, pages 127-146. ACM, December, 1985. Also available in *Concurrency Control and Reliability in Distributed Systems*, Van Nostrand Reinhold Company, New York, and as Technical Report CMU-CS-85-117, Carnegie-Mellon University, September 1985.

[Stonebraker 84] Michael Stonebraker. Virtual Memory Transaction Management. *Operating Systems Review* 18(2):8-16, April, 1984.

[Stonebraker and Neuhold 77] M. Stonebraker and E. Neuhold. A Distributed Data Base Version of INGRES. In *Proceedings of the Second Berkeley Workshop on Distributed Data Management and Computer Networks*, pages 19-36. Lawrence Berkeley Lab, University of California, Berkeley, California, May, 1977.

[Tandem 82] *ENCOMPASS Distributed Data Management System* Tandem Computers, Inc., Cupertino, California, 1982.

[Thompson 86] Dean Thompson. Coding Standards for Camelot. June, 1986. Camelot Working Memo 1.

[Traiger 82] Irving L. Traiger. Virtual Memory Management for Database Systems. *Operating Systems Review* 16(4):26-48, October, 1982. Also available as Technical Report RJ3489 IBM Research Laboratory, San Jose, California, May, 1982.

[Watson 81] R.W. Watson. Distributed system architecture model. In B.W. Lampson (editors), *Lecture Notes in Computer Science.* Volume 105: *Distributed Systems - Architecture and Implementation: An Advanced Course*, chapter 2, , pages 10-43.Springer-Verlag, 1981.

[Weihl 84] William E. Weihl. *Specification and Implementation of Atomic Data Types.* PhD thesis, Massachusetts Institute of Technology, March, 1984.

[Weinstein et al. 85] Matthew J. Weinstein, Thomas W. Page, Jr., Brian K. Livezey, Gerald J. Popek. Transactions and Synchronization in a Distributed Operating System. In *Proceedings of the Tenth Symposium on Operating System Principles*, pages 115-126. ACM, December, 1985.

[Williams et al. 81] R. Williams, et al. *R*: An Overview of the Architecture.* IBM Research Report RJ3325, IBM Research Laboratory, San Jose, California, December, 1981.

[Zimmermann 82] Hubert Zimmermann. A Standard Network Model. In Paul E. Green, Jr. (editor), *Computer Network Architectures and Protocols*, chapter 2, pages 33-54.Plenum Press, 1982.

WORM PROGRAMS*

T. Kindberg, A.V. Sahiner, Y.Paker

Polytechnic of Central London,
School of Computer Science,
115 New Cavendish St.,
London W1M 8JS

1 Introduction

1.1. The Reasons for Worms

The initial work on 'worm programs' was done by John Shoch and Jon Hupp at Xerox PARC [1]. The motivation for worms comes from the existence of computer networks in which conventional sharing of resources such as disc drives and printers take place, but in which no attempt is made to share the processing workload amongst the available processors. Shoch and Hupp thought of their Ethernetwork of Alto minicomputers at Xerox PARC as a gigantic multiprocessor, some of whose processing elements were in general being wasted at any one time. A worm program is one which can take maximum advantage of the population of free processors ('free' in the Xerox context means free according to constraints placed by other network users) by expanding its operations to encompass them as they become available, and according to its needs. This approach is to be contrasted with, for example, the Cambridge Distributed Computing System as described in [2], in which a processor from a pool is allocated to a user at the beginning of a session; worms on the other hand must be able to operate at a number of machines and respond dynamically to changes in processor availability at run time; moreover they may operate remotely from any computer to which their user happens to be logged-on. Control of worm programs at run time, in other words, is to be essentially decentralised.

Given the ability to occupy more than one processor, and to seek out the most appropriate (eg least- used) processors in a network, worms may be considered to have four rather useful abilities or attributes:-

1) full and balanced usage of a network's processing resources (which may be heterogeneous);

* This work has been supported by a grant from the Science and Engineering Research Council

NATO ASI Series, Vol. F28
Distributed Operating Systems. Theory and Practice
Edited by Y. Paker et al.

2) parallel processing;

3) tolerance of processor failure in certain applications;

4) adaptability to short- and long-term network changes.

Whilst our work involves an implementation using a particular network of computers (see 'PCL earth' below), the software structures we are producing are independent of the underlying physical connection medium, and are defined for any processor/operating system capable of supporting multiple processes and a means of inter-process communication.

1.2. Basic Terms

1.2.1. The Earth.

Term definition. A set of completely connected processors, taken together with their interconnections and peripherals, which is available for running worm programs is called an 'earth'.

The processors may, for example, be either loosely- or tightly-coupled; they may lie on a number of different networks connected by gateways. As stated above, assumptions about the processors are kept to a minimum:

to participate in an earth, each processor must run an operating system kernel which supports multiple processes and inter-process communication (these facilities may either be provided specially or may perhaps be obtained from an existing operating system).

Our intention is to produce a design which can be implemented on as many existing networks as possible, and which is to be used also for implementation on networks built specifically for running worm programs.

1.2.2. Worms and the Worm mechanisms

It is important to consider as separate developments the notion of worm programs themselves, and that of the underlying worm mechanisms. The latter are responsible for monitoring and providing for the overall run-time behaviour of worm programs in terms of their processor- and other resource usage, and the worm programs themselves are applications making use of these mechanisms. Our project has sought to develop a 'worm operating system', which we call Wormos. Thus it is the concern of Wormos, a distributed operating system, to provide facilities for worm programs as they run in the earth: Wormos turns the earth into a 'worm computer'. A worm programmer may then concern him- or herself with a particular application (worm program), and use the worm mechanisms through Wormos.

1.2.3. The Worms Themselves

Our intention is to provide a general framework in which programmers can create their worms in a flexible and well-understood way. Each worm is to be constructed as a set of separate programs called 'segments'.

> Term definition. A worm consists of individual program units called segments, each of which can be run at a single processor in the earth. An executing image of a segment at a processor is called a segment incarnation. (The latter are sometimes just called 'segments' for short, where no confusion can arise).

2 The PCL earth.

The PCL earth (Fig. 1) is based around a five-node Cambridge Ring Local Area Network (LAN), on which are connected the following machines:

- A SUN 2/120 graphics workstation, running the Unix* 4.2 bsd operating system.
- Four 'bare' machines, each containing Motorola 68000 processor boards with local memory and a Cambridge Ring node controller on a Multibus. We are building a multi-processor machine from one of these, using several 68000 processors with shared memory.
- The Polytechnic has recently invested in a number of SUN series three machines, connected by an Ethernet and using several fileservers. Our SUN 2 is also connected to this Ethernet, and our intention is to use it as a gateway between the Cambridge Ring and the Ethernet, so as to enable us to experiment with an earth built from disimilar local area networks.

The Unix machine is used for general program development, and for our work on including Unix-based machines as part of an earth. The bare machines are being used specifically for running worm programs. The operating system used on the bare machines is downloaded from Unix via the ring, using PCL-developed ROMs in the 68000 cards.

* Unix is a trademark of AT & T.

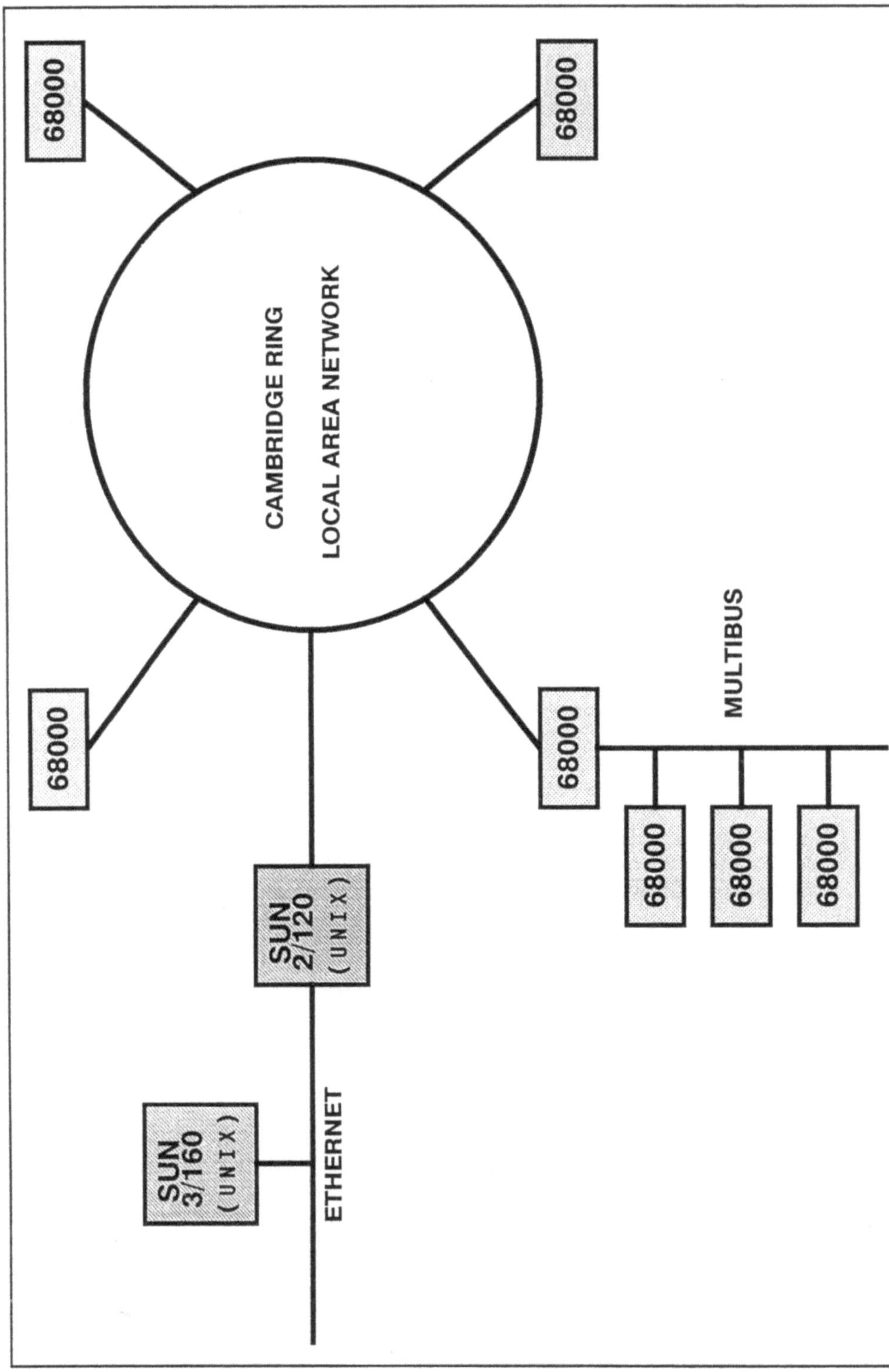

Fig.1. The PCL Earth.

3 Worms

3.1. The Overall Structure of a Worm

To construct a worm program, a programmer must provide:-

a) Programs for the different segments of the worm.

b) Instructions as to the required loading pattern of each segment. For example, each segment may have one or more incarnations at run-time, and constraints on the multiplicity of each segment's incarnations may be given. Also, segments may have to run at particular processors in the earth.

c) Information as to the communications linkage to be made between the segments at the time of incarnation, and details as to any complexes of connected segments to be incarnated together at run time.

d) Constraints must also be given about the rights each segment has with regard to other segments, for example the right to incarnate and terminate other segments.

b)-d) above are determined using what is called the DNA of a worm, which will be discussed further below.

Specifying a worm's DNA is in part comparable to using the Configuration Language used in the CONIC system [3]. However there the run-time configuration of different program modules among the available processors is explicitly determined, and moreover it is centrally controlled. Worms,in contrast, are to adapt dynamically to a changing earth and are subject at run time to decentralised operating system control.

The segments and DNA are separately produced and compiled (Fig. 2). A worm program is created by producing a worm egg. This contains no executable code itself, but is a data structure giving information as to the whereabouts of the executable code, and details of part of the DNA.

3.2. The Segments

We are using a model of segment incarnations as communicating processes, with reference to the work of both C.A.R. Hoare [4] and P. Brinch-Hansen [5]. This is desirable for a number of reasons:

- Process management and communications are exactly those

widely available and minimal facilities which we are presupposing as being supported in our earths;

- the communicating processes model enables a programmer to think in terms of parallel operations in writing a worm application;

- such parallelism is of a degree which is consonant with the overheads due to communications in the kinds of earth we are considering;

- the semantics of message-passing are conveniently such that the processes need have no knowledge of where in the system they and their peers reside;

- the work of Hoare and Brinch-Hansen has shown that a rich set of applications can be devised from a small set of primitive constructs such as 'guarded regions' [6] which have been developed in their work with communicating processes; and moreover these are applications which can be reasoned about in a systematic way [7].

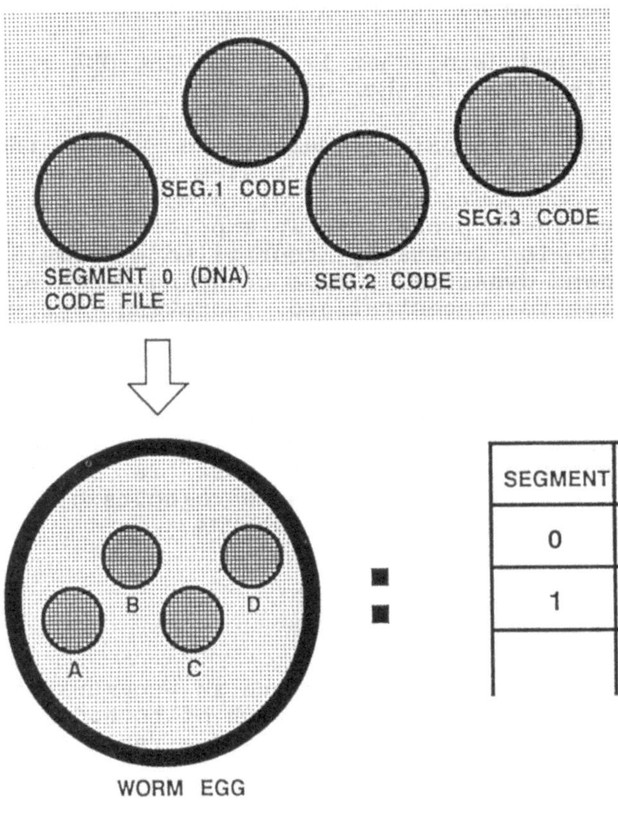

SEGMENT	CODE	SEGMENT DNA
0	A	~
1	B	~

Fig.2. A Worm program is created by producing a worm egg

As a first step, we are assuming that segments will be written in the language 'C', with extra facilities such as inter-process communication (IPC) provided through system calls.

Instead of each segment having to name other segments explicitly, as in [4], but to allow for more complex interactions than the 'client - server' relationships described in [5], we intend each segment to be a function of its input and output data linkage points, called 'streams'. Just as a Unix program may write to its standard output, for example, and this may be made to correspond to the standard input of another program using a pipe, we intend that worms should be constructed by connecting input and output streams of segments in a similar way. Also, segments will access all devices and servers (in particular, fileservers) by using streams connected to them.

Data arriving at a stream will in general be cast into a particular format by a segment; this raises the issue of being able to represent data types consistently between heterogenous machines with different internal representations (for example, byte orderings differ between a VAX and a Motorola 68000-based machine). This problem does not arise in our earth, but can be solved by the addition of a communications sub-layer which marshals data into a standard format before inter-processor transmission, and unmarshals it at the receiving end.

3.3. The DNA

There are two forms of DNA in any worm: the segment DNA, which is described for each segment at the time of producing a worm egg, and the worm DNA which is one of the segments, but one which has special rights. Their respective roles will be described in what follows.

3.3.1. Segment Incarnation Requirements

The possibility of using a variety of processors requires a programmer to put constraints upon the number of incarnations of each segment, and where each will run. Several motives will contribute to these specifications. For example, some segment incarnations should reside locally to whatever hardware they particularly require to use; fault-tolerant applications will require incarnations at different processors so as to be able to cope with the failure of one of them; and the exploitation of parallelism will require a certain distribution of segments among the given processors. In writing a set of segments to run in parallel, a programmer can try to make the segment partitioning of the computation such that the parallelism is maximally exploited for a given problem. However, such arrangements will produce a speedup which is in part a function of the overheads of inter-process communication. For a given earth it should be possible to experiment with different arrangements of incarnations in order to gain the maximum advantage in that particular earth, by altering whether or not incarnations are to reside at the same or different processors, for example. This would be a heuristic response to the peculiarities of a given earth and a given set of segments.

This information is provided as part of each segment's DNA, and described at the time of creating a worm egg. One can specify:

1) The type of processing element the segment may run on;

2) Any special hardware requirements in addition to this (e.g. a certain minimum amount of main memory);

3) A list of sub-groups of processors where the segment may run;

4) Constraints upon the incarnation multiplicity required: e.g. exactly one; no limit;

5) The maximum number of incarnations per processing element.

Only one segment is directly incarnated by the operating system, and that is the DNA segment, which is automatically incarnated at the beginning of a worm's run-time. This is moreover the only segment which has the right to incarnate other segments, and indeed it is up to the DNA segment to incarnate all the others explicitly. The operating system keeps the DNA segment informed of changes both in the earth and in the state of segment incarnations. For example, a new processor may come on-line during the run, which the worm may want to utilise; or a segment may terminate, perhaps due to an exception, perhaps naturally.

This is the worm model we are presently using, chosen for its relative simplicity. More complicated schemes to be examined include:

(i) wherein the DNA segment can confer on other segments the right to incarnate and/or terminate other incarnations; or, indeed, wherein there is no single DNA segment, but rather each segment has specific rights established in its segment DNA.

(ii) Priorities might also be specified, so that certain segments are given precedence over others by the operating system in meeting their incarnation requirements.

(iii) Segment complexes could be described so that, say, a complex of three incarnations inter-connected in a certain way can be thought of as a single entity, and this entire complex incarnated using a single command.

(iv) Incarnations of certain segments could be constrained to run on the same or different processors. Rules could be assigned, as in J. Conway's game of 'Life', to determine which combinations of incarnations can or cannot be present at the same processing element. Similar rules could indeed be specified as applying to incarnations of the segments of different worms at the same machine. For example, a slow worm is one whose segments run only while the processing element in which they find themselves is not required by other worms; if such a demand does arise, then they are terminated by the operating system, but may run again when other processing resources become available.

(v) In our model, a segment incarnation remains at a single processor throughout its life. However it is in principle perfectly possible, of course, for a segment incarnation to migrate from one processor to another during its run-time, due to load changes.

There is a wealth of research to be done in these areas, and all the above are possibilities we intend to investigate.

3.3.2. Data Connection

Consider, under Unix, two programs P and Q. If we use the pipe mechanism to form the job

P ¦ Q

then we might consider this to be a worm formed out of the two 'segments', P and Q. (Fig. 3a) P and Q may have been written quite independently, with P writing to its standard output, and Q reading data from its standard input.

Now let us add the further possibilities that each may deal with more than one input stream and more than one output stream, and also that streams may be connected to several other streams (Fig. 3b). To use this new 'multiple piping' possibility, a programmer will specify a more complicated set of links between outputs and inputs, the worm's 'data connection graph'.

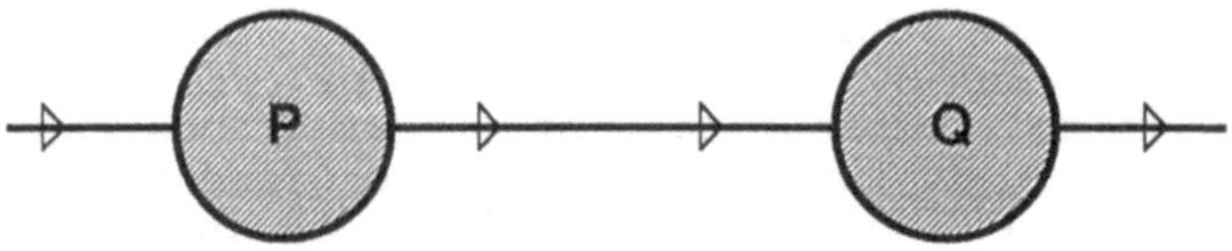

Fig.3a. A simple 2 segment worm formed by piping together 2 programs under Unix.

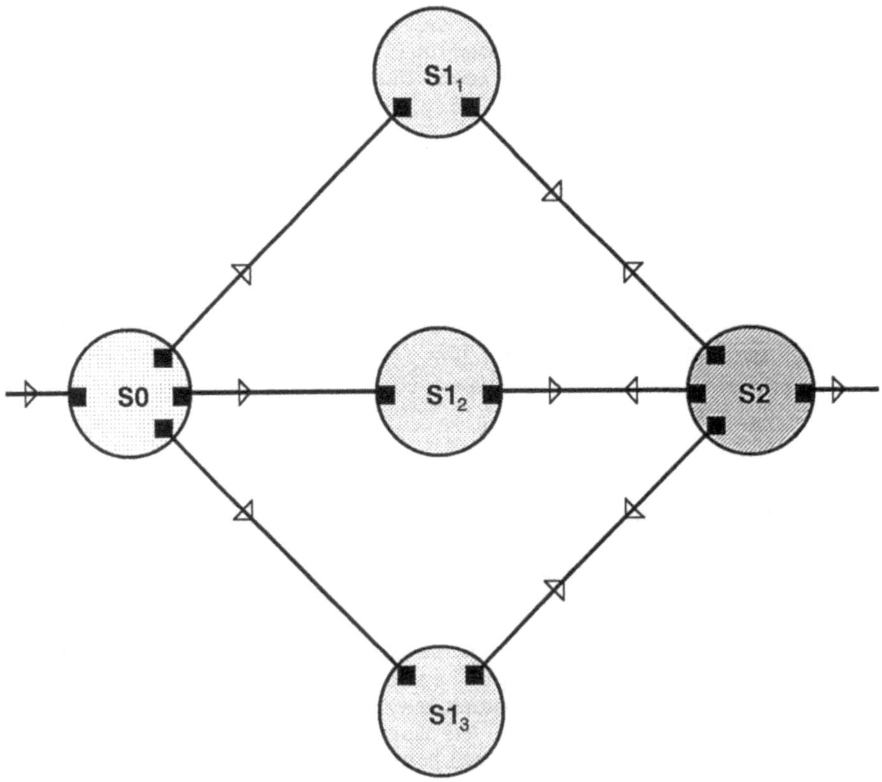

FIG.3b. A 3-segment worm, showing its data connections

The worm's data connection graph is, abstractly, a set of triples:

(connection_type, seg1.stream1, seg2.stream2)

such that the two named streams are connected in the fashion determined by the connection type. Data sent to the first stream arrives at the second. The connection type is used to specify a service type to use between the two end-points (datagram, acknowledged datagram etc.).

Segments may either explicitly make these connections at run-time, or they can be specified in the segment DNA in the worm egg, in which case the operating system will create the connection before the running of the segments concerned commences, at incarnation time. Note that in the latter case a connection is specified between segments, rather than segment incarnations. We are considering the possibility that at run-time the connections could be one-to-many: data sent from one stream would be multicast to corresponding streams on a set of incarnations. Thus multiple incarnations of a segment could be addressed as a single object by other segments and function in step. This would be most useful for fault-tolerant applications. Connections directed at a single segment incarnation from multiple incarnations of another segment would be managed using a 'family' or array of streams at the single segment.

4 Wormos

4.1. Wormos Facilities.

Wormos is a distributed operating system to support worm programs. It is to be able to support distributed processes (the segment incarnations), giving each transparent access to those objects and resources in the earth for which rights have been granted to it. Each 'object and resource' is either a process itself, or is, for example, a device to which access can only be obtained via a monitor process (i.e. a process which has exclusive direct access to the device, and which co-ordinates other processes' use of the device). Thus all top-level activity in Wormos is constituted by communicating processes.

The facilities Wormos must provide for running worms are in outline as follows:-

1) Earth monitoring. The earth is subject to change by the subtraction and addition of processors, either in administering demands arising from general network use or through failure. Wormos should be capable of adapting to such changes in the earth, or at least discovering and noting them.

2) Segment propagation. Segment executable code must be distributed appropriately around the earth during a worm's run-time.

3) Processor allocation. Incarnations must be produced at sites consistent with the requirements of each segment. A load-balancing algorithm should be run.

4) Segment monitoring. The overall population of segment incarnations must be monitored, and the status of each must be determined at appropriate times.

5) Termination. It must be possible at all times for any given segment incarnation(s) to be terminated; and it must be possible to establish whether or not a worm has terminated.

6) Inter-segment communication. Segments must be able to pass data to each other without being concerned with low-level network protocols. This facility is to be built on top of a system of message-passing used by Wormos itself, incorporating a notion of 'port' following [8] (see 'Communications' below).

7) I/O devices. Segments should have access to network peripheral resources through address-independent references, as in any distributed system.

8) Joint decision making. Implicit in most of the above is a mechanism whereby joint decisions can be made concerning the status of distributed entities where each site contains only partial information. An example of this would be determining the set of processors at which incarnations of a particular segment are active.

4.2. Wormos Structure.

In order that Wormos may run in a given earth, it is necessary that software called Sub-Wormos runs at each processor in the earth. It is the co-operative interaction between Sub-Wormos's that constitutes the distributed operating system called Wormos (Fig. 4). Performance considerations aside, it is a matter of indifference how many Sub-Wormos's are running in an earth: part of Sub-Wormos's functionality is to monitor the presence of other Sub-Wormos's, and it is the mutually identified group of Sub-Wormos's that functions as Wormos in any earth. Thus any processor for which a Sub-Wormos has been implemented can be part of an earth for running worms.

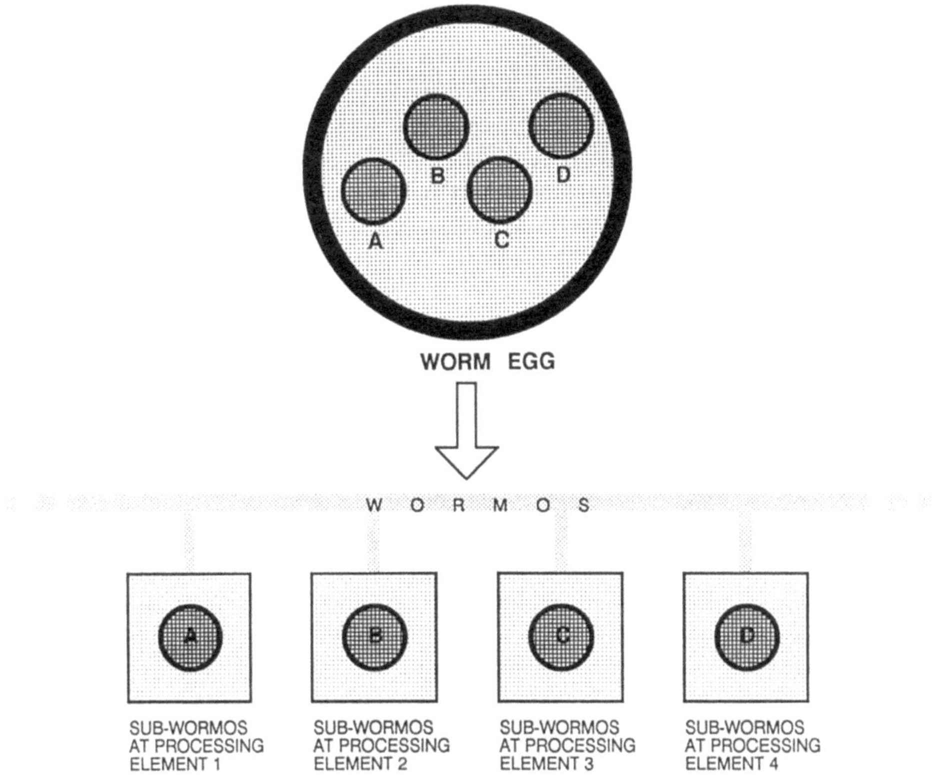

Fig.4. The Structure of WORMOS

4.3. Sub-Wormos

The functionality of Sub-Wormos is defined in terms of a set of communicating processes. These are supported by a kernel, and they provide the Wormos facilities described above through their interaction, both between each other and with counterpart processes in Sub-Wormos's at other processors (Fig. 5). These processes, called system processes, are in outline as follows:-

1) Earthmonitor

This establishes and maintains information about the state of the earth. At start-up (boot-time) an earth map is loaded. There is a map for each network to which the processor is connected. This is a data structure which contains details of all the processors on the network which may run a Sub-Wormos and thus participate in running Wormos. Of course, at any one time some of these may be 'down'. Each processor on the network loads the same map, and thus a uniform interface to the network is presented to the Sub-Wormos's, giving a uniform logical-to-physical addressing scheme.

Processors are described in terms which are required for the run-time interpretation of DNA, for example:

Node:	103
Physical address (Cambridge Ring):	12
Processor type:	PM68k
Processor groups:	2
'Special':	vdu attached, memory = 512k.

In addition to processor descriptions, the addresses of network 'services' such as fileservers are included in the map. Each processor is assumed to be on no more than two networks, and those on two are termed 'gateway processors'. The earthmap includes the addresses of processors to use as gateways to other networks.

The main function of Earthmonitor, apart from loading the earthmap and hence initialising the Sub-Wormos data-base, is to establish which other processors are up and running Sub-Wormos. This it does by probing its logical network neighbours with messages until it gets a certain response. This response enables the processor to participate thereafter in a token-passing scheme whose aim is to give the processors a consistent view of the 'active earth', and detect processor crashes via repeated failures to respond.

Apart from processing these probing and token-passing messages, Earthmonitor also deals with:

- Worm registration messages. A worm using a given processor must have a local 'worm shadow' process assigned to it, whose first task is to register with Earthmonitor, giving its local address and specifying any particular events which it is interested in. The worm shadow will also register its termination.

- In the event of a fresh processor coming on-line to Wormos, or a processor being deemed to have crashed, Earthmonitor will inform all local worm shadows who have registered as being interested in such events.

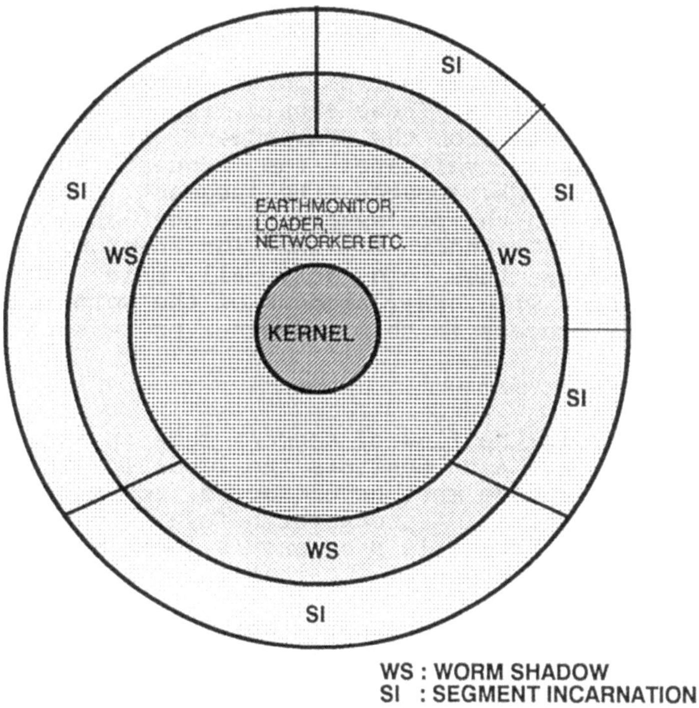

Fig.5. Segment incarnations running at sub-wormos

2) <u>Worm Shadows</u>

Each worm has a set of processors assigned to running it at any one time, and in each of these, for each worm, there is a process called a 'worm shadow'. The worm shadows corresponding to a particular worm liaise to run it, providing a 'virtual earth' for it. They perform a number of functions:

- Keeping track of which segments are incarnated where, and the locations of segment code;
- Informing the DNA segment of the termination of a local segment, with the reason for the termination.
- Processing messages from Earthmonitor notifying changes in the state of the earth;
- Forwarding 'notifications' from local segments to the DNA segment. These inform the DNA segment that a certain processing stage has been reached, signifying, for example, that more segments should be incarnated;
- Processing requests from local segments to incarnate other segments. These should, in our first worm model, only emanate from the DNA segment. At such times the worm shadow validates the request according to the segment's DNA, locates the segment executable code, guesses which processors are best able to run it and puts out a 'tender' for the incarnation, which these processors then bid for. All this is done by cooperation with other shadows of the worm, and using the Loader process in this and other processors.

3) <u>Loader</u>

Loader controls the flow of segment code in and out of local primary memory and monitors the local loading level. Each worm segment's code must be extracted from a filestore and sent to a suitable processor before it can run. Code may best be copied from this processor's local memory to other processors for subsequent incarnations. Loader:

- Reports on its processor's ability to incarnate a segment, both in terms of its available memory capacity and its current loading by other segments;
- Instructs a slave process to load a segment into memory, when agreed with a remote Loader;
- Instructs a slave process to send segment code, when this has been agreed.
- Having agreed to the incarnation of the first segment

belonging to a particular worm, creates a Worm Shadow process for it;

- Processes 'Early Bird' messages. These cause Loader to terminate all processes serving a particular worm;

4) Networker

It is not in general the concern of segments to acknowledge received data, or that of either sending or receiving segments to ensure that data arrives in the same order as was sent, without duplication. Networker is a process to implement such low-level protocols on behalf of worm segments. Networker processes connection requests and flow control once connections have been made.

Earthmonitor, Loader and Networker must be constantly present in any running Sub-Wormos; and the Worm Shadows come and go with the worms as described above. In addition to these, particular resources such as fileservers and network gateways are accessed in Sub-Wormos through system processes which manage them.

5 Implementations

5.1. Sub-Wormos

A Sub-Wormos can be implemented in any environment that provides a process management structure and suitable means of inter-process communication (IPC) (between any processes, whether in the same or different processors). These facilities are provided for Sub-Wormos through a local kernel. We are working on the development of three implementations of Sub-Wormos, which differ mainly in their kernels, but also in terms of the system processes present.

1) 68000 Sub-Wormos. This is for running as the native operating system on our 'bare' single-68000 machines referred to above. It is to be a full implementation of the standard system processes, supported by a kernel which includes a driver for our Cambridge Ring network. The kernel is an adaptation of a small operating system kernel called XINU [9], which is Unix-like in its organisation.

2) multi-68000 Sub-Wormos. Each processor in such a machine is to run a version of Sub-Wormos which is very much like 68000 Sub-Wormos, except for the network facilities used. Each will contain a driver which sends data between the processors on the 'Multibus network' via shared Multibus memory. Only one processor, however, will have access to the external (ring) network, and so the Sub-Wormos running on this will be different

in that it will run a gateway process for data passed between the external and Multibus networks.

3) Unix Sub-Wormos A Cambridge Ring driver has been developed for our SUN2 machine, and this together with Berkeley Unix sockets [10] has been used to develop suitable IPC mechanisms for a Sub-Wormos to be implemented with Unix acting as its 'kernel' and the Sub-Wormos system processes implemented as Unix user processes. The functionality of Unix sub-wormos is the same as 68000 sub-wormos, except that a special system process, called earthgate, is being written to implement an interface to the earth for users and administrators in running worm programs and booting machines etc.

Only slight adaptations to the Transmission communications layer (see below) need be made in order that this Unix sub-wormos can run on the SUN3 machines.

5.2. Unix tools

We are producing software for administering the earth and producing worm programs as follows:

1) Earthuser. This enables a user to establish which processors are active in the earth, and to boot processors which are not;

2) Makeworm. This allows a worm programmer interactively to create a worm egg, having written and compiled the segments of the worm;

3) Worm. This is to execute the worm whose worm egg is given as an argument. This program becomes the Worm Shadow for the worm which incarnates the DNA segment, thus initiating the worm's growth.

5.3. Communications

There are three Communications layers, the:-

Streams,

Ports and

Transmission layers.

The top layer provides a service corresponding to the OSI Transport layer (Fig. 6). The following assumptions are made about the earth's connections:

i. The earth consists of a number of networks (LANs and bus-based schemes), inter-connected by gateways.

ii. Each network has a logical number to identify it, as does each node on each network. 'Gateway' nodes may have more than one logical station number, one for each network to which they are attached.

iii. Each network node has only one host processor attached.

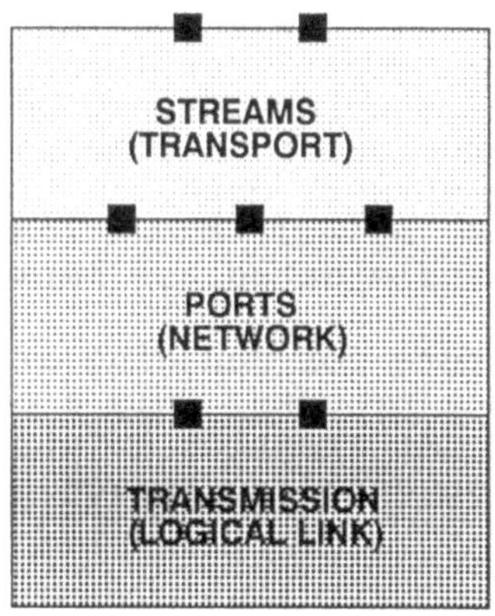

Fig.6. WORMOS Communications Layers

5.3.1. The top layer: Streams.

This is to provide inter-segment connections as described above. It is intended that, in this layer, segments need know only address-independent names for directing their data, and that data sent arrives coherently: i.e. in the correct order and without duplication or omissions (or according to the service specified at connection). As in Unix, no record boundaries are presupposed.

Each 'stream' is a small integer provided by the system, a service access point for the Streams layer. It is translated into a node and port number, to which the data is sent via the 'ports' layer. The streams layer is implemented by Networker at the remote address, which acknowledges data and implements flow control on behalf of the remote process for which the data is ultimately intended.

5.3.2. The Ports Layer (OSI Network Layer)

This provides an (unacknowledged) datagram service for packets addressed to a 'port' (service access point) at any node in the earth. The service corresponds to the OSI Network Layer. It is provided by a combination of a) Transmission service for intra-network datagram travel, and b) a set of gateway processes at well-known (earthmap-defined) network addresses which handle datagrams between networks.

A port is a structure for managing arriving messages. Each port belongs to a process. Only a port's owner may receive data from a port. At creation an upper limit is specified on the number of outstanding messages a port may hold at any one time.

5.3.3. The Transmission (OSI Data Link) Layer.

This provides a connectionless service using service access points also called ports in machines on the same network.

6 An Example Worm

The following example illustrates the use of a worm program in the solution of an image-processing problem which is being explored by our team at PCL.

6.1. The Match Worm

Analysis of 3-d scenes for the recognition and positioning of rigid objects in 3-d space is an important problem for Robotics and Navigation applications. Using range data to solve this problem is relatively new in the field of computer vision. Range data is basically an array of numbers, referred to as a range image or depth map, where the numbers denote the distances of the sensor (e.g. a stereo camera system or a laser range finder) to object surfaces within the field of view. Since the depth information depends only on geometry it includes important clues to recognize and locate 3-d objects by their shape. The first step in using a range image is to extract primitives (e.g. 3-d lines, planes, cylinders, edges, etc.) in order to construct descriptions of objects in the scene. For recognition purposes these descriptions are then matched against a set of existing descriptions called "models".

A four segment "match worm" has been designed to carry out this task. The input to the worm is two descriptions: one belonging to an object in a given scene and the other to a possible model of this object. In our application since only polyhedral objects are considered, simple descriptions which have only one component are used. These are the end points of the line segments that lie on the boundaries of the planar surfaces, in other words the end points of the edges. The worm carries out its task by using a scheme based on estimation and verification of hypotheses. Each hypothesis is an estimation of the position and orientation (a translation and a rotation) of the model that will possibly put it in correspondance with the object in 3-d space. Verification is done by applying this translation and rotation to each edge that exists in the model description and looking for a match for it in the given object description. At the end of the verification phase each hypothesis is assigned a "goodness of fit" rating. Finally the object under consideration is identified, its edges are labelled and its position and orientation are determined in relation to the best rated hypothesis. If all of the hypotheses rate below a predetermined threshold this means that the model is not the correct one for this particular object. In a computer vision system which has the objective of recognizing objects (that are placed in the field of view of its sensors) from a library of a limited number of models, a number of match worms can be utilized: each simply testing the validity of a particular model that exists in the library.

The match worm consists of four segments (including the worm DNA) (Fig. 7). Their roles are in outline as follows:

> The DNA segment (segment 0). This incarnates one incarnation each of segment 1 and segment 3, and multiple copies of segment 2.
>
> There is one incarnation only of this segment, and it may reside anywhere in the PCL earth.
>
> Segment 1. This reads the files associated with the object and model descriptions and makes a preliminary analysis to determine the set of hypotheses about the transformation which will possibly bring the model into correspondance with the object. Having done this, it assigns the job of testing these hypotheses to the incarnations of segment2. Segment 1 is supplied by the DNA segment with the number of incarnations of segment 2, and uses this parameter in assigning the hypothesis-testing among the segment 2 incarnations.
>
> This segment's DNA specifies that it should run at the SUN machine where the image files are kept.
>
> Segment 2. Incarnations of this segment form the work force of the match worm. The matching process is mainly a tree search problem but because of the dimensionality involved it can be a bottleneck in any vision system. Segment 2 incarnations of the match worm provide the means to improve computational efficiency by exploiting the parallelism that is inherent in the nature of the tree search. In testing the hypotheses assigned to them, as described above, they write their partial results to segment 3.
>
> These segments are intended to run at the 'bare' machines in our earth, which act as a bank of processors for running worm segments.
>
> Segment 3. The single incarnation of this segment is responsible for guiding the course of hypothesis testing as the calculation proceeds, updating tables as partial results from segment 2 incarnations arrive. The verification of a particular hypothesis is stopped when the degree of fit is found to be worse than the current best. Segment 3 can re-allocate work to segment 2 incarnations at such times. The final results are written to disk by this segment.
>
> Segment 3 could run at any processor in our earth.

It would be possible to combine the functions of the DNA

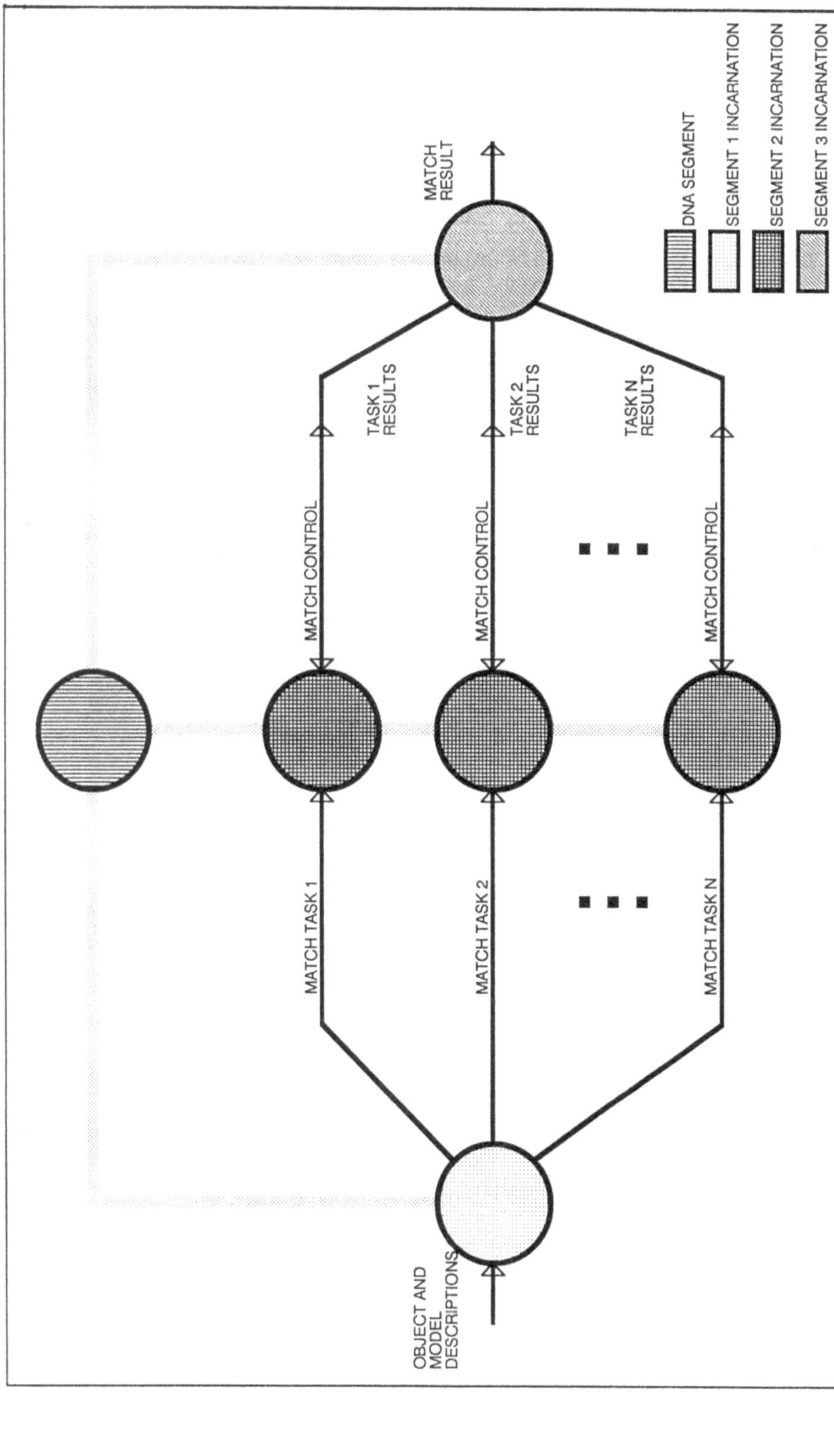

Fig.7. The Match Worm

segment and segment 1 into one segment, and similarly with segment 1 and segment 3. However we have kept them separate deliberately so as to make the functionality of each segment as specific as possible.

7 Conclusion

Detailed algorithms for distributed control etc. have not been given here, largely because these have not yet been fully worked out. Rather, what has been described is an architecture which for the present defines a 'software laboratory', in which many experiments have still to be made before firm conclusions can be reached. These experiments concern:

i) the testing of algorithms to use for each Wormos facility as described above, and

ii) how precisely to formulate the worm programming model so that it is both relatively straightforward to use and flexible enough for a wide class of applications.

Although much of our work, therefore, lies still ahead of us, we are presently putting together a preliminary version of the operating system on our earth. We intend our work to be driven, once this is completed, by the practical experiences gained from allowing a range of users to write worm programs using our system.

8 References

[1] Shoch and Hupp "The 'Worm' Programs - Early Experience with a Distributed Computation" Communications of the ACM Volume 25 no. 3 (March '82)

[2] R.M. Needham and A.J. Herbert, "The Cambridge Distributed Computing System" Addison-Wesley London (1982)

[3] J. Kramer et al "CONIC: An Integrated Approach to Distributed Computer Control Systems" Imperial College Research Report no. DOC 82/6, April 1982

[4] C.A.R. Hoare, "Communicating Sequential Processes" Communications ACM Volume 21 no. 8 (August '78)

[5] Per Brinch Hansen, "Distributed Processes: A Concurrent Programming Concept" Communications ACM Volume 21, no. 11 (November '78)

[6] E.W. Dijkstra "Guarded Commands, nondeterminacy, and formal derivation of programs" Communications ACM Volume 18, no. 8 (August '75)

[7] C.A.R. Hoare et al "A Theory of Communicating Sequential Processes" Technical Monograph PRG-16, Computing laboratory, University of Oxford.

[8] R.F. Rashid, "Accent: A Distributed Operating System Kernel for a Network of Personal Computers" Carnegie-Mellon University Technical Report, June 1984.

[9] D. Comer "Operating System Design - The XINU approach" Prentice Hall 1984

[10] Leffler, Joy, Fabry "4.2BSD Networking Implementation Notes" Computer Systems Research Group, Dept. of Electrical Engineering and Computer Science, University of California, Berkeley.

NATO ASI Series F

Vol. 1: Issues in Acoustic Signal – Image Processing and Recognition. Edited by C. H. Chen. VIII, 333 pages. 1983.

Vol. 2: Image Sequence Processing and Dynamic Scene Analysis. Edited by T. S. Huang. IX, 749 pages. 1983.

Vol. 3: Electronic Systems Effectiveness and Life Cycle Costing. Edited by J. K. Skwirzynski. XVII, 732 pages. 1983.

Vol. 4: Pictorial Data Analysis. Edited by R. M. Haralick. VIII, 468 pages. 1983.

Vol. 5: International Calibration Study of Traffic Conflict Techniques. Edited by E. Asmussen. VII, 229 pages. 1984.

Vol. 6: Information Technology and the Computer Network. Edited by K. G. Beauchamp. VIII, 271 pages. 1984.

Vol. 7: High-Speed Computation. Edited by J. S. Kowalik. IX, 441 pages. 1984.

Vol. 8: Program Transformation and Programming Environments. Report on an Workshop directed by F. L. Bauer and H. Remus. Edited by P. Pepper. XIV, 378 pages. 1984.

Vol. 9: Computer Aided Analysis and Optimization of Mechanical System Dynamics. Edited by E. J. Haug. XXII, 700 pages. 1984.

Vol. 10: Simulation and Model-Based Methodologies: An Integrative View. Edited by T. I. Ören, B. P. Zeigler, M. S. Elzas. XIII, 651 pages. 1984.

Vol. 11: Robotics and Artificial Intelligence. Edited by M. Brady, L. A. Gerhardt, H. F. Davidson. XVII, 693 pages. 1984.

Vol. 12: Combinatorial Algorithms on Words. Edited by A. Apostolico, Z. Galil. VIII, 361 pages. 1985.

Vol. 13: Logics and Models of Concurrent Systems. Edited by K. R. Apt. VIII, 498 pages. 1985.

Vol. 14: Control Flow and Data Flow: Concepts of Distributed Programming. Edited by M. Broy. VIII, 525 pages. 1985.

Vol. 15: Computational Mathematical Programming. Edited by K. Schittkowski. VIII, 451 pages. 1985.

Vol. 16: New Systems and Architectures for Automatic Speech Recognition and Synthesis. Edited by R. De Mori, C.Y. Suen. XIII, 630 pages. 1985.

Vol. 17: Fundamental Algorithms for Computer Graphics. Edited by R.A. Earnshaw. XVI, 1042 pages. 1985.

Vol. 18: Computer Architectures for Spatially Distributed Data. Edited by H. Freeman and G.G. Pieroni. VIII, 391 pages. 1985.

Vol. 19: Pictorial Information Systems in Medicine. Edited by K. H. Höhne. XII, 525 pages. 1986.

Vol. 20: Disordered Systems and Biological Organization. Edited by E. Bienenstock, F. Fogelman Soulié, G. Weisbuch. XXI, 405 pages.1986.

Vol. 21: Intelligent Decision Support in Process Environments. Edited by E. Hollnagel, G. Mancini, D.D. Woods. XV, 524 pages. 1986.

Vol. 22: Software System Design Methods. The Challenge of Advanced Computing Technology. Edited by J.K. Skwirzynski. XIII, 747 pages. 1986.

NATO ASI Series F

Vol. 23: Designing Computer-Based Learning Materials. Edited by H. Weinstock and A. Bork. IX, 285 pages. 1986.

Vol. 24: Database Machines. Modern Trends and Applications. Edited by A. K. Sood and A. H. Qureshi. VIII, 570 pages. 1986.

Vol. 25: Pyramidal Systems for Computer Vision. Edited by V. Cantoni and S. Levialdi. VIII, 392 pages. 1986.

Vol. 26: Modelling and Analysis in Arms Control. Edited by R. Avenhaus, R. K. Huber and J. D. Kettelle. VIII, 488 pages. 1986.

Vol. 27: Computer Aided Optimal Design: Structural and Mechanical Systems. Edited by C. A. Mota Soares. XIII, 1029 pages. 1987.

Vol. 28: Distributed Operating Systems. Theory und Practice. Edited by Y. Paker, J.-P. Banatre and M. Bozyiğit. X, 379 pages. 1987.

MIX
Papier aus verantwortungsvollen Quellen
Paper from responsible sources
FSC® C105338

If you have any concerns about our products,
you can contact us on
ProductSafety@springernature.com

In case Publisher is established outside the EU,
the EU authorized representative is:
Springer Nature Customer Service Center GmbH
Europaplatz 3, 69115 Heidelberg, Germany

Printed by Libri Plureos GmbH
in Hamburg, Germany